Look Your Best with WordPerfect® 5.1

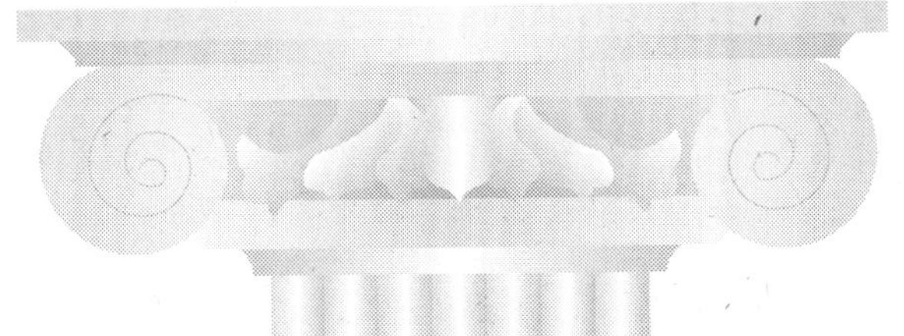

Designs by Julia B. Beinhorn

Text by George R. Beinhorn

Look Your Best with WordPerfect 5.1

Library of Congress Catalog No.: 91-67631

ISBN 0-88022-814-8

95 94 93 92 4 3 2 1

Interpretation of the printing code: the rightmost double-digit number is the year of the book's printing; the rightmost single-digit number, the number of the book's printing. For example, a printing code of 92-1 shows that the first printing of the book occurred in 1992.

This book is based on WordPerfect Version 5.1.

Publisher: Lloyd J. Short

Acquisitions Manager: Rick Ranucci

Managing Editor: Paul Boger

Product Development Manager: Thomas H. Bennett

Book Designers: Scott Cook and Michele Laseau

Production Team: Claudia Bell, Michelle Cleary, Mark Enochs, Brook Farling, Audra Hershman, Laurie Lee, Anne Owen, Juli Pavey, Cindy Phipps, Kevin Spear, Johnna VanHoose, Lisa Wilson, Phil Worthington

ABOUT THE AUTHORS

Julia B. Beinhorn has been a professional graphic designer for 15 years, with clients in the publishing and recording industries.

George R. Beinhorn is a writer, editor, and commercial photographer. He is the author of Que's *Using Professional Write Plus for Windows*, *Look Your Best with WordPerfect for Windows*, and the revision author of *Using Q & A*, 4th Edition. He writes the "Pro Tips" word processing column for *PC Computing* magazine.

George R. Beinhorn and Julia B. Beinhorn serve as document design consultants for business clients and may be reached through Que Corporation.

CREDITS

Product Director
Charles O. Stewart III

Production Editor
Kelly D. Dobbs

Editors
Tracy Barr
Donald R. Eamon
Susan M. Shaw
Micci E. Swick-Volk

Technical Editor
Eric Baatz

Composed in Garamond and MCP Digital by Que Corporation.

ACKNOWLEDGMENTS

Julia B. Beinhorn wishes to thank Mrs. Julian Beakley and George R. Beinhorn for their generosity and support.

George R. Beinhorn wishes to thank Julia Beakley Beinhorn and J. Donald Walters for their help and friendship.

The authors owe a huge debt of gratitude to technical editor Eric Baatz and to Que's editing staff. May camels arrive at their door-steps laden with diamonds and gold.

The authors wish to thank the following suppliers:

Canon USA for the SC-1 Adobe PostScript cartridge that was used to create the figures for this book. The Canon LBP series of printers were chosen for the unexcelled quality of their type and gray screens.

Logitech, Inc., for the superb ScanMan 256 scanner.

TRADEMARK ACKNOWLEDGMENTS

Que Corporation has made every effort to supply trademark information about company names, products, and services mentioned in this book. Trademarks indicated below were derived from various sources. Que Corporation cannot attest to the accuracy of this information.

1-2-3 and Lotus are registered trademarks of Lotus Development Corporation.

Apple, LaserWriter, LaserWriter Plus, and Macintosh are registered trademarks of Apple Computer, Inc.

Bitstream and Fontware are registered trademarks of Bitstream Inc.

CompuServe is a registered trademark of H&R Block.

dBASE IV is a trademark of Ashton-Tate Corporation.

Diablo 630 is a registered trademark of Xerox Corporation.

Hewlett-Packard, HP Graphics Gallery, and HP Scanning Gallery are registered trademarks of Hewlett-Packard Company.

IBM, PC, XT, AT, PS/2, and PC DOS are registered trademarks of International Business Machines Corporation.

ITC Bookman, ITC Zapf Dingbats, and ITC Zapf Chancery are registered trademarks of International Typeface Corporation.

Linotronic is a trademark and Helvetica, Times, and Palatino are registered trademarks of Allied Corporation.

Microsoft, Microsoft Excel, MS-DOS, Microsoft Word, and Microsoft Mouse are registered trademarks of Microsoft Corporation.

PageMaker is a registered trademark of Aldus Corporation.

PostScript is a registered trademark of Adobe Systems Incorporated.

Ventura Publisher is a registered trademark of Ventura Software, Inc.

WordPerfect and WordPerfect Library are registered trademarks of WordPerfect Corporation.

Trademarks of other products mentioned in this book are held by the companies producing them.

CONTENTS at a GLANCE

CONTENTS

THE TRADITIONAL BUILDER

Plexes On Rise

Tight money has now buyers moving in together

Victorian Sunshine

Add-on solaria now a popular trend for older homes

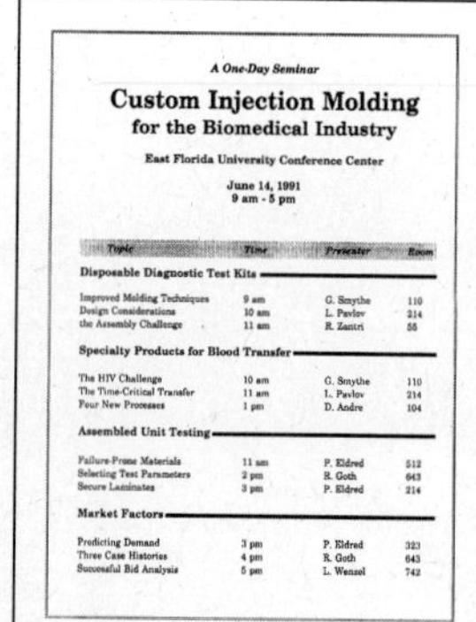

A One-Day Seminar

Custom Injection Molding
for the Biomedical Industry

East Florida University Conference Center

June 14, 1991
9 am - 5 pm

Topic	*Time*	*Presenter*	*Room*
Disposable Diagnostic Test Kits			
Improved Molding Techniques	9 am	G. Smythe	110
Design Considerations	10 am	L. Pavlov	214
the Assembly Challenge	11 am	R. Zantri	55
Specialty Products for Blood Transfer			
The HIV Challenge	10 am	G. Smythe	110
The Time-Critical Transfer	11 am	L. Pavlov	214
Four New Processes	1 pm	D. Andre	104
Assembled Unit Testing			
Failure-Prone Materials	11 am	P. Eldred	512
Selecting Test Parameters	2 pm	R. Goth	643
Secure Laminates	3 pm	P. Eldred	214
Market Factors			
Predicting Demand	3 pm	P. Eldred	323
Three Case Histories	4 pm	R. Goth	643
Successful Bid Analysis	5 pm	L. Wenzel	742

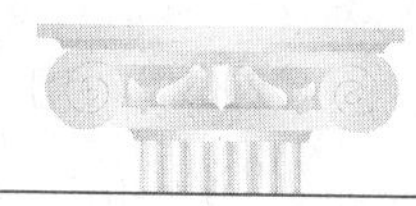

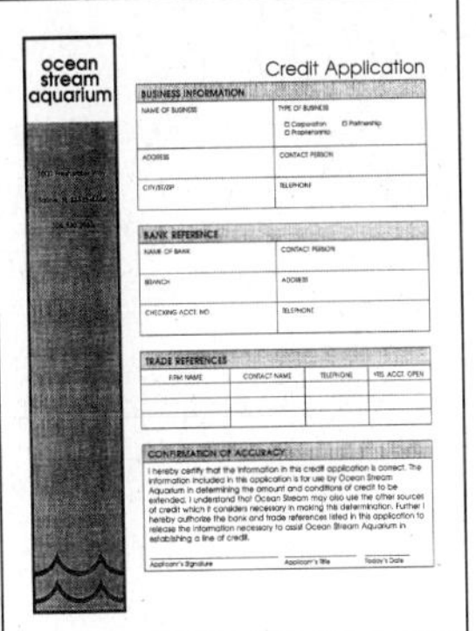
ocean
stream
aquarium
Credit Application

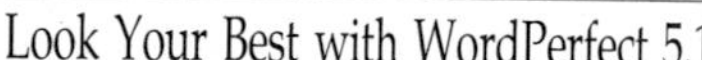

Longhorn Sports
Year-End Preferred Customer
Sale!
December 28-31
8-11 am
You're among the top 25% of our customers for 1992! In appreciation of your support, you're invited to a special closed-door year-end sale.
Save up to 50%
on our famous maker brands. Top-of-the-line items in all sports drastically reduced.
Shoes
Avia, Nike, Puma, Brooks, Converse, ASICS, Reebok, Vans, New Balance, Adidas, Saucony, LA Gear, Sperry, Rockport
Pro Team Gear
NFL, NBA, NL, AL, NHL
Exercise Equipment
Tunturi, Soloflex, Nautilus, Nordic Track
Sports Outfitting
Running, Cycling, Canoeing, X-C Skiing, Racquet Sports, Swimming, Tennis, Aerobics, Cross-Training
Longhorn Sports
12482 Altissima Blvd.
El Dorado, CO 80004
(555) 789-0123

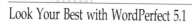

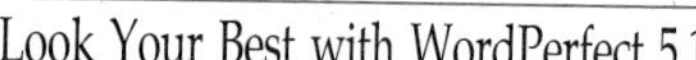

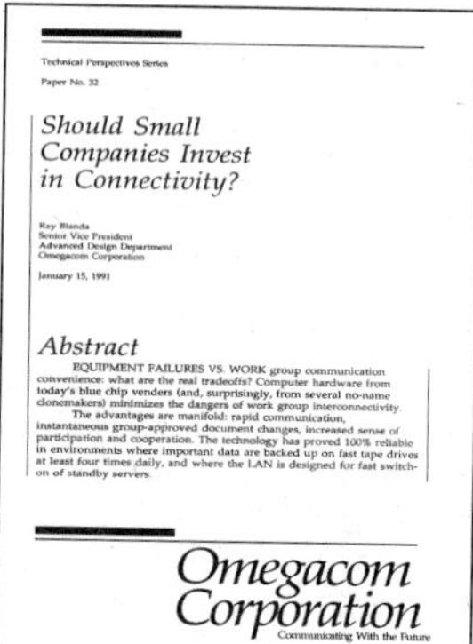

Technical Perspectives Series

Paper No. 32

Should Small Companies Invest in Connectivity?

Ray Blanda
Senior Vice President
Advanced Design Department
Omegacom Corporation

January 15, 1991

Abstract

EQUIPMENT FAILURES VS. WORK group communication convenience: what are the real tradeoffs? Computer hardware from today's blue chip venders (and, surprisingly, from several no-name clonemakers) minimizes the dangers of work group interconnectivity.

The advantages are manifold: rapid communication, instantaneous group-approved document changes, increased sense of participation and cooperation. The technology has proved 100% reliable in environments where important data are backed up on fast tape drives at least four times daily, and where the LAN is designed for fast switch-on of standby servers.

Omegacom Corporation
Communicating With the Future

west bay

senior runner

Dr. Allen in San Jose

Women's Racing

New Feature

Gearing Up

Age Group Mileage

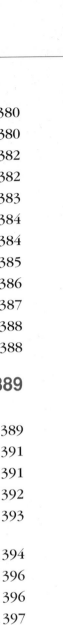

Introduction

This book was written for WordPerfect users who must create documents that will be judged for their appearance as well as their contents. Few things are as frustrating as having the tools to create great-looking documents and not knowing how to use them.

In the step-by-step chapters within this book, you find proof positive that WordPerfect can indeed help you create good-looking documents. Between knowing the basics of WordPerfect and being able to look good in print is a long step that not many can make on their own.

The sample documents in this book were created by Julia Beinhorn, a graphic designer with more than 20 years' experience. If you have had no graphic design experience, you still can use this book to create attractive press releases, newsletters, and brochures.

Who Should Use This Book?

You cannot escape the fact that looking good in print requires good design skills. Good design, in turn, demands talent and experience. This book, therefore, was conceived not as a graphic design tutorial but as a desktop publishing "cookbook." The book was written for people who cannot spare five years to learn graphic design. Use this book as intended, and the author confidently promises that you soon will be turning out documents to enhance your business image.

How To Use This Book

How do beginning cooks use their cookbooks? By following the recipes exactly, being careful to measure each ingredient precisely. Similarly, if you follow the keystroke instructions included with each document in the step-by-step chapters, you will achieve "tasty" document designs without fail—just change the company names, text, and illustrations to meet your particular needs.

After you have created a few documents by following the step-by-step instructions, you can begin to experiment with changing the sample layouts in accordance with basic graphic design principles, as described in the first four chapters.

Read the first four chapters of this book carefully, because they should help you understand how the principles of graphic design are applied to create the sample documents. Awareness of design principles turns each document into a mini-course in applied design.

Authors of books on desktop publishing sometimes make extravagant claims, "Buy this book, and you will become an effective, successful desktop publisher." This book takes a different approach that will give you the successful, satisfying experience of using WordPerfect to create well-designed documents.

Remember, however, that the total number of conceivable document designs is infinite, and no single book can ever cover them all. At some point, you may decide that the recipe you need isn't in this book. You then must choose whether to tackle the project yourself or to hire a professional graphic designer. Chapter 1 should help you make that decision.

Think of this book as a graphic designer who is looking over your shoulder, giving advice and encouragement, showing you step-by-step keystrokes, explaining principles, and showing you how to look good in WordPerfect 5.1.

If you are new to WordPerfect, or if you have not used the program's desktop publishing features extensively, you still can use this book, by re-creating the keystrokes exactly as they are given in the step-by-step chapters. For an in-depth understanding of desktop publishing with WordPerfect, however, you should review the appropriate chapters in the *WordPerfect Workbook* supplied with the program. For a review of desktop publishing

features, also read Ralph Blodgett's *WordPerfect Power Pack*, published by Que, 1990.

How This Book Is Organized

Look Your Best with WordPerfect 5.1 is organized into six parts. Part I discusses general layout and design rules that you should be aware of when creating your own documents. Parts II through VI take you through the step-by-step process of creating progressively more complex documents.

Part I: Graphic Design: The Art and Science of Good Taste

Part I introduces basic graphic arts concepts that you must know to produce attractive, effective documents.

Chapter 1, "Creating a Business Image," discusses why creating an attractive visual image for your business communications is as important as choosing a catchy business name.

Chapter 2, "Understanding Typography," shows you how to use type in ways that invite the reader to receive your message, because when readers find documents hard to read, they stop reading.

Chapter 3, "Understanding Page Design," shows you how to balance page elements for a harmonious, visually appealing effect. This chapter helps you avoid creating poorly designed pages that repel the eye.

Chapter 4, "Working with the Sample Designs," gives important instructions and tips that make your work easier, as you adapt the sample designs for your own business communications.

Part II: Creating Business Documents

Part II, "Creating Business Documents," gives instructions for adding a special touch of design flare to routine, hard-working documents that must communicate important information effectively.

Chapter 5, "Producing Letterheads," shows you how to design an effective letterhead that matches your business image: sober, playful, artistic, or staid.

Chapter 6, "Producing Envelopes," gives instructions for placing your business logo on envelopes and helps you avoid trying to crank out envelopes on a typewriter.

Chapter 7, "Producing Résumés," tells you how to lay out resumes, the most important business documents you will ever design, so that they impress prospective employers.

Chapter 8, "Producing Press Releases," shows you how to design press releases that will catch editors' eyes and convey your business's visual identity.

Chapter 9, "Producing Invitations," presents sample invitations, both of which are effective, for a playful and for a formal event.

Chapter 10, "Producing Programs and Schedules," gives sample designs that you can adapt for information that is simple or complex and helps you avoid the special problems encountered when trying to present data in an organized, readable way.

Chapter 11, "Producing Directories," shows you how to format lookup information for easy access and optimal readability.

Part III: Creating Business Forms

Part III, "Creating Business Forms," gives instructions for designing the most common kinds of documents that you must work with every day. Attractively designed business forms can add a special touch of class to your business image—especially if the form will be seen by your clients.

Chapter 12, "Producing Invoices," gives sample designs that you can adapt to produce an invoice that represents you well in the wider business community.

Chapter 13, "Producing Fax Cover Sheets," helps you to bring order to the presentation of important information about the Fax sender and receiver.

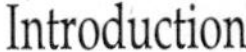

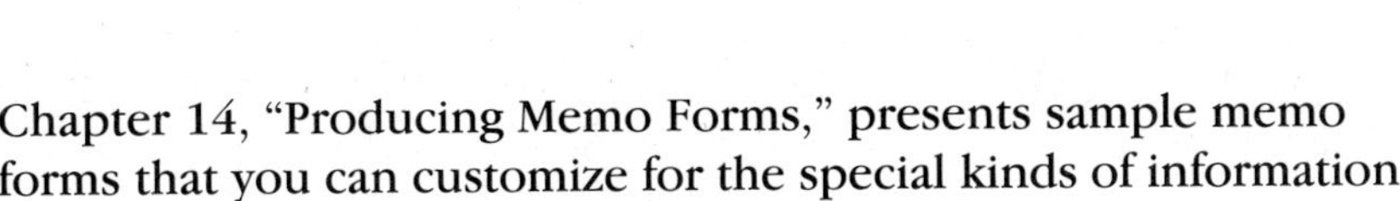

Chapter 14, "Producing Memo Forms," presents sample memo forms that you can customize for the special kinds of information that keep your company running smoothly.

Chapter 15, "Producing Time Sheets," shows you how to use WordPerfect's table feature to make flexible times sheets that you can alter at a moment's notice.

Chapter 16, "Producing Credit Forms," shows you sample designs that use multiple tables and shaded cells to organize credit data in a business-like manner.

Chapter 17, "Producing Organizational Charts," demonstrates a little-known application of the table feature that enables you to easily design organizational charts.

Part IV: Creating Sales Documents

Part IV, "Creating Sales Documents," ventures into territory that is generally considered the domain of "real" desktop publishing software. Sales literature must attract attention in an emphatic but harmonious manner. The sample sales documents demonstrate how you can achieve advanced visual effects with WordPerfect.

Chapter 18, "Producing Flyers," gives you a start on announcing your products and services effectively and with style

Chapter 19, "Producing Brochures," shows you how to pack the maximum amount of information into the limited confines of a sales brochure.

Chapter 20, "Producing Product and Price Lists," presents readability principles that give you a competitive advantage when producing attractive lists.

Part V: Creating Long Documents

Long documents present a special design challenge: to package hundreds or even thousands of words in ways that hold the reader's attention. Part V, "Creating Long Documents," shows you

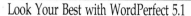

how to format reports, booklets, and instruction sheets that baby the reader's eyes.

Chapter 21, "Producing Reports," shows you how to format reports that convey essential information in ways that get attention.

Chapter 22, "Producing Booklets," applies the rules of typography and page design to make booklets effective and attractive.

Chapter 23, "Creating Instruction Sheets," shows you how surprisingly easy it is to create instruction sheets that present step-by-step information in a logical, readable manner with WordPerfect tables and graphic boxes.

Part VI: Creating Newsletters

Newsletters are what most people think of when they hear the term desktop publishing. Part VI, "Creating Newsletters," proves that WordPerfect can match high-end desktop publishing programs for creating simple and moderately complex newsletters.

Chapter 24, "Producing Simple Newsletters," shows how even a simple newsletter may involve extremely precise application of design principles. You learn a tremendous amount about formatting your own newsletters by following the steps for the sample document.

Chapter 25, "Producing Complex Newsletters," presents a sample design that serves as an advanced, hands-on tutorial in using type and graphics in a tasteful and orderly manner to create knockout newsletter designs.

Appendixes

Appendix A, "Glossary of Desktop Publishing Terms," gives you access to and an understanding of the world of design by defining the terms that make up the puzzling language spoken by graphic designers.

Appendix B, "Compose Codes for Zapf Dingbats," provides a complete list of the Compose key assignments that enable you to use Zapf Dingbats in your documents.

Appendix C, "Decimal Equivalents," provides a handy bridge between your fractional ruler and WordPerfect's decimal world. WordPerfect accepts measurements in fractions or decimals but converts any fractions to decimals. If you later decide to fine-tune a measurement, this appendix will help you remember the original fraction.

Where To Find More Help

To pack this book with as many practical hands-on document designs as possible, the text avoids reviewing the basic operation of WordPerfect's features. If you get stuck while attempting to create your own document designs, try the following resources:

- *WordPerfect Reference*
- *WordPerfect Workbook*
- WordPerfect Technical Support Lines:

Dot-Matrix Printers	800-541-5160
Laser Printers	800-541-5170
Other Printers	800-541-5097
Features	800-541-5096
Graphics/Tables/Equations	800-321-3383
Installation	800-533-9605
Macros, Merge, Labels	800-541-5129
Update to 5.1	800-451-5151

- WordPerfect Bulletin Board 801-225-4414
- Related books from Que include the following titles:

  Using WordPerfect 5.1
  WordPerfect QueCards
  WordPerfect 5.1 Quick Reference
  WordPerfect 5.1 Tips, Tricks, and Traps
  WordPerfect 5.1 Workbook and Disk
  WordPerfect Power Pack

November 1992 Vol 3 No. 11

FOUNDING MEMBERS

Salkin Construction

Brown Restorers

Vintage Homes, Inc.

THE TRADITIONAL BUILDER

❖ *Newsletter of Peninsula Restorers and Period Builders Association* ❖

Plexes On Rise

Tight money has new buyers moving in together

HI OMNES LINGUA, institutis, legibus inter se differunt. Gallos ab Aquitanis Garumna flumen, a Belgis Matrona et Sequana dividit. Horum omnium fortissimi sunt Belgae, propterea quod a cultu atque humanitate provinciae longissime absunt, minimeque ad eos mercatores saepe commeant atque ea quae ad effeminandos animos pertinent important, proximique sunt Germanis, qui trans Rhenum incolunt, quibuscum continenter bellum gerunt. Que de causa Helvetii quoque reliquos Gallos virtute praecedunt, quod fere cotidianis proeliis cum Germanis contendunt, cum aut suis finibus eos prohibent, aut ipsi in eorum finibus bellum gerunt. Eorum una pars, quam Gallos obtinere dictum est, initium capit a flumine Rhodano; continetur Garumna flumine, Oceano, finibus Belgarum; attingit etiam ab Sequanis et Helvetiis flumen Rhenum; vergit ad septentriones. Belgae ab extremis Galliae finibus oriuntur; pertinent ad Inferiorem partem fluminis Rheni; spectant in septentriones et orientem solem. Aquitania a Garumna flumine ad Pyrenaeos montes et eam partem Oceani quae est ad Hispaniam pertinent; spectat inter occasum solis et septentriones. Apid Helvetios longe nobilissimus fuit et ditissimus Orgetorix. Is, M. Messala, M. Pisone consulibus, regni cupiditate inductus coniurationem nobilitatis fecit et civitati persuasit ut de finibus suis cum omnibus copiis exirent: Perfacile esse, cum virtute. Que de causa Helvetii quoque reliquos Gallos virtute praecedunt. Eorum una pars, quam Gallos obtinere dictum est, initium capit a flumine Rhodano. ❖

Victorian Sunshine Builders specializes in add-on solaria for traditional homes.

Victorian Sunshine

Add-on solaria now a popular trend for older homes

ID HOC FACILIUS iis persuasit quod undique loci natura Helvetii contionentur: una ex parte flumine Rheno latissimo atque altissimo, qui agrum Helvetium a Germanis dividit; altera ex parte monte Iura altissimo, qui est inter Sequanos et Helvetios; teria lacu Lemanno et flumine. Gallos ab Aquitanis Garumna flumen, a Belgis Matrona et Sequana dividit. Horum omnium fortissimi sunt Belgae, propterea quod a cultu atque humanitate provinciae longissime absunt, minimeque ad eos mercatores saepe commeant atque ea quae ad effeminandos animos pertinent important, proximique sunt Germanis, qui trans Rhenum incolunt, quibuscum continenter bellum. Eorum una pars, quam Gallos obtinere dictum est, initium capit a flumine Rhodano; continetur Garumna. ❖

Part I

Graphic Design: The Art and Science of Good Taste

Includes

1

Creating a Business Image

The four chapters in Part I provide a crash course in design principles that can help you design good-looking documents. The remainder of the book gives step-by-step instructions for designing sample documents.

Looking good with WordPerfect is impossible without an awareness of the basic principles of graphic design. What *is* graphic design? Avoiding abstract definitions, graphic design is the art and science of designing attractive, readable newsletters, advertisements, magazine article pages, forms, brochures, flyers, and other business publications. Chapters 1 through 4 give you the principles to evaluate what looks good and why. With that design-awareness, plus hands-on practice with the step-by-step chapters, you will acquire a good basis for designing your own good-looking business documents.

How Image Affects Your Business

Consider the case of the Chevrolet Nova. When the mid-sized Chevy was introduced in the 1960s, no one at General Motors considered what would happen when it was exported to Spanish-speaking countries. In Spanish, *no va* means "It doesn't go." Needless to say, sales were sluggish south of the border.

Words matter. Appearances matter, too. Consider the following case history. Although fictitious, this situation probably occurs thousands of times every day.

A company needs a sales brochure. The sales manager writes and turns the copy over to the word processing department with instructions to "make it look nice—I need it back tomorrow morning." The word processor's awareness of graphic design is rudimentary, and the brochure reflects it.

Meanwhile, a competing company has trained its WordPerfect users in the basics of graphic design. Customers compare the two companies' brochures side-by-side. Although the product lines are functionally identical, the professionally designed brochure exudes competence, care, friendliness, and efficiency, but the hastily produced brochure says, "We don't respect you enough to put on our best tie. Here we are with spaghetti sauce on our shirt, our shoes unshined, and our hair dirty and untrimmed. Will you buy our product anyway?"

Figures 1.1 and 1.2 show the difference that graphic design can make in a simple business report. The *before* version shows a report format that was common circa 1985, when laser printers first entered the business environment. This report is not too bad, considering the limited font cartridges supplied with the original Hewlett-Packard LaserJet. However, the extremely long, double-spaced lines are a carryover from the days of the IBM Selectric, when reports were typed in 10-point Courier. Long, unreadable lines were inexcusable even in 1985, when WordPerfect 4.0 already had acquired newspaper-style columns.

The *after* version (fig. 1.2) was created with WordPerfect and output to a PostScript printer, following the step-by-step instructions given in Chapter 14. The improved report format is easier to read because it follows the design rules for font size and line length that you learn in Chapter 2. This format also is visually pleasing, thanks to its attractive use of page design basics that you learn in Chapter 3.

If you had received these reports from competing companies, which one would you read first? The company that took the time and trouble to apply design principles would surely have a competitive edge.

Graphic design is the art of keeping your shirt clean and your shoes shined, in print. Appearances affect your prospects of success. Certainly, some products—machine bearings, industrial cleaners, stamping presses, and so on—need little visual embellishment. Even if your product is strictly practical, the way you tell potential customers about it—whether copied from sloppy, typewritten, coffee-stained fourth-generation sheets or attractively laid out in laser-printed columns—carries a message about what you think of the customer and how you run your business.

Technical Perspectives Series

Paper No. 32:

Should Small Companies Invest in Connectivity?

Ray Blanda
Senior Vice President
Advanced Design Department
Omegacom Corporation

ABSTRACT

Equipment failures versus group communication convenience: what are the real tradeoffs? Computer hardware from today's blue chip venders (and, surprisingly, from several no-name clonemakers) minimizes the dangers of work group interconnectivity.

The advantages are manifold: rapid communication, instantaneous group-approved document changes, increased sense of participation and cooperation. The technology has proved 100% reliable in environments where important data are backed up on fast tape drives at least four times daily, and where the LAN is designed for fast switch-on of standby servers.

INTRODUCTION

Hi omnes lingua, institutis, legibus inter se differunt. Gallos ab Aquitanis Garumna flumen, a Belgis Matrona et Sequana dividit. Horum omnium fortissimi sunt Belgae, propterea quod a cultu atque humanitate provinciae longissime absunt, minimeque ad eos mercatores saepe commeant atque ea quae ad effeminandos animos pertinent important, proximique sunt Germanis, qui trans Rhenum incolunt, quibuscum continenter bellum gerunt.

FIG. 1.1 A laser-printed report formatted with three fonts and a page design common when laser printers first appeared, around 1985. (Part 1 of 3)

Should Small Companies Invest in Connectivity? **P. 2**

Que de causa Helvetii quoque reliquos Gallos virtute praecedunt, quod fere cotidianis proeliis cum Germanis contendunt, cum aut suis finibus eos prohibent, aut ipsi in eorum finibus bellum gerunt.

THE PROBLEM

Eorum una pars, quam Gallos obtinere dictum est, initium capit a flumine Rhodano; continetur Garumna flumine, Oceano, finibus Belgarum; attingit etiam ab Sequanis et Helvetiis flumen Rhenum; vergit ad septentriones. Belgae ab extremis Galliae finibus oriuntur; pertinent ad Inferiorem partem fluminis Rheni; spectant in septentriones et orientem solem. Aquitania a Garumna flumine ad Pyrenaeos montes et eam partem Oceani quae est ad Hispaniam pertinent; spectat inter occasum solis et septentriones.

Apid Helvetios longe nobilissimus fuit et ditissimus Orgetorix. Is, M. Messala, M. Pisone consulibus, regni cupiditate inductus coniurationem nobilitatis fecit et civitati persuasit ut de finibus suis cum omnibus copiis exirent: Perfacile esse, cum virtute omnibus praestarent, totius Galliae imperio potiri. Id hoc facilius iis persuasit quod undique loci natura Helvetii contionentur: una ex parte flumine Rheno latissimo atque altissimo, qui agrum Helvetium a Germanis dividit; altera ex parte monte Iura altissimo, qui est inter Sequanos et Helvetios; teria lacu Lemanno et flumine Rhodano, qui provinciam nostram ab Helvetiis dividit.

THE SOLUTIONS

His rebus fiebat ut et minus late vagarentur et minus facile finitimis bellum inferre possent; qua ex parte homines bellandi cupidi magno dolore afficiebantur. Pro multitudine autem hominum et pro gloria bellie atque fortitudinis angustos se fines habere arbitrabantur, qui in longitudinem milia passuum CCXL, in latitudinem CLLXXX patebant.

His rebus adducti et auctoritate Orgetorigis permoti constitu erunt ea quae ad proficiscendum pertinerent comparare, iumentorum et carrorum quam maximum numerum coemere, sementes quam maximas facere, ut in itinere copia frumenti suppeteret, cum proximis vicitatibus pacem et amicitiam confirmare.

FIG. 1.1 A laser-printed report formatted with three fonts and a page design common when laser printers first appeared, around 1985. (Part 2 of 3)

Should Small Companies Invest in Connectivity? P. 3

HARDWARE GIFTS, GIVENS, GRIPES

Ad eas res conficiendas biennieum sibi satis esse duxerunt; in tertium annum profectionem lege confirmant. Ad eas res conficiendas Orgetorix deligitur. Is sibi legationem ad civitates suscipit. In eo itinere persuadet Castico, Catamantaloedis filio, Sequano, cuius pater regnum in Sequania multos annos obtinuerat et a senatu populi Romani amicus appellatus erat, ut regnum in civitate sua occuparet, quod pater ante habuerat; itemque Dumnorigi Haeduo, fratri Diviciaci, qui eo tempore.

TYPICAL COST BREAKDOWN

Ea res est Hevetiis per indicium enuntiata. Moribus suis Orgetorigem ex vinculis cansam dicere coegerun; damnatum poenam sequi oportebat, ut igni cremaretru. Die constituta causae dictionis Orgetorix ad iudicium omnem suam familiam, ad homionum milia decem, undique coegit, et omnes clientes obaeratosque suos, quorum magnum numerum habebat, eodem conduxit; per eos, ne causam diceret, se eripuit. Cum civitas ob eam rem incitata armis ius suum exsequi conaretur, multitudinemque hominum ex agris magistratus cogerent, Orgetorix mortuus est; neque abest suspicio, ut Helvetii arbitrantur, quin ipse sibi mortem consciverit.

CONCLUSION

Post eius mortem nihilo minus Helvetii id quod constituerant facere conantur, ut e finibus suis exeant. Ubi iam se ad eam rem paratos esse arbitrati sunt, oppida sua omnia, numero ad duodecim, vicos ad quadringentos, relique privata, aedificia incendunt; frumentum omne, praeterquam quod secum portaturi erant, comburunt, ut, domum reditionis spe sublata, paratiores ad omnia pericula subeunda essent; trium mensium molita cibaria sibi quemque domo efferre iubent. Persuadent Rauracis et Tulingis et Latobrigis, finitimis, uti eodem usi consilio, oppidis suis vicisque exustis, una cum iis proficiscantur; Boiosque, qui trans Rhenum incoluerant et in agrum oricum transierant Noreiamque oppugnabant, receptos ad se socios sibi asciscunt.

FIG. 1.1 A laser-printed report formatted with three fonts and a page design common when laser printers first appeared, around 1985. (Part 3 of 3)

Technical Perspectives Series

Paper No. 32

Should Small Companies Invest in Connectivity?

Ray Blanda
Senior Vice President
Advanced Design Department
Omegacom Corporation

January 15, 1991

Abstract

EQUIPMENT FAILURES VS. WORK group communication convenience: what are the real tradeoffs? Computer hardware from today's blue chip venders (and, surprisingly, from several no-name clonemakers) minimizes the dangers of work group interconnectivity.

The advantages are manifold: rapid communication, instantaneous group-approved document changes, increased sense of participation and cooperation. The technology has proved 100% reliable in environments where important data are backed up on fast tape drives at least four times daily, and where the LAN is designed for fast switch-on of standby servers.

FIG. 1.2 A report based on the design principles for optimal readability and attractive page design. (Part 1 of 3)

2

Introduction

HI OMNES LINGUA, institutis, legibus inter se differunt. Gallos ab Aquitanis Garumna flumen, a Belgis Matrona et Sequana dividit. Horum omnium fortissimi sunt Belgae, propterea quod a cultu atque humanitate provinciae longissime absunt, minimeque ad eos mercatores saepe commeant atque ea quae ad effeminandos animos pertinent important, proximique sunt Germanis, qui trans Rhenum incolunt, quibuscum continenter bellum gerunt.

Que de causa Helvetii quoque reliquos Gallos virtute praecedunt, quod fere cotidianis proeliis cum Germanis contendunt, cum aut suis finibus eos prohibent, aut ipsi in eorum finibus bellum gerunt.

The Problem

EORUM UNA PARS, quam Gallos obtinere dictum est, initium capit a flumine Rhodano; continetur Garumna flumine, Oceano, finibus Belgarum; attingit etiam ab Sequanis et Helvetiis flumen Rhenum; vergit ad septentriones. Belgae ab extremis Galliae finibus oriuntur; pertinent ad Inferiorem partem fluminis Rheni; spectant in septentriones et orientem solem. Aquitania a Garumna flumine ad Pyrenaeos montes et eam partem Oceani quae est ad Hispaniam pertinent; spectat inter occasum solis et septentriones.

Apid Helvetios longe nobilissimus fuit et ditissimus Orgetorix. Is, M. Messala, M. Pisone consulibus, regni cupiditate inductus coniurationem nobilitatis fecit et civitati persuasit ut de finibus suis cum omnibus copiis exirent: Perfacile esse, cum virtute omnibus praestarent, totius Galliae imperio potiri. Id hoc facilius iis persuasit quod undique loci natura Helvetii contionentur: una ex parte flumine Rheno latissimo atque altissimo, qui agrum Helvetium a Germanis dividit; altera ex parte monte Iura altissimo, qui est inter Sequanos et Helvetios; teria lacu Lemanno et flumine Rhodano, qui provinciam nostram ab Helvetiis dividit.

The Solutions

HIS REBUS FIEBAT ut et minus late vagarentur et minus facile finitimis bellum inferre possent; qua ex parte homines bellandi cupidi magno dolore afficiebantur. Pro multitudine autem hominum et pro gloria bellie atque fortitudinis angustos se fines habere arbitrabantur, qui in longitudinem milia passuum CCXL, in latitudinem CLLXXX patebant.

His rebus adducti et auctoritate Orgetorigis permoti constitu erunt ea quae ad proficiscendum pertinerent comparare, iumentorum et carrorum quam maximum numerum coemere, sementes quam maximas facere, ut in itinere copia frumenti suppeteret, cum proximis vicitatibus pacem et amicitiam confirmare.

Hardware Gifts, Givens, Gripes

AD EAS RES conficiendas biennieum sibi satis esse duxerunt; in tertium annum profectionem lege confirmant. Ad eas res conficiendas Orgetorix deligitur. Is sibi legationem ad civitates suscipit. In eo itinere persuadet Castico, Catamantaloedis filio, Sequano, cuius pater regnum in Sequania multos annos obtinuerat et a senatu populi Romani amicus appellatus erat, ut regnum in civitate sua occuparet, quod pater ante habuerat; itemque Dumnorigi Haeduo, fratri Diviciaci, qui eo tempore.

Should Small Companies Invest In Connectivity?

FIG. 1.2 A report based on the design principles for optimal readability and attractive page design. (Part 2 of 3)

Typical Cost Breakdown

EA RES EST HEVETIIS per indicium enuntiata. Moribus suis Orgetorigem ex vinculis cansam dicere coegerun; damnatum poenam sequi oportebat, ut igni cremaretru. Die constituta causae dictionis Orgetorix ad iudicium omnem suam familiam, ad homionum milia decem, undique coegit, et omnes clientes obaeratosque suos, quorum magnum numerum habebat, eodem conduxit; per eos, ne causam diceret, se eripuit. Cum civitas ob eam rem incitata armis ius suum exsequi conaretur, multitudinemque hominum ex agris magistratus cogerent, Orgetorix mortuus est; neque abest suspicio, ut Helvetii arbitrantur, quin ipse sibi mortem consciverit.

Conclusion

POST EIUS MORTEM nihilo minus Helvetii id quod constituerant facere conantur, ut e finibus suis exeant. Ubi iam se ad eam rem paratos esse arbitrati sunt, oppida sua omnia, numero ad duodecim, vicos ad quadringentos, relique privata, aedificia incendunt; frumentum omne, praeterquam quod secum portaturi erant, comburunt, ut, domum reditionis spe sublata, paratiores ad omnia pericula subeunda essent; trium mensium molita cibaria sibi quemque domo efferre iubent. Persuadent Rauracis et Tulingis et Latobrigis, finitimis, uti eodem usi consilio, oppidis suis vicisque exustis, una cum iis proficiscantur; Boiosque, qui trans Rhenum incoluerant et in agrum oricum transierant Noreiamque oppugnabant, receptos ad se socios sibi asciscunt.

FIG. 1.2 A report based on the design principles for optimal readability and attractive page design. (Part 3 of 3)

Word Processing versus Desktop Publishing

Desktop publishing is the art of producing documents on small computers, using tools traditionally associated with formal typography and graphic design. As word processing programs have acquired desktop publishing features, unadulterated word processing software has become increasingly rare.

Ten years ago, you might have printed reports on a dot-matrix printer with two or three fonts and a few line illustrations. Today, with WordPerfect and a laser printer, you can select from hundreds of fonts and insert spreadsheet charts and graphic images in your documents. You can print text in columns, place text and pictures where you want them on the page, and preview the results with the View Document feature. WordPerfect 5.1 has some of the most advanced desktop publishing features of any DOS word processing software.

When would you ever need a *real* desktop publishing program like Ventura Publisher or Aldus Pagemaker?

As word processing programs have improved, so has desktop publishing software. PageMaker and Ventura enable you to work on an on-screen version of your document that looks almost exactly like the final, printed result. With WordPerfect for DOS, you still must use View Document to preview your work, a considerable inconvenience. The latest versions of PageMaker and Ventura enable you to specify spot color, rotate type in small increments, use advanced typographic features, and import spreadsheet charts that change automatically when you edit the original chart in Microsoft Excel or Lotus 1-2-3 for Windows.

The desktop publishing features of the Microsoft Windows version of WordPerfect have some of the flavor, if not the depth, of PageMaker and Ventura, and they are easier and quicker to use. Meanwhile, desktop publishing software offers unique benefits for the experienced graphic designer or for the ambitious amateur who must crank out complex documents on a regular basis.

WordPerfect users need not despair. You do a bit more work to create good-looking document designs with WordPerfect, and you can do a great many things with desktop publishing programs that you cannot do with WordPerfect, but a well-designed document looks the same—whether you create it with WordPerfect or with desktop publishing software. Figure 1.3 shows a newsletter page designed in PageMaker and reproduced in WordPerfect 5.1 without compromising a single feature of the design. (Instructions for creating this newsletter are in Chapter 25.)

Graphic Design: The Art of Looking Good in Print

Everyone is familiar with the laws of grammar: for example, an adverb usually should follow the verb, not the subject, lest the meaning of the sentence be changed. The time-tested rules of visual presentation, however, are less familiar to many people, because they have little occasion to learn and practice them.

In pre-computer days, most business reports were typewritten with a Courier 10-pitch daisywheel, and as long as the text was double-spaced, it was readable. When the first laser printers appeared, many companies changed their report format to single-spaced 10- or 12-point Times Roman without changing column width or line spacing, which made for hard-to-read text.

Graphic design is the art of avoiding such horrendous errors; and much more than that, graphic design is the art of harmonious presentation. Graphic design principles ask: "What arrangement of words and pictures is easiest to read and looks most pleasing?" Finding answers to that simple question is the subject of a four-year college-level course of study.

Clearly established rules exist for using type, designing pages, and choosing and placing photos, charts, and line drawings. At times, you can safely break the rules, but only after carefully considering the effect on the reader. WordPerfect makes applying the rules easy. Chapters 2 through 4 give you a crash course in graphic design basics, with tips for applying them in WordPerfect.

This book takes a cookbook approach. If you follow the step-by-step directions for the sample documents in Chapters 5 through 25, you will achieve gratifying results. In most cases, you will want to customize the sample designs—adding your company's logo, using different illustrations, and so on. If you know the basics of design, you can adapt the sample documents with little trouble.

November 1992 Vol 3 No. 11

FOUNDING MEMBERS

Salkin Construction

Brown Restorers

Vintage Homes, Inc.

THE TRADITIONAL

BUILDER

❖ *Newsletter of Peninsula Restorers and Period Builders Association* ❖

Plexes On Rise

Tight money has new buyers moving in together

HI OMNES LINGUA, institutis, legibus inter se differunt. Gallos ab Aquitanis Garumna flumen, a Belgis Matrona et Sequana dividit. Horum omnium fortissimi sunt Belgae, propterea quod a cultu atque humanitate provinciae longissime absunt, minimeque ad eos mercatores saepe commeant atque ea quae ad effeminandos animos pertinent important, proximique sunt Germanis, qui trans Rhenum incolunt, quibuscum continenter bellum gerunt. Que de causa Helvetii quoque reliquos Gallos virtute praecedunt, quod fere cotidianis proeliis cum Germanis contendunt, cum aut suis finibus eos prohibent, aut ipsi in eorum finibus bellum gerunt. Eorum una pars, quam Gallos obtinere dictum est, initium capit a flumine Rhodano; continetur Garumna flumine, Oceano, finibus Belgarum; attingit etiam ab Sequanis et Helvetiis flumen Rhenum; vergit ad septentriones. Belgae ab extremis Galliae finibus oriuntur; pertinent ad Inferiorem partem fluminis Rheni; spectant in septentriones et orientem solem. Aquitania a Garumna flumine ad Pyrenaeos montes et eam partem Oceani quae est ad Hispaniam pertinent; spectat inter occasum solis et septentriones. Apid Helvetios longe nobilissimus fuit et ditissimus Orgetorix. Is, M. Messala, M. Pisone consulibus, regni cupiditate inductus coniurationem nobilitatis fecit et civitati persuasit ut de finibus suis cum omnibus copiis exirent: Perfacile esse, cum virtute. Que de causa Helvetii quoque reliquos Gallos virtute praecedunt. Eorum una pars, quam Gallos obtinere dictum est, initium capit a flumine Rhodano. ❖

Victorian Sunshine Builders specializes in add-on solaria for traditional homes.

Victorian Sunshine

Add-on solaria now a popular trend for older homes

ID HOC FACILIUS iis persuasit quod undique loci natura Helvetii contionentur: una ex parte flumine Rheno latissimo atque altissimo, qui agrum Helvetium a Germanis dividit; altera ex parte monte Iura altissimo, qui est inter Sequanos et Helvetios; teria lacu Lemanno et flumine. Gallos ab Aquitanis Garumna flumen, a Belgis Matrona et Sequana dividit. Horum omnium fortissimi sunt Belgae, propterea quod a cultu atque humanitate provinciae longissime absunt, minimeque ad eos mercatores saepe commeant atque ea quae ad effeminandos animos pertinent important, proximique sunt Germanis, qui trans Rhenum incolunt, quibuscum continenter bellum. Eorum una pars, quam Gallos obtinere dictum est, initium capit a flumine Rhodano; continetur Garumna. ❖

FIG. 1.3 A newsletter front page created with WordPerfect.

Suppose that you need a design that is different from any of the samples in this book. You must determine how important the final product is. Some jobs should *always* be professionally designed, whether by an outside studio or an on-call design consultant. These jobs include corporate annual reports, wedding invitations, formal invitations, and so on.

If you believe you can design the document yourself, ask yourself whether the proposed design departs radically from the samples in this book or from professional designs that you have seen or that you have successfully emulated in the past. You may be wise to buy a few hours of a designer's time. When your company's image is at stake, it's generally better to err on the side of caution.

TIP

Before hiring a graphic designer, ask to see the designer's portfolio. Some designers specialize, and their work may not be consistent with your business. A designer who has done beauty product packaging for 10 years may be woefully out of touch with current trends in the electronics industry.

Desktop Publishing with WordPerfect

Desktop-published documents, whether well or poorly designed, contain just three elements: type, boxes (for photos and graphic images), and lines. These elements enable you to have tremendous variety in document design. Fortunately, WordPerfect 5.1 supports them all.

To give you some idea of the enormous flexibility of WordPerfect's desktop publishing features, consider the many ways that you can use type, boxes, and lines. With type, you can create visually dominant design elements such as newsletter headings. Figure 1.4 shows a fax form from Chapter 19 that uses type as the principle design element.

LPCP

LandPro
Commercial
Properties

5793 LANDING BAY CIRCLE
ATLANTIC COMMONS, MA 01234-6453
VOICE: (102) 777-8765
FAX: (102) 777-8766

FAX TRANSMISSION

To

Location

Voice #

Fax #

From

Location

Voice #

Fax #

Number of pages (including this page)

Date

Time

COMMENTS:

FIG. 1.4 A fax form that uses type as the principle design element.

Boxes can be borderless, with thick or thin borders, and may contain text, photographs, line drawings, spreadsheet figures, graphic images, charts, or graphs. Thin vertical graphic lines can be used to separate columns, and thick horizontal graphic lines can separate major headings from body text. As with type, you also can use boxes and lines to decorate your pages. The newsletter page in figure 1.5 uses eight boxes that hold photos and text and two graphic lines. (Design steps for this newsletter are given in Chapter 24.)

The three major page design features—type, boxes, and lines—form the core of WordPerfect's desktop publishing features. WordPerfect's tables feature also is tremendously useful, particularly for designing forms.

This book does not provide a detailed, keystroke-level review of WordPerfect's desktop publishing features. As you work through the examples in Chapters 5 through 25, you should get a good review of these features. The following sections of the Word-Perfect reference manual describe features used throughout the step-by-step chapters. When you attempt your own designs, you may find it helpful to read these sections for a deeper understanding. You also may find helpful tips for working with WordPerfect features in Chapter 4 of this book.

Advance
Attributes
Cartridges and Fonts
Columns, Display
Columns, Newspaper
Columns, Parallel
Compose
Display Pitch
Display Setup
Font
Graphics, Create
Graphics, Define a Box
Graphics, Edit
Graphics, Formats and Programs
Graphics Lines
Graphics Options
Graphics Screen Type
Justification
Kerning
Line Format
Line Height
Line Spacing
Margins, Left and Right
Margins, Top and Bottom
Master Documents
Paper Size/Type
Print (all aspects)
Print Quality
Printer Functions
Printing, Landscape
Rewrite
Screen Capture Program
Style
Style, Create
Tab
Tab Set
Table, Create
Table, Edit Structure
Table, Format Columns and Cells
Table, Math
View Document
View Document, Options
Widow/Orphan
Word and Letter Spacing

4 West Bay senior runner

Energy & Sports Physiology

Concedendum non putabat; neque homines inimico animo, data facultate per provinciam itineris faciendi, temperaturos ab iniuria et maleficio existimabat. Tamen, ut spatium intercedere posset, dum milites quos imperaverat convenirent, legatis respondit diem se ad deliberandum sumpturum; si quid vellent, ad Id. April. reverterentur.

Aquitania a Garumna flumine ad Pyrenaeos montes et eam partem Oceani quae est ad Hispaniam pertinent; spectat inter occasum solis et septentriones.

Apid Helvetios longe nobilissimus fuit et ditissimus Orgetorix. Is, M. Messala, M. Pisone consulibus, regni cupiditate inductus coniurationem nobilitatis fecit et civitati persuasit ut de finibus suis cum omnibus copiis exirent: Perfacile esse, cum virtute omnibus praestarent, totius Galliae imperio potiri. Id hoc facilius iis persuasit quod undique loci natura Helvetii contionentur: una ex parte flumine Rheno latissimo atque

Ab extremis Galliae finibus oriuntur; pertinent ad Inferiorem partem fluminis

Apid Helvetios longe nobilissimus fuit et ditissimus Orgetorix.

Erant omnino itinera duo quibus itineribus domo exire possent.

agrum Helvetium a Germanis dividit; altera ex parte monte Iura altissimo, qui est inter Sequanos et Helvetios; teria lacu Lemanno et flumine Rhodano, qui provinciam nostram ab Helvetiis

dividit. His rebus flebat ut et minus late vagarentur et minus facile finitimis bellum inferre possent; qua ex parte homines bellandi cupidi magno dolore afficiebantur. Pro multitudine autem hominum.

west bay
senior runner
589 South North Avenue
San Francisco, CA 94100-9876

U.S. Postage
PAID
Permit No. 000
San Francisco, CA

Address Correction
and Forwarding Requested

FIG. 1.5 A newsletter page that uses two graphic lines and eight boxes to create functional and decorative effects.

Using Help

As you work with WordPerfect's desktop publishing features, remember that information is as close as the F3 (Help) key. For example, to get help about Word and Letter Spacing, press F3 to display the help screen and then press W to move to the appropriate section of the help list. Word/Letter Spacing is shown with its command keystrokes: Shift-F8, 4, 6, 3. Without leaving the help screen, press Shift-F8, 4, 6, 3 to display specific help about Word/Letter Spacing. Then press Enter to exit help.

You also can get help about Word/Letter Spacing *after* you press the command keystrokes (Shift-F8, 6, 4, 3) to choose that feature from the Format menu. With the `Word Spacing` or `Letter Spacing` prompt displayed in the status line, press F3 to get context-sensitive help about the selected feature.

How To Learn Desktop Publishing

Attractive documents have a clean, harmonious, deceptively simple look. Like great performances in athletics and dance, they seem effortless. But years of training lie behind a good athlete's or graphic designer's inspiring performances. One famous designer used six fonts from three typefaces in a column of magazine text, while maintaining a harmonious effect. You may not be able to match such a world-class performance, but you can learn a great deal about document design by following the step-by-step procedures for creating the professionally designed documents in Chapters 5 through 25.

You cannot learn desktop publishing merely by studying the appropriate sections of the WordPerfect manual; nor can you learn desktop publishing just by reading this book. It takes practice. For some readers, learning graphic design may be a low priority. They may want only to copy a good design for a flyer, memo, or report. If you aspire to design your own documents, however, you need to practice.

Professional graphic artists collect good designs. When you attend a trade show, stuff a plastic bag full of brochures. When you see an especially attractive report, save it. Tear pages out of old magazines. Study any printed literature that particularly strikes you. Ask lots of questions. "Why did the designer put white space here? What font is this? What's the size? The line length? Is this typeface Palatino Italic or Zapf Calligraphic?" Studying the work of professional designers is an invaluable way to learn. Better yet, find a designer who can critique your work.

How To *Do* Desktop Publishing

Learning the theory behind desktop publishing is one thing. Putting that theory to practice is quite another. The difference is as great as that between reading what a museum brochure says about a sculpture and being knee-deep in marble chips with hammer and chisel in hand.

When computers came along, everyone thought that they would make writing and number-crunching easy. Actually, computers only made it faster. When desktop publishing came along, everyone thought it would free users from rulers and rubber cement. Actually, designers got rid of glue pots and X-Acto knives, but they are still using their rulers.

Desktop Publishing's Nit-Picky Side

Like any job, desktop publishing has its own, special rhythms. If you resist those rhythms, you will find the publishing process frustrating, but if you can understand and accept those rhythms, you will find that the process will help you to be more productive.

Newcomers to desktop publishing sometimes are dismayed by how much of their time is spent solving problems that have more to do with the tiny, nit-picking details than with grand experiences of artistic creativity. The only way to find happiness as a desktop publisher is to accept this nit-picking aspect of the work and to learn to love it.

Specifically, you will find yourself spending a great deal of time in Reveal Codes, doing nit-picky chores like editing box and line codes, changing column specifications, and trying out different font sizes. An entire section of the Format: Other menu structure deserves to be known as WordPerfect's *nit-picking features bundle*.

This section includes Advance, Kerning, Word and Letter Spacing, Word Spacing Justification Limits, Leading Adjustment, and Border Options.

PageMaker users don't have it much easier. They also must place drop caps and left-border subheads with extreme care.

TIP

Make lists. This process simplifies the process of working with fine details. If a page contains seven text boxes, four horizontal lines, and three vertical lines, Reveal Codes doesn't tell you which code belongs to which box or line. As you create each box, write down its number and description. This practice greatly speeds up the process of finding and changing a specific line or box.

TIP

Work methodically. For example, when you create a drop cap (a large, capital letter at the start of an article), work on one problem at a time. First, align the bottom of the drop cap with the baseline of the adjacent line of body text, using Advance. Then adjust the white space between the drop cap and body text, by changing the size of the drop-cap box.

The Desktop Publishing Work Cycle

You save time if you organize your desktop publishing projects for a logical, step-by-step work flow:

1. Plan the document.

   Before you turn on the computer, sketch your design on paper. This is essential. Repositioning page elements with WordPerfect can take many keystrokes and a great deal of measuring. A pencil sketch helps you set margins and place text, line, and boxes close to their final position. Chapter 3 gives advice about planning an underlying page "grid" on which all page elements are placed. As you plan a document, ask yourself some questions about the person(s) who will read it:

> Is it intended for a business audience? If so, you may want to use conservative typefaces and illustrations. Will you ask the reader to spend money? If so, you may need to include a great deal of persuasive copy and give less space to illustrations. Does the document have time value? If so, you may want to place dates and event announcements near the top of the page in bold type. Will the document include a self-mailer? If so, you need to plan the layout so that it folds correctly. (You also may want to make sure that photos and headlines don't overlap the fold line inside the document.) Are tables included? If so, they may communicate more effectively if you convert them to charts.

2. Create major document and page elements first. As you work with the sample documents in Chapters 5 through 25, you should notice that the first line of each WordPerfect file contains margin settings, followed by header and footer codes, and then page-anchored boxes. WordPerfect requires that these codes be placed in the first line of the page, but there are good reasons to create them first. With margins set and headers, footers, and boxes in place, you can begin placing titles and body text and using View Document to get an accurate view of your work. If you cannot judge the position of report headings, for example, you may end up with side-by-side headings after you place a few photo boxes.

TIP

Create and then adjust. Don't be afraid to be way off with your first estimate of line or box placement, for example. Suppose that you want to place a heavy horizontal line under a title. You measure the spacing and create a horizontal line and then check your work in View Document. The line has landed in the middle of the title and is much too far to the right. Edit the line code and add or subtract from the Horizontal Position and Vertical Position settings. The point is that this is how graphic design is done: by gradual adjustments. Many times in the step-by-step chapters, you will find the statement: "This measurement was arrived at by experimentation."

After you set margins, headers, footers, and boxes, create the major page heading, if any (a newsletter banner or flyer headline, for example). Finally, place the body text, including subheads, vertical lines between columns, and horizontal lines between sections.

TIP

Work from printouts. You will save time if you print your early draft pages and use a ruler to position or reposition boxes and lines. Don't try to guess spacing from the View Document screen. View Document may not accurately display the position of large title text that you have fine-tuned with Advance, Leading Adjustment, and Word/Letter Spacing. Be sure to check your work with a printout before proceeding to the next step.

3. Fine-tune the design. This step is vital and one that beginning desktop publishers often neglect. See Chapter 4 for a checklist for fine-tuning your documents.

TIP

Measure. Chapter 4 gives tips for working with units of measure and setting measurements in box and line definition menus. Most importantly, don't rely on View Document to show you how to space page elements. Print out your work and use a ruler. This practice saves a great deal of time, because the View Document screen isn't 100-percent accurate.

TIP

When you use View Document to view the results of your work, check fine details by pressing 2 to display the page at 200-percent of actual size. Don't rely on View Document for the finest details—to check those, print your work. View Document can tell you whether a box and adjoining text are far out of alignment, however.

2

Understanding Typography

Desktop publishing software provides enormous freedom—freedom from glue pots, scissors, and T-squares; freedom from hefty typographer's fees; and freedom from print production delays and breakdowns. This freedom, however, comes with a price. When you use WordPerfect for desktop publishing, you leave word processing and enter the world of graphic design, a world with its own laws and limitations. To succeed in this world of graphic design, you have to know the laws and their application.

The most basic laws of graphic design concern type: how to choose it and how to use it. Publication researchers discovered factors that make documents attractive and easy on the eye. This chapter summarizes those findings.

Typography

You don't need the skills and experience of a graphic designer to create readable documents. Most publications, such as newsletters, reports, letters, memos, catalogs, and price lists, are filled with type rather than graphic images, tables, lines, boxes, photographs, and screens. When the type is unpleasant to read, the reader stops and puts the document down, but when the type is inviting, he or she reads on. Type can be formal or informal, staid or playful, dull or decorative. No matter which typefaces you use or how you use them, they must be readable. Research shows that using type in certain ways makes documents more readable, which in turn makes your documents more effective.

Typefaces versus Fonts

In the discussions of type throughout this book, you see the terms *font* and *typeface* repeatedly. Although many people use the terms interchangeably, a typeface is actually a family of fonts. Times Roman is a typeface. Times Roman Bold, Times Roman Italic, and Times Roman Bold Italic are fonts. 96-point Times Roman Bold Italic is a font, and 10-point Times Roman Bold Italic is another font.

A typeface can have many variations in addition to bold, italic, and bold italic. For example, PostScript printers come with eleven Helvetica fonts: Bold, Bold Oblique Italic, Condensed Bold, Condensed Bold Oblique, Condensed Medium, Condensed Oblique, Narrow, Narrow Bold, Narrow Bold Oblique, Narrow Oblique, and Oblique.

If your printer supports the feature, WordPerfect can create outline and shadowed type and small caps. To use these enhancements, follow these steps:

1. Press Ctrl-F8 (Font), A (Appearance).
2. Choose an enhancement from the menu.

You also can use the Print Color feature on the Font menu to create various types of shading, if your non-color printer supports the feature. Figure 2.1 shows some of the type variations you can create with a Canon LBP8-III or compatible printer. You cannot produce these effects with a PostScript printer.

Until recently, most laser printers came with fonts in specific point sizes: 10-point Helvetica, 9-point Times Roman, and so on. Many newer models, however, have scalable font technology that enables you to choose any font size, typically from 2 points (1/36") to 800 points (11.11") or larger, just by choosing the size from the Base Font menu. For example, to choose 32.5-point Times Roman, follow these steps:

1. Press Ctrl-F8 (Font), F (Base Font).
2. Move the cursor to Times Roman in the font list and press Enter.
3. Type *32.5*" at the `Point size` prompt and press Enter.

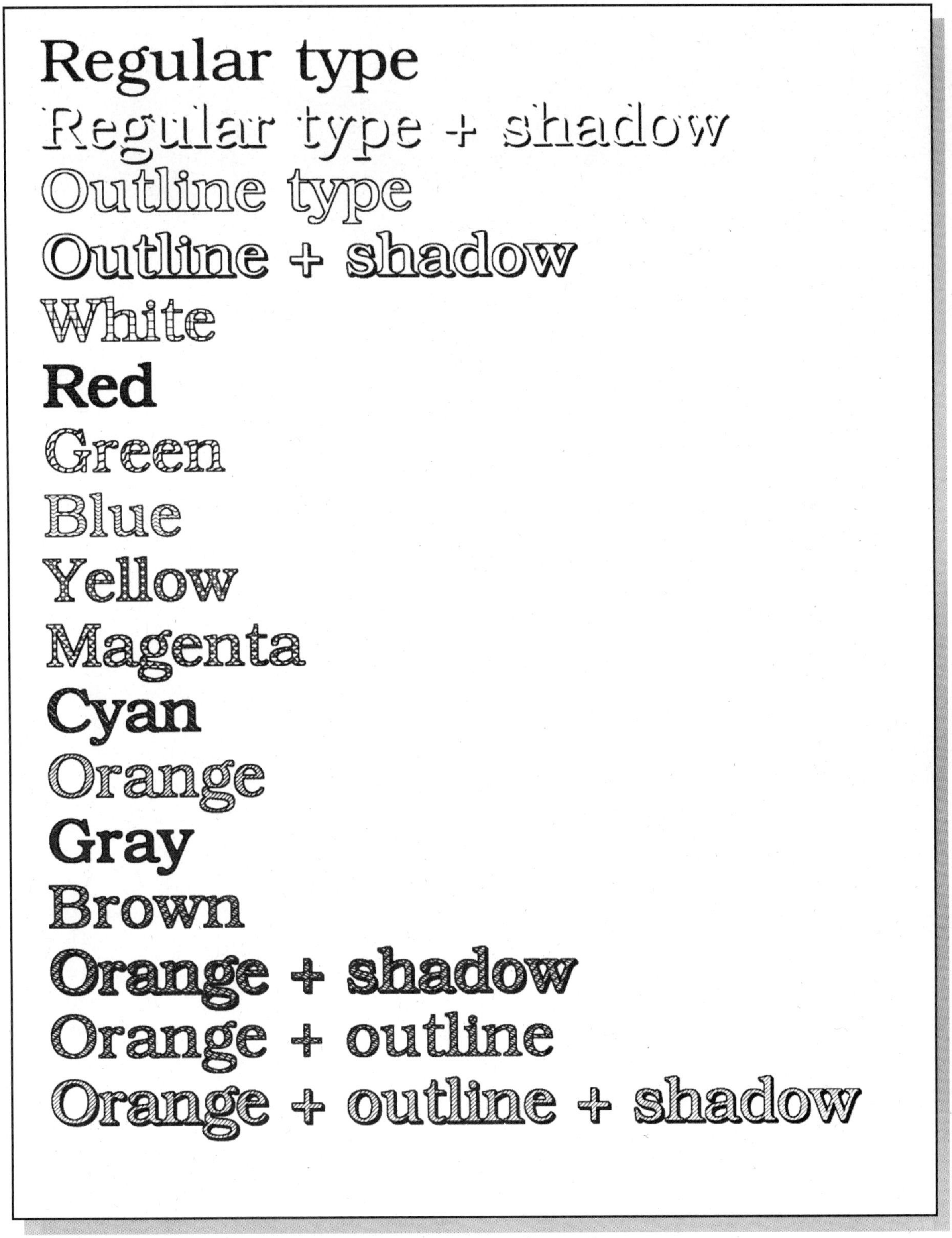

Regular type
Regular type + shadow
Outline type
Outline + shadow
White
Red
Green
Blue
Yellow
Magenta
Cyan
Orange
Gray
Brown
Orange + shadow
Orange + outline
Orange + outline + shadow

FIG. 2.1 Font Appearance and Color variations.

The View Document feature displays font sizes in their relative proportions but displays all serif fonts with the same screen font and all sans serif fonts with the same screen font. You cannot distinguish on the View Document screen whether a serif font is Times Roman or Bookman.

Serif versus Sans Serif Typefaces

Type comes in two styles: serif and sans serif. A *serif* is a small line that extends from a letter. Figure 2.2 shows a typeset word labeled with the terms used to describe the parts of the letters.

FIG. 2.2 The elements of type.

Sans serif, French for *without serif*, type lacks serifs. Figure 2.3 shows popular serif and sans serif faces.

Research shows that sans serif type is harder to read than serif type, possibly because the horizontal strokes at the bottom of serif letters guide the eye back to the beginning of the next letter. As a general rule, use sans serif type only for brief sections of text such as pull quotes or headlines. Figure 2.4 shows a sample of serif and sans serif type.

In figure 2.4, see how much larger the Helvetica text appears, although both paragraphs use 10-point type. Helvetica letters have an unusually large *x-height*. You learn more about type sizes in the next section.

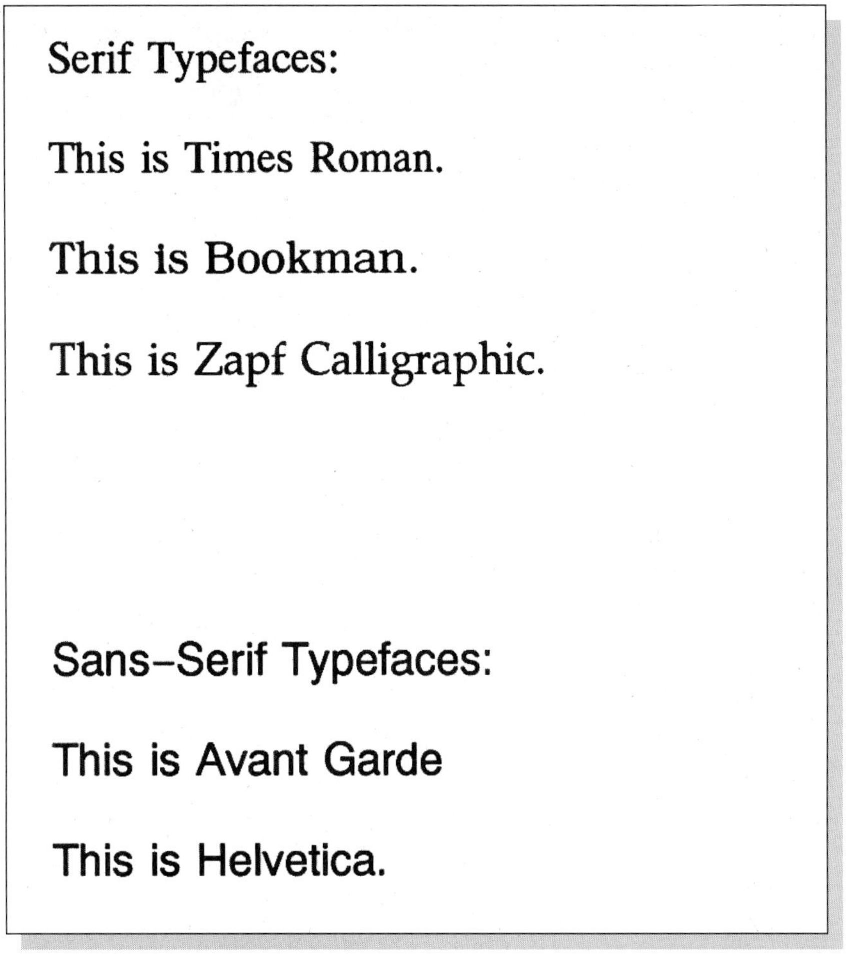

Serif Typefaces:

This is Times Roman.

This is Bookman.

This is Zapf Calligraphic.

Sans-Serif Typefaces:

This is Avant Garde

This is Helvetica.

FIG. 2.3 Serif and sans serif fonts.

Type Size

Type size greatly affects the readability of a document. Readability studies show that the best size for body text is between 9 and 12 points. Figure 2.5 shows text set in 8-point, 10-point, and 12-point Times Roman.

This is a sample of 10-point Times Roman. This typeface was designed for optimum readability. Its popularity has stood the test of time: evidence that it is indeed among the most readable typefaces. Times Roman is a serif typeface. It was designed approximately 45 years ago.

This is a sample of 10-point Helvetica. It, too, was designed for readability. But research has shown that sans serif typefaces are not as readable as serif type, possibly because there are no serifs at the bottoms of letters to guide the eye back to the start of the next line.

FIG. 2.4 Serif type is more readable than sans serif type.

TIP

Some fonts look larger than other fonts of the same measured size because the larger appearing font's x-height is larger. The x-height, shown in figure 2.2, is the height of letters that don't have ascenders or descenders—for example, e, a, o, x, r. The effect of x-height on font appearance is shown in figure 2.4.

This is an example of 8-point Times Roman. It is too small for body text. The optimal size for three-column body text is between 9 and 11 points. For wider columns you should choose a larger size. A good choice for a two-column layout would be 11- or 12-point Times Roman.

This is an example of 10-point Times Roman. It's just right for body text. The optimal size for three-column body text is between 9 and 11 points. For wider columns you should choose a larger size. A good choice for a two-column layout would be 11- or 12-point Times Roman.

This is an example of 12-point Times Roman. It is too big for three-column body text. The optimal size for three-column body text is between 9 and 11 points. For wider columns you should choose a larger size. A good choice for a two-column layout would be 11- or 12-point Times Roman.

FIG. 2.5 Type size greatly affects readability.

TIP

Some fonts look darker than others, and this difference may affect their readability. A visual comparison of several paragraphs set in fonts of differing darkness helps you decide which is the more readable font. Figure 2.6 shows paragraphs set in Times Roman and New Century Schoolbook.

This is 10–point Times Roman. It is a classic serif face with a relatively large x–height, and therefore very readable. Notice that it's lighter than New Century Schoolbook. That's because the strokes of the letters are thinner. Both are readable, but a page set in New Century Schoolbook looks darker.

This is 10–point New Century Schoolbook. It is darker than Times Roman. That makes pages set in this face look darker, but it also gives New Century Schoolbook a decorative look, especially when it's used for large headlines.

Which should you use? You be the judge.

FIG. 2.6 Times Roman is lighter than New Century Schoolbook.

Leading

The space between lines, *leading* (pronounced ledding), affects readability. With too little leading, text appears overly dense and unreadable; with too much leading, text looks sloppy. Readability studies indicate that body text looks best with one or two points of extra leading. For example, 11-point leading in 20-pica (3 1/3") lines is very readable. (A *pica* is approximately 1/6".)

WordPerfect sets the leading to two points more than the size of the type. You can override the default setting with the Leading Adjustment feature. Figure 2.7 shows the effect of a change in leading on the appearance of a printed paragraph. Notice that the paragraph on the right contains seven lines, and the one on the left contains eight lines.

WordPerfect automatically adds leading of 2 points greater than the size of the type. For example, this is 10-point Times Roman with 12-point leading. The leading is appropriate for the font and the column width, which is 11 picas.	This is 10-point Times Roman with 14-point leading. This leading is too "airy" for such a narrow column. But if you need to set type in wide columns, adding extra leading may help maintain readability.

FIG. 2.7 Too much leading makes text look "airy."

Be careful when you use Leading Adjustment. You must specify leading in points, or WordPerfect assumes that the leading adjustment that you enter is in inches, usually with disastrous results. The instructions in this book specify measurements in inches ("), which is WordPerfect's default. If you have changed the units of measure to "inches" or another unit, you will find it easier to work with the sample designs if you change the unit to ". Press Shift-F1, E, U, D, ", Enter, S, ", Enter, F7.

To adjust the leading, follow these steps:

1. Press Shift-F8 (Format), O (Other), P (Printer Functions), L (Leading Adjustment).

2. At the `Primary` prompt, enter the amount of extra leading you want to insert between lines of text that WordPerfect wordwraps with a soft return.

   For example, if you enter *2p*, WordPerfect adds two points of extra leading in addition to the default leading amount of two points greater than the font size. If the font is 12-point Times Roman, WordPerfect sets the leading to 14 points. If you then add two more points of extra leading with the Leading Adjustment feature, you get 16 points of leading. To subtract leading, type a minus sign before the leading adjustment amount, for example, *–3p*.

   Remember that to specify points you must add a *p* after the leading adjustment amount, or WordPerfect interprets your instructions in inches:

3. At the `Secondary` prompt, enter the amount of extra leading after a hard return.

4. Press F7 to return to the document screen.

Table 2.1 presents research results for leading and type size to obtain the most readable body text.

Table 2.1
Leading Ranges for Type Sizes

Type size (in points)	*Minimum leading (in points)*	*Maximum leading (in points)*
6	6	7
8	8	10
10	10	14
11	12	15
12	14	18
14	17	22

TIP

Large type sometimes requires a leading adjustment for a compact, designed effect. Figure 2.8 shows text for an advertisement heading and a news headline, set normally and with minus three points of leading. Minus leading makes the headline look squeezed but improves the product name. Many design decisions hinge on specific circumstances rather than hard and fast rules.

Line Length

Too long lines make it hard to find the start of the next line of text. Too short lines also are hard to read, because the eye spends too much time jumping from one line to the next.

The most readable line length depends on the size of the font currently in use. Research shows that 10-point type is most readable when set in lines 18.9 picas long (about 3 1/3"; a pica is 1/6").

When 10-point text is set in 13.9-pica lines, readability falls by 10 percent. For 10-point text in 43.9-pica lines, readability drops another 11.4 per cent.

City Supervisors Bite Budgetary Bullet in '92

City Supervisors Bite Budgetary Bullet in '92

FIG. 2.8 Leading Adjustment moves lines closer together.

A traditional graphic designer's rule-of-thumb dictates body type be set in lines no longer than twice the width in picas of the current font size in points. For example, 10-point type should be set in lines no wider than 20 picas. However, as the following table shows, the rule-of-thumb doesn't work well for very small or very large text sizes.

Table 2.2
Line Lengths for Type Sizes

Type size (in points)	*Minimum length (in picas)*	*Maximum length (in picas)*
6	8	10
8	9	13
10	13	16
11	13	18
12	14	21
14	18	24
18	24	30

TIP

If you must use very long lines, make the text more readable by using a larger typeface and adding extra leading. Figure 2.9 shows text set in long lines using 10-point text with normal leading and 12-point text with two points of added leading.

Type Alignment

Should you set text justified or ragged right? Readability studies show little difference between the two, except for the following:

- Slow readers find justified text harder to read.
- Sans serif fonts are easier to read when set ragged right.

When you are trying to decide between ragged right or justified text, consider the tone of the publication you are designing. Generally, justified text looks neater and more formal than ragged right text. A brochure aimed at convincing bank customers to take out automobile loans, therefore, should be businesslike but friendly, and ragged right may be the best choice. A more formal report on state-wide housing trends for the bank's board of directors probably should be justified.

Of air–born honey, gift of heaven, I now take up the tale. Upon this theme no less look thou, Maecenas, with indulgent eye. A marvellous display of puny powers, high–hearted chiefs, a nation's history, its traits, its bent, its battles and its clans, all, each, shall pass before you, while I sing. Slight though the poet's theme, not slight the praise, so frown not heaven, and Phoebus hear his call.

Of air–born honey, gift of heaven, I now take up the tale. Upon this theme no less look thou, Maecenas, with indulgent eye. A marvellous display of puny powers, high–hearted chiefs, a nation's history, its traits, its bent, its battles and its clans, all, each, shall pass before you, while I sing. Slight though the poet's theme, not slight the praise, so frown not heaven, and Phoebus hear his call.

FIG. 2.9 Increased leading and font size improves readability.

TIP

Extremely ragged line endings slow the reader. To avoid overly loose (ragged) lines, use WordPerfect's hyphenation feature. Figure 2.10 shows the same paragraph, set with and without hyphenation.

TIP

To justify text, WordPerfect adds space between words and letters to create flush-right line ends. When type is set in narrow columns, this can create too much space between words, resulting in *airy* text that is hard to read. Generally, you should not justify narrow columns. When you must set justified text in narrow columns, be sure to turn hyphenation on.

First find your bees a settled sure abode, where neither winds can enter (winds blow back the foragers with food returning home) nor sheep and butting kids tread down the flowers, nor heifer wandering wide upon the plain dash off the dew, and bruise the springing blades. Let the gay lizard too keep far aloof his scale–clad body from their honied stalls, and the bee–eater, and what birds beside, and Procne smirched with blood upon the breast from her own murderous hands.	First find your bees a settled sure abode, where neither winds can enter (winds blow back the foragers with food returning home) nor sheep and butting kids tread down the flowers, nor heifer wandering wide upon the plain dash off the dew, and bruise the spring–ing blades. Let the gay lizard too keep far aloof his scale–clad body from their honied stalls, and the bee–eater, and what birds beside, and Procne smirched with blood upon the breast from her own murderous hands.

FIG. 2.10 Hyphenation cures overly ragged line endings.

When using justified text, you can adjust the Word Spacing Justification Limits. WordPerfect uses this feature to stop adding extra space between words to justify text and to begin adding space between letters. To change the setting, follow these steps:

1. Move the cursor to the top of the justified text.
2. Press Shift-F8 (Format), O (Other), P (Printer Functions), J (Word Spacing Justification Limits).
3. At the `Compressed to` prompt, press Enter to accept the default (60 %).
4. At the `Expanded to` prompt, type *200%* or some other figure lower than the default of 400 %.
5. Press Enter and then F7 to return to the document screen.

Figure 2.11 shows the effect of hyphenation and adjusted word spacing on the same justified paragraph. In the left column, hyphenation is turned off, and the default Word Spacing Justification Limits is used. In the right column, hyphenation is turned on and the Word Spacing Justification Limits is set to 200 percent.

Me you have killed because you wanted to escape the accuser, and not to give an account of your lives. But that will not be as you suppose; far otherwise. For I say there will be more accusers of you than there are now; accusers whom hitherto I have restrained; and as they are younger they will be more severe with you, and you will be more offended at them.	Me you have killed because you wanted to escape the accuser, and not to give an account of your lives. But that will not be as you suppose; far otherwise. For I say there will be more ac-cusers of you than there are now; accusers whom hitherto I have restrained; and as they are younger they will be more severe with you, and you will be more offended at them.

FIG. 2.11 Effect of hyphenation and adjusted word spacing.

TIP

Too much hyphenation is as disruptive as too little. Before printing your work, check that WordPerfect hasn't hyphenated more than two adjoining lines. Where it has, delete one of the hyphens by editing the text or overriding hyphenation for the word. To override hyphenation, move the cursor to the first letter in the word and press Home, / (Slash). WordPerfect moves the word to the next line, and you can delete the hyphen.

Kerning, Letter Spacing, and Word Spacing

Kerning is the amount of space between adjacent letters. Certain letter pairs can look too widely spaced, especially when used in large sizes. WordPerfect can tighten the spacing between the most troublesome letter pairs. To turn on automatic kerning, press Shift-F8 (Format), O (Other), P (Printer Functions), K (Kerning), Y (Yes), F7.

Automatic kerning may not be sufficient to tighten problem letter pairs in large fonts, particularly when you want to create a very tight, designed effect. In such cases, you can use the Word Spacing, Letter Spacing, and Advance features to remove space between certain letters selectively. Figure 2.12 shows the effect of applying these features.

With automatic kerning turned on, WordPerfect adjusts only those letter pairs defined as problems in the PRS setup file for your printer. As figure 2.12 shows, turning on automatic kerning may not help at all when kerning pairs are not set correctly in the PRS definition file for your printer.

1. Yerby Bros. Woodstove Store

2. Yerby Bros. Woodstove Store

3. Yerby Bros. Woodstove Store

4. Yerby Bros. Woodstove Store

FIG. 2.12 Some kerning adjustments to improve readability.

Figure 2.12 shows the effect, on two problem letter pairs (Ye and Wo), of turning on kerning, adjusting word and letter spacing, and using Advance:

- Line 1 shows how WordPerfect prints the company name in 36-point Times Roman.
- Line 2 shows the effect of turning kerning on. Kerning pairs have not been set for the printer, a Canon LBP8-III.
- Line 3 shows the effect of setting word and letter spacing to 90 percent of optimal. The text looks tighter, but Ye and Wo are still much too loosely spaced.
- Line 4 shows the effect of using Advance to shift the *e* seven points closer to the *Y* and the *o* three points closer to the *W*.

These methods are used to tighten the text of many headlines, titles, and company names in the sample designs in Chapters 5 through 25.

Character Enhancements

How often should you use boldface, italics, or underlining? Readability studies show that the answer is seldom.

People read italics 20 words per minute slower than normal text. Confine italics to photo captions, foreign words, the titles of publications, pull quotes, and other brief text. Figure 2.13 shows the same paragraph set in normal and italics.

Boldface has no place in body text, unless you are striving for a disruptive, choppy effect. Reserve boldface for headings, being careful not to overwhelm the reader with too much. Be particularly careful to avoid *tombstoning*, where two headlines end up side by side in adjacent columns. Try to place headlines to provide an interesting design element to the page. Often you can do this by alternating the position of articles or putting one article in a one- or two-column sidebar.

Use underlining only with non-proportionally spaced typewriter fonts. No underline character is used in formal typography. Underlined Times Roman text, for example, looks terrible, as seen in figure 2.14. The underline cuts descenders, letters such as q, p, g, and y, and markedly decreases readability. Several of the sample designs, for example, the newsletters in Chapters 24 and 25, use horizontal graphics lines under headings, but in no case do the lines run close enough to cut through descenders.

And let green cassias and far-scented thymes, and savory with its heavy-laden breath bloom round about, and violet-beds hard by sip sweetness from the fertilizing springs. For the hive's self, or stitched of hollow bark, or from tough osier woven, let the doors be strait of entrance; for stiff winter's cold congeals the honey, and heat resolves and thaws, to bees alike disastrous; not for naught so haste they to cement the tiny pores that pierce their walls, and fill the crevices with pollen from the flowers, and glean and keep to this same end the glue, that binds more fast than bird-lime or the pitch from Ida's pines.	*And let green cassias and far-scented thymes, and savory with its heavy-laden breath bloom round about, and violet-beds hard by sip sweetness from the fertilizing springs. For the hive's self, or stitched of hollow bark, or from tough osier woven, let the doors be strait of entrance; for stiff winter's cold congeals the honey, and heat resolves and thaws, to bees alike disastrous; not for naught so haste they to cement the tiny pores that pierce their walls, and fill the crevices with pollen from the flowers, and glean and keep to this same end the glue, that binds more fast than bird-lime or the pitch from Ida's pines.*

FIG. 2.13 Italicized text slows reading by 20 words per minute.

Why would you wantonly use underlined type, except to cut descenders?

FIG. 2.14 Underlining decreases readability.

Type set in all capitals is very hard to read, according to advertising studies. If you must use capitalized text, use initial capitals and small capitals, as shown in figure 2.15.

Advertising research shows that reading comprehension falls by 30 percent for reversed text (white text on a black background). As with boldface type, use reversed type for brief headings, section titles, and logos—never for body text. Be especially careful when selecting a font and type size for reversed text. A bold, sans serif or heavy serif works best, because reversed letters smaller than 14-point tend to plug up with ink during printing, as do serifs printed in reverse (see fig. 2.16). Reversed type should be large, short, and sans serif, with the exception of serif type such as New Century Schoolbook Bold, which has heavy serifs.

FIG. 2.15 Small caps are easier to read than uppercase text.

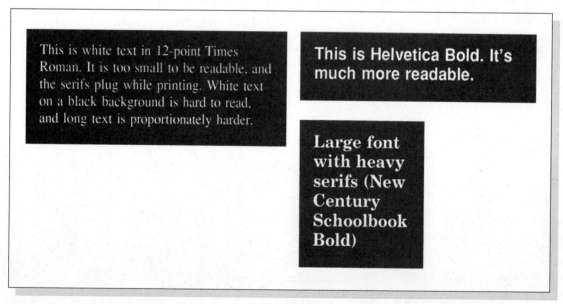

FIG. 2.16 Large sans serif or heavy serif text is more readable.

With WordPerfect 5.1, you can print reversed text only with PostScript or Hewlett Packard LaserJet III-compatible laser printers. To create reversed text, perform the following steps:

1. Select 100% gray shading in the options box.
2. Press Alt-F9, B, O, G; type *100%*; and press Enter, F7.

To create a text box, perform the following steps:

1. Press Alt-F9, B, C, E to enter the box editor.
2. Choose White as the text color. Press Ctrl-F8, C,W, Enter and type the text.
3. Press F7 twice to return to the editing screen.

TIP

If you must use reversed text, use a 100 percent black background, because lowering text-to-background contrast with a gray screen reduces readability. In fact, type reversed over a light gray background screen may become completely illegible. To avoid *losing* black type on a gray screen, never use gray shading darker than 10 percent (5 percent or 6 percent is preferable). Advertising research shows that anything that decreases type-to-background contrast interferes with readability.

Be careful when you print text over a screen. For maximum readability, use a bold, serif font over a light screen, and keep the text short (see fig. 2.17).

Fonts

In the early years of desktop publishing, computer users rushed to acquire every available font for their laser printers, and the results are notorious. During that period of *fontmania*, a famous graphic designer wrote an article for a desktop publishing magazine in which he demonstrated the value of restraint by using a single typeface, Times Roman, to create an extremely sophisticated, attractive document.

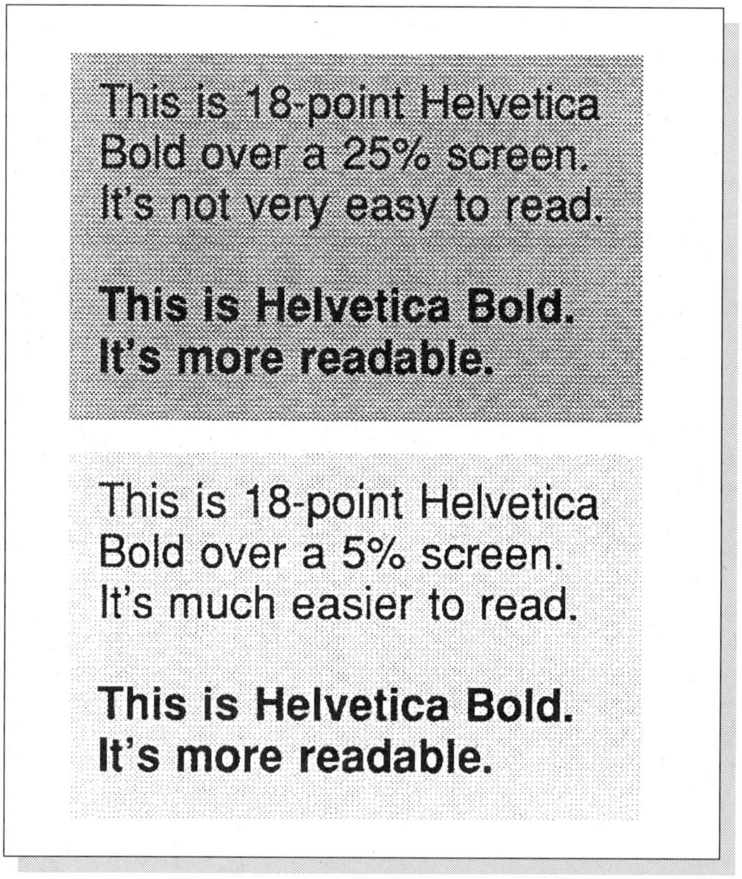

This is 18-point Helvetica Bold over a 25% screen. It's not very easy to read.

This is Helvetica Bold. It's more readable.

This is 18-point Helvetica Bold over a 5% screen. It's much easier to read.

This is Helvetica Bold. It's more readable.

FIG. 2.17 *Bold, serif text on a light screen is more readable than text on a dark screened background.*

Attractive documents reflect restrained good taste. Whether you're creating a poster for a 1960s nostalgia rock concert or an invitation to a garden society tea party, your work has visual appeal to the extent that it achieves a harmonious integration of design elements. The quickest way to create disharmony in print is to use clashing fonts, fonts from several different typefaces, or fonts in many sizes.

If you must use more than one font in a document, use just two: one for the main title and body text and another for the section subheads. Strangely enough, fonts that are slightly different may clash more glaringly than fonts that are very dissimilar. One of the most popular combinations is Times Roman for text and Helvetica for subheadings. Times is a classic traditional serif typeface, and Helvetica is unadorned and modern. In figure 2.18, the text at the top shows how Times Roman and Helvetica work well together, and the text on the bottom shows how Times Roman and Bookman clash.

Montana Out for '91!

Steve Young takes over

49ER COACH SEIFFERT announced this morning that Joe Montana will be on injured reserve for the remainder of the '91 NFL season. Elbow surgery performed last week will keep the 49ers' veteran star quarterback away from the practice field until late December, Seiffert said.

YOUNG TO START

Steve Young, outstanding at Brigham Young but relegated to the shadow of Montana since coming to the 49ers, will have his first start in five years in Saturday's game against the

Montana Out for '91!

Steve Young takes over

49ER COACH SEIFFERT announced this morning that Joe Montana will be on injured reserve for the remainder of the '91 NFL season. Elbow surgery performed last week will keep the 49ers' veteran star quarterback away from the practice field until late December, Seiffert said.

YOUNG TO START

Steve Young, outstanding at Brigham Young but relegated to the shadow of Montana since coming to the 49ers, will have his first start in five years in Saturday's game against the

FIG. 2.18 Similar typefaces may clash, and dissimilar ones may harmonize.

Every font has a personality, and your font choices affect the reader's perception of you and your work. Limit your use of Arnold Bocklin, a playful *party* font, to appropriate designs, such as a flyer for a crafts fair. Traditional fonts, such as Bookman or New Century Schoolbook, may be slightly too informal for formal documents such as invitations. Avant Garde can look too modern in a conservative business context.

3

Understanding Page Design

Designing documents is a surprisingly subtle art. Great designers make it look so easy, yet each page may require dozens of small adjustments and hours of careful thought.

In the step-by-step chapters of this book, the preliminary planning has been done for you. At some point, you probably will want to venture out on your own, adapting the sample designs to your projects or using them as templates for creating a new look. In this chapter, you learn the basic principles of page design, from creating an underlying page plan, a *grid*, to creating a harmonious arrangement of graphic elements and text.

Creating a Grid

Page design determines the basic arrangement of text, boxes, and lines on a page. Whether designing an invoice, catalog, book, or flyer, the first step in page design is creating an underlying *grid* on which text and graphics are placed.

A grid is the *floor plan* holding together the pages of your document consistently and harmoniously. In a newsletter, for example, the grid establishes major layout elements:

- Number of columns
- Space between columns
- Position and design of headers and footers
- Position of repeating lines on the page

The grid also can include small page elements:

- Fonts
- Spacing used for subheads, pull quotes, and body text
- Spacing between text and illustrations

Figure 3.1 shows three pages of a newsletter with the parts of the grid labeled:

1. *Dateline:* Publication date.
2. *Main heading:* Publication title.
3. *Drop cap:* Inset capital letter that draws the eye to the start of an article.
4. *Headline:* Title of an article.
5. *Deck (also called a subhead or tag line):* Further information about the article.
6. *Rule line:* Surrounds a page or block of text or divides page elements horizontally or vertically. Rule lines also may be used decoratively.
7. *Picture window:* Indicates the position of a photographic halftone negative to be stripped into the page by the printer.
8. *Caption:* Description of a photo or illustration.
9. *Dingbat (or vegetable):*Graphic symbol used decoratively and/or to end separate articles or items in a list.
10. *Body Text:* Text of an article.
11. *Alley:* Space between columns.
12. *Running header:* Can include page number, publication title, issue date, and so forth. When printed at the bottom of the page, this information is called a *footer*.
13. *Sidebar:* Text set apart from regular body text, usually in a box surrounded with a rule line. Sidebars sometimes are printed over a light-colored or gray screen.
14. *Gutter:* The space between pages in the middle of a two-page spread.
15. *Photo layout:* A group of photos, usually of related objects or events, for the purpose of illustrating an article.
16. *Indicia:* Mailing information required by U.S. Postal Service regulations.

November 1992 Vol 3 No. 11 — 1

FOUNDING MEMBERS

Salkin Construction

Brown Restorers

Vintage Homes, Inc.

—2 THE TRADITIONAL

BUILDER

❖ *Newsletter of Peninsula Restorers and Period Builders Association* ❖

3

4—Plexes On Rise

5—Tight money has new buyers moving in together

HI OMNES LINGUA, institutis, legibus inter se differunt. Gallos ab Aquitanis Garumna flumen, a Belgis Matrona et Sequana dividit. Horum omnium fortissimi sunt Belgae, propterea quod a cultu atque humanitate provinciae longissime absunt, minimeque ad eos mercatores saepe commeant atque ea quae ad effeminandos animos pertinent important, proximique sunt Germanis, qui trans Rhenum incolunt, quibuscum continenter bellum gerunt. Que de causa Helvetii quoque reliquos Gallos virtute praecedunt, quod fere cotidianis proeliis cum Germanis contendunt, cum aut suis finibus eos prohibent, aut ipsi in eorum finibus bellum gerunt. Eorum una pars, quam Gallos obtinere dictum est, initium capit a flumine Rhodano; continetur Garumna flumine, Oceano, finibus Belgarum; attingit etiam ab Sequanis et Helvetiis flumen Rhenum; vergit ad septentriones. Belgae ab extremis Galliae finibus oriuntur; pertinent ad Inferiorem partem fluminis Rheni; spectant in septentriones et orientem solem. Aquitania a Garumna flumine ad Pyrenaeos montes et eam partem Oceani quae est ad Hispaniam pertinent; spectat inter occasum solis et septentriones. Apid Helvetios longe nobilissimus fuit et ditissimus Orgetorix. Is, M. Messala, M. Pisone consulibus, regni cupiditate inductus coniurationem nobilitatis fecit et civitati persuasit ut de finibus suis cum omnibus copiis exirent: Perfacile esse, cum virtute. Que de causa Helvetii quoque reliquos Gallos virtute praecedunt. Eorum una pars, quam Gallos obtinere dictum est, initium capit a flumine Rhodano. ❖ —9

6— 7—  —10

8— *Victorian Sunshine Builders specializes in add-on solaria for traditional homes.*

Victorian Sunshine

Add-on solaria now a popular trend for older homes

ID HOC FACILIUS iis persuasit quod undique loci natura Helvetii contionentur: una ex parte flumine Rheno latissimo atque altissimo, qui agrum Helvetium a Germanis dividit; altera ex parte monte Iura altissimo, qui est inter Sequanos et Helvetios; teria lacu Lemanno et flumine. Gallos ab Aquitanis Garumna flumen, a Belgis Matrona et Sequana dividit. Horum omnium fortissimi sunt Belgae, propterea quod a cultu atque humanitate provinciae longissime absunt, minimeque ad eos mercatores saepe commeant atque ea quae ad effeminandos animos pertinent important, proximique sunt Germanis, qui trans Rhenum incolunt, quibuscum continenter bellum. Eorum una pars, quam Gallos obtinere dictum est, initium capit a flumine Rhodano; continetur Garumna. ❖

11

FIG. 3.1 Three-page newsletter with grid elements labeled. (Part 1 of 3)

12—**West Bay senior runner** 3

14

capit a flumine Rhodano; continetur Garumna flumine, Oceano, finibus Belgarum; attingit etiam ab Sequanis et Helvetiis flumen Rhenum; vergit ad septentriones.

Childcare Circle

Aquitania a Garumna flumine ad Pyrenaeos montes et eam partem Oceani quae est ad Hispaniam pertinent; spectat inter occasum solis et septentriones.

Apid Helvetios longe nobilissimus fuit et ditissimus Orgetorix. Is, M. Messala, M. Pisone consulibus, regni

Nutritionist Patricia Labelle will speak at Hurley Center January 20, 8 p.m.

cupiditate. inductus coniurationem nobilitatis fecit et civitati persuasit ut de finibus suis cum omnibus copiis exirent: Perfacile esse, cum virtute omnibus praestarent, totius Galliae imperio potiri. Id hoc facilius iis persuasit quod undique loci natura Helvetii contionentur: una ex parte flumine Rheno latissimo atque altissimo, qui agrum Helvetium a Germanis dividit; altera ex parte monte Iura altissimo, qui est inter Sequanos et Helvetios; teria lacu Lemanno et flumine Rhodano, qui provinciam nostram ab Helvetiis dividit. His rebus flebat ut et minus late vagarentur et minus facile finitimis bellum inferre possent; qua ex parte homines bellandi cupidi magno dolore afficiebantur. Inductus coniurationem nobilitatis fecit et civitati persuasit ut de finibus suis cum omnibus copiis exirent.

Caesar, quod memoria tenebat L. Cassium consulem occisum exercitumque eius ab Helvetiis poulsum et sub iugum missum, concedendum non putabat; neque homines inimico animo, data facultate per provinciam itineris faciendi, temperaturos ab iniuria et maleficio existimabat.

Diets Don't Work

Provinciae toti quam maximum potest militum numerum imperat (erat omnino in Gallia ulteriore legio una), pontem qui erat ad Genavam iubet rescindi. Ubi de eius adventu Helvetii certiores facti sunt, legatos ad eum mittunt, nobilissimos civitatis, cuius legationis Nammeius et Verucloetius principem locum obtinebant, qui dicerent sibi esse in animo sine ullo maleficio iter per provinciam facere, propterea quod alud iter haberent nullum; rogare ut eius voluntate id sibi facere liceat.

Health Series

Tamen, ut spatium intercedere posset, dum milites quos imperaverat convenirent, legatis respondit diem se ad deliberandum sumpturum; si quid vellent, ad Id. April. reverterentur.

Hi omnes lingua, institutis, legibus inter se differunt. Gallos ab Aquitanis Garumna flumen, a Belgis Matrona et Sequana dividit. Horum omnium fortissimi sunt Belgae, propterea quod a cultu atque humanitate provinciae longissime absunt, minimeque ad eos mercatores saepe commeant atque. Dictum est, initium capit a flumine Rhodano; continetur Garumna flumine, Oceano, finibus Belgarum; attingit etiam.

Family runs at Loren Hills make childcare a non-issue.

coming events

Phone Oren Robertson for details and carpool arrangements for events: 423-9876.

january

7	Masters Invitational
14	SloPoke Fun Run
15	Devil May Care 10K
21	Fool's Gold 50K
22	Orlaga Youth Benefit 20K
28	Winter Carnival 5, 10, 20K

february

4	Mothers' Marathon
4	WBSR Hillside Carnival
5	Tule Trail to W. Beach 30K
5	Inkadinka 20K
11	Fast & Furious 25K
12	E. Wilford 15-miler
18	Father & Son 10K
18	1992 Blue Ribbon Marathon
25	Wild 'N Wooly X-C (20K)

13

FIG. 3.1 Three-page newsletter with grid elements labeled. (Part 2 of 3)

4 West Bay **senior runner**

Energy & Sports Physiology

Concedendum non putabat; neque homines inimico animo, data facultate per provinciam itineris faciendi, temperaturos ab iniuria et maleficio existimabat. Tamen, ut spatium intercedere posset, dum milites quos imperaverat convenirent, legatis respondit diem se ad deliberandum sumpturum; si quid vellent, ad id. April. reverterentur.

Aquitania a Garumna flumine ad Pyrenaeos montes et eam partem Oceani quae est ad Hispaniam pertinent; spectat inter occasum solis et septentriones.

Apid Helvetios longe nobilissimus fuit et ditissimus Orgetorix. Is, M. Messala, M. Pisone consulibus, regni cupiditate inductus coniurationem nobilitatis fecit et civitati persuasit ut de finibus suis cum omnibus copiis exirent: Perfacile esse, cum virtute omnibus praestarent, totius Galliae imperio potiri. Id hoc facilius iis persuasit quod undique loci natura Helvetii contionentur: una ex parte flumine Rheno latissimo atque

Ab extremis Galliae finibus oriuntur; pertinent ad Inferiorem partem fluminis

15

Apid Helvetios longe nobilissimus fuit et ditissimus Orgetorix.

Erant omnino itinera duo quibus itineribus domo exire possent.

agrum Helvetium a Germanis dividit; altera ex parte monte Iura altissimo, qui est inter Sequanos et Helvetios; teria lacu Lemanno et flumine Rhodano, qui provinciam nostram ab Helvetiis

dividit. His rebus fiebat ut et minus late vagarentur et minus facile finitimis bellum inferre possent; qua ex parte homines bellandi cupidi magno dolore afficiebantur. Pro multitudine autem hominum.

west bay

senior runner

589 South North Avenue
San Francisco, CA 94100-9876

U.S. Postage
PAID
Permit No. 000
San Francisco, CA

16

Address Correction
and Forwarding Requested

FIG. 3.1 Three-page newsletter with grid elements labeled. (Part 3 of 3)

Entire books have been written about designing grids. In a nutshell, the most important rules for a good design are consistency and simplicity. Add consistency to your documents with the following guidelines:

- Make all subheadings the same size.
- Use headers and/or footers.
- Use decorative vertical lines in the same position on each page.
- Minimize mixing of different typefaces and font sizes.
- Keep the same margins.
- Keep consistent spacing between body text and subheadings and between text and illustrations.

The report in figure 3.2 uses consistent placement and sizing of page elements, including text, to create a restful, inviting effect. Research shows that a consistent design helps the reader find information on the page.

Simplicity is the essence of good taste. This statement is as true for document design as it is for interior decor or formal attire. A simple grid guides readers through text and graphics in a straightforward, visually pleasing way; whereas an overly complex grid loses readers in a visual maze. Figure 3.3 shows a booklet design based on a simple grid. Notice the consistent placement and sizing of photos, square bullets, and subheadings. Other grid elements include the single-column format, consistent spacing between photos and text, the use of ragged-right text throughout, and consistent font sizes and styles for subheadings.

Using White Space

One of the most common design errors is misuse or non-use of white space. *White space* is just what the name implies: space on the page left empty of text, graphic images, lines, or other printed elements.

Leaving too little white space on the page creates a dense, no-nonsense, information-packed appearance. That works well for a law review or a newspaper, but this type of design is completely inappropriate for an informal club newsletter.

Technical Perspectives Series

Paper No. 32

Should Small Companies Invest in Connectivity?

Ray Blanda
Senior Vice President
Advanced Design Department
Omegacom Corporation

January 15, 1991

Abstract

EQUIPMENT FAILURES VS. WORK group communication convenience: what are the real tradeoffs? Computer hardware from today's blue chip venders (and, surprisingly, from several no-name clonemakers) minimizes the dangers of work group interconnectivity.

The advantages are manifold: rapid communication, instantaneous group-approved document changes, increased sense of participation and cooperation. The technology has proved 100% reliable in environments where important data are backed up on fast tape drives at least four times daily, and where the LAN is designed for fast switch-on of standby servers.

FIG. 3.2 Consistency helps readers find information on the page. (Part 1 of 3)

2

Introduction

HI OMNES LINGUA, institutis, legibus inter se differunt. Gallos ab Aquitanis Garumna flumen, a Belgis Matrona et Sequana dividit. Horum omnium fortissimi sunt Belgae, propterea quod a cultu atque humanitate provinciae longissime absunt, minimeque ad eos mercatores saepe commeant atque ea quae ad effeminandos animos pertinent important, proximique sunt Germanis, qui trans Rhenum incolunt, quibuscum continenter bellum gerunt.

Que de causa Helvetii quoque reliquos Gallos virtute praecedunt, quod fere cotidianis proeliis cum Germanis contendunt, cum aut suis finibus eos prohibent, aut ipsi in eorum finibus bellum gerunt.

The Problem

EORUM UNA PARS, quam Gallos obtinere dictum est, initium capit a flumine Rhodano; continetur Garumna flumine, Oceano, finibus Belgarum; attingit etiam ab Sequanis et Helvetiis flumen Rhenum; vergit ad septentriones. Belgae ab extremis Galliae finibus oriuntur; pertinent ad Inferiorem partem fluminis Rheni; spectant in septentriones et orientem solem. Aquitania a Garumna flumine ad Pyrenaeos montes et eam partem Oceani quae est ad Hispaniam pertinent; spectat inter occasum solis et septentriones.

Apid Helvetios longe nobilissimus fuit et ditissimus Orgetorix. Is, M. Messala, M. Pisone consulibus, regni cupiditate inductus coniurationem nobilitatis fecit et civitati persuasit ut de finibus suis cum omnibus copiis exirent: Perfacile esse, cum virtute omnibus praestarent, totius Galliae imperio potiri. Id hoc facilius iis persuasit quod undique loci natura Helvetii contionentur: una ex parte flumine Rheno latissimo atque altissimo, qui agrum Helvetium a Germanis dividit; altera ex parte monte Iura altissimo, qui est inter Sequanos et Helvetios; teria lacu Lemanno et flumine Rhodano, qui provinciam nostram ab Helvetiis dividit.

The Solutions

HIS REBUS FIEBAT ut et minus late vagarentur et minus facile finitimis bellum inferre possent; qua ex parte homines bellandi cupidi magno dolore afficiebantur. Pro multitudine autem hominum et pro gloria bellie atque fortitudinis angustos se fines habere arbitrabantur, qui in longitudinem milia passuum CCXL, in latitudinem CLLXXX patebant.

His rebus adducti et auctoritate Orgetorigis permoti constitu erunt ea quae ad proficiscendum pertinerent comparare, iumentorum et carrorum quam maximum numerum coemere, sementes quam maximas facere, ut in itinere copia frumenti suppeteret, cum proximis vicitatibus pacem et amicitiam confirmare.

Hardware Gifts, Givens, Gripes

AD EAS RES conficiendas biennieum sibi satis esse duxerunt; in tertium annum profectionem lege confirmant. Ad eas res conficiendas Orgetorix deligitur. Is sibi legationem ad civitates suscipit. In eo itinere persuadet Castico, Catamantaloedis filio, Sequano, cuius pater regnum in Sequania multos annos obtinuerat et a senatu populi Romani amicus appellatus erat, ut regnum in civitate sua occuparet, quod pater ante habuerat; itemque Dumnorigi Haeduo, fratri Diviciaci, qui eo tempore.

Should Small Companies Invest In Connectivity?

FIG. 3.2 Consistency helps readers find information on the page. (Part 2 of 3)

3

Typical Cost Breakdown

EA RES EST HEVETIIS per indicium enuntiata. Moribus suis Orgetorigem ex vinculis cansam dicere coegerun; damnatum poenam sequi oportebat, ut igni cremaretru. Die constituta causae dictionis Orgetorix ad iudicium omnem suam familiam, ad homionum milia decem, undique coegit, et omnes clientes obaeratosque suos, quorum magnum numerum habebat, eodem conduxit; per eos, ne causam diceret, se eripuit. Cum civitas ob eam rem incitata armis ius suum exsequi conaretur, multitudinemque hominum ex agris magistratus cogerent, Orgetorix mortuus est; neque abest suspicio, ut Helvetii arbitrantur, quin ipse sibi mortem consciverit.

Conclusion

POST EIUS MORTEM nihilo minus Helvetii id quod constituerant facere conantur, ut e finibus suis exeant. Ubi iam se ad eam rem paratos esse arbitrati sunt, oppida sua omnia, numero ad duodecim, vicos ad quadringentos, relique privata, aedificia incendunt; frumentum omne, praeterquam quod secum portaturi erant, comburunt, ut, domum reditionis spe sublata, paratiores ad omnia pericula subeunda essent; trium mensium molita cibaria sibi quemque domo efferre iubent. Persuadent Rauracis et Tulingis et Latobrigis, finitimis, uti eodem usi consilio, oppidis suis vicisque exustis, una cum iis proficiscantur; Boiosque, qui trans Rhenum incoluerant et in agrum oricum transierant Noreiamque oppugnabant, receptos ad se socios sibi asciscunt.

FIG. 3.2 Consistency helps readers find information on the page. (Part 3 of 3)

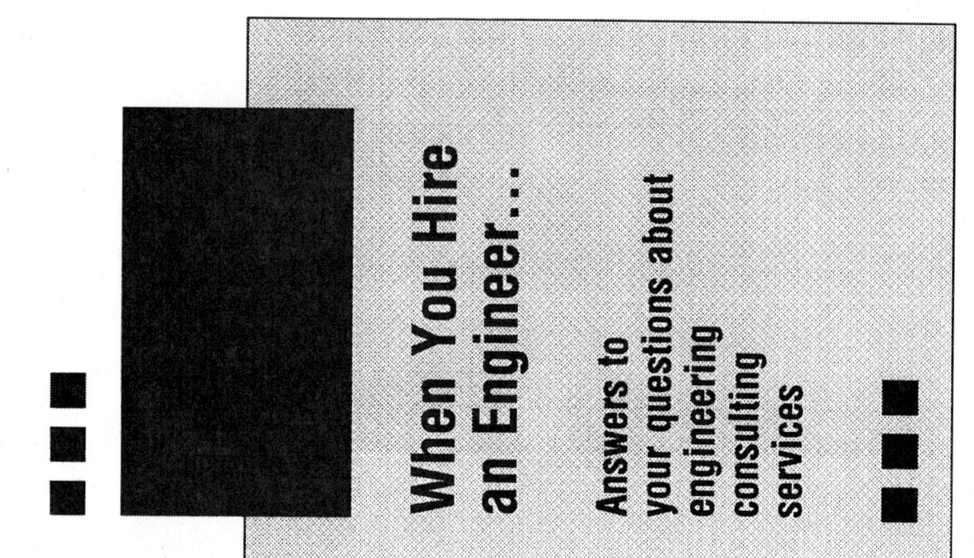
Helvetii possent: se suis copiis suoque exercitu illis regna conciliaturum confirmat. Hac oratione adducti inter se fidem et ius iurandum dant et, regno occupato, per tres potentissimos ac firmissimos populos totius Galliae sese potiri posse sperant.
CEQA/NEPA Compliance/Regulatory and Permitting Assistance
Et omnes clientes obaeratosque suos, quorum magnum numerum habebat, eodem conduxit; per eos, ne causam diceret, se eripuit. Cum civitas ob eam rem incitata armis ius suum exsequi conaretur, multitudinemkque hominum ex agris magistratus cogerent, Orgetorix mortuus est; neque abest suspicio, ut Helvetii arbitrantur, quin ipse sibi mortem consciverit.
Air Quality Evaluation and Remedial Design
Persuadent Rauracis et Tulingis et Latobrigis, finitimis, uti eodem usi consilio, oppidis suis vicisque exustis, una cum iis proficiscantur; Boiosque, qui trans Rhenum incoluerant et in agrum oricum transierant Noreiamque oppugnabant, receptos ad se socios sibi asciscunt.
Ea res est Hevetiis per indicium enuntiata. Moribus suis Orgetorigem ex vinculis cansam dicere coegerun; damnatum poenam sequi oportebat, ut igni cremaretru. Die constituta causae dictionis.
When You Hire an Engineer . . .
Answers to your questions about engineering consulting services
Consulting Engineers Association of Nebraska
15124 Grand Prairie Road, Suite 502
Omaha, NE 66766
(503) 788-6655

FIG. 3.3 Simplicity and consistency make a readable design. (Part 1 of 2)

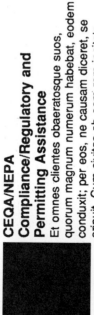

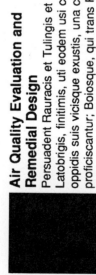

Hi omnes lingua, institutis, legibus inter se differunt. Gallos ab Aquitanis Garumna flumen, a Belgis Matrona et Sequana dividit. Horum omnium fortissimi sunt Belgae, propterea quod a cultu atque humanitate provinciae longissime absunt, minimeque ad eos mercatores saepe commeant atque ea quae ad effeminandos animos pertinent important, proximique sunt Germanis, qui trans Rhenum incolunt, quibuscum continenter bellum gerunt.

Remedial Investigations

Pro multitudine autem hominum et pro gloria bellie atque fortitudinis angustos se fines habere arbitrabantur, qui in longitudinem milia passuum CCXL, in latitudinem CLLXXX patebant.

Apid Helvetios longe nobilissimus fuit et ditissimus Orgetorix. Is, M. Messala, M. Pisone consulibus, regni cupiditate inductus coniurationem nobilitatis fecit et civitati persuasit ut de finibus suis cum omnibus copiis exirent: Perfacile esse, cum virtute omnibus praestarent, totius Galliae imperio potiri. Id hoc facilius iis persuasit quod undique loci natura Helvetii contionentur: una ex parte flumine Rheno latissimo atque altissimo, qui agrum Helvetium a Germanis dividit; altera ex parte monte Iura altissimo, qui est inter Sequanos et Helvetios; teria lacu Lemanno et flumine Rhodano, qui provinciam nostram ab Helvetiis dividit. His rebus fiebat ut et minus late vagarentur et minus facile finitimis bellum inferre possent; qua ex parte homines bellandi cupidi magno dolore afficiebantur.

Solid and Hazardous Waste Management/Feasibility Studies

His rebus adducti et auctoritate Orgetorigis permoti constitu erunt ea quae ad proficiscendum pertinerent comparare, iumentorum et carrorum quam maximum numerum coemere, sementes quam maximas facere, ut in itinere copia frumenti suppeteret, cum proximis vicitatibus pacem et amicitiam confirmare. Ad eas res conficiendas biennieum sibi satis esse duxerunt; in tertium annum profectionem lege confirmant.

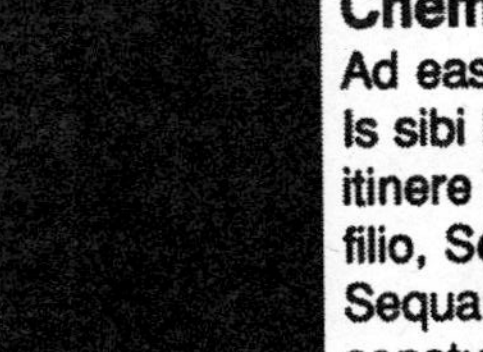

Chemical and Process Engineering

Ad eas res conficiendas Orgetorix deligitur. Is sibi legationem ad civitates suscipit. In eo itinere persuadet Castico, Catamantaloedis filio, Sequano, cuius pater regnum in Sequania multos annos obtinuerat et a senatu populi Romani amicus appellatus erat, ut regnum in civitate sua occuparet, quod pater ante habuerat; itemque Dumnorigi Haeduo, fratri Diviciaci, qui eo tempore principatum in civitate obtinebat ac maxime plebi acceptus erat, ut idem conaretur persuadet, eique filiam suam in matrimonium dat.

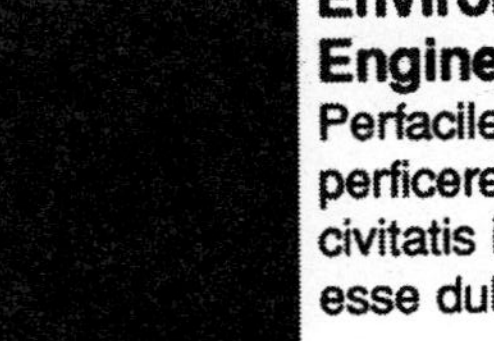

Environmental and Civil Engineering

Perfacile factu esse illis probat conata perficere, propeterea quod ipse suae civitatis imperium obtenturus esset: Non esse dubium quin totius Galliae plurimum

FIG. 3.3 Simplicity and consistency make a readable design. (Part 2 of 2)

Effective use of white space can give your documents a relaxing, open look. Breaking up white space or filling it with type just because not doing so seems wasteful is almost always a mistake. Granted, a tight budget may dictate that you fill every available inch of space, but bear in mind that white space performs a valuable function, by adding an element of restfulness and harmony. Figure 3.4 shows the effect of breaking up white space. The article heading and subhead are more visually effective when placed either closer to the top of the white space or closer to the body text.

Establishing Text Flow

Your job as document designer is to lead the reader's eye in a comfortable path from one page element to another, keeping the established scanning habits of the human eye in mind. You can avoid design pitfalls by remembering that people read from left to right and from top to bottom of a page:

- Does your placement of a title seem a trifle bizarre? Ask yourself whether it helps or hinders normal left-to-right, top-to-bottom eye flow.
- Must the reader's eye perform an acrobatic leap from a heading to body text? If so, perhaps a large initial letter at the start of the text can provide a helpful guidepost.
- Does the placement of a chart create ambiguity about where the body text resumes? If so, remember that a seasoned document designer probably would move the chart rather than risk irritating the reader.

Figure 3.5 shows a document page that uses design features to guide the reader's eye from one text element to the next. Notice how the flow of body text runs naturally from the top to bottom and from left to right, reflecting the standard reading habits of Western readers. Also notice how the boldface text, horizontal lines, and parallel columns create a visually clear arrangement of data elements.

Commercial Contractors Discover 1910

Teak and brass take time but pay well

Newel posts of polished black oak make the Smithson home, built in 1913, an enduring sight.

CUM CIVITAS ob eam rem incitata armis ius suum exsequi conaretur, multitudinemkque hominum ex agris magistratus cogerent, Orgetorix mortuus est; neque abest suspicio, ut Helvetii arbitrantur, quin ipse sibi mortem consciverit. Post eius mortem nihilo minus Helvetii id quod constituerant facere conantur, ut e finibus suis exeant. Ubi iam se ad eam rem paratos esse arbitrati sunt, oppida sua omnia, numero ad duodecim, vicos ad quadringentos, relique privata, aedificia incendunt; frumentum omne, praeterquam quod secum portaturi erant, comburunt, ut, domum reditionis spe sublata, paratiores ad omnia pericula subeunda essent; trium mensium molita cibaria sibi quemque domo efferre iubent. Persuadent Rauracis et Tulingis et Latobrigis, finitimis, uti eodem usi consilio, oppidis suis vicisque exustis, una cum iis proficiscantur; Boiosque, qui trans Rhenum incoluerant et in agrum oricum transierant Noreiamque oppugnabant, receptos ad se socios sibi asciscunt. Erant omnino itinera duo quibus itineribus domo exire possent: unum per Sequanos, angustum et difficile. Id hoc facilius iis persuasit quod undique loci natura Helvetii contionentur: una ex parte flumine Rheno latissimo atque altissimo, qui agrum Helvetium a Germanis dividit; altera ex parte monte Iura altissimo, qui est inter Sequanos et Helvetios; teria lacu Lemanno et flumine Rhodano, qui provinciam nostram ab Helvetiis dividit. ❖

Commercial Contractors Discover 1910

Teak and brass take time but pay well

Newel posts of polished black oak make the Smithson home, built in 1913, an enduring sight.

CUM CIVITAS ob eam rem incitata armis ius suum exsequi conaretur, multitudinemkque hominum ex agris magistratus cogerent, Orgetorix mortuus est; neque abest suspicio, ut Helvetii arbitrantur, quin ipse sibi mortem consciverit. Post eius mortem nihilo minus Helvetii id quod constituerant facere conantur, ut e finibus suis exeant. Ubi iam se ad eam rem paratos esse arbitrati sunt, oppida sua omnia, numero ad duodecim, vicos ad quadringentos, relique privata, aedificia incendunt; frumentum omne, praeterquam quod secum portaturi erant, comburunt, ut, domum reditionis spe sublata, paratiores ad omnia pericula subeunda essent; trium mensium molita cibaria sibi quemque domo efferre iubent. Persuadent Rauracis et Tulingis et Latobrigis, finitimis, uti eodem usi consilio, oppidis suis vicisque exustis, una cum iis proficiscantur; Boiosque, qui trans Rhenum incoluerant et in agrum oricum transierant Noreiamque oppugnabant, receptos ad se socios sibi asciscunt. Erant omnino itinera duo quibus itineribus domo exire possent: unum per Sequanos, angustum et difficile. Id hoc facilius iis persuasit quod undique loci natura Helvetii contionentur: una ex parte flumine Rheno latissimo atque altissimo, qui agrum Helvetium a Germanis dividit; altera ex parte monte Iura altissimo, qui est inter Sequanos et Helvetios; teria lacu Lemanno et flumine Rhodano, qui provinciam nostram ab Helvetiis dividit. ❖

FIG. 3.4 Filling or dividing white space is always a mistake.

Forthright Financial
FANDOR FARMS AREA OFFICE
2212 So. Western Avenue, Suite 502
Auburn, CA 95908
(916) 299-6425

Employee Directory

NAME	DEPARTMENT	EXTENSION
Cisneros, Armando Lucy (pediatrician), Alex 7, Deanna 10, Joe 13, golf, scuba, UCLA (economics, Phi Beta Kappa)	***Accounting*** Supervisor	***546***
Desrogers, Jacqueline Single, painting, Sorbonne (economics, honors)	***Planning*** Vice President	***66***
Egan, Faith Ed (contractor), Andrew 18, ultramarathoning, X-C skiing, Stanford (economics, Biz School)	***Technical Services*** Team Leader	***48***
Lamarr, Kevin Maryanne (housewife), Cindy 1½, Peter 4, Darren 7, Whitney 13, golf, Univ. New Mexico (accounting, law)	***President***	***1***
Rankin, Jolynne Frank (architect), Ashley 8, Rod 14, Greg 23, bicycling, jogging, Univ. Minnesota (philosophy, business)	***Customer Services*** Department Manager	***43***
Stanfield, Harold Single, bodybuilding, swimming, ultramarathoning, Harvard (Rhodes Scholar, mathematics, Biz School)	***Financial Services*** Chief Auditor	***18***
Tanaguchi, Alan Mary (chemical engineer), Ana 10, Toshi 12, surf fishing, backpacking, UCLA (statistics, Ph.D. economics)	***Financial Trends*** Chief Statistician	***32***
Ullyot, Marjorie Edward (doctor), Jimmy 10, Alix 13, triathlon, swimming, running (Arizona State U., business)	***Customer Service*** Department Manager	***777***

FIG. 3.5 Use design elements to guide the reader through text.

Repeating Elements

As you design documents, keep uppermost in mind the reader's need to lift useful information from the page in a visually pleasant, nondisruptive way. The reader may admire your craft but will resent anything, no matter how decorative, that interferes with access to information. Repeating design elements, such as headers and footers, page numbers, and section headings guide the reader and eliminate confusion.

In figure 3.6, notice how repeating elements guide the eye through the installation steps. The left column consists of three boxed illustrations in a clear vertical sequence, and the right column uses square bullets and boldface headings to create a consistent format for the installation instructions. In this design, the consistent use of fonts, headings, and font sizes combines with the consistent use of single-lined boxes to simplify the presentation of potentially confusing information.

Using Illustrations

Aptly used visual images add interest, persuasiveness, and power to printed documents. Like poorly applied typography, however, ineptly used illustrations can degrade rather than enhance your publications.

Illustrations—whether photos, clip art images, or spreadsheet charts—evoke feelings and images that the reader associates with your company. For example, imagine two line art drawings of a golfer. One shows an overweight duffer missing the ball, and the other shows a successful pro making an approach shot before a gallery of admiring fans. The tone of the images you use, whether crude or professional, comic or serious, strongly affects the image your publications convey. Never take chances with questionable illustrations.

Figure 3.7 shows two images from the DrawPerfect Figure Library. Both show a seated office worker drawn in the same style, but they evoke very different thoughts.

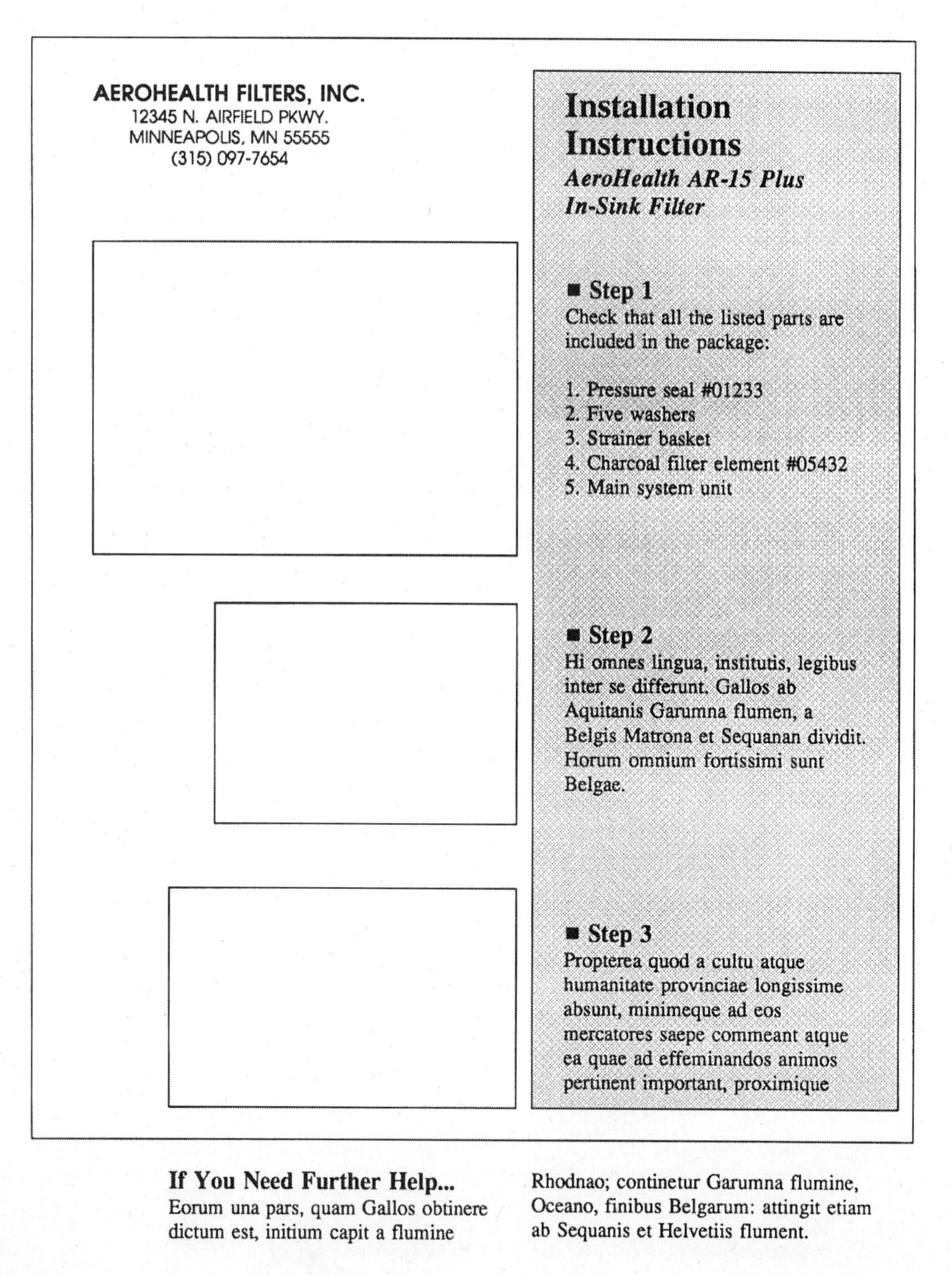
AEROHEALTH FILTERS, INC.
12345 N. AIRFIELD PKWY.
MINNEAPOLIS, MN 55555
(315) 097-7654
Installation Instructions
AeroHealth AR-15 Plus In-Sink Filter
■ Step 1
Check that all the listed parts are included in the package:
1. Pressure seal #01233
2. Five washers
3. Strainer basket
4. Charcoal filter element #05432
5. Main system unit
■ Step 2
Hi omnes lingua, institutis, legibus inter se differunt. Gallos ab Aquitanis Garumna flumen, a Belgis Matrona et Sequanan dividit. Horum omnium fortissimi sunt Belgae.
■ Step 3
Propterea quod a cultu atque humanitate provinciae longissime absunt, minimeque ad eos mercatores saepe commeant atque ea quae ad effeminandos animos pertinent important, proximique
If You Need Further Help...
Eorum una pars, quam Gallos obtinere dictum est, initium capit a flumine Rhodnao; continetur Garumna flumine, Oceano, finibus Belgarum: attingit etiam ab Sequanis et Helvetiis flument.

FIG. 3.6 Repeating elements guide the reader through text.

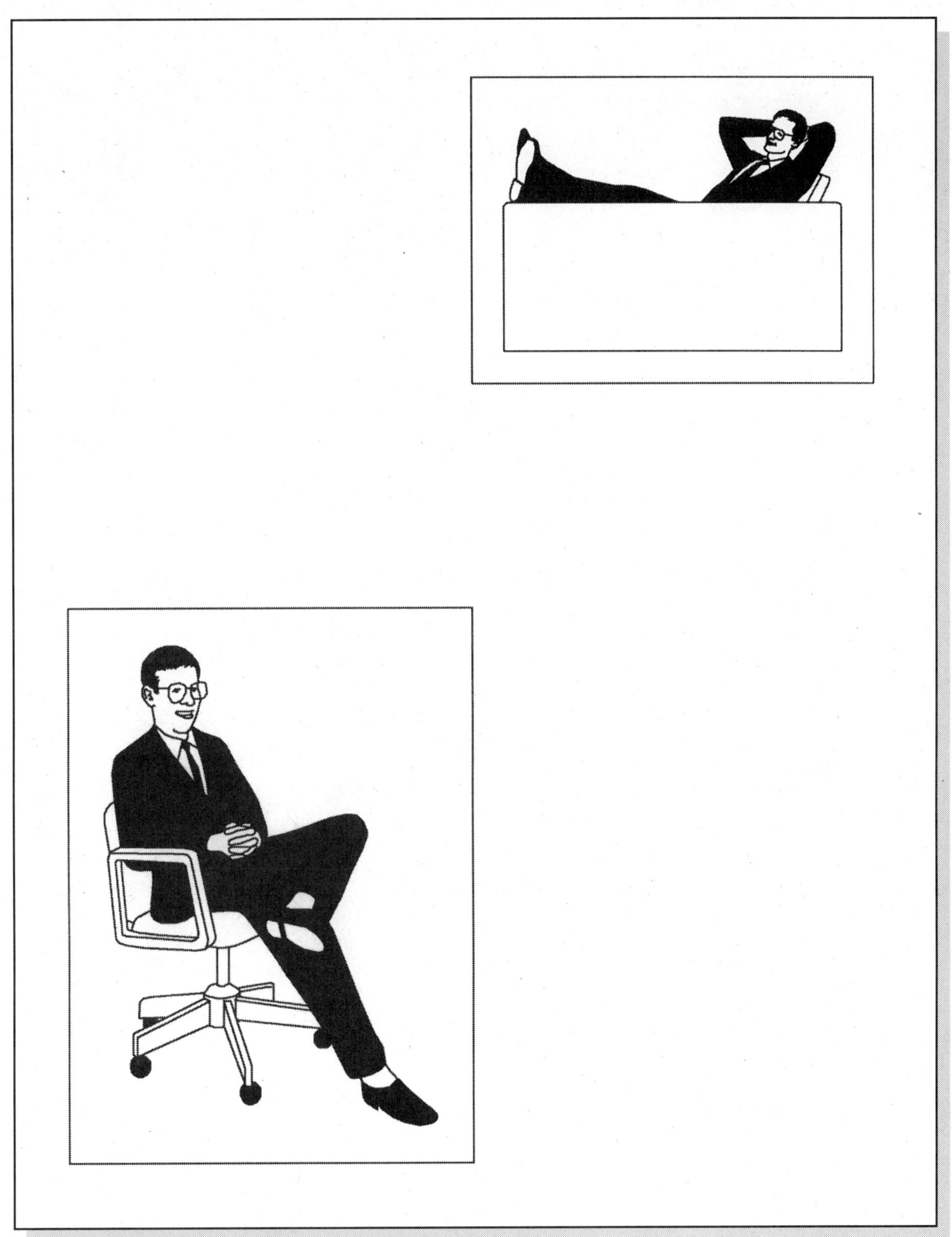

FIG. 3.7 Similar images may evoke very different responses.

The following factors influence the effectiveness of an illustration:

- *Quality.* Never use an out-of-focus photograph (unless you have snapped aliens abducting chickens from a neighbor's yard).
- *Direction.* Artwork can guide the reader's eye to important page elements, such as article headings, subheads, and sidebars. When the action in an illustration faces left, for example, place important material to the left of the illustration.
- *Inequality.* When placing several illustrations on the same page, make the more important illustration larger than the others and place the figure where the eye falls on it first. When the photos are of equal importance—a series of head shots, for example—make them the same size and line them up horizontally or vertically on the page. When you see a photo layout such as the one in figure 3.8, your eye first looks for the dominant photo. Therefore, don't place equal-sized headshots in an artistic layout, because this arrangement frustrates the reader.
- *Shape.* Use horizontal and vertical images for variety but avoid squares—they are static and boring. Notice in figure 3.8 that the photos are all rectangular but that some are vertical and some horizontal.
- *Cropping.* Crop, or remove, extraneous detail from your photographs and line drawings. The reader is more interested in Mrs. Miller than in her cluttered living room. However, to avoid a cramped look, leave a sensible amount of *breathing room* in the frame. Advertising research shows that enlarged close-ups of the human face tend to repel the viewer.

Creating Balance

Balance your designs so that all the emphasis is not placed in one corner or in the upper or lower half of the page. This balance is particularly important for side-by-side pages. Each page can look terrific, but viewing them together reveals elements that clash: headlines that align horizontally; too much emphasis on the upper half of both pages; adjacent photos that cancel each other; and so on.

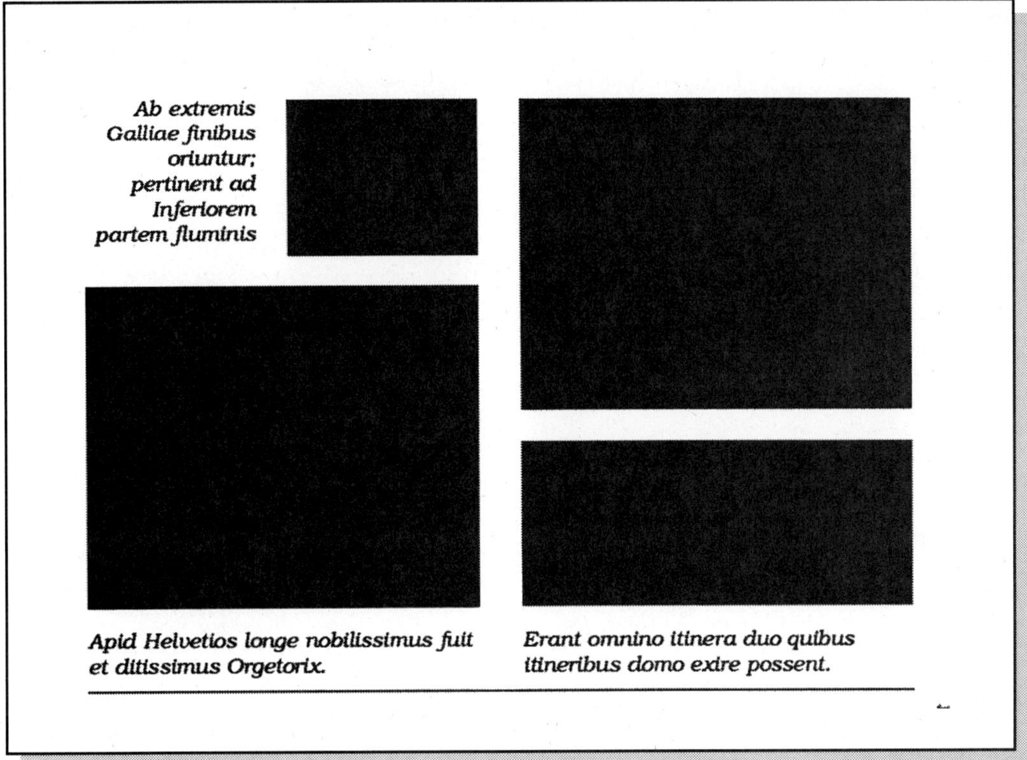
Ab extremis
Galliae finibus
oriuntur;
pertinent ad
Inferiorem
partem fluminis
Apid Helvetios longe nobilissimus fuit et ditissimus Orgetorix.
Erant omnino itinera duo quibus itineribus domo exire possent.

FIG. 3.8 In photo layouts, make one photo larger than the rest.

In figure 3.9, notice how the two-page spread is carefully balanced. This balance didn't happen by accident; the designer deliberately balanced the page elements:

- Photos are placed in the outside columns; they are different sizes and are placed at different horizontal levels.
- The large photo at upper right provides a dominant focus.
- The three drop caps (A, C, C) are deliberately arranged in a triangle. A drop cap was omitted for the first article on page three, because it broke up the eye-pleasing triangular pattern.
- At the bottom of the first page shown, the single-column article relieves the tedium of four narrow columns.
- The line and long subheading across the middle of page 2 nicely balances the vertical format of page 3.

2

Dest and Hess Restore the Asparte Mansion

Contract won on strength of portfolio, say cousins

Built in 1874-76, the Asparte Mansion is a Marsden Vale landmark.

AD EAS RES conficiendas biennieum sibi satis esse duxerunt; in tertium annum profectionem lege confirmant. Ad eas res conficiendas Orgetorix deligitur. Is sibi legationem ad civitates suscipit. In eo itinere persuadet Castico, Catamantaloedis filio, Sequano, cuius pater regnum in Sequania multos annos obtinuerat et a senatu populi Romani amicus appellatus erat, ut regnum in civitate sua occuparet, quod pater ante habuerat; itemque Dumnorigi Haeduo, fratri Diviciaci, qui eo tempore principatum in civitate obtinebat ac maxime plebi acceptus erat, ut idem conaretur persuadet, eique filiam suam in matrimonium dat.

Perfacile factu esse illis probat conata perficere, propeterea quod ipse suae civitatis imperium obtenturus esset: Non esse dubium quin totius Galliae plurimum Helvetii possent: se suis copiis suoque exercitu illis regna conciliaturum confirmat. Hac oratione adducti inter se fidem et ius iurandum dant et, regno occupato, per tres potentissimos ac firmissimos populos totius Galliae sese potiri posse sperant.

Ea res est Hevetiis per indicium enuntiata. Moribus suis Orgetorigem ex vinculis cansam dicere coegerun; damnatum poenam sequi oportebat, ut igni cremaretru. Die constituta causae dictionis Orgetorix ad iudicium omnem suam familiam, ad homionum milia decem. Belgae ab extremis Galliae finibus oriuntur; pertinent ad Inferiorem partem fluminis Rheni; spectant in septentriones et orientem solem. Aquitania a Garumna flumine ad Pyrenaeos montes et eam partem Oceani quae est ad Hispaniam pertinent; spectat inter occasum solis et septentriones. Apid Helvetios longe nobilissimus fuit. ❖

Commercial Contractors Discover 1910

Teak and brass take time but pay well

Newel posts of polished black oak make the Smithson home, built in 1913, an enduring sight.

CUM CIVITAS ob eam rem incitata armis ius suum exsequi conaretur, multitudinemkque hominum ex agris magistratus cogerent, Orgetorix mortuus est; neque abest suspicio, ut Helvetii arbitrantur, quin ipse sibi mortem consciverit. Post eius mortem nihilo minus Helvetii id quod constituerant facere conantur, ut e finibus suis exeant. Ubi iam se ad eam rem paratos esse arbitrati sunt, oppida sua omnia, numero ad duodecim, vicos ad quadringentos, relique privata, aedificia incendunt; frumentum omne, praeterquam quod secum portaturi erant, comburunt, ut, domum reditionis spe sublata, paratiores ad omnia pericula subeunda essent; trium mensium molita cibaria sibi quemque domo efferre iubent. Persuadent Rauracis et Tulingis et Latobrigis, finitimis, uti eodem usi consilio, oppidis suis vicisque exustis, una cum iis proficiscantur; Boiosque, qui trans Rhenum incoluerant et in agrum oricum transierant Noreiamque oppugnabant, receptos ad se socios sibi asciscunt. Erant omnino itinera duo quibus itineribus domo exire possent: unum per Sequanos, angustum et difficile. Id hoc facilius iis persuasit quod undique loci natura Helvetii contionentur: una ex parte flumine Rheno latissimo atque altissimo, qui agrum Helvetium a Germanis dividit; altera ex parte monte Iura altissimo, qui est inter Sequanos et Helvetios; teria lacu Lemanno et flumine Rhodano, qui provinciam nostram ab Helvetiis dividit. ❖

FIG. 3.9 Photos, drop caps, and lines provide balance. (Part 1 of 2)

3

Specialty Styles Turn the Corner

New Mexico? Old South? Maine? Texas? Sense of place keeps builders busy

EXTREMUM OPPIDUM Allobrogum est proximumque Helvetiorum finibus Genava. Ex eo oppido pons ad Helvetios pertinet. Allobrogibus sese vel persuasuros, quod nondum bono animo in populum Romanum viderentur, existimabant, vel vi coacturos ut per suos fines eos ire paterentur. Omnibus rebus ad profectionem comparatis, diem dicunt qua die ad ripam Rhodani omnes conveniant. Is dies erat a.d.v. Kal. April., L. Pisone A. Gabinio consulibus.

Caesari cum id nuntiatum esset, eos per provinciam nostram iter facere conari, maturat ab urbe profisci, et quam maximis potest itineribus in Galliam ulteriorem contendit et ad Genavam pervenit. Provinciae toti quam maximum potest militum numerum imperat (erat omnino in Gallia ulteriore legio una), pontem qui erat ad Genavam iubet rescindi. Ubi de eius adventu Helvetii certiores facti sunt, legatos ad eum mittunt, nobilissimos civitatis, cuius legationis Nammeius et Verucloetius principem locum obtinebant, qui dicerent sibi esse in animo sine ullo maleficio iter per provinciam facere, propterea quod aliud iter haberent nullum; rogare ut eius voluntate id sibi facere liceat.

His rebus adducti et auctoritate Orgetorigis permoti constitu erunt ea quae ad proficiscendum pertinerent comparare, iumentorum et carrorum quam maximum numerum coemere, sementes quam maximas facere, ut in itinere copia frumenti suppeteret, cum proximis vicitatibus pacem et amicitiam confirmare. Ad eas res conficiendas biennieum sibi satis esse duxerunt. ❖

New Mexico adobe in Central City? Yes, in Crosstree Park Estates, near Rock River.

CAESAR, QUOD memoria tenebat L. Cassium consulem occisum exercitumque eius ab Helvetiis poulsum et sub iugum missum, concedendum non putabat; neque homines inimico animo, data facultate per provinciam itineris faciendi, temperaturos ab iniuria et maleficio existimabat. Tamen, ut spatium intercedere posset, dum milites quos imperaverat convenirent, legatis respondit diem se ad deliberandum sumpturum; si quid vellent, ad Id. April. reverterentur.

Perfacile factu esse illis probat conata perficere, propeterea quod ipse suae civitatis imperium obtenturus esset: Non esse dubium quin totius Galliae plurimum Helvetii possent: se suis copiis suoque exercitu illis regna conciliaturum confirmat. Hac oratione adducti inter se fidem et ius iurandum dant et, regno occupato, per tres potentissimos ac firmissimos populos totius Galliae sese potiri posse sperant. Ea Hevetiis per indicium enuntiata. Moribus suis Orgetorigem. Is sibi legationem ad civitates suscipit. In eo itinere persuadet Castico, Catamantaloedis filio, Sequano, cuius pater regnum in Sequania multos annos obtinuerat et a senatu populi Romani amicus appellatus erat, ut regnum in civitate sua occuparet. ❖

Freeport Crafts Sponsors Classes

Three master cabinetmakers offer full schedule

Shop owners give weekend time for master classes.

FIG. 3.9 Photos, drop caps, and lines provide balance. (Part 2 of 2)

You probably will not achieve a perfect balance at first try. Usually, you need to play with the layout, trying various arrangements, moving photos and changing their sizes, adding or removing a drop cap, placing an article in a one-column boxed sidebar, and so on, to achieve balance.

TIP

Because WordPerfect requires so many keystrokes to redesign a page, you work more quickly when you do the bulk of your original page planning with pencil and paper.

To achieve a balanced design, you may need to cut words from an article or add more text—a normal, time-honored design procedure. This process can create temporary friction between writer and designer, but both should realize that words communicate more effectively when they are artistically arranged. Your document designs project an image that can be as important in the communication process as the information you are trying to convey.

Working with the Sample Designs

The step-by-step procedures in Chapters 5 through 25 give you hands-on instructions for creating professionally designed documents with WordPerfect. When you need a memo or a fax form in a hurry, follow the keystroke-by-keystroke directions and insert your company's name and address.

Some designs require more time to create than others. For one design, you need, for example, to fill a sample newsletter with your text and photos. To customize this design, you need to become comfortable with basic WordPerfect features and working procedures.

This chapter provides tips and techniques for working with the sample documents.

Using Type

Type is the simplest—and the most underrated—design element. Many of the attractive documents in the step-by-step chapters use type as an important design element.

You don't need a huge typeface library to create good-looking designs. Actually, all the sample documents in this book were created with only five popular fonts supplied with many popular laser printers: Times Roman, Helvetica, Avant Garde, Palatino, Bookman, and New Century Schoolbook. You can achieve good results with any of these designs by substituting Times Roman and

Helvetica. Remember that the appropriateness and creative use of the fonts you choose, not the number of fonts you use, makes a document attractive.

Times Roman, Helvetica, and the other fonts mentioned in the preceding paragraph have withstood the test of time because these fonts are easily readable on-screen and on paper. Figure 4.1 shows a listing of the six typefaces and the most common font variations in which the fonts are used.

Choosing a Printer

If you don't own a laser printer and you want to do desktop publishing, consider buying one. The documents you print represent you, and the quality of laser-printing is now widely expected.

A printer with scalable fonts is an even better buy. Scalable fonts enable font size changes with just a few keystrokes. PostScript printers have scalable fonts, as do many recent models of the Hewlett-Packard LaserJet. The sample documents for this book were printed on a Canon LBP8-III printer equipped with a PostScript cartridge. The Canon printer produces sharp text and excellent quality gray screens. Figure 4.2 shows scalable font sizes selected by resetting the base font. You can reset the base font in the following way by pressing Ctrl-F8 (Font), F (Base Font).

Examining Printer Variations and the Sample Designs

Because of minor variations between laser printers, select the printer that you plan to use to print a document *before* you begin the document creation process. If you create a document with one printer and then switch to another printer, WordPerfect's default font substitution feature may lengthen or shorten the text because of slight differences in font design, causing one or more lines to wrap to the next column or page or shortening a column and disturbing the design.

TIP

The designs in this book were created with a PostScript-compatible printer. If you own a Hewlett-Packard LaserJet or Canon LBP series or compatible printer, the names of the fonts given in this text may be unfamiliar. The following list of typeface names may help you determine the font equivalent to use to produce results similar to the examples shown here.

PostScript printers use the original manufacturer's names for typefaces, such as Times Roman and Helvetica. Because of copyright considerations, the Hewlett-Packard and Canon companies license similar fonts from other vendors who must use different names for typefaces.

The sample designs use three primary typefaces: Times Roman, Helvetica, and Palatino. A few designs also use Avant Garde, Bookman, and New Century Schoolbook. The following list gives the equivalent typeface names for PostScript, Hewlett-Packard, and Canon printers:

PostScript	*Hewlett-Packard*	*Canon*
Times Roman	CG Times	Dutch
Helvetica	Univers	Swiss
Palatino		Zapf Calligraphic
Avant Garde		Avant Garde
Bookman		Bookman (with SC-1 font card)
New Century Schoolbook		New Century Schoolbook (with SC-1 font card)

Times Roman
Times Roman Bold
Times Roman Bold Italic
Times Roman Italic

Helvetica
Helvetica Bold
Helvetica Bold Oblique
Helvetica Condensed Bold
Helvetica Condensed Bold Oblique
Helvetica Condensed Medium
Helvetica Condensed Oblique
Helvetica Narrow
Helvetica Narrow Bold
Helvetica Narrow Bold Oblique
Helvetica Narrow Oblique
Helvetica Oblique

Palatino
Palatino Bold
Palatino Bold Italic
Palatino Italic

Bookman Demi
Bookman Demi Italic
Bookman Light
Bookman Light Italic

New Century Schoolbook
New Century Schoolbook Bold
New Century Schoolbook Bold Italic
New Century Schoolbook Italic

FIG. 4.1 Six typefaces and their most common font variations. (Part 1 of 2)

Avant Garde Gothic Book
Avant Garde Gothic Book Oblique
Avant Garde Gothic Demi
Avant Garde Gothic Demi Oblique

FIG. 4.1 Six typefaces and their most common font variations. (Part 2 of 2)

4 Times Roman
8 Times Roman
16 Times Roman
32 Times Roman
48 Times Roman
64 Times Roman
80 Times Ron
96 Times R

FIG. 4.2 Font size changes are easy with scalable fonts.

Notice that Palatino, which is used for a number of the sample designs, and Avant Garde, Bookman, and New Century Schoolbook, which are used rarely, are not supplied with the Hewlett-Packard LaserJet series printers. If you substitute CG Times where the instructions call for these fonts, you get excellent results. You also can purchase soft fonts or a font cartridge that contains these fonts.

Using Sample Graphic Images

Many of the sample documents in Chapters 5 through 25 use graphic images selected from the figure library of the DrawPerfect program. Thirty images are supplied with WordPerfect, but few of these images are suitable for the designs in this book. You can buy the DrawPerfect figure libraries without purchasing DrawPerfect. For information, call the WordPerfect Corporation order line at 1-800-321-4566. Five figure libraries are available: Figure, Business, Holiday, Leisure, and Education. Each library contains more than 200 images. The Figure library, with general images in a variety of categories, is used for the sample documents in this book.

Other sources of graphic images are figure libraries in other formats. You can use the WordPerfect image conversion program GRAPHCNV.EXE to import these graphic images from several other formats, but the conversion process may deteriorate image quality. WordPerfect can directly access images in several popular formats (for details, see the *WordPerfect Reference Manual*).

Creating Typeset Documents

When you need the highest print quality, have the WordPerfect documents professionally typeset. The process is simple and provides a way for you to perform desktop publishing even if you don't have access to a laser printer.

You need a typesetter who can print PostScript files from disk. Many typesetters use Macintosh-compatible equipment but can convert files from IBM disks.

To set up WordPerfect for typesetting, install a WordPerfect printer driver for the Apple LaserWriter Plus printer. The LaserWriter Plus is a PostScript printer, as are the most common typesetting machines. You can send all files you print to disk in LaserWriter format directly to the typesetting machine.

When you select the Apple LaserWriter Plus, you can install the Apple LaserWriter Plus driver and tell WordPerfect to print files to disk by following these steps:

1. In the WordPerfect document screen, press Shift-F7 (Print), S (Select Printer).

   If the Apple LaserWriter Plus is listed in the Print: Select Printer menu, proceed to step 4.

2. Press A (Additional Printers). When the Apple LaserWriter Plus appears in the Select Printer: Additional Printers list, highlight the printer name and press S (Select), Enter.

   At the Printer Helps and Hints screen, press F7 (Exit).

3. If the Apple LaserWriter Plus doesn't appear in the Select Printer Additional Printers list, exit WordPerfect and use the setup program to select the LaserWriter printer. Repeat steps 1 and 2.

4. At the Select Printer: Edit screen, press P (Port), O (Other).

   At the `Device` or `Filename` prompt, type the name of a file to receive output from the LaserWriter driver, such as *TYPESET.TXT*. Press F7, F7, S, and F7 to select the Apple LaserWriter Plus printer and return to the document screen.

All text that you print with the Apple LaserWriter Plus selected is sent to the file named in step 4, TYPESET.TXT.

For text printed with the LaserWriter selected, WordPerfect sends PostScript output to a disk file that you can take to a commercial printer for typesetting.

When you design documents for typesetting, be sure that you first select the Apple LaserWriter Plus driver so that View Document gives an accurate preview of the design:

1. Press Shift-F7 (Print), S (Select Printer).

2. Move the cursor to highlight Apple LaserWriter Plus, press S (Select) and press F7.

After selecting the Apple LaserWriter Plus, you can create desktop-published documents in WordPerfect by using any of the 35 scalable PostScript fonts. You can check the work in View Document (Shift-F7 and V), but you cannot print the work on a non-PostScript printer. You can use PostScript emulation hardware and/or software, such as the QMS JetScript, to print proofs of the work on non-PostScript printers.

Using Reveal Codes

Producing desktop-published documents with WordPerfect involves spending many happy hours working in Reveal Codes. To make the work easier, enlarge the Reveal Codes window by pressing Shift-F1, D (Display), E (Edit-Screen Options), and R (Reveal Codes Window Size).

Type the number of lines for the Reveal Codes screen (try **18** for starters) and then press Exit (F7) twice to return to the document. When you turn on Reveal Codes (Alt-F3), three rows of document text appear, two rows for the status line and ruler, and 18 rows of Reveal Codes. Many of the sample documents have 10 lines or more of hidden codes at the start of the file. Expanding the Reveal Codes window gives you more elbow room to find and edit codes with less scrolling.

Working with Columns

The following tips can help you get the most out of working with columns when creating the sample documents in the following chapters.

TIP

Many of the sample documents use columns. Although you may own a fast computer, you can work faster in columns when you turn off side-by-side column display by pressing Shift-F1 (Setup), D (Display), E (Edit-Screen Options), S (Side-by-Side Columns Display), N (No), F7 (Exit).

TIP

WordPerfect's default column margins, known as *gutters*, leave too much space between columns. This problem is remedied when you define columns by setting Distance Between Columns on the Text Column Definition Screen to 3/16" or 1/4", rather than the default 1/2" gutter.

TIP

After you define columns, you may need to change column margins. When this happens, don't delete the existing column definition code.

Move the cursor to the right of the old code (if you turned on columns after you defined them, the cursor is on the `[Col On]` code). Define columns again.

To display the Text Column Definition screen, press Alt-F7, C, and D.

The settings for the old column definition appear because you didn't delete the old code. This display can save time when you need to change only one or two column margins. After making changes, return to the Reveal Codes screen and delete the first `[Col Def...]` code.

Working with Measurements

WordPerfect enables you to choose a favorite unit of measure: inches, centimeters, points, twelve-hundredths of an inch, or WordPerfect 4.2 units (lines and columns).

Computerized desktop publishing doesn't mean that you can throw the ruler away. No program—not even PageMaker—makes desktop publishing possible without carefully measuring page elements with a ruler. Actually, a good ruler can save you a great deal of time.

This book uses inches as the unit of measure. Americans grow up using inches, and common paper sizes in the U.S. are measured in inches. Setting WordPerfect to display measurements in inches, therefore, is recommended.

To set inches as the unit of measure, press Shift-F1 (Setup), E (Environment), U (Units of Measure), D (Display and Entry of Numbers), " (inches), S (Status Line Display), " (inches), F7.

TIP

Buy the best ruler for desktop publishing, a ruler that has inches on *all* edges. Rulers that have multiple scales for inches, centimeters, points, and agates can drive you crazy. Each time you pick up the ruler, you accidentally may choose the agate scale. Don't buy aluminum rulers because these tools can smudge clean printouts. Also make sure that you get a ruler with 1/32" markings.

Working with Boxes

Many of the sample documents use page-anchored graphic text boxes. As you work with these examples, remember that the hidden codes for page-anchored boxes *must* be placed on the first line of the page, before all hard returns, or WordPerfect moves the box to the next page.

On complex pages, place fixed, page-anchored design elements in page-anchored boxes—for example, sidebars, letterheads, and tables. You then can edit text around boxes and lines without worrying about accidentally moving text. Page-anchored boxes stay put.

As you create boxes, you may need to change a few settings in the box options screen. Before you bring up the Options: Text (or Figure) Box menu, move the cursor to the right of the existing options code. WordPerfect then shows the previous settings in the menu, and you don't have to re-enter previous settings that don't need changing.

TIP

You may have 10 box and line codes strung together at the top of a page. To make finding a specific box or line easier, make a list of the box and line numbers and the contents or position of each element on the page, as the elements are created.

When a box contains text or a caption, you can move instantly into the text or caption editor from anywhere in the document by pressing Home, Home, Home, and the up-arrow key to move to the top of the document, ahead of all hidden codes.

Then you can use Extended Search to locate text in the caption or box:

1. Press Home, F2 (Extended Search).
2. Type the text for which you want to search.
3. Press F2. WordPerfect places you in the box or caption editor where you can make changes.
4. To return to the document screen, press F7.

Using Macros and Styles

Documents created for day-to-day business use have two phases: design and production. After designing the basic format of a newsletter, for example, your focus changes to the production of regular issues. While you design the documents, you may perform many operations for the first and only time, such as creating a box for the main heading, choosing typefaces and font sizes, and arranging page elements in a grid.

Production work involves repetitive tasks, such as changing the font for subheadings, text, and photo captions, positioning drop caps, and sizing photos. WordPerfect's macro and style functions can speed up these routine operations.

For document production, styles may do a better job than macros, because macros require an invocation key or macro name; whereas styles are chosen from a menu.

Styles and macros are ideal for repetitive complex procedures, such as creating newsletter and report headings. With just a few keystrokes, you can specify multiple font changes, advance codes, create a text box for a drop cap, and fine-tune the positioning of body text.

Styles have a special advantage for document creation: to change the font for every subhead, edit the corresponding style.

Managing DTP Files

Don't make the mistake of spending days designing and producing the first issue of a newsletter and then lose all this work during a power outage. Professional designers keep at least three copies of current designs: a working copy on the hard disk, a working backup copy on a floppy disk, and an archival backup copy on a second floppy disk.

Disks go bad, which is why keeping at least two backups is good practice. You sometimes can recover trashed files with a utility program, but the process is tedious, and the document's design work usually comes out garbled.

Back up the designs often. Save the on-screen document file to the hard disk after every major change and save a copy on the working disk every 5 to 10 minutes. At least four times a day, save an archival copy. If you backed up all work on disks just before a power failure occurs, you can remain serene while those around you panic.

Fine-Tuning Your Designs

If you fail to correct a single small design fault, such as inconsistent spacing between text and photos, you can be sure that at least one reader will notice the problem and find you guilty of sloppy work. The human eye is remarkably adept at noticing tiny misalignments and inconsistencies. Designers are absolutely ruthless in chasing down rough edges, spacing errors, and misaligned page elements. After the major design work is done, a designer may spend hours ensuring that everything is precisely aligned.

To get a feeling for the fine-tuning process, follow the design steps for the complex newsletter in Chapter 25 that requires many precise alignments. You may be surprised by the attention to detail needed to make a document look polished and professional.

The following check list may help you fine-tune documents.

1. Do elements align? Check the alignment of photos with text, drop cap baselines with adjacent text and heading baselines, horizontal lines with tops and bottoms of columns, and so on. Figure 4.3 shows the eye-pleasing effect of the careful aligning of text and graphic elements with each other to create an appealing banner.

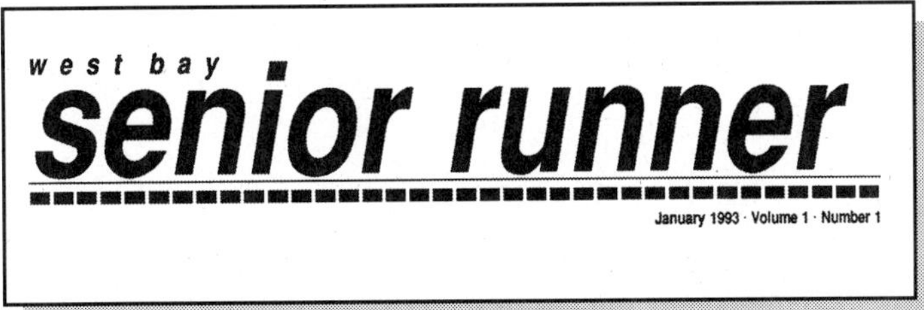

FIG. 4.3 Alignment creates a sense of order.

2. Do you see ragged edges? Does text that runs around photos have a smooth edge, or do paragraph indents create a ragged border? If so, edit the text or move the photo. Have you hyphenated ragged-right text? Do the lines of a multiple-line heading balance, or is one line much longer than the other? Figure 4.4 shows the unpleasant effect of overly ragged edges versus a cleaner, less distracting version of the same document.
3. Is spacing consistent? Is the white space between photos and text the same throughout the document? Is the border between text columns, lines, and boxes consistent? Are headlines the same distance from body text?

Hi omnes lingua, institutis, legibus inter se differunt. Gallos ab Aquitanis Garumna flumen, a Belgis Matrona et Sequana dividit. Horum omnium fortissimi sunt Belgae, propterea quod a cultu atque humanitate provinciae longissime absunt, minimeque ad eos mercatores saepe commeant atque ea quae ad effeminandos animos pertinent important, proximique sunt Germanis, qui trans Rhenum incolunt, quibuscum continenter bellum gerunt.

Remedial Investigations

Pro multitudine autem hominum et pro gloria bellie atque fortitudinis angustos se fines habere arbitrabantur, qui in longitudinem milia passuum CCXL, in latitudinem CLLXXX patebant.

Apid Helvetios longe nobilissimus fuit et ditissimus Orgetorix. Is, M. Messala, M. Pisone consulibus, regni cupiditate inductus coniurationem nobilitatis fecit et civitati persuasit ut de finibus suis cum omnibus copiis exirent: Perfacile esse, cum virtute omnibus praestarent, totius Galliae imperio potiri. Id hoc facilius iis persuasit quod undique loci natura Helvetii contionentur: una ex parte flumine Rheno latissimo atque altissimo, qui agrum Helvetium a Germanis dividit; altera ex parte monte lura altissimo, qui est inter Sequanos et Helvetios; teria lacu Lemanno et flumine Rhodano, qui provinciam nostram ab Helvetiis dividit. His rebus fiebat ut et minus late vagarentur et minus facile finitimis bellum inferre possent; qua ex parte homines bellandi cupidi magno dolore afficiebantur.

FIG. 4.4 Ragged edges look sloppy. (Part 1 of 2)

Hi omnes lingua, institutis, legibus inter se differunt. Gallos ab Aquitanis Garumna flumen, a Belgis Matrona et Sequana dividit. Horum omnium fortissimi sunt Belgae, propterea quod a cultu atque humanitate provinciae longissime absunt, minimeque ad eos mercatores saepe commeant atque ea quae ad effeminandos animos pertinent important, proximique sunt Germanis, qui trans Rhenum incolunt, quibuscum continenter bellum gerunt.

Remedial Investigations

Pro multitudine autem hominum et pro gloria bellie atque fortitudinis angustos se fines habere arbitrabantur, qui in longitudinem milia passuum CCXL, in latitudinem CLLXXX patebant.

Apid Helvetios longe nobilissimus fuit et ditissimus Orgetorix. Is, M. Messala, M. Pisone consulibus, regni cupiditate inductus coniurationem nobilitatis fecit et civitati persuasit ut de finibus suis cum omnibus copiis exirent: Perfacile esse, cum virtute omnibus praestarent, totius Galliae imperio potiri. Id hoc facilius iis persuasit quod undique loci natura Helvetii contionentur: una ex parte flumine Rheno latissimo atque altissimo, qui agrum Helvetium a Germanis dividit; altera ex parte monte lura altissimo, qui est inter Sequanos et Helvetios; teria lacu Lemanno et flumine Rhodano, qui provinciam nostram ab Helvetiis dividit. His rebus fiebat ut et minus late vagarentur et minus facile finitimis bellum inferre possent; qua ex parte homines bellandi cupidi magno dolore afficiebantur.

Solid and Hazardous Waste Management/Feasibility Studies

FIG. 4.4 Fixing inconsistent spacing removes distractions. (Part 2 of 2)

4. Do you see too much space between columns? WordPerfect's default column spacing of 1/2" is much too wide unless you place vertical lines between columns. For body text of 9 to 11 points, 3/16" or 1/4" column spacing looks much better. To correct this problem, change the Distance Between Columns setting in the Text Column Definition menu. Other spacing problem areas are as follows:

   - Too much space between drop caps and adjacent text. Change the size of the text box that contains the drop cap.

   - Too little space between text and lines, lines around the page, lines between sections, vertical lines in the margins, or between columns. Experiment with extra space and check the results in the View Document screen. The product and price list in figure 4.5 uses precise spacing of text and graphics to create a harmonious effect.

5. Is white space trapped (enclosed between page elements that may look better if grouped together)? As a rule, leave a large area of, rather than dividing, white space. Headlines look better when placed at the top or bottom of an area of white space, rather than dividing the white space by placing the headline in the middle. In figure 4.6, you see that the headline and graphic are tightly grouped together. Placing this headline at the top of a memo form leaves a large, restful area of white space at the top of the page.

6. Are subheadings tombstoned (aligned horizontally on the page)? If so, edit the text; switch sections; move, delete, or insert a new photo; put one section in a separate box or in one or two columns, separated from the rest of the page by a horizontal line.

7. Do two-page spreads work together? When you sketch the pages, make sure that two-page spreads contain no conflicting visual elements, such as adjacent or unattractively aligned photos or headlines, or more than one dominant photo or major headline on the spread. As you lay out the design, check spreads frequently with the Facing Pages option in View Document.

BLITZLICHT

PRODUCTS FOR THE PHOTO PRO

Products and Prices Spring 1992

Studio Flash Systems

BL 4800 Studio Flash **$1500.00**
Includes 4800 unit, 5" umbrella reflector, protective cover, sync cord, power cable.

BL 3600 Studio Flash **$1250.00**
Includes 3600 unit, 5" umbrella refalector, protective cover, sync cord, power cable.

BL 2400 Studio Flash **$1000.00**
Includes 2400 unit, 5" umbrella reflector, protective cover, sync cord, power cable.

Reflectors and Umbrellas

11" Diameter Reflector **$25.00**
Very effective for situations requiring long-throw, narrow-beam lighting. Bright finish.

20" Diameter Reflector **$35.00**
Good choice for portraits requiring moderate light definition and feathering. (Medium-soft portrait light.) Removable center shield for bouncelight.

42" Silver Bounce Umbrella **$35.00**
Very high output, with smooth, even coverage. Best shoice for portraits. Soft bouncelight source for beauty, products. Gives very wide coverage.

New! Advanced Control Unit

BlitzChip Control Box **$150.00**
Controls up to six Blitzlicht strobes from central console. Vary power, modeling, dump.

WARRANTY

Blitzlicht guarantees to repair or replace, free of charge, for a period of two years, any part found to be defective due to faulty materials or workmanship.

TERMS AND CONDITIONS

Blitzlicht products are shipped with an unconditional 30-day money-back guarantee.

On credit card orders, please include expiration date and a phone number where we can reach you during the day. For fastest service, order on our toll-free line using your Mastercard or VISA.

All prices subject to change without notice.

BLITZLICHT
4321 E. Meadowlark
Farmer's Mill, WI 54321
Voice: (508) 987-2345
Fax: (508 987-2344

Call toll-free:
1-800-987-6543

FIG. 4.5 Precise spacing creates a sense of harmony.

8. Finally, proofread the text. Don't rely heavily on WordPerfect's speller, which may overlook errors, such as *by* for *buy*, *there* for *their*, and double capitalization (THe). Nothing detracts from an attractive design more quickly than typographical errors.

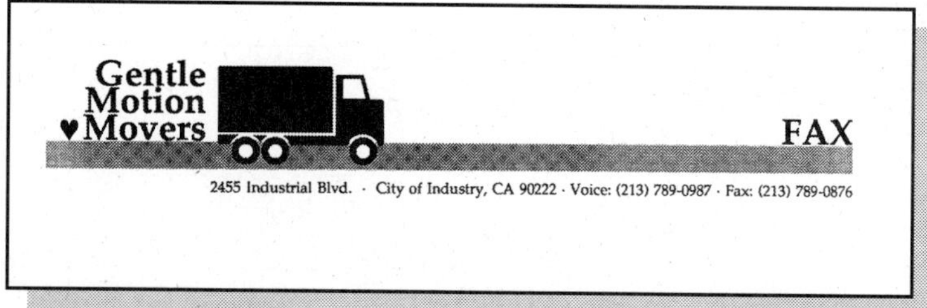

FIG. 4.6 Don't divide white space with a headline.

Customizing the Designs for Your Printer

The sample designs in the chapter that follow use hundreds of measurements to position type, lines, and figures on the page. The designs were created with a PostScript printer. If you are using a different printer, such as the Hewlett-Packard LaserJet III, you may need to fine-tune the measurements given in the text.

Suppose that the instructions tell you to use Advance to move the insertion point up 5/16". When you print or check the page in the View Document screen, you may find that the Advance code places a horizontal line on top of the preceding text instead of beneath it. To correct this problem, you need to reduce the amount of the Advance and check the results with View Document.

You also may find that measurements change if you use fonts different from those specified for the designs or if you use cloned versions of the actual fonts specified in the designs.

Although giving precise measurements for every printer on the market and every font combination available is impossible, you should find that the instructions in this book provide a starting point from which you can duplicate the designs with a small amount of fine-tuning.

A One-Day Seminar

Custom Injection Molding
for the Biomedical Industry

East Florida University Conference Center

June 14, 1991
9 am - 5 pm

Topic	Time	Presenter	Room
Disposable Diagnostic Test Kits			
Improved Molding Techniques	9 am	G. Smythe	110
Design Considerations	10 am	L. Pavlov	214
the Assembly Challenge	11 am	R. Zantri	55
Specialty Products for Blood Transfer			
The HIV Challenge	10 am	G. Smythe	110
The Time-Critical Transfer	11 am	L. Pavlov	214
Four New Processes	1 pm	D. Andre	104
Assembled Unit Testing			
Failure-Prone Materials	11 am	P. Eldred	512
Selecting Test Parameters	2 pm	R. Goth	643
Secure Laminates	3 pm	P. Eldred	214
Market Factors			
Predicting Demand	3 pm	P. Eldred	323
Three Case Histories	4 pm	R. Goth	643
Successful Bid Analysis	5 pm	L. Wenzel	742

Part II

Creating Business Documents

Includes

5

Producing Letterheads

A widespread dogma among business people holds that letterheads, envelopes, and business cards should be professionally designed and printed. Laser-printed correspondence doesn't stand up well to close scrutiny, and if you are in an appearance sensitive business such as fine cabinetry, women's fashions, or financial counseling, even a well-designed, laser-printed letterhead can project carelessness.

If you are confident in your artistic abilities, go ahead and design logos, letterheads, and envelopes but have them professionally printed. You can "print" your design to a PostScript disk file and take the disk to a print shop. Because sending files out for professional typesetting is such an important option for desktop publishers, you should consider this process. You can find step-by-step instructions in Chapter 4.

Letterhead No. 1: A Rural Clinic

For some businesses, laser printing is sufficient. Figure 5.1 shows a simple letterhead for a busy, rural clinic that cares less about its image than about the people it treats. The bulk of the clinic's correspondence consists of medical referrals and billing reminders, none of which needs embossed logos and high-resolution type. When your business doesn't require a polished image, for example freight-forwarding, nonprofit community services, or auto wrecking, laser-printed documents are adequate.

SIERRA FAMILY MEDICAL CENTER
Urgent Care · Family Practice
15195 TYLER FOOTE CROSSING RD
NEVADA CITY, CA 95959

TELEPHONE: (916) 292-3478

PETER VAN HOUTEN, MD
Medical Director
Family Practice

DAVID KESSLER, DO
Osteopathic Physician
Family Practice

SUE LOPER-POWERS, RN, NP
Women's Health Care
Nurse Practitioner

LAURA HERMANN, RN, FNP
Family Nurse Practitioner

LENNIE MARTIN, RN, FNP
Family Nurse Practitioner

FIG. 5.1 *Simple but effective business letterhead.*

The letterhead in figure 5.1 is simple but intriguing and can be customized for any business that needs a simple, businesslike design.

Creating letterheads is a good introduction to desktop publishing with WordPerfect, because letterhead creation provides experience with typography, the most basic element of graphic design. In this section, you create the letterhead shown in figure 5.1.

Begin by changing the typeface and adjusting the margins. Follow these steps:

1. To change the font to 12-point Times Roman, press Ctrl-F8, F; move the cursor to Times Roman in the Base Font list; press Enter; type *12*; and press F7.

   Note: Keystroke instructions for changing the font are given only in the first three chapters of this section.

2. To print the name and address high on the page, you need to change the top page margin. Press Shift-F8, P, M; type *9/16*"; and press Enter, Enter, F7.

To create the title and address in the heading, follow these steps:

1. Press Shift-F6 (Center).
2. Type the title *SIERRA FAMILY MEDICAL CENTER* and press Enter.
3. Press Shift-F6 (Center).
4. Type *Urgent Care* and press the space bar.
5. Use Compose to create a bullet—a small, round typesetter's symbol used to set off items in vertical or horizontal lists. Press Ctrl-V.

   At the `Key =` prompt, type *4,3* and press Enter and the space bar.

   Type *Family Practice* and press Enter.

6. To change the font to 9-point Times Roman, press Ctrl-F8, F; move the cursor to Times Roman in the Base Font list; press Enter; type *9*; and press F7.
7. Press Shift-F6 and type *15195 TYLER FOOTE CROSSING RD*.
8. Press Enter, Shift-F6 (Center) and type the names of the city, state, and the ZIP code.

The telephone number is separated from the rest of the address by a horizontal line with a space, below the address and above the phone number; the space is less than what you get by pressing Enter twice. This customized space is obtained by using the Line Height feature to change the line height. Follow these steps:

1. Press Shift-F8.
2. Press L, H, F and type *.05*".
3. Press Enter, F7.

   In the Reveal Codes screen (Alt-F3), WordPerfect inserts the code: `[Ln Height:0.05"]`. Press Enter to insert *vertical* space before the horizontal line.

TIP

The number for line height, 0.05", was found by experimentation. Fine-tuning document designs always involves some trial and error, whether you are working with WordPerfect or PageMaker.

4. To create the horizontal line, press Alt-F9, L, H.
5. In the Graphics: Horizontal Line screen, make the following settings:

Horizontal Position	Center
Vertical Position	Baseline
Length	.273"
Width	.008"
Gray Shading	100%

6. Press F7 to return to the document screen.
7. Before pressing Enter, change the line height to .058" by pressing Shift-F8, L, H, F; typing *.058*"; and pressing Enter, F7.
8. Press Enter three times.
9. Press Shift-F6 (Center) and type *TELEPHONE: (916)292-3478*.

10. Before pressing Enter, change the line height back to the automatic setting. Press Shift-F8, L, H, A, F7.

The staff names and titles are created next. Follow these steps:

1. Press Enter four times.
2. Change the left margin for the staff names and titles that appear in the left margin. Press Shift-F8, L, M and type *7/16*".

   Press Enter, Enter, F7.
3. To change the font to 6-point Times Roman, press Ctrl-F8, F and move the cursor to Times Roman in the Base Font list.

   Press Enter; type *6*; and press F7.
4. Type the first staff member's name *PETER VAN HOUTEN, MD*. Press Enter.
5. Press Ctrl-F8, A, I to turn on italics.
6. Type Dr. Van Houten's title *Medical Director*. Press Enter.
7. Type *Family Practice*.
8. Press the right-arrow key to turn off italics.
9. Press Enter three times and type the next staff member's name. Repeat steps 4 through 8 for the remainder of the staff list.

The cursor is now far down the page and far into the left margin. The clinic wants to type letters on the letterhead, displayed on-screen, and then laser-print text and letterhead simultaneously. With the letterhead displayed, you move the cursor into the typing area by using the Advance feature and following these steps:

1. Move the cursor to a designated line on the page. Press Shift-F8, O, A, I and type *1.6*". Press F7 twice.
2. To change the font to 12-point Courier, press Ctrl-F8, F and move the cursor to Courier in the Base Font list. Press Enter; type *12*; and press F7.
3. To change the margins, press Shift-F8, L, M. Type *1.8*" and press Enter. Type *1*" and press F7, F7.

The first page of the letter uses a nonstandard left margin of 1.8" to indent body text past the staff list in the left border. A reminder is needed for anyone using the form to reset the margins on subsequent pages. To have Wordperfect remind you by displaying a warning in a nonprinting WordPerfect Comment box on-screen, complete the following steps:

1. Press Ctrl-F5, C, C.
2. Type a warning in the Document Comment editing screen. The comment for the medical clinic's letterhead is as follows:

```
<<<CHANGE MARGINS TO 1", 1" PAGE 2!!! HEADERS ALSO!!!>>>

Begin typing below:
```

3. Press F7 to leave the comment editing screen.

After retrieving the letterhead form into the editing screen, follow these steps:

1. Press Home, Home, and the down-arrow key to move the cursor to the top of the typing area.

   The cursor rests below the letterhead text, but thanks to the Advance command, WordPerfect prints the body text in the correct location.

2. The nonprinting comment reminds the typist to press Enter and change the left margin at the top of page two.

Letterhead No. 2: A Janitorial Service

Another small business that may not suffer from laser-printing its letterhead is the Night Lights Janitorial Service, an office cleaning service run by enterprising single women who met (of course) in night school.

First Design: All Type

The first design, shown in figure 5.2, uses type strictly. If the essence of style is simplicity, this is a stylish letterhead. You can insert your company's name in this generically simple yet attractive letterhead, with full confidence of presenting a respectable image.

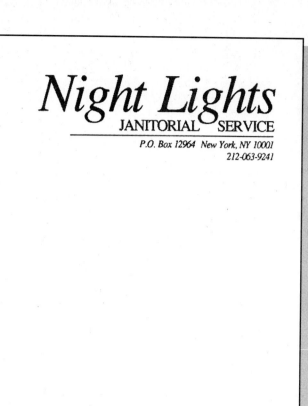

FIG. 5.2 Simple but stylish letterhead for a janitorial service.

When designing documents, begin by sketching the underlying page grid. A grid is a pencil-and-paper drawing that shows the position of columns, main headings, artwork, and lines. In a multipage catalog or newsletter, the grid gives each page a consistent look. Headers repeat on each page in the same position and in the same typeface. A line at the top of each page separates headers from body text and provides a pleasing, relaxing visual continuity.

Letterheads usually are simple, but they still need a grid, and the first Night Lights letterhead design is no exception. In preliminary sketches, the artist first tried various positions for the company's name and address and sketched in various type sizes on plain white paper. Several versions of the type were printed on a laser printer, cut out with scissors, and placed in various positions on the page. With each trial, a date line and a rectangular area representing body text were marked. The result appears in figure 5.2.

Begin creating the first design by setting the page margins and changing the font. Follow these steps:

1. To set the page margins, press Shift-F8, L, M, Enter. Type *.5* and press Enter, Enter.

   Press P, M and type *5*. Press Enter, Enter, F7.

2. To change the font to 56-point Times Roman Italic, press Ctrl-F8, F and move the cursor to Times Roman Italic in the Base Font list.

   Press Enter, type *56*, and press F7.

3. Press Alt-F6 (Flush Right).

Type set in a very large font generally looks as though there is too much space between the words and letters. Remedy this situation with the Word Spacing/Letter Spacing function. Complete the following steps:

1. Press Shift-F8, O, P, W, P.

2. Type *90* and press Enter.

3. Press P, type *90*, and press Enter, F7.

4. Type *Night Lights* and press Enter.

   This process sets word spacing to 90% of the default, sets letter spacing to 90% of the default, and gives the logotype a tighter, more designed look.

The next line "JANITORIAL SERVICE" rests under *Night Lights*, with the lowercase *g* in *Lights* positioned between "JANITORIAL" and "SERVICE." To achieve this effect, position "JANITORIAL SERVICE" carefully, using the Advance feature. Follow these steps:

1. Advance the next line up 1/8", under *Night Lights*. Press Shift-F8, O, A, U. Type *1/8"* and press Enter, F7.
2. To change the font to 16-point Times Roman, press Ctrl-F8 and move the cursor to Times Roman in the Base Font list.

   Press Enter, type *16*, and press F7.
3. Press Alt-F6 (Flush Right) and type *JANITORIAL SERVICE*, pressing the space bar four times to separate the words.
4. Press Enter to move to the next line.

The graphic line that separates "JANITORIAL SERVICE" from the address also must be moved up to create a tight, unified effect for the letterhead:

1. Press Shift-F8, O, A, U.
2. Type *5/16"* and press Enter, F7.

To create the horizontal line, follow these steps:

1. Press Alt-F9, L, H.
2. In the Graphics: Horizontal Line screen, make the following settings:

Horizontal Position	Right
Vertical Position	Baseline
Length of Line	3"
3. Accept the default values for the other settings by pressing Enter to move to the next line.

Use Advance again to move the insertion point down far enough below the line to allow space for the first line of the address. Follow these steps:

1. Press Shift-F8, O, A, D; type *5/8"*; and press Enter, F7.
2. To change the font to 10-point Times Roman Italic, press Ctrl-F8, F and move the cursor to Times Roman Italic in the Base Font list.

   Press Enter, type *10*, and press F7.

3. Press Alt-F6 (Flush Right) and type the first line of the address.
4. Type the remaining line of the address, pressing Enter and Alt-F6 (Flush Right).

When typing letters on this letterhead form in the editing screen and printing letter text and letterhead simultaneously, you need to set appropriate margins for letter body text. Follow these steps:

1. Press Shift-F8, L, M, Enter.
2. Type *1*"; press Enter, Enter, P, M; type *1*"; and press Enter, Enter.
3. Press F7.

The letterhead definition is now complete.

> **TIP**
>
> Save a backup copy. You need to keep a spare empty form in reserve for when you accidentally save letter text under the blank form name.

Second Design: Reversed Text with Graphics Boxes

The next version of the Night Lights letterhead, shown in figure 5.3, uses reversed (white) text printed in a black graphics box. You can print reversed type with WordPerfect 5.1 only on a PostScript or Hewlett-Packard LaserJet III or compatible printer. This design also looks good without the reversed text, however.

P.O. Box 12964 · New York, NY 10001
212-623-9241

FIG. 5.3 *Night Lights letterhead with reversed text.*

The company address is printed in the bottom margin of the page—a common technique for letterheads.

Begin by setting narrow top and bottom margins:

1. Press Shift-F8, P, M.
2. Type .5" and press Enter.
3. Type .5" and press Enter, F7.

To create the black box, complete the following steps:

1. Press Alt-F9, B, O, and in the Options: Text Box menu, make the following settings:

Border Style	Set all to None
Outside Border Space	Set all to 0"
Inside Border Space	Set all to 0"
Gray Shading	Set to 100%

2. Press F7 to return to the document screen.
3. Press Alt-F9, B, C, and in the Definition: Text Box screen, make the following settings:

Anchor Type	Page, Number of pages to skip: 0
Vertical Position	Top
Horizontal Position	Margin, Center
Size	Set Both, 3.63" wide × 0.75" high

4. Press E to enter the text box editing screen and press Enter to move to the second line.

TIP

The Center Page function is not available in the text box editing screen, so you must use press Enter and Advance to center text vertically in a box.

To type the main heading *NIGHT LIGHTS*, follow these steps:

1. To change the text color to white, press Ctrl-F8, C, W, Enter.

2. Press Shift-F6 (Center).
3. To change the font to 42-point Times Roman, press Ctrl-F8, F and move the cursor to Times Roman in the Base Font list.

   Press Enter, type *42*, press F7, and type *N*.
4. Change the font to 28-point Times Roman and type *IGHT LIGHT*.
5. Change the font to 42-point Times Roman and type the letter *S*.
6. Press F7 twice to return to the document screen.

Create the subheading "JANITORIAL SERVICE." A bug prevents WordPerfect from centering the text correctly under the box or from accepting an Advance command to position the text. However, you can create another box under the first box and use Advance to position text correctly in the graphics box text editing screen:

1. Move the cursor to the right of the first box code.
2. To set the gray shading in the box, press Alt-F9, B, O. In the Options: Text Box screen, change Gray Shading to 0%. Press F7 to return to the document screen.
3. Press Alt-F9, B, C, and in the Definitions: Text Box screen, make the following settings:

Vertical Position	1.15"
Horizontal Position	Margins, Center
Size	6" wide × 3/8" high

4. Press E to enter the text box editor.
5. To position the text with the Advance command, press Shift-F8, O, A, R; type *1.17*"; and press Enter, F7.
6. To change the font to 14-point Times Roman Bold, press Ctrl-F8, F and move the cursor to Times Roman Bold in the Base Font list. Press Enter, type *14*, and press F7.

Notice that the letters in "JANITORIAL SERVICE" are widely spaced. You create this effect with the Word/Letter Spacing function. Follow these steps:

1. To set word and letter spacing to 180% of normal, press Shift-F8, O, P, W, P. Type *180*; press Enter, P; type *180*; and press Enter, F7.
2. Type *JANITORIAL SERVICE*.
3. To reset word and letter spacing to Optimal, press Shift-F8, O, P, W, O, O, F7. Press F7 to return to the document screen.

To create the thick gray horizontal line under "JANITORIAL SERVICE," follow these steps:

1. Press Alt-F9, L, H
2. In the Graphics: Horizontal Line screen, make the following settings:

Horizontal Position	Set Position, 2 7/16"
Vertical Position	Set Position, 1.53"
Length of Line	3 5/8"
Width of Line	3/32"
Gray Shading	30%

Press F7 to return to the document screen.

The logo portion of the letterhead is complete. To insert the address in a text box at the bottom of the page, you can move the cursor to the bottom of the page and type the address, but that procedure complicates the creation of body text in the letterhead form because entering text ahead of the address pushes the address forward.

The address can be placed in a footer that prints only on page one but that makes creation of footers on subsequent pages inconvenient, because a new footer must be inserted and positioned after the address footer code.

A page-anchored box prints where placed, independent of cursor movement. To create the page-anchored box for the address, follow these steps:

1. Press Alt-F9, B, O, and in the Options: Text Box screen, make the following settings:

Border Style	Set all to None
Outside Border Space	Set all to 0"
Inside Border Space	Set all to 0"
Gray Shading	0%

2. Press F7 to return to the document screen.
3. Press Alt-F9, B, C and in the Definition: Text box screen, make the following settings:

Anchor Type	Page, Number of pages to skip: 0
Vertical Position	Set Position, 10 1/4"
Horizontal Position	Margin, Center
Size	6" wide × .45" high

4. Press E to enter the text box editor.
5. To set the font to 12-point Times Roman, press Ctrl-F8, F and move the cursor to Times Roman in the Base Font list. Press Enter, type *12*, and press F7.
6. Press Shift-F6 (Center) and type *P.O. Box 12964*.
7. Between the P.O. box number and the city, you need to insert a bullet. After the box number, press the space bar and then press Ctrl-V (Compose). At the `Key =` prompt, type *4,3* and press Enter.
8. Press the space bar again and type *New York, NY 10001*.
9. Press Enter to go to the next line.
10. Press Shift-F6 (Center) and type *212-623-9241*.
11. Press Exit twice to return to the document screen.

To reset the top and bottom page margins for typing text on subsequent pages, complete the following steps:

1. Press Shift-F8, P, M.
2. Type *1*" and press Enter.
3. Type *1*" and press Enter, F7.

Third Version: Using a Graphics Image

The third variation on the Night Lights letterhead, shown in figure 5.4, uses a graphics image. The use of a graphic adds sophistication, but this design actually is the easiest of the three to create.

> **TIP**
>
> If your printer is slow in printing graphics, and you plan to be printing letterhead in WordPerfect, think twice about using a graphics image in your letterhead.

The letterhead image and text are held in a narrow column at the left side of the page. Begin the design by setting the margins and defining the columns.

1. To define the margins, press Shift-F8, L, M.

   Type .5" and press Enter.

   Type .5" and press Enter.

   Press Enter, P, M.

   Type .5" and press Enter.

   Type .5" and press Enter, F7.

2. To define the columns, press, Alt-F7, C, D. In the Text Column Definition menu, accept the defaults but change the Margins settings:

Column 1	1/2"(left), 2-1/8"(right)
Column 2	2.5"(left), 7"(right).

3. Press Enter, O, Enter to turn columns on and return to the document screen.

P.O. BOX 12764
NEW YORK
NY 10001
212-063-9241

FIG. 5.4 *Night Lights letterhead with a graphics image.*

To create the figure box that holds the imported image of office buildings, follow these steps:

1. Press Alt-F9, F, O, and in the Options: Figure screen, make the following settings:

Border Style	Set all to None
Outside Border Space	Set all to 0"
Inside Border Space	Set all to 0"
Gray Shading	0%

2. Press F7 to return to the document screen.
3. Press Alt-F9, F, C, and in the Definition: Figure screen, make the following settings:

Filename	CITY.WPG
Contents	Graphic
Anchor Type	Page, Number of pages to skip: 0
Vertical Position	Top
Horizontal Position	Columns, 1, Center
Size	Set Width, Auto Height, 1 5/8" wide × 1.35" (high)

4. Press F7 to return to the document screen.

Create the type by following these steps:

1. Press Enter.
2. To change the font to 35-point Times Roman, press Ctrl-F8, F and move the cursor to Times Roman in the Base Font list.
3. Press Enter, type *35*, and press F7.

Fit the first line of type "NIGHT LIGHTS" closely under the graphic image. To position the type *1/4*" higher with Advance, follow these steps:

1. Press Shift-F8, O, A, U; type *1/4*"; and press Enter, F7.
2. Press Shift-F6 (Center) and type *NIGHT*.
3. Press Enter to move to the next line.

"LIGHTS" should fit tightly under "NIGHT," so use Advance again to move the word 1/8" higher:

1. Press Shift-F8, O, A, U.
2. Type *1/8"* and press Enter, F7.
3. Type the word *LIGHTS* and press Enter.

The subtitle, "JANITORIAL SERVICE," also requires fine-tuning with Advance. Notice that the letters are spaced further apart than usual. You can create this effect easily with the Word/Letter Spacing feature:

1. To change the font to 14-point Times Roman, press Ctrl-F8, F and move the cursor to Times Roman in the Base Font list. Press Enter, type *14*, and press F7.
2. To move the line up 1/16" with Advance, press Shift-F8, O, A, U; type *1/16"*; and press Enter, F7.
3. The word SERVICE should fit tightly under "JANITORIAL." Change the leading (line spacing) but use the Leading Adjustment feature to reduce the line spacing by 2 points (1/32").

   Press Shift-F8, O, P, L, Enter; type *–2p*; and press Enter, F7.
4. To adjust the letter spacing to add 10% extra space between letters, press Shift-F8, O, P, W, O, P; type *110*; and press Enter, F7.
5. Type *JANITORIAL SERVICE* and press Enter.
6. To reset the letter spacing to Optimal, press Shift-F8, O, P, W, O, O, F7.

To create the address, follow these steps:

1. Use Advance to move the insertion point for the address near the bottom of column one, to a point nine inches from the top of the page. Press Shift-F8, O, A, I; type *9"*; and press Enter, F7.

TIP

You can use Enter to move the cursor to the bottom of the page but that puts a large number of `[HRt]` codes in the Reveal Codes screen. Moving the cursor past all those hard returns while editing is annoying.

2. To change the font to 10-point Times Roman, press Ctrl-F8, F and move the cursor to Times Roman in the Base Font list. Press Enter, type *10*, and press F7.
3. To adjust the line spacing with the Leading Adjustment feature, press Shift-F8, O, P, L, Enter; type *4p*; and press Enter, F7.

> **TIP**
>
> Include the lowercase p after the number, indicating that the unit of measurement is points, or Wordperfect adds four inches of space between lines!

4. Type the address, pressing Shift-F6 (Center) at the beginning of each line and Enter at the end of each line.
5. To turn columns off, press Alt-F7, C, F.

When you are typing letters directly on the letterhead form, press Home, Home, and the down-arrow key to move the insertion point to the top of the page and to the right of the graphic image. The following Advance, leading adjustment, margin setting, and font codes place the cursor in the proper position and change the font to 10-pitch Courier, with normal leading, which is appropriate for body text:

1. Press Shift-F8, O, A, U.
2. Type *9"* and press Enter, Enter.
3. Press L, M; type *3"*; press Enter; type *1"*; and press Enter, Enter.
4. Press O, P, L, 0, Enter, 0, Enter, F7.
5. Press Ctrl-F8, F; choose 10-pitch Courier from the Base Font list; and press F7.

To type letters longer than one page, you need to reset the left margin beginning on page two. When you reach the end of page one, do the following:

1. Press Enter to end the last line on the page with a hard return and press Delete to remove the space at the beginning of the first line on page two.
2. Press Shift-F8, L, M, 1, Enter, Enter, F7.

TIP

You may want to add a reminder to the non-printing comment box you just created, telling you to reset the margin at the top of page two.

The comment box with the message appears in the document screen. When typing a letter, follow these steps:

1. Retrieve the file.
2. Press Home, Home, and the down-arrow key to move the cursor to the bottom of the file, just below the comment box.

TIP

You may prefer to assign the file retrieval and cursor-movement commands to a macro.

Version 4: Night Lights Letterhead with Reversed Graphics Image

One final bit of graphic design magic is possible due to the courtesy of the WordPerfect graphic image editor. The name of the company NIGHT LIGHTS suggests trying a reverse in the image of office buildings, so they appear to have their lights on after dark (see fig. 5.5).

P.O. BOX 12764
NEW YORK
NY 10001
212-063-9241

FIG. 5.5 Night Lights letterhead with graphics image reversed.

Follow these steps to create the letterhead in figure 5.5:

1. Turn on Reveal Codes (Alt-F3) and move the cursor just past the `[Fig Opt]` code for the image. Press Alt-F9, F, O.

   In the Options: Figure screen, set Gray Shading to 100% and press F7 to return to the document screen.

2. To invert the image, press Alt-F9, F, E. Type *1* and press Enter, E.

   In the graphic image editing screen, press I to invert the image and press F7 twice to return to the document screen.

3. Print a copy of the letterhead.

Figure 5.5 shows how the image prints, with only the windows of the buildings showing against a solid black sky. The image reversal gives the logo an interesting abstract effect. At the very least, this image reversal suggests the variations made possible by the image editor.

6

Producing Envelopes

Designing envelopes is easy after you have designed a letterhead—you need only create a WordPerfect envelope paper size and type, change the layout slightly, and start printing.

In this chapter, you design an envelope to accompany each of the letterheads you designed in Chapter 5.

The first two steps of envelope design, defining the envelope paper size and type and the envelope margins, are exactly the same for all the envelopes defined in this chapter. To avoid repetition, these steps are given here just once.

To define the envelope paper size, follow these steps:

1. Press Shift-F8, P, S.
2. In the Format: Paper Size/Type menu, press A, E, S, E.
3. Press Enter, F7 to return to the document screen.

   When you display the Reveal Codes screen (Alt-F3), you see the hidden code for the envelope definition.

To set the envelope margins, follow these steps:

1. Press Shift-F8, L, M.
2. Type *1/3*" and press Enter.
3. Type the appropriate right margin setting for the name and address and press Enter.
4. Press F7 to return to the document screen.

TIP

You have to set the right margin when, as in figure 6.2, the letterhead text is formatted flush-right or centered. Otherwise, you can press Enter at the right margin setting to accept the WordPerfect default.

TIP

The left margin setting of 1/3" is for laser printers, which cannot print any closer to the edge of the paper than 1/3". If you are using a nonlaser printer, you can experiment with various margin settings and choose the one that looks best.

TIP

Some laser printers may not impress the image well with a 1/3-inch margin, and the type may flake off. If you have this problem, first try printing envelopes with the printer's straight-through paper path. If that doesn't work, try setting the margin at 1/2".

Envelope No. 1: A Rural Clinic

Figure 6.1 shows an envelope created from the first letterhead design, shown in figure 5.1.

SIERRA FAMILY MEDICAL CENTER
Urgent Care · Family Practice
15195 TYLER FOOTE CROSSING RD
NEVADA CITY, CA 95959

FIG. 6.1 Envelope design for rural clinic.

Night Lights
JANITORIAL SERVICE
P.O. Box 12964 New York, NY 10001
212-063-9241

FIG. 6.2 Envelope design for all-type Night Lights letterhead.

To create the envelope design shown in figure 6.1, follow these steps:

1. Choose the envelope paper size and type; press Shift-F8, P, S.

   Move the cursor to `Envelope - Wide` and press S to select `Envelope-Wide`. Press F7 to return to the document screen.

2. Set the left and top margins as described at the beginning of the chapter.
3. Switch to Document 2 by pressing Shift-F3. Retrieve the letterhead design shown in figure 5.1.
4. To select the address for retrieval into Document 1, turn on Reveal Codes (Alt-F3) and press Home, Home, Home, and the up-arrow key. Press Alt-F4 (Block) and move the cursor to the end of the ZIP code. Press Ctrl-F4 (Move), B, C.
5. Clear the screen in Document 2, switch back to Document 1, and retrieve the address by pressing F7, N, Y, Enter.
6. In Reveal Codes (Alt-F3), remove all of the `[Center]` codes. Press Alt-F3 to turn off Reveal Codes and return to the document screen.

Check your work in View Document by pressing Shift-F7 and then V. You see the return address positioned in the upper left corner of the envelope.

Night Lights Envelope with Mostly Text

The envelope design accompanying the all-type Night Lights letterhead of figure 5.2 is shown in figure 6.2. The text for this envelope is set flush-right, as in the letterhead.

The steps are similar to those for the envelope in figure 6.1, except that an appropriate right margin must be set for the flush-right address.

In step 2 of the procedure for the rural clinic, set the left margin to 1/3" and the right margin to 5 5/8" by following these steps:

1. Press Shift-F8, L, M.
2. Type *1/3*" and press Enter
3. Type *5 5/8*" and press Enter.
4. Press F7 to return to the document screen.

Night Lights Envelope with Reversed Text and Graphics Boxes

Figure 6.3 shows design variation number two of the Night Lights envelope, associated with the letterhead shown in figure 5.3.

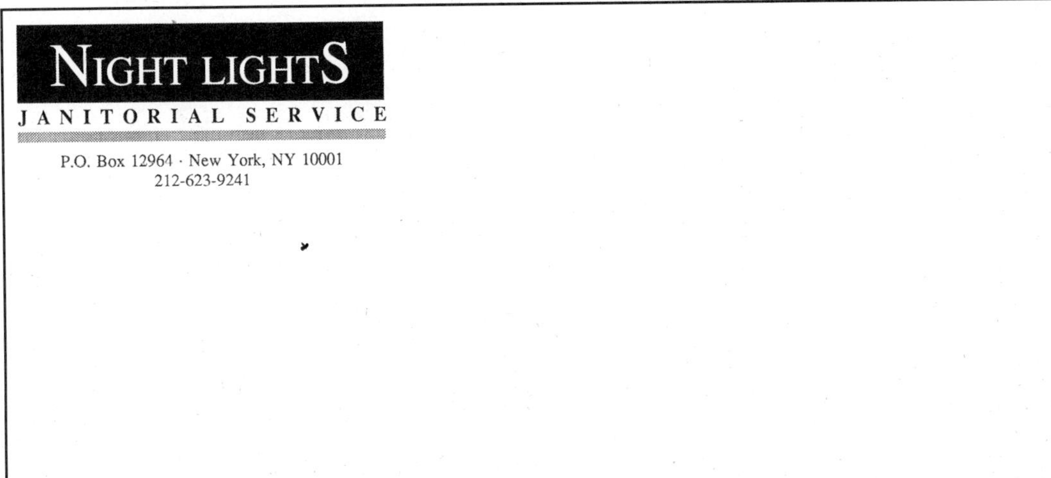

***FIG. 6.3** Envelope with reversed text and text boxes.*

> **TIP**
>
> Depending on your laser printer and the envelope stock you use, you may or may not have trouble printing the reversed logo. (The black areas may show white scuff marks.) You can, of course, change the reversed logo to black-on-white. The only other alternative is to have your envelopes commercially printed.

This design calls for a bit more fine-tuning to get it to print in the correct position on envelope stock. Follow these steps:

1. Choose the envelope paper size and type. Press Shift-F8, P, S. Move the cursor to `Envelope - Wide` and press S. Press F7 to return to the document screen.

2. Set the left and top margins as described at the beginning of this chapter.

3. Switch to Document 2 (Shift-F3), retrieve the letterhead design shown in figure 5.3, and turn on Reveal Codes (Alt-F3).

   Notice that the letterhead was created almost entirely using boxes and lines. Edit the letterhead to reposition the letterhead text for printing on envelopes.

4. Copy the letterhead text into Document 1. Press Home, Home, Home, the up-arrow key, Alt-F4, Home, Home, the down-arrow key, Ctrl-F4, B, C, Shift-F3, Enter.

5. To edit text box 1, press Alt-F9, B, E; type *1*; and press Enter. Press H, M, L to change the Horizontal Position to Margin, Left.

   Press F7 to return to the document screen.

6. To edit text box 2, press Alt-F9, B, E. Type *2* and press Enter. Press H, M, L to change the Horizontal Position to Margin, Left.

   Press E, and in the box editing screen, press Alt-F3 (Reveal Codes). Find and delete the `[AdvRgt:1.17"]` code. Press F7 twice to return to the document screen.

7. To edit text box 3, press Alt-F9, B, E; type *3*; and press Enter.

   Press V, S; type *1 3/4"*; and press Enter to set Vertical Position to 1 3/4".

   Press H, S; type *1/2"*; and press Enter to set Horizontal Position to 1/2".

   Press S, B; type *4 5/8"*; and press Enter, Enter to change the width of the box to 4 5/8".

   Press F7 to return to the document screen.

8. To change the horizontal position of the shaded line to 1/3", move the cursor onto the horizontal line code and press Alt-F9, L, O, H, S.

   Type *1/3"* and press Enter.

   Press F7 to return to the document screen.

9. Check your work in the View Document screen by pressing Shift-F7, V.

Night Lights Envelope Using a Graphic Image

Figure 6.4 shows the Night Lights envelope associated with the letterhead shown in figure 5.4.

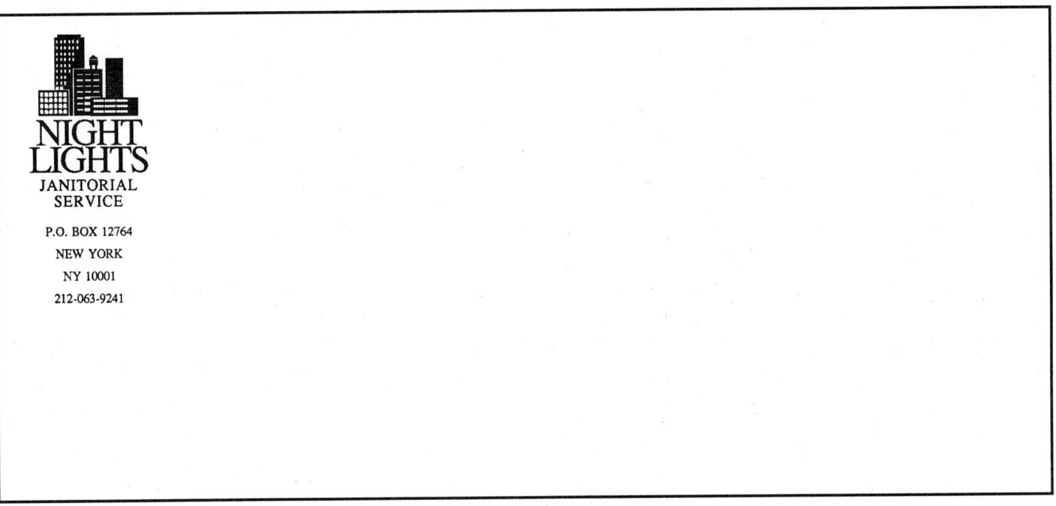

FIG. 6.4 Night Lights envelope using a graphic image.

Because this design is the most visually complex Night Lights design, you may think it is the hardest to convert for envelopes. This design is, in fact, the easiest. The figure is already positioned near the left edge of the form. All you need do is shrink the graphic image and type sizes. Follow these steps:

1. Choose the envelope paper size and type. Press Shift-F8, P, S.

   Move the cursor to `Envelope - Wide` and press S.

   Press F7 to return to the document screen.

2. Set the left margin as described at the beginning of this chapter.

3. Switch to Document 2 (Shift-F3), retrieve the letterhead design shown in figure 5.4, and turn on Reveal Codes (Alt-F3).

4. To shrink the graphic image, press Alt-F9, F, E. Type *1* and press Enter, S, B, Enter.

   Type *3/4*" and press Enter.

   Press F7 to return to the document screen.

5. Remain in Reveal Codes, find the font code that sets "Night Lights" to 35-point Times Roman. Delete that font code and set the font to 24-point Times Roman.

6. Find the font code that sets "JANITORIAL SERVICE" to 14-point Times Roman. Delete that font code and set the font to 10-point Times Roman.

7. Find the font code that sets the address to 10-point Times Roman. Delete that font code and set the font to 8-point Times Roman.

8. Find the `[AdvToLn:9"]` code preceding the address and delete it.

Instructions are not given for converting figure 5.5, because that letterhead is exactly the same as the conversion of figure 5.4, except for the reversal of the graphic image.

7

Producing Résumés

A resume may be the most consequential document you will ever create. A resume must present you at your best—your abilities, attitudes, experiences, and goals.

Employment directors expect resumes to be concise. The rule of thumb is that a resume should be no longer than one page. If the employment director needs more information, he will request it.

The resume samples described in this chapter use typography, graphic lines, and graphic boxes to make information as easily accessible as possible to the reader.

Résumé No. 1: A Chemical Engineer

This design is quite appropriate for virtually any job applicant and meets the minimum requirement for resumes—clear, sequential presentation of information (see fig. 7.1). This design also uses typography and graphic lines in an attractive, eye-pleasing way.

GEORGE C. HORENSTEIN
Chemical Engineer

240-C Aberdeen Towers
Citrus Meadow, FL 33321
(305) 444-6688

PERSONAL	Hi omnes lingua, institutis, legibus inter se differunt. Gallos ab Aquitanis Garumna flumen, a Belgis Matrona et Sequana dividit. Horum omnium fortissimi sunt Belgae, propterea quod a cultu atque humanitate provinciae longissime absunt, minimeque ad eos mercatores saepe commeant atque ea quae ad effeminandos animos pertinent important.
EDUCATION	Que de causa Helvetii quoque reliquos Gallos virtute praecedunt, quod fere cotidianis proeliis cum Germanis contendunt, cum aut suis finibus eos prohibent, aut ipsi in eorum finibus bellum gerunt.
PRESENT POSITION	Que de causa Helvetii quoque reliquos Gallos virtute praecedunt, quod fere cotidianis proeliis cum Germanis contendunt, cum aut suis finibus eos prohibent, aut ipsi in eorum finibus bellum gerunt.
EMPLOYMENT HISTORY	Que de causa Helvetii quoque reliquos Gallos virtute praecedunt, quod fere cotidianis proeliis cum Germanis contendunt, cum aut suis finibus eos prohibent, aut ipsi in eorum finibus bellum gerunt.
HONORS	Que de causa Helvetii quoque reliquos Gallos virtute praecedunt, quod fere cotidianis proeliis cum Germanis contendunt, cum aut suis finibus eos prohibent, aut ipsi in eorum finibus bellum gerunt.
PROFESSIONAL SOCIETIES	Que de causa Helvetii quoque reliquos Gallos virtute praecedunt, quod fere cotidianis proeliis cum Germanis contendunt, cum aut suis finibus eos prohibent. De causa Helvetii quoque reliquos Gallos virtute praecedunt, quod fere cotidianis proeliis cum Germanis contendunt, cum aut suis finibus eos prohibent, aut ipsi in eorum finibus bellum gerunt.
REFERENCES	Que de causa Helvetii quoque reliquos Gallos virtute praecedunt, quod fere cotidianis proeliis cum Germanis contendunt, cum aut suis finibus eos prohibent, aut ipsi in eorum finibus bellum gerunt. De causa Helvetii quoque reliquos Gallos virtute praecedunt, quod fere cotidianis proeliis cum Germanis contendunt, cum aut suis finibus eos prohibent, aut ipsi in eorum finibus bellum gerunt.

FIG. 7.1 A basic resume.

Setting Up the Page

You begin this resume design by setting line and page margins to WordPerfect's default of 1" at the top, bottom, and sides of the page. Complete the following steps:

1. To set line margins, press Shift-F8, L, M; type *1*"; press Enter; type *1*"; and press Enter, Enter.

   These keypresses return you to the Format menu.

2. To set the page margins, press P, M; type *1*"; press Enter; type *1*"; and press Enter, F7.

Choosing a Base Font

Next, you need to choose a base font. The sample uses Times Roman 10-point for body text and 12-point for the applicant's name and section titles, so you should choose 12-point Times Roman:

1. Press Ctrl-F8, F and move the cursor to Times Roman on the Base Font list.
2. Press S.
3. At the `Point Size` prompt, type *12* and press F7 to return to the document screen.

Setting Up Parallel Columns

Notice in figure 7.1 that the applicant name and address align flush-right at the same column as the subheads. This resume design is a perfect application for WordPerfect's parallel columns feature. Complete the following steps to set up parallel columns:

1. Press Alt-F7, C, D to display the Text Column Definition menu.
2. Press T, B to select Parallel with Block Protect.

TIP

For resumes, you generally should choose Parallel with Block Protect rather than Parallel. When you reach the end of a page and part of a parallel column entry spills over onto the next page, Parallel with Block Protect moves the entire current group of parallel columns onto the next page. Choosing Parallel, however, enables several lines of text to continue on the next page without moving the entire group along with those stray lines. Because resumes should be just one page long, you probably will not use this feature, but when an employment director asks you for an expanded resume, you already will have the proper setting entered in your resume file.

3. Accept the Number of Columns default setting of 2. Press D to select Distance Between Columns and type *.25*" to put 1/4" of space between the parallel columns. Press Enter to return to the `Selection` prompt.

4. Press M to set column margins. For the Column 1 left and right margins, enter *1*" and *2.75*". For the Column 2 left and right margins, enter *3*" and *7.5*". Press Enter to return to the `Selection` prompt.

   WordPerfect measures margins from the left edge of the page.

5. Press Enter, O to turn columns on. WordPerfect returns you to the document screen.

Entering the Text

Now you can begin typing the text of the resume. In this first basic design, the text is divided into three main areas: the applicant's name, title, and address; the subheadings that divide areas within the body of the resume; and the body text.

TIP

You need to switch between the 10-point and 12-point fonts using the Base Font feature rather than the Size option on the Font menu. The Size option enables you to switch only between a group of pre-determined percentages of the base font size. The default percentage sizes are as follows:

Fine	60%
Small	80%
Large	120%
Very Large	150%
Extra Large	200%
Super/Subscript	60%

You can customize the size percentages used in the Font Size menu by pressing Shift-F1 to display the setup menu and then selecting Initial Settings, Print Options, and Size Attribute Ratios and changing the settings. Setting a percentage of 120% is impractical, however, just so that you can select 12-point type with the Font Size menu while using a 10-point base font. Because you will seldom use the 120% setting, it is much quicker just to reset the base font to 12-point Times Roman.

Exception: If you frequently create documents that require you to switch between 10- and 12-point type, for example, you should definitely change the default Size Attribute Ratios, because using the Font Size menu saves you time.

Applicant's Name, Title, and Address

The applicant's name and address are set flush-right within the left column. The name is set in small caps. Complete the following steps:

1. Press Alt-F6 to specify flush-right text.
2. Press Ctrl-F8, F and move the cursor to Times Roman in the Base Font list. Press Enter, type *12* at the prompt, and press F7.

If your printer cannot print small caps, the resume still looks fine if you type the name in upper- and lowercase.

3. Type the applicant's name (*George C. Horenstein*) and then press the right-arrow key to move the cursor past the `[sm cap]` code so that you can type the applicant's title in upper- and lowercase letters.

4. Press Enter to move the cursor to the next line.

   Notice that the applicant's title (Chemical Engineer) is separated from the name with a visually appropriate amount of space between the lines. To achieve this effect, press Enter to move the cursor to the next line before you switch to 10-point Times Roman and type *Chemical Engineer*. The line spacing that WordPerfect inserts when you press Enter with a 12-point font selected is greater than the line spacing entered for a 10-point font. When you switch to 10-point Times Roman and begin typing the title, WordPerfect will have inserted extra space between the lines.

5. Press Ctrl-F8, F to display the Base Font list and move the cursor to Times Roman. Press Enter, type *10* at the `Point size` prompt, and press F7 to return to the document.

6. Press Alt-F6 to select flush-right text and type the applicant's title (*Chemical Engineer* in the sample).

7. Press Enter twice to enter extra space before the first line of the address.

8. Type the address, pressing Enter between lines and Alt-F6 to select flush-right text at the start of each line.

TIP

Remember that you can check your progress with the View Document screen: press Shift-F7, V to display a copy of your text as it appears when printed.

Subheadings and Body Text

Next, you need to begin entering the subheadings that divide the various areas on the applicant's resume. Press Enter four times to insert space between the address and the first section heading (*Personal* in the sample). Then complete the following steps:

1. Press Ctrl-Enter twice to move the cursor into the second column and then back to the first column. (No second column follows the applicant's name, title, and address, so you need to move the cursor through an empty second column after the telephone number.)
2. Press Alt-F6 to specify flush-right text.
3. Press Ctrl-F8, F; choose Times Roman from the Base Font list; press Enter; type *12* at the `Point size` prompt; and press Enter to return to the document.
4. Press Ctrl-F8, A, C to type in small caps and then type the first subheading (*Personal* in the sample). Press the right-arrow key to turn off small caps.
5. Press Ctrl-Enter to move the cursor to the second column. Press Ctrl-F8, F; choose Times Roman from the Base Font list; press Enter; type *10* at the `Point size` prompt; and press Enter to return to the document. Type the text for the first subheading.

If you review your work at this point, by printing or viewing it in the View Document screen, you should notice that the subhead and text are aligned at the tops of the letters. This alignment places the baselines of the 12-point heading and 10-point text out of alignment. Although this point may seem minor and terribly nit-picky, it is precisely the kind of thing that drives graphic designers nuts. Very small misalignments can give your documents an unprofessional look. Looking good often involves tiny adjustments.

To fix the misalignment between subheadings and text, complete the following steps:

1. Move the cursor to the first letter of the 10-point text in the right column.
2. Press Shift-F8, O, A, D to select the Advance Down function. At the `Adv. down` prompt, type *2p* to move the 10-point text down 2 points so that it aligns correctly with the baseline of the adjoining 12-point subheading.

Press Enter, F7 to return to the document screen. If you check your work in the View Document screen, you can see that the subheading and text now align on the baseline.

> **TIP**
>
> You can format the text for each heading using straight text and word wrap, as shown in figure 7.1, or you can use tabs to format lists of colleges attended and degrees received, awards and honors, society memberships, and so on.

When you have finished typing in the second parallel column, press Ctrl-Enter to return to the left margin and begin typing the second column, using the font, flush right, and small caps settings you used for the first item.

Dividing Lines

In the sample resume, subheadings are separated with horizontal lines. Creating these lines is easy to do:

1. With the cursor at the end of the first subdivision's text, press Enter twice to insert extra space before the dividing line.
2. Press Alt-F9, L, H to display the Graphics: Horizontal Line menu. Accept all the entries as given by pressing F7 to return to the document.
3. Press Ctrl-Enter to return to the left column.
4. Type the remainder of the resume by repeating the steps given earlier for setting the font, flush right, and small caps for the resume items, as well as for moving between parallel columns.

Résumé 2: A Graphic Designer

The resume shown in figure 7.2 clearly represents a creative person. This design would not be suitable for someone who is applying for a job as a bank vice-president.

> **TIP**
>
> When creating documents that contain repeated design elements, such as graphic lines and frequent font changes, you can save time by assigning these elements to macros or styles. For details, see the WordPerfect Reference Manual.
>
> When you must repeat a few formatting elements within a short document, you don't need to use macros or styles. Turn on Reveal Codes (Alt-F3) and copy a group of repeating elements (press Alt-F4; highlight a block; and press Ctrl-F4, B, C). Then move the cursor to the location of the next repetition and press Enter to insert the copy. To insert further copies, move the cursor to the next location and press Ctrl-F4, R, B to retrieve the block again. You then can replace the repeated text with new text for each section.
>
> When you just need to repeat a few lines or Base Font codes, the quickest way often is to block the font or line code in Reveal Codes and then to save the font or line code to a file and retrieve the code into the document as needed:
>
> - Press Alt-F3 (Reveal Codes) and position the cursor on the code.
> - Press Alt-F4 (Block) and press the right-arrow key to move the cursor ahead of the code.
> - Press F10 (Save), type a name for the temporary file, and press Enter.
> - To retrieve the code, press Shift-F10, type the code's file name, and press Enter.

The design features a logo composed of white (*reversed*) text in a black box. You can create reversed type with WordPerfect 5.1 only if you are using a PostScript or Hewlett-Packard LaserJet III or compatible printer. Some other printers, such as the Canon LBP8-III, can use reverse, shaded text in a black box (for example, a 6 percent shade) but cannot create white (0 percent shade) text in a reverse.

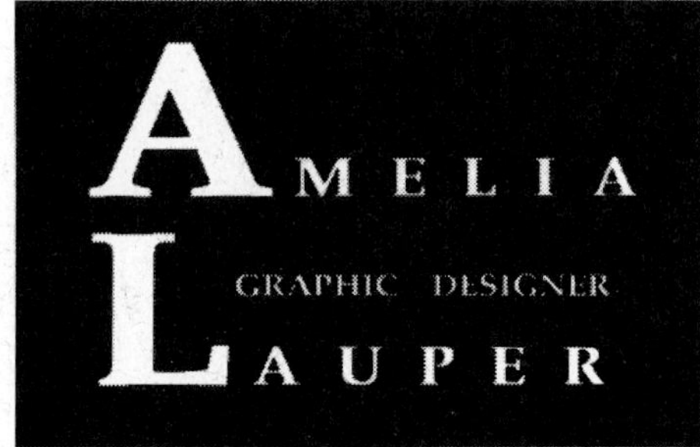

25 Grace Lane Parkway #302
Forest Hills, KS 55678
(456) 987-6543

E D U C A T I O N

Of air-born honey, gift of heaven, I now take up the tale. Upon this theme no less look thou, Maecenas, with indulgent eye.

E M P L O Y M E N T H I S T O R Y

A marvellous display of puny powers, high-hearted chiefs, a nation's history, its traits, its bent, its battles and its clans, all, each, shall pass before you, while I sing. Slight though the poet's theme, not slight the praise, so frown not heaven, and Phoebus hear his call.

M A J O R C L I E N T S

First find your bees a settled sure abode, where neither winds can enter (winds blow back the foragers with food returning home) nor sheep and butting kids tread down the flowers, nor heifer wandering wide upon the plain dash off the dew, and bruise the springing blades.

R E F E R E N C E S

Let the gay lizard too keep far aloof his scale-clad body from their honied stalls, and the bee-eater, and what birds beside, and Procne smirched with blood upon the breast from her own murderous hands.

A W A R D S

For these roam wide wasting all substance, or the bees themselves strike flying, and in their beaks bear home, to glut those savage nestlings with the dainty prey. But let clear springs and moss-green pools be near.

FIG. 7.2 A more creative resume.

Creating the Logo

The main design challenge of this resume is to create the logo, which makes "arty" use of type in varied sizes and with nonstandard letter and line spacing.

Note: This procedure is complex. Designing logos usually is. If you follow the steps, however, you can learn a great deal about using advanced WordPerfect features such as Letter Spacing, Graphics, Fonts, and Advance.

This design uses a Palatino typeface available with PostScript printers. If your printer does not have Palatino, it may have an equivalent font. For example, the version of Palatino supplied with Canon LBP series printers is called Zapf Calligraphic. If you do not have any version of Palatino, you can choose another font, such as Times Roman.

In keeping with the applicant's creative personality, the resume uses margins that differ from WordPerfect's defaults. To set the margins, press Shift-F8, L, M; type *1 3/8*"; press Enter; type *1 3/8*"; press Enter, Enter, P, M; type *.5*"; press Enter; type *.5*"; and press Enter, F7.

Logo Text

Now, you can type the text for the logo. Notice that the first and last names have expanded letter spacing. Because two drastically different font sizes are used in the name, you need to adjust letter spacing individually for the larger and smaller fonts.

1. Use the Letter Spacing feature to add extra space after the first letter of the first name. Press Shift-F8, O, P, W.
2. At the `Word Spacing` prompt, press O to choose Optimal.
3. At the `Letter Spacing` prompt, press P to select `Percent of Optimal`.
4. At the `Percent of Optimal` prompt, type *115* to tell WordPerfect to add 15% more letter spacing between the first and second letters of the first name. Press Enter, F7.
5. To switch to a 72-point Palatino Bold font, press Ctrl-F8, F; select Palatino Bold from the Base Font list; and press Enter.

6. At the `Point size` prompt, type *72* and press Enter to return to the document. Type the first letter of the first name (*A* in the sample).

   Don't specify white type until you have created the black box, or you cannot preview your work with View Document.

TIP

If you don't have Palatino Bold, try another typeface that matches your visual *personality*. If you are reversing the type over a black box, don't choose a font with fine serifs, such as Times Roman, because the serifs may *plug* with ink during the printing process. (Serifs in large typefaces are more likely to be plugged by commercial offset presses than with laser printers.)

7. Use the Letter Spacing feature once more to add space between the remaining letters of the first name. Press Shift-F8, O, P, W.
8. At the `Word Spacing` prompt, press O to choose Optimal.
9. At the `Letter Spacing` prompt, press P to choose Percent of Optimal, and at the `Percent of Optimal` prompt, type *200* to tell WordPerfect to print letters with 100% more letter spacing than normal. Press Enter, F7.
10. Choose a smaller font for the remaining letters of the first name. Press Ctrl-F8, F; move the cursor to Palatino Bold in the Base Font list; and press Enter.
11. At the `Point size` prompt, type *18* and press Enter to return to the document. Then type the remaining letters of the first name, in all caps. Press Enter.

Now, you need to copy the first line, including codes, to the second line:

1. Turn on Reveal Codes (Alt-F3). With the cursor in the first line, press Home, Home, and the left-arrow key to move the cursor to the left end of the line, ahead of all hidden codes. Press the right-arrow key twice to place the cursor to the right of the margin settings.

2. Press Alt-F4, Home, Home, and the right-arrow key to block the entire line, including hidden codes at the right end of the line.
3. Press Ctrl-F4, B, C to copy the block.
4. Press the down-arrow key to move the cursor to the second line and press Enter to insert the copy at the cursor.
5. Finally, use Del to erase the first name and type the last name in its place. (WordPerfect warns you if you accidentally try to delete any hidden codes.)

If you check your work in the View Document screen (Shift-F7, V), you should see that the lines are too far apart. In the sample, the L in Lauper is tucked very close under the A in Amelia. To move the last name up, complete the following steps:

1. With the cursor in the second line, press Home, Home, Home, and the left-arrow key to move the cursor to the start of the line, ahead of all codes.
2. Press Shift-F8, O, A, U, and at the `Adv. up` prompt, type *3/16"*. (The exact number may vary, depending on the typeface you have chosen.)
3. Press Enter, F7 to return to the document screen.

WordPerfect very considerately translates fractions into decimals for you. If you check View Document again, you should see that the second name has been moved up, closer to the first name.

Applicant's Title

You still need to create and position the applicant's title (*GRAPHIC DESIGNER* in the sample):

1. With the cursor in the second line of text, press Home, Home, and the right-arrow key to move to the right end of the line, past any hidden codes. Then press Enter to create a line.
2. Turn off added letter spacing. Press Shift-F8, O, P, W. At the `Word Spacing` prompt, press O to choose Optimal.
3. At the `Letter Spacing` prompt, press P to choose Percent of Optimal, and at the `Percent of Optimal` prompt, press O to choose Optimal.

4. Press F7 to return to the document.
5. To switch to a 10-point Palatino Bold font and type the title, press Ctrl-F8, F; move the cursor to Palatino Bold in the Base Font list; and press Enter.
6. At the `Point size` prompt, type *10*. Press Enter to return to the document and type the title, in caps, entering two extra spaces between the words.

You now need to position the title. First print out a copy and measure the horizontal and vertical distances between the current position of the title and the estimated position after you have used the Advance feature to reposition it between the first and last names.

1. With the cursor in the title line (*GRAPHIC DESIGNER* in the sample), press Home, Home, Home, and the left-arrow key to move the cursor to the beginning of the line, ahead of any hidden codes.
2. Move the cursor to the end of the applicant's title by pressing Home, Home, and the right-arrow key.
3. Press Shift-F8, O, A, U; type *13/16*"; press Enter, A, R; type *5/8*"; and press Enter, F7.

   If you check your work with View Document (Shift-F7, V), you should see that WordPerfect has moved the title between the first and last names.

   Because you entered advance codes to position the applicant's title, you now need to enter advance codes to return the cursor to the point where you entered the advance codes.
4. Press Shift-F8, O, A, D; type *13/16*"; press Enter, A, L; type *5/8*"; and press Enter, F7.

Finally, as the last step in creating the logo's text, save your work to a file. (Be sure to save a backup copy—you don't want to lose the end-product of so much labor!)

The Reversed Box

Next, you need to create the reversed box. First, set the Text Box options by completing the following steps:

1. First, clear the screen so that you can create a Text Box and import the logo text into it. Press F7, N, N.
2. Press Alt-F9, B, O. In the Options: Text Box screen, make the following changes to the default settings:

Border Style	Set all to None
Outside Border Space	Set all to 0"
Inside Border Space	Accept the default of 0.167"
Gray Shading	100% (black)

   Setting the outside border space to 0 enables the black box fill to extend all the way out to the vertical and horizontal positions that you set in step 1 of the following procedure.
3. Press F7 to return to the document.

To actually create the box, do the following:

1. Press Alt-F9, B, C. In the Definition: Text Box screen, make the following changes to the default settings:

Contents	Text
Anchor Type	Page, Number of pages to skip: 0
Vertical Position	Top
Horizontal Position	Set Position, 1 3/8"
Size	2 7/8" wide × 2" high
Wrap Text Around Box	Yes

2. Press E. In the box editing screen, press Shift-F10, type the name of the file where you saved the logo's text, and press Enter.
3. To change the color of the logo's text to white, press Home, Home, and the up-arrow key. Then press Ctrl-F8, C, W, Enter.
4. Press F7 twice to return to the editing screen.
5. Save the file and check your work with View Document (Shift-F7, V).

Adding the Address and Body Copy

The quickest way to center the address under the logo is by setting temporary margins aligned with the left and right edges of the logo's box, centering the text, and then returning the margins to their previous values.

With the cursor at the end of the file, press Enter to insert an extra line after the logo. Then complete the following steps:

1. Press Shift-F8, L, M; type *1 3/8*"; press Enter; type *4 1/4*"; and press Enter, F7.

   Note: WordPerfect measures margins from the left and right edges of the page.

2. For the address, you need to use a light sans serif font, such as 9-point Helvetica. Press Ctrl-F8, F; move the cursor to Helvetica in the Base Font list; press Enter; type *9* at the `Font size` prompt; and press Enter.
3. Type the address and phone number, pressing Shift-F6 (Center) at the beginning of each line.
4. After typing the address and phone number, press Enter to create a line and reset the margins: press Shift-F8, L, M; type *1 3/8*"; press Enter; type *1 3/8*"; and press Enter, Enter.
5. Press Enter four times to insert space between the logo and body copy.
6. Change the font to the same typeface and size that you used for the applicant's title ("GRAPHIC DESIGNER" in 10-point Palatino Bold in the sample).
7. To set the letter spacing to 200% of normal, press Shift-F8, O, P, W, O, P; type *200*; and press F7, F7.
8. Press F8 (Underline) and type the first subheading (*EDUCATION* in the sample) in all caps. Press F8 to stop underlining.

To reset letter spacing to Optimal, do the following:

1. Press Shift-F8, O, P, W, O, O, F7.

2. Press Enter twice to add extra space after the subheading.

Switch to the same font you used for the address (Helvetica in the sample), but choose a larger 11-point size:

1. Press Ctrl-F8, F; move the cursor to Helvetica in the Base Font list; press Enter; type *11* at the `Point size` prompt; and press Enter.
2. Press F4 (Indent) three times to indent the body text for the first subheading.
3. Type the body text. Press Enter twice to insert extra space between the body text and the next subheading.

Repeat the preceding steps to create each of the remaining sections. As suggested earlier, you can shorten the process by blocking a subheading, complete with font codes, and saving a copy of the block to a file. To do this, move the cursor to the first code in the subheading, press Alt-F4, move the cursor to the last code, press F10, type a file name, and press Enter. To format each new subheading, retrieve the file (Shift-F10, *filename*, Enter) and replace the old subheading's text with the text for the next subheading.

Creating Variations of the Logo

Because this design uses a reverse, and you can print reverses with WordPerfect only if you own a PostScript, Hewlett-Packard LaserJet III, or compatible printer, two variations of the logo are included here. Both of these variations use normal, black-on-white, unreversed type.

Figure 7.3 shows how the logo prints if you omit the white color codes and specify 0% black as the gray shading for the box.

The logo as shown in figure 7.3 looks a bit stark. Figure 7.4 shows the logo with the addition of two horizontal graphic lines.

To create the first line, move the cursor below the box code and press Enter to create a line.

FIG. 7.3 The same logo without the white color codes and with 0% black specified as the gray shading.

FIG. 7.4 The same logo with two graphic lines added.

TIP

You cannot create graphics lines in the Graphics Box editing screen, because WordPerfect does not enable you to create a graphic box or line within another box or line. Instead, you must create the lines outside the box and specify vertical and horizontal line positions in the Graphics: Horizontal Line menu that will print the lines in the box. (If you enter the graphics line codes in the Graphics Box editing screen, WordPerfect doesn't print the lines.)

To add the first line, complete the following steps:

1. With the cursor positioned after the graphics box, press Alt-F9, L, H to display the Graphics: Horizontal Line menu.
2. In the Graphics: Horizontal Line menu, make the following settings:

Horizontal Position:	Set, 1.65"
Vertical Position:	Set, 1.42"
Length:	2.34"
Width:	0.031"
Gray Shading:	100%

   (These figures were arrived at by experimentation.) Depending on the font you used and where you positioned the type in the box, you may need to preview your work repeatedly with View Document and adjust the numbers to size and position the lines.

TIP

If you need to make changes to the line, don't delete the existing hidden line code and re-enter all the line specifications from scratch. Instead, turn on Reveal Codes (Alt-F3) and move the cursor on the line code. Then press Alt-F9, L, O to edit the code. The existing settings for the line appear in the Graphics: Horizontal Line screen.

3. Press F7 to return to the document.
4. Press the right-arrow key to move the cursor after the graphic line's hidden code.

You now need to position a second line under the applicant's last name:

1. With the cursor positioned after the first line, press Alt-F9, L, H to display the Graphics: Horizontal Line menu.
2. In the Graphics: Horizontal Line menu, make the following settings:

Horizontal Position:	Set, 1.65"
Vertical Position:	Set, 2.27"
Length:	2.21"
Width:	1/32"
Gray Shading:	100%

Again, you may need to adjust these numbers, depending on the fonts you have used and where you positioned the type.

3. Press F7 to return to the document.

> **TIP**
>
> A final suggestion: If you are really ambitious, and you have a PostScript or LaserJet III printer, you can specify white color for the graphic lines and print them over the original, reversed logo text.

8

Producing Press Releases

Probably no other type of document is as widely distributed and as seldom read as the press release. The average lifespan of a press release amounts to a mere three seconds—the time required to open the envelope and toss the release into the circular file.

The poor design of most press releases is partly to blame for this shockingly short lifespan. Certainly, a press release isn't a glamorous document. The first design requirement of a press release is that it be functional—double-spaced, designed in a readable typeface, and uncluttered with distracting design elements.

Although tradition may say that press releases should be totally unadorned, no rule exists that says you cannot make press releases more attractive and readable by aptly using design principles for optimum readability. You can choose a readable typeface and shorten lines, making the lines more readable; you can use an attractive logo to quickly communicate your ideas; and you can include subheadings that arouse interest and guide the reader's eye through the press release.

Well-designed press releases, even those releases hastily relegated to the editor's overflowing wastepaper basket, can serve a useful purpose. An attractive logo announcing the company's name and business may be remembered because a well-designed logo gives an impression of importance that, however fleeting, registers in the reader's mind. A subconscious thought, "This company seems solid; we better do something on them someday," may be born.

You don't need to use an elaborate, complicated design scheme to create attractive, eye-catching press releases. The two press releases in this chapter use only type, graphic lines, and columns as visual elements, but they present a strong, memorable image.

Press Release No. 1: A Freight Expediter

The company that produced the first press release is in the business of moving industrial freight. The logo reflects a practical, no-nonsense, hard-working image. The very clear and readable positioning of the unusual logotype and the `For Immediate Release` text at the top of the release creates an impressive design likely to catch the attention of a busy editor.

To create the press release shown in figure 8.1, you first must set up the narrow column for the logo. Rather than use newspaper-style or parallel columns, you need to set left and right margins temporarily for a narrow column.

1. To set the left margin at 1 1/2" and the right margin at 4 1/4", press Shift-F8, L, M; type *1 1/2*"; press Enter; type *4 1/4*"; and press Enter, F7.

   (To make the body text more readable, the left margin is a bit wider than WordPerfect's default.)

2. Change the font to 18-point Times Roman Italic, press Shift-F6 (Center), and type *For Immediate Release*. Press Enter three times to insert space before the logo.

Adding the Logo

To add the logo, you need to create the first heavy horizontal line by doing the following:

1. Press Alt-F9, L, H.
2. In the Graphics: Horizontal Line menu, accept the default settings but change the width of the line to 1/8".
3. Press F7 to return to the document; then press Enter twice to move down to the next line.

For Immediate Release

Advanced Delivery Concepts

Worldwide Freight Expediters
12349 Auckland Harbor Blvd.
Seattle, WA 99018-3243
(206) 899-9876
Contact: Jan Whyte

ADC Adds "Jet Exec" Service

And now, O men who have condemned me, I would fain prophesy to you; for I am about to die, and that is the hour in which men are gifted with prophetic power. And I prophesy to you who are my murderers, that immediately after my death punishment far heavier than you have inflicted on me will surely await you. Me you have killed because you wanted to escape the accuser, and not to give an account of your lives. But that will not be as you suppose; far otherwise. For I say there will be more accusers of you than there are now; accusers whom hitherto I have restrained; and as they are younger they will be more severe with you, and you will be more offended at them. For if you think that by killing men you can avoid the accuser censuring your

FIG. 8.1 A press release for a worldwide freight carrier.

Next, you need to create the logotype (ADC Advanced Delivery Concepts) by doing the following:

1. To switch the font to 56-point Helvetica, press Ctrl-F8, F; then move the cursor to Helvetica in the Base Font list, press Enter, type *56*, and press F7.

2. Change the font's appearance to Outline by pressing Ctrl-F8, A, O.

3. Set letter spacing to 65 percent by pressing Shift-F8, O, P, W, Enter, P; type *65*; press Enter, F7; and then type *ADC*.

4. Check your work in View Document (Shift-F7, V).

The logotype is too far below the heavy line. Use Advance to position the logotype 1/8" closer:

1. Move the cursor in front of the font code preceding ADC and press Shift-F8, O, A, U; type *1/8"*; and press Enter, F7

2. Move the cursor to the right of ADC and press the right-arrow key to move beyond the ending `[outln]` font code.

3. Reset letter spacing to Optimal by pressing Shift-F8, O, P, W, O, O, F7.

4. To change the font to 15-point Helvetica Bold, press Ctrl-F8, F; then move the cursor to Helvetica Bold in the Base Font list, press Enter, type *15*, and press F7.

To position the type within the logo, you use parallel columns:

1. Move the cursor in front of the font code preceding ADC and press Alt-F7, C, D. In the Text Column Definition menu, change the settings to the following:

Type	Newspaper
Number of Columns	2
Distance Between Columns	1/8"
Margins	1.6", 3", 3.2", 4.25"

   Generally, you arrive at the margin figures by trial and error.

2. Press F7; then press O to turn columns on.

3. Move the cursor past the `[Wrd/Ltr Spacing:Optimal, Optimal]` code and press Ctrl-Enter (Hard Page).

4. Change the font to 15-point Helvetica Bold. Press Ctrl-F8, move the cursor to Helvetica Bold, press Enter, type *15*, and press F7.

5. Change the line spacing. Press Shift-F8, O, P, Enter; type *–2p*; press Enter, F7. Type *Advanced Delivery Concepts*, pressing Enter after each word.

6. Press Alt-F7, C, F to turn columns off. The cursor jumps back to the left margin.

7. To create the second heavy line, in the Reveal Codes screen, highlight the code for the first heavy line, press Del to delete the code, and then press F1, 1 to restore it. Press Home, Home, and the down-arrow key to move to the end of the file. Then press F1, 1 to restore another copy of the line code.

   Check your work in the View Document screen (Shift-F7, V).

To create the rest of the title and address, do the following:

1. With the cursor placed after the second heavy line code, press Enter twice to insert a blank line; then switch to a smaller font. Press Ctrl-F8, F; move the cursor to Helvetica Bold in the Base Font list; press Enter; type *12*, and press F7.

2. Press Shift-F6 (Center), type *Worldwide Freight Expediters*, and press Enter.

   Check your work in View Document (Shift-F7, V). The text you entered (Worldwide Freight Expediters) is too far from the heavy horizontal line. Move the text up a line; now the text is too close to the heavy horizontal line. Move the text back down a line and insert an Advance code to position the text precisely.

3. With the cursor in the same line as Worldwide Freight Expediters, press Home, Home, Home, and the left-arrow key to move the cursor to the left end of the line, in front of any hidden codes. Move the line up 1/8" by pressing Shift-F8, O, A, U; typing *1/8"*; and pressing Enter, F7.

4. To type the rest of the address, move the cursor to the end of Worldwide Freight Expediters and press Enter.

5. Change to Times Roman 11-point Italic. Press Ctrl-F8, F; move the cursor to Times Roman Italic; press Enter; type *11*; and press F7.

6. Press Shift-F6 (Center), type the first line of the address, press Enter, and type the remainder of the address, continuing to use Center.

Designing the Body

After you place the logo, you need to design the body of the newsletter as follows:

1. Press Enter four times; then set the margins for the body text. Press Shift-F8, L, M; type *1.5*"; press Enter; type *1.5*"; and press Enter, F7.
2. Change the font to 12-point Helvetica Bold. Press Ctrl-F8, F; move the cursor to Helvetica Bold; press Enter; type *12*; and press F7. Type *ADC Adds "Jet Exec" Service*.
3. Press Enter three times to insert two blank lines; then change line spacing to 2. Press Shift-F8, L, S, 2, Enter, F7.
4. Change the font to 12-point Courier. Press Ctrl-F8, F; move the cursor to Courier; press Enter; type *12*; and press F7.
5. Type the body of the press release.

Press Release No. 2: A Legal Graphics Service

This press release clearly indicates the company's products and services. The display type consists almost exclusively of a conservative and businesslike, but moderately artistic, italic face—which suits the company's business of providing art for the legal profession. By merely changing the type, you can adapt this design for other businesses. Times Roman regular display type, for example, would be suitable for a financial consulting firm.

Although the effect is sophisticated, this design presents fewer design challenges than the preceding press release.

FOR IMMEDIATE RELEASE

Rapid Art
Legal Graphics

1329 River Bend Center

Chicago, IL 60113

(699) 043-4321

Contact: Geri Akke (699) 023-4321

Attorneys rely on art firm for courtroom advantage.

Hi omnes lingua, institutis, legibus inter se differunt. Gallos ab Aquitanis Garumna flumen, a Belgis Matrona et Sequana dividit. Horum omnium fortissimi sunt Belgae, propterea quod a cultu atque humanitate provinciae longissime absunt, minimeque ad eos mercatores saepe commeant atque ea quae ad effeminandos animos pertinent important, proximique sunt Germanis, qui trans Rhenum incolunt, quibuscum continenter bellum gerunt.

Que de causa Helvetii quoque reliquos Gallos virtute praecedunt, quod fere cotidianis proeliis cum Germanis contendunt, cum aut suis finibus eos prohibent, aut ipsi in eorum finibus bellum gerunt. Eorum una pars, quam Gallos obtinere dictum est, initium

Charts

Diagrams

Graphs

Illustration

Enlargements

Scale Models

Photography

Video

FIG. 8.2 A press release for a legal graphics service.

Designing the Page

To create this press release, you first must set the margins and create the vertical line at the left side of the page by doing the following:

1. Set the left margin at 1 3/4". Press Shift-F8, L, M; type *1 3/4"*; and press Enter, Enter, F7.

   This step sets the margin for the text, not the vertical line. You set the horizontal position of the vertical line by using the Graphics: Vertical Line menu.

2. Set the top and bottom margins at 1/2" and 3/4" respectively. Press Shift-F8, P, M; type *1/2"*; press Enter; type *3/4"*; and press Enter, F7.

3. To create the vertical graphic line, press Alt-F9, L, V. In the Graphics: Vertical Line menu, make the following settings:

Horizontal Position	Set Position, 1 7/16"
Vertical Position	Full Page
Width of Line	1/24"

4. Press F7.

Adding Headings and Subheadings

Now you can add and format the heading text by doing the following:

1. To place the "FOR IMMEDIATE RELEASE" text, you first must set a temporary right margin. Press Shift-F8, L, M, Enter; type *.5"*; and press Enter, F7.

2. Change the font to 12-point Helvetica. Press Ctrl-F8, F; move the cursor to Helvetica in the Base Font list; press Enter; type *12*; and press F7.

3. Press Alt-F6 (Flush Right) and type *FOR IMMEDIATE RELEASE*, pressing the space bar three times between the words.

   Before you press Enter to start a new line, change the font to 72-point Times Roman Bold Italic and change the right margin to 1 1/8". The reason for changing the font before pressing Enter is so that WordPerfect can insert the appropriate line spacing for the large font that you use on the next line.

4. To change the font, press Ctrl-F8, F; move the cursor to Times Roman Bold Italic in the Base Font list; press Enter; type *72*; and press F7.
5. To change the margin, press Shift-F8, L, M, Enter; type *1 1/8"*; and press Enter, F7.

   When you enter a margin setting at the end of a line, WordPerfect inserts a hard return code and places the margin code at the beginning of the next line.
6. Press Alt-F6 (Flush Right) and type *Rapid Art*.
7. After you type *Rapid Art* but before you press Enter, change the font to 30-point Times Roman Italic. Press Ctrl-F8, F; move the cursor to Times Roman Italic in the Base Font list; press Enter; type *30*; and press F7.

   You must change the font before moving to the next line so that when you press Enter WordPerfect inserts line spacing appropriate for the font you selected.
8. Press Enter, Alt-F6 (Flush Right) and type *Legal Graphics*.
9. Check your work in View Document (Shift-F7, V). The Legal Graphics subtitle still isn't close enough to "Rapid Art." Position the subtitle 1/8" higher with Advance. Move the cursor in front of `Legal Graphics`. Press Shift-F8, O, A, U; type *1/8"*; and press Enter, F7.
10. Press Enter to move to the next line.

Using Parallel Columns

You format the remainder of the press release with parallel columns—a wide column for the body text of the press release and a narrow column for the company's address and the list of services at the right side of the page.

1. To create columns, press Alt-F7, C, D. In the Text Column Definition screen, make the following settings:

Type	Parallel
Number of Columns	2
Distance Between Columns	3/8"
Margins	1 3/4", 5 3/4", 6", 7 3/4"

You select Parallel instead of Parallel With Block Protect so that the block protect feature moves an entire parallel section of copy to the next page if any single column's text extends onto the next page. You don't need that feature here because body text is typed in the first column, which is likely to extend onto a second page. The second column, which appears only on page 1, holds a list of services.

2. Press F7, O to turn columns on and return to the document screen.

3. Press Enter twice; then change the font to 12-point Helvetica Bold. Press Ctrl-F8, F; move the cursor to Helvetica Bold in the Base Font list; press Enter; type *12*; and press F7. Type the following contact line:

   Contact: Geri Akke (699) 023-4321

4. Press Enter two times and type the topic line:

   Attorneys rely on art firm for courtroom advantage.

5. Press Shift-F8, L, J, L, F7. Press Enter twice; then switch to a 12-point (10-pitch) Courier font. Press Ctrl-F8, F; move the cursor to Courier in the Base Font list (or Courier 10-Pitch if your printer doesn't have scalable fonts); press Enter; type *12*; and press F7.

6. Set line spacing to 2. Press Shift-F8, L, S, 2, Enter, F7. Type the body text.

To save this release form as a template for other press releases, save the form before you type any body copy. To send out a press release, retrieve the form and type body copy in the first column. When you reach the bottom of page one, press Home, Home, and the down-arrow key to move to the end of the form. Insert a hard page break (Ctrl-Enter) and type the remainder of the release, beginning on page two. Figure 8.3, shown later in this chapter, gives a sample design for continuing pages, followed by instructions for creating the design.

Finishing the First Page

To finish creating the press release, do the following:

1. Place the cursor at the end of the body text on page one and press Ctrl-Enter to move to the top of the second column. Then switch line spacing to single.
2. Press Shift-F8, L, S, 1, Enter, F7.
3. Press Enter to insert space between "Legal Graphics" and the first line of the address; then switch to 12-point Times Italic.
4. Press Ctrl-F8, F; move the cursor to Times Roman Italic in the Base Font list; press Enter; type *12*; and press F7.
5. Type the address flush-left in the second column, pressing Enter twice between address lines.
6. After typing the address, press Enter three times and then switch to 20-point Times Roman Italic. Type the service list flush-left, pressing Enter twice between items.
7. At the end of the services list, switch to 12-point Courier (or 10-pitch if your printer doesn't support scalable type). Press Ctrl-F8, F; move the cursor to Courier (or Courier 10-pitch) in the Base Font list; press Enter; type *12* if you are using scalable type (if not, the font size prompt doesn't appear); and press F7.

   Switching to the body text font here is wise, in case you forget to go back to Courier for body text on subsequent pages. For the same reason, set the line spacing to 2 now.
8. To set line spacing to 2, press Shift-F8, L, S, 2, Enter, F7.
9. Check your work in View Document (Shift-F7, V).

Continuing the Press Release

Now you can design the continuing pages. Figure 8.3 shows the format. Because many readers consider elaborate design on continuing pages excessive and because these readers are likely to resent the time required to wade through a complex design, the design of the press release should be kept very simple.

Rapid Art Legal Graphics - For Immediate Release *P. 2*

Is, M. Messala, M. Pisone consulibus, regnicupiditate inductus coniurationem nobilitatis fecit et civitati persuasit ut de finibus suis cum omnibus copiis exirent: Perfacile esse, cum virtute omnibus praestarent, totius Galliae imperio potiri. Id hoc facilius iis persuasit quod undique loci natura Helvetii contionentur: una ex parte flumine Rheno latissimo atque altissimo, qui agrum Helvetium a Germanis dividit; altera ex parte monte Iura altissimo, qui est inter Sequanos et Helvetios; teria lacu Lemanno et flumine Rhodano, qui provinciam nostram ab Helvetiis dividit. His rebus fiebat ut et minus late vagarentur et minus facile finitimis bellum inferre possent; qua ex parte homines bellandi cupidi magno dolore afficiebantur. Pro multitudine autem hominum et pro gloria bellie atque fortitudinis angustos se fines habere arbitrabantur, qui in longitudinem milia passuum CCXL, in latitudinem CLLXXX patebant.

His rebus adducti et auctoritate Orgetorigis permoti constitu erunt ea quae ad proficiscendum pertinerent comparare, iumentorum et carrorum quam maximum numerum coemere, sementes quam maximas facere, ut in itinere copia frumenti suppeteret, cum proximis vicitatibus pacem et amicitiam confirmare. Ad eas res conficiendas biennieum sibi satis esse duxerunt; in tertium annum profectionem lege confirmant. Ad eas res conficiendas Orgetorix deligitur. Is sibi legationem ad civitates suscipit. In eo itinere persuadet Castico, Catamantaloedis filio, Sequano, cuius pater regnum .

FIG. 8.3 Continuing the press release to another page.

To continue a press release on another page, do the following:

1. After completing step 9 in the preceding instructions, place the cursor at the end of column two and turn off columns by pressing Alt-F7, C, F.
2. Press Ctrl-Enter to create a hard page break and move the cursor to the top of page two.
3. Subsequent pages can have a normal 1-inch right margin. To change the margins, place the cursor at the left margin in the first line of page two. Press Shift-F8, L, M; type *1.75*"; press Enter; type *1*"; and press Enter, F7.

   Inserting a margin code before the header also changes the margins for the header.
4. Create the header. Press Shift-F8, P, H, A, P. Press F7 (Exit) to leave the header.
5. Copy the vertical line from page one into the header on page two. Press Home, Home, and the up-arrow key to move to the top of the document. Turn on Reveal Codes (Alt-F3) and move the cursor onto the vertical graphics line code. Press Del to delete the code; then press F1, 1 to restore the code. Press Shift-F8, P, H, A, E to edit the header. With the cursor in the header editing screen, press F1, 1 to restore a copy of the vertical line.

   The vertical line is now part of the header and appears on each page of the document, starting on page two.

   With the cursor still in the header editing screen, type the text to be repeated in the header on each page of the press release.
6. Change the font to 12-point Times Roman Italic. Press Ctrl-F8, F; move the cursor to Times Roman Italic in the Base Font list; press Enter; type 12; and press F7. Type *Rapid Art Legal Graphics - For Immediate Release*. Press Alt-F6 (Flush Right), type *P.*, and press and space bar and Ctrl-B. Press Enter to insert an extra blank line in the header. (Extra space between header and body text improves the appearance of the page.)
7. Press F7 twice to return to the document screen.

8. Check your work with View Document (Shift-F7, V).

   When you begin to type copy on page two, always check the Reveal Codes screen first to make sure that you don't insert text in front of the margin and header codes. If you do insert text in front of the margin and header codes, the header and new margins do not take effect at the top of the second page.

9

Producing Invitations

An invitation can be sedate, whimsical, or anything in between. Because most WordPerfect users probably create invitations for business purposes, the design examples in this chapter lean toward the formal. The first sample invitation is classic in design, but modern in essence; the second sample invitation is simple, yet informative.

Invitation No. 1: An Expensive Furniture Store

The invitation shown in figure 9.1 uses reversed type in a box. You cannot print this invitation unless you own a PostScript or Hewlett-Packard LaserJet III-compatible printer. But don't worry—this invitation looks almost as nice in black-on-white. To accommodate all readers, instructions are given for designing this invitation with and without reversed type.

If a document calls for precise placement of text, lines, and boxes, making several preliminary sketches can be especially helpful. Professional designers routinely doodle their designs on paper before entering the designs on the computer. This first invitation is a case in point. Because this design calls for careful placement of lines and boxes, entering the invitation directly in WordPerfect may take hours of trial and error before the outcome is satisfactory. (Because this design should be taken to a printer and offset-printed on heavy linen paper, the placement of the invitation on the page doesn't matter.)

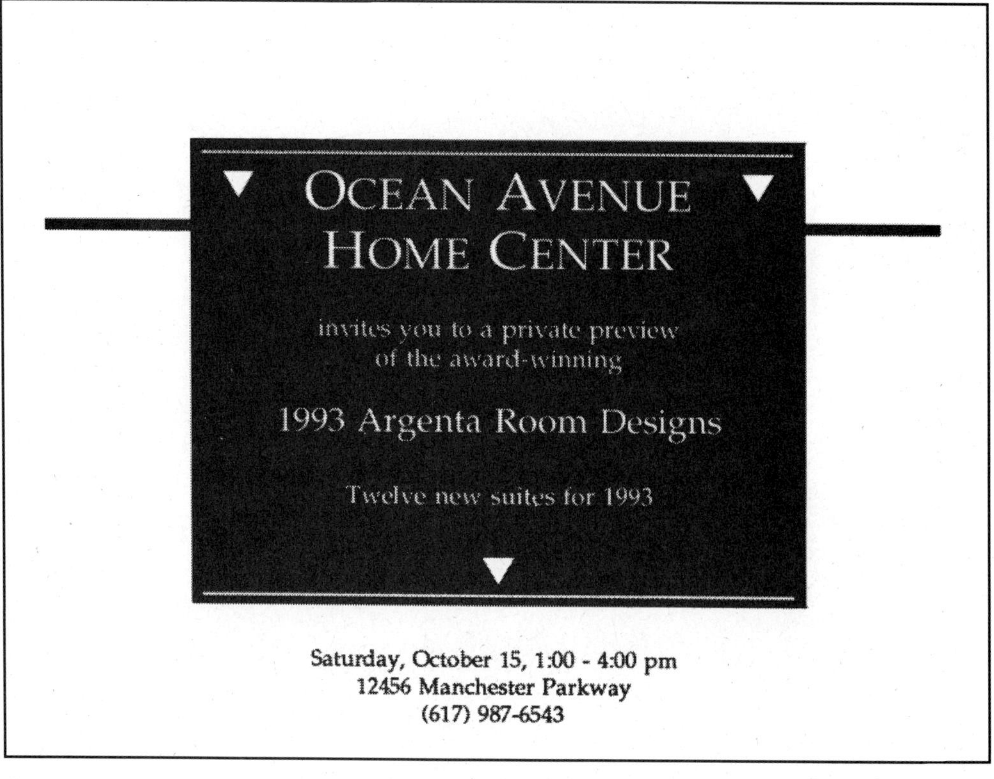

FIG. 9.1 A white-on-black invitation.

Creating the Boxes and Lines

To create this invitation, begin by creating the large box with thin lines:

1. Press Alt-F9, B, O. In the Options: Text Box screen, make the following changes:

Border Style	Set all to Single
Gray shading	0%

2. Press Alt-F9, B, C. In the Definition: Text Box screen, make the following changes:

Anchor Type	Page, Number of pages to skip: 0
Vertical Position	Top
Horizontal Position	Margin, Left

Size	Set Both, 5.5" wide x 4.25" (high)
Wrap Text Around Box	Yes

TIP

To place one box or graphic line on top of another on the same page, you must place the two (or more) codes immediately after each other on the first line of the page. If you fail to do this, WordPerfect moves the second element to the next page.

To create the smaller, reversed box, do the following:

1. Press Alt-F9, B, O. In the Options: Text Box screen, make the following settings:

Border Style	None, None, Single, Single
Gray shading	100%

2. Press F7 to return to the document; then press Alt-F9, B, C. In the Definition: Text Box screen, make the following settings:

Anchor Type	Page, Number of pages to skip: 0
Vertical Position	Set Position, 1 5/8"
Horizontal Position	Set Position, 2 1/16"
Size	Set Both, 3 7/16" wide x 2 5/8" (high)

3. Press F7 to return to the document.

To make the top reversed line, do the following:

1. Position the cursor immediately following the box codes in the first line on the page; otherwise, WordPerfect prints the line on the second page.

2. Press Alt-F9, L, H. In the Graphics: Horizontal Line screen, make the following settings:

Horizontal Position	Set Position, Offset from left of page: 2 1/8"
Vertical Position	Set Position, 1.85"

Length of Line	3.31"
Width of Line	.02"
Gray shading	0%

TIP

With a PostScript printer, such as the one used to create the illustrations for this book, WordPerfect does not display a 0% line in the View Document screen, but the line prints correctly. To check the position of the line, set gray shading temporarily to 6%.

3. Press F7 to return to the document. Check your work with View Document (Shift-F7, V).

To create the line at the bottom of the reversed box, do the following:

1. Position the cursor immediately following the first graphics line code in the first line on the page; otherwise, WordPerfect prints the line on the second page.
2. Press Alt-F9, L, H. In the Graphics: Horizontal Line screen, make the following settings:

Horizontal Position	Set Position, Offset from left of page: 2 1/8"
Vertical Position	Set Position, 4.35"
Length of Line	3.31"
Width of Line	.02"
Gray shading	0%

3. Press F7 to return to the document. Check your work with View Document (Shift-F7, V).

Placing the Text within the Box

To format the text to be placed within the larger box, do the following:

1. In Reveal Codes (Alt-F3), move the cursor onto the box code for the reversed box and press Alt-F9, B, E, Enter, E to display the Graphics Text Box editing screen.
2. Set the font color to white by pressing Ctrl-F8, C, W, Enter.
3. Set the font to Palatino 16-point. Press Ctrl-F8, F; move the cursor to Palatino in the Base Font list; press Enter; type *16*; and press F7.

You need to add the inverted triangles to the left and right of the main head. To create the first inverted triangle, do the following:

1. Press Ctrl-V (Compose); type *12,116* (12, comma, 116); and press Enter.
2. Press Alt-F6 (Flush Right) and create another dingbat.
3. Press Ctrl-V (Compose); type *12,116* (12, comma, 116); and press Enter.

The inverted triangle is a Zapf Dingbat, available with PostScript printers. Zapf Dingbats are assigned to Compose character set 12; the inverted triangle is 12,116. If you don't have this character, pick another decorative character. The character set chart in the appendix of the WordPerfect Reference lists many decorative characters. If you own a PostScript printer, see Appendix B of this book for a list of Zapf Dingbats and their code assignments in WordPerfect character set 12, which you can access with Compose.

To add the name of the host within the box, do the following:

1. Press Enter and use Advance to move the insertion point up 1/4". Press Shift-F8, O, A, U, 1/4", Enter, F7.
2. To change to 22-point Palatino, press Ctrl-F8, F; move the cursor to Palatino in the Base Font list; press Enter; type *22*; and press F7.
3. Turn on small caps. Press Ctrl-F8, A, C. Press Shift-F6 (Center), type *Ocean Avenue*, and press Enter.
4. Press Shift-F6 (Center), and type *Home Center*. Press the right-arrow key to turn off small caps.

Finish adding the text to the invitation:

1. Press Enter and change the font to Palatino 10-point. Press Ctrl-F8, F; move the cursor to Palatino in the Base Font list; press Enter; type 10; and press F7. Press Enter again.

2. Press Shift-F6 (Center) and type *invites you to a private preview*.

3. Press Enter, press Shift-F6 (Center), and type *of the award-winning*.

4. Press Enter twice and change the font to 14-point Palatino. Press Ctrl-F8, F; move the cursor to Palatino in the Base Font list; press Enter; type 14; and press F7. Press Shift-F6 (Center) and type *1993 Argenta Room Designs*.

5. Press Enter twice and switch to 10-point Palatino. Press Ctrl-F8, F; move the cursor to Palatino in the Base Font list; press Enter; type 10; and press F7. Press Shift-F6 (Center) and type *Twelve new suites for 1993*.

6. Press Enter twice and switch to 16-point Palatino. Press Ctrl-F8, F; move the cursor to Palatino in the Base Font list; press Enter; type *16*; and press F7.

To add the last inverted triangle at the bottom of the box, do the following:

1. Advance the cursor down 1/16" to position the inverted triangle at the bottom of the box with its downward-pointing tip almost touching the horizontal line. (The distance is determined by experimentation.)

2. Press Shift-F8, O, A, D, 1/16", Enter, F7.

3. Press Shift-F6 (Center) and create the dingbat. Press Ctrl-V; type *12,116* (12, comma, 116); and press Enter. Press F7 twice to return to the document screen.

Save your work and check it in View Document (Shift-F7, V). To check work involving fine positioning, you always should print out the document. View Document displays Zapf Dingbats as empty squares, for example, so you must make a printout to check the positioning of the inverted triangles.

Finishing the Invitation

To create the thick "handles" (the two heavy horizontal lines) next to the reversed box, do the following:

1. Make sure that the cursor is in the first line, immediately following the `[TextBox;2;;]` code. Press Alt-F9, L, H. In the Graphics: Horizontal Line screen, change the settings to the following:

Horizontal Position	Set Position, 1 1/4"
Vertical Position	Set Position, 2 1/4"
Length of Line	1"
Width of Line	1/16"
Gray shading	100%

   Press F7 to return to the document screen.

2. To create the second line, repeat step 1; however, in the Graphics: Horizontal Line screen, make the following changes:

Horizontal Position	Set Position, 5 1/4"
Vertical Position	Set Position, 2 1/4"
Length of Line	1"
Width of Line	1/16"
Gray shading	100%

   Press F7 to return to the document screen.

To create the date and location text at the bottom of the large box with thin borders:

1. Turn on Reveal Codes; position the cursor on the hidden code for the first box; and press Alt-F9, B, E, Enter, E.

2. Advance the cursor down 3 1/2" by pressing Shift-F8, O, A, D, 3.5", Enter, F7.

3. Switch to 9-point Palatino. Press Ctrl-F8, F; move the cursor to Palatino in the Base Font list; press Enter; type *9*; and press F7. Press Shift-F6 (Center) and type *Saturday, October 15, 1:00 - 4:00 pm*. Press Enter, Shift-F6 and type the street address. Repeat for the phone number. Press F7 twice to return to the document screen.

4. Check your work by printing it.

Using Black Text on a White Background

As promised earlier, even those who don't own a PostScript or H-P LaserJet III-compatible printer can produce an attractive version of this invitation. Figure 9.2 shows a version of the design that uses straight, unreversed text.

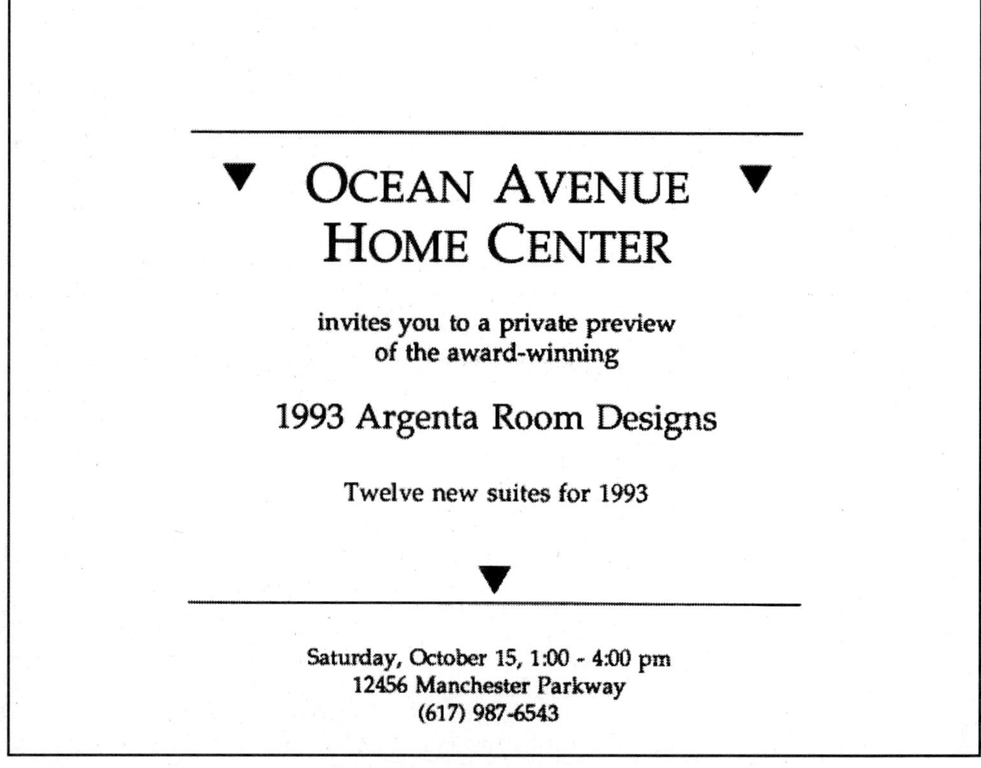

FIG. 9.2 A black-on-white invitation.

Create the design as described previously but change the following settings:

- Specify 0% gray shading for the smaller box.
- Omit the thick horizontal lines (the "handles") that stick out at the sides of the smaller box.
- Omit the thin horizontal lines positioned just inside the top and bottom edges of the smaller box.

- In the graphic box editing screen for the smaller box, omit the white color code.
- Because the thin horizontal lines are omitted, you must move the bottom inverted triangle down until it almost touches the bottom line of the smaller box. With the cursor in front of the last Zapf Dingbat code (12,116), press Shift-F8, O, A, D; type *1/8*"; and press Enter, F7.

Invitation No. 2: An Engineering Society Picnic

This design is much simpler than the previous one, even though it involves one tricky element: the positioning of one box on top of another box (see fig. 9.3).

Creating the Boxes

First, create the larger box. Remember, to place one box on top of another with a page anchor type, you must place the box codes on the first line of the page. To create the larger box, do the following:

1. Press Alt-F9, B, O. In the Options: Text Box screen, change the settings to the following:

Border Style	Set all to Single
Gray shading	0%

2. Press F7 to return to the document screen. Press Alt-F9, B, C. In the Definition: Text Box screen, make the following settings:

Anchor Type	Page, Number of pages to skip: 0
Vertical Position	Top
Horizontal Position	Margins, Left
Size	Set Both, 4 1/4" wide x 5 1/2" (high)

FIG. 9.3 An invitation created with over-lapping boxes.

3. Press F7 to return to the document screen.

TIP

The options for the first box are the same for the second, so repeating step 1 is unnecessary.

To create the second, smaller box, do the following:

1. Press Alt-F9, B, C.
2. In the Definition: Text Box screen, change the settings to the following:

Anchor Type	Page, Number of pages to skip: 0
Vertical Position	Set Position, 1 1/16"
Horizontal Position	Set Position, 1 1/4"
Size	Set Both, 3 3/4" wide x 4 15/16" (high)

Adding the Text

To add the text to the invitation, you first need to press E. Then type the text and do the following:

1. Press Alt-F7, C, D. In the Text Column Definition screen, change the settings to the following:

Type	Parallel
Number of Columns	2
Distance Between Columns	1/8"
Margins	1/4", 2 1/8", 2 3/8", 3 5/16"

2. Press F7, O to turn columns on.
3. Press Enter to insert space; then switch to 9-point Avant Garde Gothic Book. Press Ctrl-F8, F; move the cursor to Avant Garde Gothic Book in the Base Font list; press Enter; type 9; and press F7. Press Alt-F6 (Flush Right) and type *Saturday April 4 1 pm* (insert two spaces between the day, date, and time).
4. Press Enter twice and switch to 18-point Avant Garde Gothic Book. To tighten line spacing for the lines that follow, insert a 2-point (1/36") leading adjustment code. Press Shift-F8, O, P, L, Enter; type *-2p*; and press Enter, F7.

   Press Ctrl-F8, F; move the cursor to Avant Garde Gothic Book; press Enter; type *18*; and press F7.
5. Type the next five lines (*New Mexico...Annual*), pressing Enter between lines and aligning the lines flush right by pressing Alt-F6 at the beginning of each line. At the end of

the last line, switch to 30-point Avant Garde Gothic Book. Press Ctrl-F8, F; move the cursor to Avant Garde Gothic Book in the Base Font list; press Enter; type 30; and press F7.

6. Press Enter, Alt-F6 (Flush Right) and type *PICNIC*.
7. Press Ctrl-Enter to move to the next column.
8. Switch to 9-point Avant Garde Gothic Book. Press Ctrl-F8, F; move the cursor to Avant Garde Gothic Book in the Base Font list; press Enter; type 9; and press F7. Press Enter four times and type the remaining text flush-left, pressing Enter twice between items as shown in figure 9.3.

10

Producing Programs and Schedules

Programs and schedules must be functional and attractive, helping the reader navigate times, places, and events. Schedules generally show times and places; programs may only show events. The sample schedule presented in this chapter gives titles, times, and places for lectures at a technical seminar for biomedical product manufacturers. The program in this chapter announces a concert. Both designs are flexible and prove that spending days sweating over desktop-published documents to achieve first-class results is not necessary. With typographical changes and the judicious use of graphics, you can adapt these samples for conferences, crafts fairs, film series, and so on.

Sample Program: A Music Concert

A glance at figure 10.1 reveals that the concert is a formal event. Centered text and italic type usually look formal. The design of this program is extremely simple, but effective. This program is designed to be copied on both sides of a single 8 1/2-by-11 sheet of attractive ivory stock paper. To avoid cutting and pasting, the cover and inside designs can be printed in landscape mode (horizontally), ready to take to a local copy center.

Wembley Village

Performing Arts Society

Spring Concert

April 13, 7 pm

Wembley Village Hall

❦

FIG. 10.1 *A program for a spring concert.*

Setting Up the Page

Begin by choosing a landscape form. Use one of WordPerfect's defaults:

1. Press Shift-F8, P, S. In the Format: Paper Size/Type menu, move the cursor to `Standard-Wide` and press Enter, F7 to return to the document screen.

   Now create the long box that holds the cover copy. To print the cover on the right half of the horizontal page, make the following settings in the Definition: Text Box menu.

2. Set the margins. Press Shift-F8, L, M; type *1/2*"; press Enter; type *1/2*"; and press Enter, Enter, P, M, O, Enter, O, Enter, F7.

3. Press Alt-F9, B, O. In the Options: Text Box screen, make the following settings:

Border Style	Set all to Double
Gray Shading	0%
Outside Border Space	Set all to 0

4. Press F7. Press Alt-F9, B, C. In the Definition: Text Box screen, make the following settings:

Anchor Type	Page, Pages to skip: 0
Vertical Position	Set Position, 1/2"
Horizontal Position	Margin, Right
Size	4.5" wide x 7.5" (high)
Wrap Text Around Box	Yes

Adding the Text

Before entering text into the box, you need to press E in the Definition: Text Box screen and then do the following:

1. In the Text Box edit screen, press Enter five times and choose 14-point Palatino Italic. Press Ctrl-F8, F; move the cursor to Palatino Italic in the Base Font list; press Enter; type *14*; and press F7. Type *Wembley Village*.

2. Press Enter twice; then press Shift-F6 (Center) and type *Performing Arts Society*.

3. Press Enter three times and choose 28-point Palatino Italic. Press Ctrl-F8, F; move the cursor to Palatino Italic in the Base Font list; press Enter; type *28*; and press F7. Press Shift-F6 (Center) and type *Spring Concert.*

4. Press Enter twice and switch to 10-Point Palatino. Press Ctrl-F8, F; move the cursor to Palatino in the Base Font list; press Enter; type *10*; and press F7.

5. Press Enter, Shift-F6 (Center) and type *April 13, 7 pm*.

6. Press Enter twice, press Shift-F6 (Center), and type *Wembley Village Hall.*

Finishing Page One

To finish the first page, you need to add the dingbat character that appears centered at the bottom of the text:

1. Press Enter twice and switch to 22-point Palatino.

2. Press Ctrl-F8, F; move the cursor to Palatino in the Base Font list; press Enter; type *22*; and press F7.

3. Press Shift-F6 (Center). If you have the Zapf Dingbat typeface, press Ctrl-V (Compose); type *12,166*; and press Enter. Press F7 twice.

   If you don't have Zapf Dingbats, choose another decorative character. The appendix to the WordPerfect reference manual lists the characters you can create with Compose. If you own a PostScript printer, see Appendix B of this book for a list of Zapf Dingbats assigned to WordPerfect character set 12 that you can print using Compose.

Creating the Inside Page

The inside page of the program uses the same box as the cover. To copy the cover to a new page, do the following:

1. With the cover design displayed in the document screen, press Home, Home, and the down-arrow key to move to the end of the file.
2. Press Ctrl-Enter to insert a hard page break and create a page.
3. Press the up-arrow key to move back to page one. Press Ctrl-F4, A, C to copy page one.
4. Press Home, Home, and the down-arrow key. Then press Enter to insert the copy of page one in page two.
5. Press Home, Home, and the down-arrow key. Then press Backspace to delete the hard page break at the end of page two.
6. Press Alt-F9, B, E, 2, Enter, E.

   You are now in the text box editing screen, where you can create the inside copy for the program by editing the front cover copy.

> **TIP**
>
> To change text that already contains base font codes that you use for new text, you don't have to use the Base Font feature. To change to a new font, press Alt-F3 to turn on Reveal Codes. Move the cursor to the code for the font you need and press Del. Press F1, 1 to restore the code; move the cursor to the location where you want to use the font; and press F1, 1 again to restore another copy of the code. This method works best for short documents where you can move around and copy codes quickly in the Reveal Codes screen.

7. Using the method described in the tip, edit the cover copy until the edited version resembles figure 10.2.

Wembley Village Performing Arts Society

Spring Concert

A Dance: "The Coming of Spring"
Poppy Kegley-Bassington

Four Arias from Puccini
Clarence Tuckweiler

Vivaldi: Gloria
The Wembley Village Chorale

Intermission

Telemann: Machet die Tore Weit
Wembley Village Ensemble and Chorale
Winston Barret, Bass
Elwin Fortis, Tenor
Maria Trattorina, Alto
Eldyce Forkner, Soprano

Ralph Vaughn Williams: Songs
Winston Barrett, Bass
Elwin Fortis, Tenor

Smetana: The Moldau, from Ma Vlast
Wembley Village Chamber Ensemble

FIG. 10.2 The inside page of the spring concert invitation.

Because you create the remainder of the design by changing the font, turning on italics, and pressing Enter, the steps are not listed here. When you are finished, the text should resemble the following in Reveal Codes:

```
[Font:Palatino Italic 14pt][HRt]

[Center]Wembley Village Performing Arts
Society[HRt]

[HRt]

[HRt]

[Font:Palatino Italic 28pt][Center]Spring
Concert[HRt]

[HRt]

[Font:Palatino 22pt][Center] [HRt]

[HRt]

[Center][Font:Palatino 11pt][ITALC]A Dance: "The
Coming of Spring"[italc][HRt]

[Center][Font:Palatino 9pt]Poppy Kegley[-
]Bassington[HRt]

[HRt]

[Center][Font:Palatino 11pt][ITALC]Four Arias from
Puccini[italc][HRt]

[Center][Font:Palatino 9pt]Clarence Tuckweiler[HRt]

[HRt]

[Center][Font:Palatino 11pt][ITALC]Vivaldi:
Gloria[italc][HRt]

[Center][Font:Palatino 9pt]The Wembley Village
Chorale[HRt]

[HRt]
```

```
[HRt]

[Center][Font:Palatino
11pt][ITALC]Intermission[italc][HRt]

[HRt]

[HRt]

[Center][Font:Palatino 11pt][ITALC]Telemann: Machet
die Tore Weit[italc][HRt]

[Center][Font:Palatino 9pt]Wembley Village Ensemble
and Chorale[HRt]

[Center]Winston Barret, Bass[HRt]

[Center]Elwin Fortis, Tenor[HRt]

[Center]Maria Trattorina, Alto[HRt]

[Center]Eldyce Forkner, Soprano[HRt]

[HRt]

[Center][Font:Palatino 11pt][ITALC]Ralph Vaughn
Williams: Songs[italc][HRt]

[Center][Font:Palatino 9pt]Winston Barrett,
Bass[HRt]

[Center][Font:Palatino 9pt]Elwin Fortis, Tenor[HRt]

[HRt]

[Center][Font:Palatino 11pt][ITALC]Smetana: The
Moldau, from Ma Vlast[italc][HRt]

[Center][Font:Palatino 9pt]Wembley Village Chamber
Ensemble[HRt]
```

Sample Schedule: A Technical Seminar

The schedule in figure 10.3 is a handout announcing a one-day seminar for a professional conference. The design is functional but attractive and contains two main components: the header and the columns of times and places. The design is flexible—you can create headers for events of many different types without harming the appearance of the piece.

Setting Up the Page

The main design challenges of the schedule are the gray bar and the heavy black graphic lines. To create the schedule, you first must create the box around the page by doing the following:

1. Set the margins at 1/2" all around. Press Shift-F8, L, M; type *1/2"*; press Enter; type *1/2"*; press Enter, Enter, P, M; type *1/2"*; press Enter; type *1/2"*; and press Enter, F7.

2. Press Alt-F9, B, O. In the Options: Text Box screen, change the settings to the following:

Border Style	Set all to Double
Outside Border Space	Set all to 0
Gray Shading	0%

3. Press F7. Press Alt-F9, B, C. In the Definition: Text Box screen, change the settings to the following:

Anchor Type	Page, Number of Pages to Skip: 0
Vertical Position	Full Page
Horizontal Position	Margin, Full
Size	Set both 7.5" wide x 10" (high)
Wrap Text Around Box	Yes

A One-Day Seminar

Custom Injection Molding
for the Biomedical Industry

East Florida University Conference Center

June 14, 1991
9 am - 5 pm

Topic	*Time*	*Presenter*	*Room*
Disposable Diagnostic Test Kits			
Improved Molding Techniques	9 am	G. Smythe	110
Design Considerations	10 am	L. Pavlov	214
the Assembly Challenge	11 am	R. Zantri	55
Specialty Products for Blood Transfer			
The HIV Challenge	10 am	G. Smythe	110
The Time-Critical Transfer	11 am	L. Pavlov	214
Four New Processes	1 pm	D. Andre	104
Assembled Unit Testing			
Failure-Prone Materials	11 am	P. Eldred	512
Selecting Test Parameters	2 pm	R. Goth	643
Secure Laminates	3 pm	P. Eldred	214
Market Factors			
Predicting Demand	3 pm	P. Eldred	323
Three Case Histories	4 pm	R. Goth	643
Successful Bid Analysis	5 pm	L. Wenzel	742

FIG. 10.3 A schedule of events for a technical seminar.

WordPerfect does not enable you to place graphic boxes or lines inside this or any box. The gray bar that holds the column headings (Topic, Time, Presenter, Room) is a heavy shaded line, and the thick black bars next to the topic sections also are graphic lines. Because you cannot create these lines inside the box, you must create the lines after entering the text in the box and then position the lines carefully with Advance.

Adding the Text

To create the text, press Alt-F9, B, E, 1, Enter, E. In the text box editing screen, set the left and right margins to 3/8" and 0"; then type the text for the schedule:

1. Press Enter twice to create space at the top of the box and change the font to 14-point New Century Schoolbook Bold Italic.
2. Press Shift-F6 (Center) and type *A One-Day Seminar*. Press Enter twice.
3. Press Shift-F6 (Center), change the font to 30-point New Century Schoolbook Bold, and type *Custom Injection Molding*.
4. Press Enter, change the font to 24-point New Century Schoolbook Bold, press Shift-F6 (Center), and type *for the Biomedical Industry*.
5. Press Enter and change the font to 14-point New Century Schoolbook Bold. Press Enter, press Shift-F6 (Center), and type *East Florida University Conference Center*.
6. Press Enter twice, press Shift-F6 (Center), and type *June 14, 1991*.
7. Press Enter, press Shift-F6 (Center), and type *9 am - 5 pm*.
8. Press Enter four times, change the font to 12-point New Century Schoolbook Bold Italic.
9. Press Tab and type *Topic*; press Tab four times and type *Time*; press Tab three times and type *Presenter*; press Tab twice and type *Room*.

   Note: Step 9 assumes WordPerfect's default tab settings of a tab stop every .5".

10. Press Enter twice, change the font to 14-point New Century Schoolbook Bold, and type *Disposable Diagnostic Test Kits*.

11. Press Enter twice and add 2 points to the line leading by pressing Shift-F8, O, P, L, Enter; typing *2p*; and pressing Enter, F7.

    This adds 2 points (1/32") of extra space between the lines. You leave this setting and press Enter to add space between lines.

12. Change the font to 12-point New Century Schoolbook and type *Improved Molding Techniques*; press Tab twice and type *9 am*; press Tab three times and type *G. Smythe*; press Tab twice and type *110*.

13. Continue typing the body text of the schedule, using the same fonts as listed previously. Press F7 twice to return to the document screen.

TIP

When you must type several short sections of text that contain the same repeated font changes, blocking a section of text containing all the needed font codes, saving it to a file, and then retrieving and editing the copy for each new section is quicker. To copy the font codes, turn on Reveal Codes (Alt-F3), move the cursor just ahead of the first font change, and press Alt-F4 (Block). Then move the cursor to the end of the section, press F10 (Save), type a file name at the prompt, and press Enter. Move the cursor to the location of the new section and retrieve the file to insert the text and font codes from the previous section. Press Shift-F10 (Retrieve), type the file name, and press Enter. Delete the old text and type the new, being careful not to delete any hidden codes. (To be sure that you don't accidentally delete any codes, type the new text in the Reveal Codes screen.)

Adding the Lines

After you have entered all the text, you still must create five horizontal lines: the gray bar for the column headings and four heavy black lines to set apart the sections. To create the gray and black lines, do the following:

1. Move the cursor ahead of the box code and insert all of the line codes there.

> **TIP**
>
> With a full-page box on the page, WordPerfect moves the lines onto the succeeding page unless you place the line codes carefully; therefore, be sure not to omit step 1.

2. To create the horizontal gray bar, press Alt-F9, L, H. In the Graphics: Horizontal Line screen, change the settings to the following:

Horizontal Position	Set Position, Offset from left of page: 1 1/16"
Vertical Position	Set Position, 3.83"
Length of Line	6 9/16"
Width of Line	1/16"
Gray Shading	10%

   These figures were determined by printing the text, carefully measuring the line positions, repeatedly returning to the Graphics: Horizontal Line screen, and making fine adjustments. To edit an existing line, place the cursor after the horizontal line code in the Reveal Codes screen (Alt-F3), not on or before the code.

   Press F7 to return to the document screen.

TIP

Avoid printing type over a box with gray shading greater than 10 percent because the text is harder to read.

3. Create the heavy black lines. In Reveal Codes (Alt-F3), move the cursor to the right of the code for the gray bar that you created in steps 1 and 2 and press Alt-F9, L, H. In the Graphics: Horizontal Line screen, change the settings to the following:

Horizontal Position	Set Position, Offset from left of page: 4 3/8"
Vertical Position	Set Position, 4.6"
Length of Line	3 1/4"
Width of Line	1/16"
Gray Shading	100%

4. Repeat Step 3 for the other three heavy black lines. In the Graphics: Horizontal Line screen, make the following settings:

	Line 2	*Line 3*	*Line 4*
Horizontal Position	5"	3.53"	2.68"
Vertical Position	5.93"	7.32"	8.71"
Length of Line	2.63"	4.1"	4.93"
Width of Line	1/16"	1/16"	1/16"
Gray Shading	100%	100%	100%

These figures were determined by carefully measuring distances on a printout of the text and then making fine adjustments repeatedly in the Graphics: Horizontal Line screen.

11

Producing Directories

Like other hardworking business documents, directories can be functional without being boring. Only a little of WordPerfect design magic is required to organize and clarify your phone lists, medical emergency procedures, employee directories, and lists of suppliers. Although most directories don't require graphic images, you can use lines, columns, and screens to make your lists attractive.

Directory No. 1: An Employee Directory

This directory presents a common problem—how to mix two kinds of data: ordinary columnar information (Name, Department, Extension) and free-form text (the employee's spouse, children, hobbies, college degrees, and alma mater). The sample design solves the problem simply, with tabular columns and a change of typeface (see fig. 11.1).

Designing the Directory

To create this directory, you first must change the margins by doing the following:

1. Press Shift-F8, P, M; type *0"*; press Enter; type *1"*; press Enter, Enter, L, M; type *1 1/8"*; press Enter; type *1 1/8"*; and press Enter, F7.

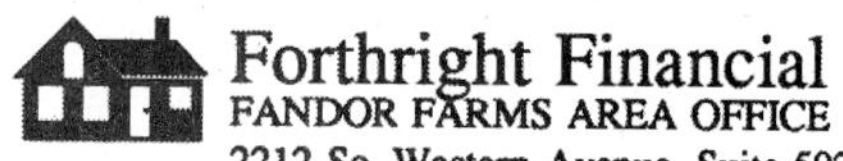

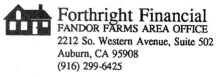

FANDOR FARMS AREA OFFICE
2212 So. Western Avenue, Suite 502
Auburn, CA 95908
(916) 299-6425

Employee Directory

NAME	DEPARTMENT	EXTENSION
Cisneros, Armando Lucy (pediatrician), Alex 7, Deanna 10, Joe 13, golf, scuba, UCLA (economics, Phi Beta Kappa)	***Accounting*** Supervisor	***546***
Desrogers, Jacqueline Single, painting, Sorbonne (economics, honors)	***Planning*** Vice President	***66***
Egan, Faith Ed (contractor), Andrew 18, ultramarathoning, X-C skiing, Stanford (economics, Biz School)	***Technical Services*** Team Leader	***48***
Lamarr, Kevin Maryanne (housewife), Cindy 1½, Peter 4, Darren 7, Whitney 13, golf, Univ. New Mexico (accounting, law)	***President***	***1***
Rankin, Jolynne Frank (architect), Ashley 8, Rod 14, Greg 23, bicycling, jogging, Univ. Minnesota (philosophy, business)	***Customer Services*** Department Manager	***43***
Stanfield, Harold Single, bodybuilding, swimming, ultramarathoning, Harvard (Rhodes Scholar, mathematics, Biz School)	***Financial Services*** Chief Auditor	***18***
Tanaguchi, Alan Mary (chemical engineer), Ana 10, Toshi 12, surf fishing, backpacking, UCLA (statistics, Ph.D. economics)	***Financial Trends*** Chief Statistician	***32***
Ullyot, Marjorie Edward (doctor), Jimmy 10, Alix 13, triathlon, swimming, running (Arizona State U., business)	***Customer Service*** Department Manager	***777***

FIG. 11.1 *An employee directory.*

TIP

When you type *0"* at the prompt, WordPerfect changes that setting to 0.3" if you are using a laser printer. 0" is specified throughout this book because it is quicker than typing *0.3"*.

TIP

To create this directory, you need to break the general design rule that states when space is tight, you should set your side margins wider and the top margin higher. Actually, this rule applies only if you must cut margins as much as possible to fit a great deal of copy onto the page. In figure 11.1, however, plenty of space is available. In this instance, the copy looks more compact with the margins set wide, and the letterhead with its graphic image looks best placed high on the page.

2. To create the thick horizontal line under the column titles (NAME, DEPARTMENT, EXTENSION), press Alt-F9, L, H.
3. In the Graphics: Horizontal Line screen, change the settings to the following:

Horizontal Position	Full
Vertical Position	Set Position, 2 1/2"
Length of Line	6 1/2"
Width of Line	1/16"

4. Press F7 to return to the document screen.

TIP

When positioning lines on your own, try making a pencil sketch first. You may be surprised how much fine-tuning this can save in getting the positioning just right.

Adding the Graphic

Next, you need to place the house graphic in the upper left portion of your document. To create the image of the house, do the following:

1. Press Alt-F9, F, O.
2. In the Options: Figure screen, change the settings to the following:

Border Style	Set all to None
Outside Border	Set all to 0"
Inside Border Space	0", 1/16", 0", 0"

3. Press F7 to return to the document screen; then press Alt-F9, F, C.
4. In the Graphics: Figure Box screen, change the settings to the following:

Filename	HOUSE.WPG
Anchor Type	Page, Number of pages to skip: 0
Vertical Position	Set Position, 3"
Horizontal Position	Margins, Left
Size	Set Both 3/4" wide × 1" high
Wrap Text Around Box	Yes

Note: The sample figures used in the designs for this book are from the DrawPerfect Figure Library, which offers a much greater variety than the figure collection supplied with WordPerfect 5.1. For information about ordering the DrawPerfect Figure Library and other figure collections, call WordPerfect Corporation.

Adding the Text

Now, add the letterhead text by completing the following steps:

1. Press F7 to return to the document screen; then use the Advance feature to move the insertion point down 1/16" to position the first line of letterhead text (Forthright Financial). Press Shift-F8, O, A, D; type *1/16"*; and press Enter, F7.

2. Change the font to 18-point Times Roman before pressing Enter.

3. Press Shift-F8, O, P, L, Enter; type *–4p*; and press Enter, F7 to reduce the line spacing so that FANDOR FARMS AREA OFFICE fits tightly under "Forthright Financial". Type *Forthright Financial*.

4. Change the font to 10-point Times Roman, press Enter, and turn the leading adjustment off by pressing Shift-F8, O, P, L, Enter, 0, Enter, F7.

5. Type *FANDOR FARMS AREA OFFICE* and press Enter. Type the remainder of the address as shown in figure 11.1, pressing Enter at the end of each line.

6. Press Enter five times, change the font to 18-point Times Roman Bold Italic, and type *Employee Directory*.

7. Press Enter, change the font to 9-point Times Roman, press Enter again, and type the column headings (*NAME*, *DEPARTMENT*, *EXTENSION*), pressing Tab to separate the headings.

   Don't worry about the exact positioning now. You can adjust the placement with the help of View Document (Shift-F7, V) after you type the first line of the list.

8. Press Enter three times, change the font to 10-point Times Roman Bold Italic, and type the first line of the list (*Cisneros, Armando*, *Accounting*, *546*). Before you press Enter at the end of the line, change the font to 10-point Times Roman.

9. Press Enter and type the first line of the employee data—*Lucy (pediatrician)*, *Alex 7*, and *Supervisor*—pressing Tab between items.

10. Press Enter and type the remainder of the employee background, pressing Enter as necessary to end each line—*Deanna 10, Joe 13, golf, scuba, UCLA (economics, Phi Beta Kappa)*.

11. Press Enter and create the first thin horizontal line by turning on Reveal Codes (Alt-F3) and pressing underline until WordPerfect enters a `[DSRt]` (dormant soft return) code.

12. Then press Backspace until the `[DSRt]` is removed. (If other lines follow, the `[DSRt]` code is replaced with a `[HRt]` code.) If you go too far, press underline until the `[DSRt]` code reappears and then press Backspace only until the `[HRt]` replaces it.

13. Press Enter and begin the next section, formatting this section as described in the preceding steps.

    To save time, block the first section, including font codes and hard returns, and save it to a temporary file; then retrieve and edit the text for each new section.

Adding Pages to the Directory

To format subsequent pages of the list, copy the list heading to a header by doing the following:

1. Turn on Reveal codes (Alt-F3) and move the cursor onto the 18-point Times Roman Bold Italic font code just above the list heading (Employee Directory).
2. Press Alt-F4 (Block) and press the down-arrow key twice, Home, Home, and the right-arrow key to move the cursor to the end of the column headings (NAME, DEPARTMENT, EXTENSION).
3. Press Ctrl-F4 (Move), B, C; then press Home, Home, Home, the up-arrow key, and the right-arrow key twice to move the cursor to the right of the margin codes at the top of the file.
4. Press Shift-F8, P, H, A, P. In the Header A editing screen, press Enter to insert the copy of the header.
5. Press Home, Home, the up-arrow key, Home, Home, the right-arrow key, and Alt-F6. Type *P.* ^*B* (hold down Ctrl and press B).

6. Press Home, Home, the down-arrow key, Enter to insert extra space at the bottom of the header.

7. Press F7, U, F7 to turn off header printing for the first page only and to return to the document screen. Figure 11.2 shows a sample second page.

Directory No. 2: A Service and Supplier Phone List

The second sample directory presents another example of mixed data (see fig. 11.3). Although this directory does not mix columns with free-form text, this directory does have two sections—one with phone numbers and the other with addresses. Because this directory contains no problems that WordPerfect cannot solve, the challenge is formatting the directory in a visually pleasing way, using basic tools, such as lines and typography.

Creating the Header

Start the directory by creating a header that will appear on each subsequent page of the document. To create the header, do the following:

1. Press Shift-F8, P, H, A, P.

2. In the Header A editing screen, change the font to 14-point Times Roman, press Ctrl-F8, A, C to turn on small caps, and type *Computer Resource Phone List*.

3. Press Alt-F6 (Flush Right) and type *P. ^B* (press Ctrl-B to enter the ^B page numbering command).

4. Press Enter and create a horizontal line by pressing Alt-F9, L, H. In the Graphics: Horizontal Line screen, press Enter to accept the defaults and return to the header editing screen.

5. Press Enter to insert extra space after the line in the header; then press F7, U, A, F7 to turn off header printing for the first page only and to return to the document screen.

Employee Directory **P. 2**

NAME	DEPARTMENT	EXTENSION
Stanfield, Harold Single, bodybuilding, swimming, ultramarathoning, Harvard (Rhodes Scholar, mathematics, Biz School)	***Financial Services*** Chief Auditor	***18***
Tanaguchi, Alan Mary (chemical engineer), Ana 10, Toshi 12, surf fishing, backpacking, UCLA (statistics, Ph.D. economics)	***Financial Trends*** Chief Statistician	***32***
Ullyot, Marjorie Edward (doctor), Jimmy 10, Alix 13, triathlon, swimming, running (Arizona State U., business)	***Customer Service*** Department Manager	***777***

FIG. 11.2 The second page of the directory.

Creating the Body

Now that you have created the header, which is repeated on each subsequent page, you can create the main body of the phone list.

1. To create the vertical line to the left of the company name, press Alt-F9, L, V.

   In the Graphics: Vertical Line screen, change the settings to the following:

Horizontal Position	Left Margin
Vertical Position	Top
Length of Line	15/16"

2. Change the font to 16-point Times Roman; press Ctrl-F8, A, C to turn on small caps; and type *HEARTH & HOME*.
3. Before you press Enter, press the right-arrow key to turn off small caps; then change the font to 9-point Times Roman. Press Enter and type the next line, *FINE FURNITURE MFG*.
4. Press Enter and type the remaining lines of the address as shown in Figure 11.3.
5. Press Enter three times; change the font to 18-point Times Roman; press Ctrl-F8, A, C to turn on small caps; and type *Computer Resource Phone List*. Press the right-arrow key to turn off small caps and then press Enter twice.
6. Press Enter. To create a horizontal line, press Alt-F9, L, H. In the Graphics: Horizontal Line screen, change the settings to the following:

Horizontal Position	Full
Vertical Position	Baseline
Width of Line	1/32"

7. Press F7 to return to the document screen.
8. Press Enter twice and define two newspaper-style columns by pressing Alt-F7, C, D. In the Text Column Definition screen, press F7, O to accept the defaults and turn on columns; then return to the document screen.

HEARTH & HOME
FINE FURNITURE MFG.
1201 Chickopee Star Route
Anseline, VT 02345
(112) 957-3642

COMPUTER RESOURCE PHONE LIST

WORDPERFECT

Bulletin Board (IBM)	801-225-4414
DrawPerfect	800-541-5098
Executive	800-321-2186
Features (5.1, 5.0)	800-541-5096
Graphics/Tables	800-321-3383
Installation (5.1, 5.0)	800-533-9605
Library/Office	800-321-3253
Macros, Merge, Labels	800-541-5129
Networks	800-321-3389
Orders	800-321-4566
Printers:	
Dot Matrix Printers	800-541-5160
Laser Printers	800-541-5170
Other Printers	800-541-5097
SoftCopy	800-526-6215
Update Info Hotline	800-321-5906

HARDWARE PROBLEMS

Ace Computer (system repair)	777-9765
T-Tech (drive repair)	775-7854
Alan Talma (modems)	775-4231

INSTRUCTION & CONSULTING

AutoCad: Nancy Peel	775-1042
Excel: Alan Schneiderman	777-0098
WordPerfect: Thelma Gutierrez	777-0504

OCR PRODUCTS

Advanced Vision Research
2201 Qume Dr.
San Jose, CA 95131

Caere Corp.
100 Cooper Ct.
Los Gatos, CA 95030

Calera Systems, Inc.
2500 Augustine Dr.
Santa Clara, CA 95054

Computer Aided Technology
7411 Hines Pl., Suite 212
Dallas, TX 75235

DataCap, Inc.
P.O. Box 5048
Evanston, IL 60204

Flagstaff Engineering, Inc.
1120 Kaibab Lane
Flagstaff, AZ 86001

Inovatic
1911 N. Fort Meyer Dr. #708
Arlington, VA 22209

Moniterm Corp.
5740 Green Circle Drive
Minnetonka, MN 55343

New Dest Corp.
1015 E. Brokaw Rd.
San Jose, CA 95131

OCR Systems
1800 Byberry Rd., Suite 1405
Huntingdon Valley, PA 19006

Ocron, Inc.
3350 Scott Blvd., Bldg 36
Santa Clara, CA 95054

Olduvai Corp.
7520 Red Rd., Suite A
S. Miami, FL 33143

FIG. 11.3 A sample directory with two sections. (Part 1 of 2)

COMPUTER RESOURCE PHONE LIST — P. 2

MONITORS

Cornerstone Technology
1883 Ringwood Ave.
San Jose, CA 95131

Moniterm
5740 Green Circle Dr.
Minnetoka, MN 55343

Princeton Publishing Labs
19 Wall St.
Princeton, NJ 08540

Sampo America
5550 Peachtree Industrial Blvd.
Norcross, GA 30071

Sigma Designs, Inc.
46501 Landing Pkwy.
Fremont, CA 94538

SCANNERS

Abaton
48431 Milmont Dr.
Fremont, CA 94538

Canon USA, Inc.
One Canon Plaza
Lake Success, NY 11042

Chicony America, Inc.
1641 W. Collins Ave.
Orange, CA 92667

Chinon America, Inc.
660 Maple Ave.
Torrance, CA 90503

CompuScan Inc.
300 Broadacres Dr.
Bloomfield, NJ 07003

Fujitsu America, Inc.
3055 Orchard Dr.
San Jose, CA 95134

Hewlett-Packard
19310 Pruneridge Ave.
Cupertino, CA 95014

Howtek, Inc.
21 Park Ave.
Hudson, NH 03051

IBM
1133 Westchester Ave.
White Plains, NY 10604

KYE International Corp.
760 Pinefalls Ave.
Walnut, CA 91789

Kyocera Unison, Inc.
1321 Harbor Bay
Alameda, CA 94501

Logitech, Inc.
6506 Kaiser Dr.
Fremont, CA 94555

Microtek Lab, Inc.
680 Knox St.
Torrance, CA 90502

Mitsubishi Electronics America, Inc.
Computer Peripherals Division
991 Knox St.
Torrance, CA 90502

New Dest Corp.
1015 E. Brokaw Rd.
San Jose, CA 95131

NISCA, Inc.
1919 Old Denton Rd.
Carrollton, TX 75006

Packard Bell
9425 Canoga Ave.
Chatsworth, CA 91311

Panasonic Industrial Co.
Two Panasonic Way
Secaucus, NJ 07094

Pentax Technologies Corp.
880 Interlocken Pkwy.
Broomfield, CO 80020

Relisys
320 S. Milpitas Blvd.
Milpitas, CA 95035

Ricoh Corp.
Peripheral Products Division
3001 Orchard Pkwy.
San Jose, CA 95134

Saba Technologies
9300 SW Gemini Dr.
Beaverton, OR 97005

Sharp Electronics Corp.
Sharp Plaza
Mahwah, NJ 07430

The Complete PC
521 Cottonwood Dr.
Milpitas, CA 95035

Truvel Corp.
8943 Fulbright Ave.
Chatsworth, CA 91311

Xerox Imaging Systems
1215 Perra Bella Ave.
Mt. View, CA 94043

DESKTOP PUBLISHING SOFTWARE

Aldus Corp.
411 First Ave. S., Suite 200
Seattle, WA 98104

Interleaf
Ten Canal Park
Cambridge, MA 02141

Xerox Desktop Software
9745 Business Park Ave.
San Diego, CA 92131

FIG. 11.3 A sample directory with two sections. (Part 2 of 2)

9. Change the font to 12-point Times Roman Bold; press Ctrl-F8, A, C to turn on small caps; and type *WORDPERFECT.* Press the right-arrow key to turn off small caps.
10. Press Enter twice, change the font to 10-point Times Roman, and type the first column of the list. Press Tab between the items and phone numbers. Press the right-arrow key to turn off small caps.
11. When you reach the end of the WordPerfect numbers, press Ctrl-Enter (Hard Page) to move to the top of column two.
12. Change the font to 12-point Times Roman Bold; press Ctrl-F8, A, C to turn on small caps; and type *HARDWARE PROBLEMS*.
13. Press Enter twice, change the font to 10-point Times Roman, and type the list in the second column, changing fonts for the "INSTRUCTION & CONSULTING" section as described in step 12.
14. At the end of the INSTRUCTION & CONSULTING section, press Alt-F7, C, F to turn columns off. Press the right-arrow key to turn off small caps.
15. Press Enter and create another horizontal line. Press Alt-F9, L, H. In the Graphics: Horizontal Line screen, change the settings to the following:

Horizontal Position	Full
Vertical Position	Baseline
Width of Line	1/32"

16. Press F7 to return to the document screen. Press Enter three times; change the font to 12-point Times Roman Bold; press Ctrl-F8, A, C to turn on small caps; and type *OCR PRODUCTS*.

Changing the Column Format

To change the directory to a three-column format for the list of suppliers, complete the following steps:

1. To define three newspaper-style columns for the OCR PRODUCTS section, press Alt-F7, C, D. In the Text Column Definition screen, change the Number of Columns setting to 3. Press F7, O to accept the defaults, turn on columns, and return to the document screen.

2. Press Enter twice, change the font to 10-point Times Roman, and type the remainder of page one, pressing Enter twice between items and allowing WordPerfect to move the cursor from one column to the next as you type.

To align the tops of the columns, check your work in View Document (Shift-F7, V) and use Enter to move the tops of columns down as needed. At the same time, you can check for addresses that WordPerfect has split between columns and use Ctrl-Enter (Hard Page) to move stray lines from the bottom of a column to the top of the next. You also can check to see whether WordPerfect has split an item between pages one and two. If an item has been split between pages, use Enter to move the split item to the top of page two.

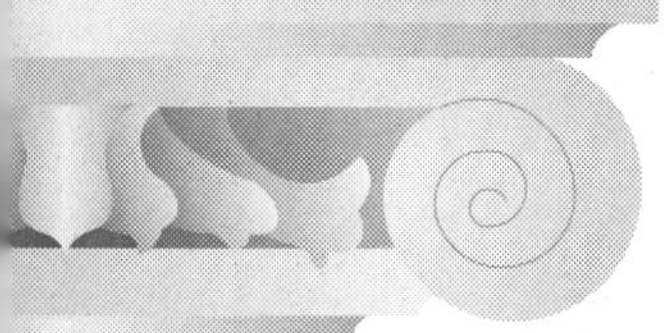

ocean stream aquarium

1000 Freshwater Way

Saline, FL 33333-4444

305 930 3963

Credit Application

BUSINESS INFORMATION	
NAME OF BUSINESS	TYPE OF BUSINESS ☐ Corporation ☐ Partnership ☐ Proprietorship
ADDRESS	CONTACT PERSON
CITY/ST/ZIP	TELEPHONE

BANK REFERENCE	
NAME OF BANK	CONTACT PERSON
BRANCH	ADDRESS
CHECKING ACCT. NO.	TELEPHONE

TRADE REFERENCES

FIRM NAME	CONTACT NAME	TELEPHONE	YRS. ACCT. OPEN

CONFIRMATION OF ACCURACY

I hereby certify that the information in this credit application is correct. The information included in this application is for use by Ocean Stream Aquarium in determining the amount and conditions of credit to be extended. I understand that Ocean Stream may also use the other sources of credit which it considers necessary in making this determination. Further I hereby authorize the bank and trade references listed in this application to release the information necessary to assist Ocean Stream Aquarium in establishing a line of credit.

Applicant's Signature ______ Applicant's Title ______ Today's Date ______

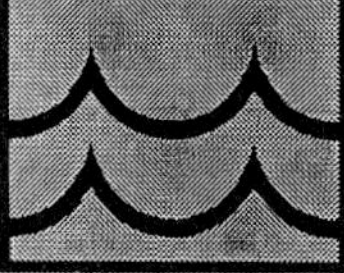

Part III

Creating Business Forms

Includes

12

Producing Invoices

The WordPerfect table feature is ideal for creating business forms. Being able to change the forms quickly is one advantage of using tables to design your business forms. If you receive an unusually large order, for example, you easily can add a few rows to your company's invoice form.

Invoice No. 1: A Time Billing Form

You create the invoice in figure 12.1 by using the table feature. With this feature, you also can expand your invoices to accommodate larger orders. The following instructions explain how to create the invoice form shown in figure 12.1.

Creating the Letterhead

As mentioned in Chapter 5, "Producing Letterheads," this chapter also includes letterheads that you can customize for your own business. To create the letterhead, do the following:

1. Press Shift-F8, P, M; type *1/2*"; press Enter; type 1"; and press Enter, F7 to set the margins.
2. To place the letterhead in a header so that the company name appears on subsequent pages, press Shift-F8, P, H, A, P.

⊗ INVOICE

⊗ THE BARRON CO.
LAN Consulting Services
11412 West Shore Drive
Raleigh, NC 30303
(999) 888-7777

INVOICE DATE

Date	Description	Time	Rate	Amount	

FIG. 12.1 An expandable invoice. (Part 1 of 2)

⊗ INVOICE P. 2

⊗ THE BARRON CO.
LAN Consulting Services
11412 West Shore Drive
Raleigh, NC 30303
(999) 888-7777

INVOICE DATE

Date	Description	Time	Rate	Amount	
			Total		

FIG. 12.1 An expandable invoice. (Part 2 of 2)

3. In the Header A editing screen, create the shaded graphic box and horizontal line at the top of the screen by pressing Alt-F9, B, O. In the Options: Text Box screen, change the settings to the following:

Border Style	Set all to None
Outside Border Space	Set all to 0"
Inside Border Space	Left 1/4", Right, Top, and Bottom 1/6"
Gray Shading	8 percent

   Although many of the boxes in other designs have 5 or 6 percent shading, this box is small and contains just one word of text in a large font; hence, the darker shading is unlikely to cause problems with readability. Using a slightly darker shade here creates a stronger design element.

4. Press F7 to return to the Header A editing screen.

5. Press Alt-F9, B, C. In the Definition: Text Box screen, change the settings to the following:

Anchor Type	Page, Number of pages to skip: 0
Vertical Position	Top
Horizontal Position	Margin, Left
Size	Set Both, 2" wide × 1/2" high

6. Press E. In the box editing screen, change the font to 18-point Times Roman.

7. Press Ctrl-V (Compose) to create the symbol. At the `Key =` prompt, type *6,80* (6, comma, 80, with no space before or after the comma). Then press Enter.

8. Press the space bar and type *INVOICE*; then press F7 twice to return to the Header A editing screen.

9. To create the horizontal line across the top of the screen, press Alt-F9, L, H. In the Graphics: Horizontal Line screen, change the settings to the following:

Horizontal Position	Set Position, 0.3"
Vertical Position	Set Position, 7/8"
Length of Line	7.9"

Width of Line	0.013"
Gray Shading	100%

10. Press F7 to return to the Header A editing screen.
11. To include the page number on subsequent pages, insert a page number code by pressing Enter; then press Alt-F6 (Flush Right).
12. Change the font to 10-point Times Roman and type *P.*; then press the space bar and Ctrl-B to insert a ^B page numbering code.

To insert the company's name, address, and the dateline, do the following:

1. Press Enter three times to position the name and address just below the horizontal line.
2. Set a tab stop 4.8" from the left side of the page to enable you to use Indent to position the graphic symbol close to the company's name. Press Shift-F8, L, T; move the cursor on the tab ruler to the 3.8" marker; and press L.
3. Press F7 twice to return to the Header A editing screen.
4. Press F4 (Indent) seven times and change the font to 18-point Times Roman. Then press Enter.
5. Press Ctrl-V (Compose) to create the symbol. At the `Key =` prompt, type *6,80* (6, comma, 80).
6. Press F6 (Indent); type the company name, *THE BARRON CO.*; and press Enter.
7. Change the font to 12-point Times Roman and type the rest of the company's name and address, pressing Enter between lines and F4 (Indent) to position the text.
8. After you enter the phone number, press Enter three times and create the horizontal line above `INVOICE DATE` by pressing Alt-F9, L, H. In the Graphics: Horizontal Line screen, change the settings to the following:

Horizontal Position	Set Position, 4.8"
Vertical Position	Baseline
Length of Line	2"

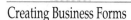

9. Press F7 to return to the Header A editing screen.

10. To create the text under the horizontal line, press Enter twice and use Advance to move the insertion point close to the line by pressing Shift-F8, O, A, U; typing *1/10"*; and pressing Enter, F7.

11. Press F4 (Indent) to position the cursor; type *INVOICE DATE* and press Enter to add space to the header.

12. Press F7 to exit the Header A editing screen and display the Format: Page screen; then press U, A to suppress header printing for page one. Press Enter to return to the Format: Page screen.

    In this invoice, the letterhead text is included in the header as well as in the main document text. As you complete an invoice, it is convenient to have the letterhead repeated on each page, as a reference in case invoice pages become separated.

    Typing an invoice date in both the document screen and the header is inconvenient. If you want to avoid this extra step, delete the dateline in the Header A screen. The invoice in figure 12.1 includes the dateline in the header because a date printed on each page of the invoice is helpful if the invoice pages become separated. If your invoices usually don't run onto subsequent pages, however, the inconvenience of not having dates in the header is slight.

13. Copy the header text onto the document screen. In the Format: Page menu, press H, A, E.

14. In the Header A editing screen, press Alt-F4, Home, Home, and the down-arrow key to block the entire header text; then press Ctrl-F4, B, C to copy the block.

15. Press F7 twice to return to the document screen and press Enter to insert the header text.

    In the Reveal Codes screen, delete the page number codes: `[Flsh Rgt][Font:Times Roman 10pt]P. ^B.`

Creating the Invoice Form

Using the table feature, create the invoice form by doing the following:

1. Press Home, Home, and the down-arrow key to move to the end of the inserted text. Press Alt-F7, T, C; type *6*; press Enter; and then type *10* and press Enter to create a table with 6 columns and 10 rows. Press F7 to exit the Table Edit menu and return to the document screen.

   Press Enter to insert additional space below "INVOICE DATE."

2. To create the table headings, move the cursor to the upper left table cell, press Shift-F6 (Center), and type *Date*.

3. Press Tab to move the cursor to the next cell, press Shift-F6 (Center), and type *Description*.

   Repeat this step for the rest of the column labels. Notice in figure 12.1 that the `Amount` label covers two columns—one column for dollars and another for cents. You must join the two cells in the first row to create this effect; instructions for joining the cells are discussed later in this chapter.

4. Press Shift-Tab to move the cursor back to the upper left cell; then press Alt-F7 to display the Table Edit menu.

5. Use Ctrl and the left- and right-arrow keys to adjust the width of the columns. (Press Tab and Shift-Tab to move right and left between cells.)

6. To delete the lines separating the cells in the row that contains the column labels (`Date`, `Description`, and so on), move the cursor to the upper left cell of the table. With the Table Edit menu displayed, press Alt-F4; then press the right-arrow key until the top row of cells is highlighted.

7. Press L, I, N to remove the inside lines across the row of cells.

8. Press Alt-F4 and the left-arrow key to highlight the top row of cells and to move the cursor to the upper left cell.

9. Press L, L, N to remove the line at the left side of the cell.

10. Press Alt-F4 and the right-arrow key to move to the rightmost cell; press L, T, N to remove the top line from the row. Then press L, R, N to remove the line at the right side of the cell.

If an invoice extends onto subsequent pages, you may want to repeat the column labels. To repeat column labels, do the following:

1. You must use the Table Edit menu to designate the top row of the table as a repeating header. Move the cursor into any cell in the top row of the table. If the Table Edit menu isn't displayed, press Alt-F7.
2. Press H. At the `Number of header rows:` prompt, press Enter to accept the default (1). WordPerfect repeats the column labels for subsequent pages.

To format your invoice with single lines, as shown in figure 12.1, do the following:

1. Move the cursor to the left cell of row two; press Alt-F4 (Block); and press Home, Home, and the down-arrow key to highlight the remainder of the table. Be careful not to start the block from row one; otherwise WordPerfect places lines around the column heading cells.
2. Press L, A, S to format all of the highlighted cells with single lines.

Notice in figure 12.1 that the `Amount` heading is centered over two columns. To create this effect, do the following:

1. To join the two rightmost columns of row one, move the cursor into the rightmost cell of the label row (row one). If the Table Edit menu isn't displayed, press Alt-F7.
2. Press Alt-F4 (Block) and the left-arrow key to highlight the rightmost two cells in row one.
3. Press J, Y to join the two cells. WordPerfect centers the Amount label in the new cell.
4. Then press L, O, N to remove the two outside lines that appear when you join the cells.

To format the `Total` line, do the following:

1. Move the cursor into the left cell of the last row of the table. If the Table Edit menu isn't displayed, press Alt-F7.

2. Press Alt-F4 (Block); then press the right-arrow key to move the cursor into the third cell from the right.
3. Press L, I, N to remove the inside lines.
4. Press Alt-F4; move the cursor into the leftmost cell; and press L, B, N to delete the bottom line of the cells.
5. Press L, L, N to remove the left line of the leftmost cell. Press F7 to exit the Table Edit screen.
6. Move the cursor into the third cell from the right of the bottom row; then press Alt-F6 (Flush Right) and type *Total*.
7. To create the double line in the Total cell, move the cursor into the rightmost cell of the bottom line. If the Table Edit menu isn't displayed, press Alt-F7.
8. Press Alt-F4 (Block); press the left-arrow key to highlight both cells; and press L, B, D to create a double line along the bottom of the cells.

   Press F7 to return to the document screen.

Adding Lines to a Table

For long invoices, you easily can add lines to the table by doing the following:

1. Move the cursor into the left cell in row two and press Alt-F7 to display the Table Edit menu.
2. Press Alt-F4, Home, and the right-arrow key to highlight the row.
3. Press P, R. At the `Number of Rows:` prompt, type the number of rows with which to replace the current row and press Enter. To create two rows, for example, type *3* and press Enter.

> **CAUTION:**
>
> Don't use the Size feature on the Table Edit menu to add rows to a table. The Size feature creates rows formatted like the bottom row of the table. If you use Size to add rows to the invoice shown in figure 12.1, for example, the new rows are formatted like the Total row.

Invoice No. 2: Product Billing

The invoice shown in figure 12.2 contains a great deal of text; however, like the invoice in figure 12.1, you easily can extend this invoice onto subsequent pages. To create table header rows to be printed on each page and to create a repeating letterhead, see the instructions for figure 12.1.

Creating the Letterhead

To create the letterhead, do the following:

1. Press Shift-F8, P, M; type *1/2*"; press Enter; type *1*"; press Enter, Enter, L, M; type *1/2*"; press Enter; type *1/2*"; and press Enter, F7 to set the margins.
2. Change the font to 30-point Times Roman and press Shift-F6 (Center).
3. Large fonts usually appear too loosely kerned (letter spaced). Tighten the letter spacing for the logotype (`Art Books, Inc.`) by pressing Shift-F8, O, P, W, O, P; type *98*; and press Enter, F7.
4. Type *Art Books, Inc.*
5. Change the font to 10-point Times Roman, press Enter, and press Shift-F6 (Center).
6. To switch to very wide letter spacing for the subheading, press Shift-F8, O, P, W, O, P; type *170*; and press Enter, F7.

TIP

By using very wide letter spacing, you can create easily and quickly an elegant, *designed* effect.

7. Type *FINE* and press the space bar twice.

Art Books, Inc.

FINE ❖ BOOKS ❖ FOR ❖ THE ❖ ARTIST

55593 W. Ocean Drive, Suite 402 Malibu, CA 90000 (800) 646-4646 (213) 464-6464

Bill to: ______________________

Ship to: ______________________

QTY	TITLE	UNIT COST	TOTAL AMOUNT
		SUBTOTAL	
		RETAIL DISC.	
		6% TAX IN CA	
		SHIPPING	
		TOTAL	

WHOLESALE CUSTOMERS

Our standard policy is a 40% discount; first orders are COD. Reorders will be invoiced at net 30 terms after an approved credit profile is on file. If you prepay your orders over $20 net, you'll get free shipping. If you place an order for more than $20 net and do not prepay, we will add a shipping charge (no handling) to your invoice. If you order less than $20 net you need to prepay your order. Please include $3 to cover shipping.

We offer volume discounts for any combination of books and other products ordered. The discount schedule is:

1-49 items:	40% discount
50-149 items:	42% discount
150+ items:	45% discount

SHIPPING

Orders are sent UPS unless you specify otherwise. Freight is always shown as your expense on your invoice, unless you have prepaid as described above.

RETURNS

Returns in resalable condition (no price stickers, undamaged, etc.) are accepted with original invoice for 1 year from date of invoice. We will issue a credit or refund within 4 weeks. Return shipping is the customer's expense. Please ship UPS.

SERVICE

Call 9-5pm PST **TOLL-FREE 800-545-7444 or FAX 916-292-3333.** We ship within 48 hours of receiving an order. If you have a problem, special request, or just want to get to know us better, give us a call.

FIG. 12.2 An invoice with a great deal more text.

8. Create the graphic symbol that separates FINE and BOOKS.

   The graphic symbol in figure 12.2 is from the Zapf Dingbat typeface, which WordPerfect assigns to character set 12 if you use a printer with Zapf Dingbats installed. See Appendix B for a list of the Zapf Dingbat assignments, which aren't documented in the WordPerfect reference manual.

   If you don't have access to Zapf Dingbats, you can choose a graphic symbol from the WordPerfect character sets. You may use number 12 from character set 5, for example. To create the symbol, press Ctrl-V (Compose). At the `Key =` prompt, type *5,12* (5, comma, 12).

9. Before you press Enter to move to the next line, change the font to 9-point Times Roman.

10. Press Enter and change letter spacing to normal by pressing Shift-F8, O, P, W, O, O, F7.

11. Press Shift-F6 (Center) and type the address, pressing the space bar twice between the address, city/state/ZIP, and telephone numbers.

12. Press Enter five times, change the font to 10-point Times Roman, and type *Bill to:*. Press Tab nine times and type *Ship to:*.

13. Press Enter; then use the underline key and the space bar to create the first horizontal line of the `Bill to:...Ship to:` section.

    Depending on your printer, you must adjust the line lengths with the underline character. As a starting point, press the underline key 45 times for each line. Press Enter twice between lines.

Creating the Invoice Form

Next you create the working section of the invoice—the table that contains space for the entry of product ordering information.

1. After creating the `Bill to:...Ship to:` section, press Enter twice.

> **TIP**
>
> Depending on the method you use to align lines, creating order forms and fill-in lines in WordPerfect with a proportionally spaced font can be extremely difficult or quite easy. Aligning the right ends of the lines is impossible if you place proportionally spaced characters in the same line with horizontal lines you created with the underline character; however, three solutions exist.
>
> With the first solution, type the text; then press Alt-F6 (Flush Right). Press the underline key until WordPerfect breaks the line with an `[SRt]` code. Use the Backspace key to delete underline characters, moving the cursor up to the row above and back again with the up-arrow and down-arrow keys until WordPerfect returns the underline characters to the preceding line. This method is frustrating and time-consuming, and good results aren't guaranteed. Although this solution seems logical, it is not recommended.
>
> With the second solution, you use the table feature to create a table with the appropriate number of rows. Type section labels in cells and use the Table Edit menu to size cells and delete vertical lines. Because you cannot adjust the size of a cell without also changing the size of its column, this method also can be troublesome. If you plan carefully, however, you can create many more cells than you need and adjust the width of each section by selectively deleting vertical lines.
>
> The third solution is the quickest and easiest. Use the underline character to create horizontal lines and place form labels (Name, Address, and so on) under or above the lines.

2. To define a table for the invoice form, press Alt-F7, T, C. At the `Number of Columns:` and `Number of Rows:` prompts, specify the number of rows and columns the table should contain. (Press Enter to leave each prompt.)

   To create figure 12.2, you need to specify a table with 12 rows and four columns. (Notice the top row that contains column headings is a table row with lines removed.)

3. Press F7 to leave the Table Edit menu.

4. Use Tab and Shift-Tab to move the cursor to the upper left table cell, press Shift-F6 (Center), and type *QTY*.

   Repeat this step for the header cells in the first row.

5. To delete the lines around the header cells, move the cursor into the left cell in row one.
6. Press Alt-F7 to display the Table Edit menu.
7. Press Alt-F4, Home, Home, and the right-arrow key to highlight the top row.
8. Press L, A, N to remove the lines from the top and sides of the cells in the row.

To create the totals section, do the following:

1. Press Alt-F7 if the Table Edit menu isn't displayed.
2. Move the cursor into the second cell from the right of the bottom row.
3. Press Alt-F4; then press the up-arrow key four times; press Home, Home, and the left-arrow key to highlight the four bottom rows and three left columns.
4. Press L, A, N to erase all the lines from the blocked cells. Notice that WordPerfect also removes the line from the top of the blocked section; you must restore this line.
5. To restore the line from the blocked section, move the cursor to the cell in the left column just below the line to be restored. Press Alt-F4 (Block) and the right-arrow key to highlight the cells with the missing line.
6. Press L, T, S to restore the single top line.

To format the table with single lines rather than WordPerfect's default double outside lines, do the following:

1. Move the cursor to the cell just below the first header label (QTY).
2. Press Alt-F7 if the Table Edit menu isn't displayed.
3. Press Alt-F4 and use the arrow keys to highlight the sections of the table to be formatted with single lines.
4. Press L, A, S to change any double lines to single lines.

To create a double line at the bottom of the TOTAL cell, do the following:

1. Move the cursor into the TOTAL cell.
2. Press Alt-F7 if the Table Edit menu isn't displayed.
3. Press L, B, D to create the double line.

To create the labels for the totals section, do the following:

1. If the Table Edit menu is displayed, press Exit to return to the table text typing mode.
2. Move the cursor into the SUBTOTAL cell, press Alt-F6 (Flush Right), and type *SUBTOTAL*. Repeat for the rest of the totals section.

To create the ordering information text at the bottom of the page, do the following:

1. Move the cursor below the table, press Enter, and define two newspaper-style columns by pressing Alt-F7, C, D. In the Text Column Definition screen, press Enter, O to accept the defaults, turn columns on, and return to the document screen.
2. To justify the text, press Shift-F8, L, J, F, F7.
3. Type the text shown in figure 12.2.

   Press F6 to turn on bold, press Enter twice between paragraphs, use Tab to format the discount table, and press Ctrl-Enter (Hard Page) to move from column one to column two.

If you receive large orders, you may need to expand the invoice by adding rows to the table. The earlier section, "Adding Lines to a Table," explains how to expand a table.

To create long invoices with this format, you can provide table headers and repeat the letterhead on subsequent pages. For specific steps, see the instructions for the invoice in figure 12.1.

13

Producing Fax Cover Sheets

Just because fax covers are simple doesn't mean that these covers must look unattractive. Some fax covers don't present relevant information in an easily accessible form: useful phone numbers are relegated to the bottom of the page; sections that belong together are randomly placed on the form; and so on. The two fax covers presented in this chapter represent an attempt to meet the requirements of good design in a functional way.

Fax Cover No. 1: A Generic Fax Form

You can customize the fax form shown in figure 13.1 by replacing the moving company's letterhead with your own. Clearly, much more time and effort went into creating the company logo than the transmittal information lines. If you need an all-purpose cover, you can use this form to create your own simple and attractive template.

Creating the Letterhead

To create the company logo, do the following:

1. Set the margins by pressing Shift-F8, P, M; typing *1/2*"; pressing Enter; typing *1*"; pressing Enter, Enter, L, M; typing *1/2*"; pressing Enter; typing *1/2*"; and pressing Enter, F7.

FAX

2455 Industrial Blvd. · City of Industry, CA 90222 · Voice: (213) 789-0987 · Fax: (213) 789-0876

Date

Attention

Company

From

Number of pages (including this page)

Message:

FIG. 13.1 A simple, yet attractive, fax cover.

2. To create the wide, shaded horizontal line at the top of the page (the "road"), press Alt-F9, L, H. In the Graphics: Horizontal Line screen, change the settings to the following:

Horizontal Position	Full
Vertical Position	Set Position, 1 1/4"
Width of line	1/4"
Gray Shading	20%

3. Press F7 to return to the document screen.
4. To create a figure box for the image of the truck, press Alt-F9, F, O. In the Graphics: Figure screen, change the settings to the following:

Border Style	Set all to None
Outside Border Space	Set all to 0 inch
Inside Border Space	Set all to 0 inch
Gray Shading	0%

5. Press F7 to return to the document screen.
6. Press Alt-F9, F, C. In the Definition: Figure screen, change the settings to the following:

Filename	SEMI.WPG
Anchor Type	Page, Number of pages to skip: 0
Vertical Position	Top
Horizontal Position	Set Position, 2"
Size	Set Both, 1 3/4" wide × 1" high

   The figure is from the DrawPerfect Figure Library.

7. Press F7 to return to the document screen.
8. Press Alt-F7, C, D to define newspaper-style columns for the logotype (Gentle Motion Movers). In the Text Column Definition menu, change the first two margin settings to 1/2" and 2".

   Although you can position the logotype by placing it in a text box, temporarily changing the margins, or using Tab Align, using columns is the quickest way.

9. Press F7, O to turn columns on and return to the document screen. Notice that `Gentle Motion Movers` is tightly leaded (spaced vertically). To create this effect, you must use the Leading Adjust feature.

10. Change the font to 24-point Palatino; then press Shift-F8, O, P, L, Enter; type *–8p*; and press Enter, F7 to adjust the leading.

    If you omit the *p*, WordPerfect subtracts 8 inches from the line leading and prints the lines on top of each other.

11. Press Alt-F6 (Flush Right), type *Gentle*, and press Enter.

12. Press Alt-F6 (Flush Right), type *Motion*, and press Enter.

13. To create the graphic of a heart at the start of the third line of the logotype (Movers), press Alt-F6 (Flush Right). Press Ctrl-V (Compose); at the `Key =` prompt, type *5,0* (5, comma, 0). Then press Enter.

14. Type *Movers* and press Alt-F9, C, F to turn columns off.

15. Press Enter. Press Alt-F6 (Flush Right). Change the font to 10-point Palatino and type the address line. Separate the street, city, and so on, as shown in figure 13.1.

    To create a bullet, press the space bar twice. Press Ctrl-V (Compose); at the `Key =` prompt, type *4,3* (4, comma, 3). Then press Enter.

16. At the end of the address line, press Shift-F8, O, P, L, 0, Enter, 0, Enter, F7 to change the line spacing back to normal.

17. Press Enter and use Advance to position the insertion point just above the thick, shaded horizontal line. Press Shift-F8, O, A, I; type *1"*; and press Enter, F7.

18. Press Alt-F6 (Flush Right), change the font to 24-point Palatino, type *FAX*, and press Enter.

Creating the Information Transmittal Section

Creating the remainder of the fax form is simple, because the rest of the form contains only information entry lines and titles. Complete the following steps:

1. Press Shift-F8, O, A, I; type *2.5"*; and press Enter, F7 to move the insertion point down for the date line.
2. To enter the date line, change the font to 12-point Palatino and use the underline key to create a horizontal line.
3. Check the length of the line in the View Document screen (Shift-F7, V). Adjust the line's length by adding or deleting underline keystrokes.

TIP

Using the underline character to create horizontal lines whose length and position don't have to be precisely defined is much quicker than using the graphics horizontal line feature.

4. Press Enter and type *Date*.
5. Press Enter twice and use the underline key to create the first horizontal line that spans the page width. Turn on Reveal codes (Alt-F3) and press the underline key until WordPerfect breaks the line with a `[DSRt]` (dormant soft return) code.
6. Press Backspace until WordPerfect replaces the `[DSRt]` with an `[HRt]` (hard return) code. Repeat the process for the remainder of the lines on the page.

TIP

You can save time spent drawing repeated horizontal lines by blocking the first line, saving it to a file, and retrieving the line to create other lines. Move the cursor to the line to save and then press Home, the left-arrow key, Alt-F4, End, F10. Type a single-letter file name, such as *L*, and press Enter. To retrieve the line, press Shift-F10, type the file name, and press Enter.

Fax Cover No. 2: A Company-Specific Fax Form

The fax cover shown in figure 13.2 includes a line for department locations; this cover is an example of how you can use space optimally and attractively, even though an existing design (the letterhead) would seem to preclude it.

The solution lies in "sticking to the grid." The *grid*—the foundation on which page elements are placed—provides a visually satisfying sense of order by aligning elements consistently on the page. For more information on using grids, refer to Chapter 3, "Understanding Page Design."

Notice in figure 13.2 how many elements are aligned. `FAX TRANSMISSION`, `To`, `Location`, `Voice #`, `Fax #`, and the comment lines at the bottom of the page are aligned flush-right. The words and lines in the From section (`From`, `Location`, `Voice #`, and `Fax #`) at the left of the page are left-aligned with the `COMMENTS:` section.

Although the logotype and `Number of pages` sections are not aligned flush right or left, the page still appears well-organized. The predominance of alignments enables you to break the rules slightly, without destroying the overall impression of order.

Creating the Letterhead

To create the letterhead, do the following:

1. Press Shift-F8, P, M; type *1/2*"; press Enter; type *1*"; press Enter, Enter, L, M; type *1/2*"; press Enter; type *1/2*"; and press Enter, F7 to set the margins.

2. Press Alt-F7, C, D, and in the Text Column Definition screen, change the margins to 1/2", 3 1/4", 4 1/2", 8". (You center the letterhead in a column on the left side of the page.)

3. Press F7, O to turn columns on and return to the document screen.

LPCP

LandPro
Commercial
Properties

5793 LANDING BAY CIRCLE
ATLANTIC COMMONS, MA 01234-6453
VOICE: (102) 777-8765
FAX: (102) 777-8766

FAX TRANSMISSION

To

Location

Voice #

Fax #

From

Location

Voice #

Fax #

Number of pages (including this page)

Date

Time

COMMENTS:

FIG. 13.2 A fax cover designed for company-specific information.

4. To create the vertical line to the right of the letterhead, press Alt-F9, L, V. In the Graphics: Vertical Line screen, change the settings to the following:

Horizontal Position	Between columns, Column 1
Vertical Position	Top
Length of Line	3"

5. Press F7 to return to the document screen.

6. Press Shift-F8, O, P, L, Enter; type *–5p*; and press Enter, F7 to tighten the leading (line spacing) of "LandPro Commercial Properties". If you tighten the leading here, you also tighten the space between LPCP and LandPro.

   Don't forget the *p*; otherwise, WordPerfect deletes inches instead of points, and the lines print on top of each other.

7. Change the font to 80-point Times Roman.

8. Tighten the spacing of the letters in the logotype. (Large fonts usually appear too loose and must be tightened.) Press Shift-F8, O, P, W, O, P; type *95*; and press Enter, F7.

9. Press Shift-F8, L, J, C, F7 to turn on center justification; then type *LPCP*.

10. Before pressing Enter, change the font to 30-point Times Roman. Press Enter, type *LandPro*, press Enter, type *Commercial*, press Enter, and type *Properties*.

11. Change the leading (line spacing) back to normal by pressing Shift-F8, O, P, L, Enter, 0, Enter, F7.

12. Change the font to 9-point Times Roman.

13. Press Enter twice and type the address, as shown in figure 13.2.

14. Press Shift-F8, L, J, L, F7 to change to left justification.

15. Press Ctrl-Enter (Hard Page) to move to the top of the next column.

Creating the Information Transmittal Section

Use the following steps to create the information entry section of the fax form:

1. Change the font to 14-point Times Roman Bold; press Alt-F6 (Flush Right); and type *FAX TRANSMISSION*.

2. Before pressing Enter, change the font to 12-point Times Roman.

3. Press Enter five times, press Alt-F6 (Flush Right), and use the underline key to create the horizontal line above `To`.

   The number of underline keystrokes for the line depends on your printer. Press the underline key 35 times and then check your work in the View Document screen (Shift-F7, V). Adjust the line length as needed.

4. Press Enter, Alt-F6 (Flush Right), and type *To*. Repeat this step to create lines for Location, Voice #, and Fax #. Be sure to press Enter twice before each horizontal line, as shown in figure 13.2.

5. At the end of the To section, press Alt-F7, C, F to turn columns off.

6. Press Enter four times and define two newspaper-style columns by pressing Alt-F7, C, D. In the Text Column Definition screen, change the margins to 1/2", 3 1/4", 4 1/2", 8".

7. Press F7, O to turn columns on and return to the document screen.

8. Press the underline key to create the line above "From." The number of keystrokes depends on your printer. Press the underline key 35 times; then check your work in the Document View screen (Shift-F7). Adjust the line length by adding or deleting underline keystrokes as needed.

9. Press Enter and type *From*.

   Repeat steps 8 and 9 to create the lines for Location, Voice #, and Fax #. Be sure to press enter twice before each horizontal line.

10. After the Fax # line, press Ctrl-Enter (Hard Page) to move the cursor to column two.
11. Press the underline key to create the line above "Number of pages (including this page)." The number of keystrokes depends on your printer. Press underline 35 times; then check your work in the View Document screen (Shift-F7, V). Add or delete underline characters as needed.
12. Press Enter and type *Number of pages (including this page)*. Repeat the process for the Date and Time lines, pressing Enter twice before each line.
13. After the Time label, press Alt-F7, C, F to turn columns off and move the cursor to the left margin.
14. Press Enter three times, type *COMMENTS:*, and press Enter twice.
15. Press Alt-F3 to turn on Reveal Codes; then press the underline key to create a horizontal line across the page. Press the key until WordPerfect breaks the line and displays a `[DSRt]` (dormant soft return) code.
16. Carefully press Backspace until WordPerfect replaces `[DSRt]` with an `[HRt]` (hard return) code.

    To speed the process of creating multiple lines, save the line to a file and retrieve it to create other lines.
17. Check your work with View Document (Shift-F7, V).

14

Producing Memo Forms

To get an idea of how many ways you can design a memo form, look in the Yellow Pages where you will find hundreds of business categories, each listing dozens of companies, each of which probably has at least one company-specific memo form. You can create personal memos containing your name, department memos expressing pride in a department's products, and generic memos containing general information only. You also can create specialized memos that make routing messages through a labyrinth of company mail stops easier.

Because most message forms are small, both samples provided in this chapter are laid out sideways (in *landscape mode*) on an 8 1/2-by-11-inch sheet of paper. Printing documents in landscape mode isn't very complicated; however, you must fine-tune the spacing of page elements. The examples in this chapter can serve you well if you need to create other two-up forms.

Memo Form No. 1: A Generic Memo

This section shows you a simple way to place two designs side by side on a page (see fig. 14.1). For this example, you place the second copy of the design in a text box.

INDUSTRIAL
TOOL & HOIST
▾ SALES ▾ SERVICE ▾ REPAIR
9999 Alondra Hwy. Compton, CA 90200 (213) 455-6667

TO: ______
FROM: ______
DATE: ______
TIME: ______
RE: ______
COMMENTS: ______

▾ Air Hoists
▾ Electric Hoists
▾ Hand Chain Hoists
▾ Winches
▾ Jib & Gantry Cranes
▾ Slings & Accessories

INDUSTRIAL
TOOL & HOIST
▾ SALES ▾ SERVICE ▾ REPAIR
9999 Alondra Hwy. Compton, CA 90200 (213) 455-6667

TO: ______
FROM: ______
DATE: ______
TIME: ______
RE: ______
COMMENTS: ______

▾ Air Hoists
▾ Electric Hoists
▾ Hand Chain Hoists
▾ Winches
▾ Jib & Gantry Cranes
▾ Slings & Accessories

FIG. 14.1 A generic memo.

Although you can use text columns, the text box method is easier. The text box editor does have some limitations: you cannot check your progress in View Document, and you must repeatedly enter and exit the editor. With the text box, however, you can make all your changes in the document screen and copy the new version in its entirety into the text box editor. Adjusting boxes vertically on the page is much easier than moving text up and down in columns. Most importantly, with the text box editor, you can place tables in a box, a capability that does not exist if you use columns.

To begin this memo, set the margins and select the landscape mode by doing the following:

1. Press Shift-F8, P, S; then move the cursor to `Standard - Wide`; and press Enter, F7 to select the landscape paper size/type definition that comes with WordPerfect.
2. Press Shift-F8, P, M; type *1/2*"; press Enter; type *1/2*"; press Enter, Enter, L, M; type *1/2*"; press Enter; type *6*"; and press Enter, F7 to set the margins.

Creating the Graphic

Again, this design uses a figure from the DrawPerfect Figure Library, because the image collection supplied with WordPerfect doesn't contain a suitable graphic.

To create the memo's graphics, do the following:

1. To create the image of the cogs on the left side of the page, press Alt-F9, F, O. In the Options: Figure screen, change the settings to the following:

Border Style	Set all to None
Outside Border Space	Set all to 0"
Inside Border Space	Set all to 0"
Gray Shading	0%

2. Press F7 to return to the document screen.
3. To import the figure, press Alt-F9, F, C. In the Definition: Figure screen, change the settings to the following:

Filename	COGS.WPG

Anchor Type	Page, Number of pages to skip: 0
Vertical Position	Set Position, 7/8"
Horizontal Position	Set Position, .3"
Size	Set Both, 1 1/4" wide × 1 1/4" high
Wrap Text Around Box	No

4. Press E. In the figure editing screen. press R (Rotate); at the `Enter number of degrees` prompt, type *350* and press Enter. At the `Mirror image?` prompt, press N.

   WordPerfect rotates the image.

5. Press F7 twice to return to the document screen.

6. To create a second copy of the gears image on the right side of the page, press Alt-F9, F, C. In the Definition: Figure screen, change the settings to the following:

Filename	COGS.WPG
Anchor Type	Page, Number of pages to skip: 0
Vertical Position	Set Position, 7/8"
Horizontal Position	Set Position, 5 3/4"
Size	Set Both, 1 1/4" wide × 1 1/4" high
Wrap Test Around Box	No

7. Press E. In the figure editing screen, press R (Rotate); at the `Enter number of degrees` prompt, type *350* and press Enter. At the `Mirror image?` prompt, press N.

8. Press F7 twice to return to the document screen.

Creating Text Boxes

To enter the text at the bottom of the memo, do the following:

1. Create a text box for the text at the bottom of the left page by pressing Alt-F9, B, O. In the Options: Text Box screen, change the settings to the following:

Border Style	Set all to None
Outside Border Space	Set all to 0"
Inside Border Space	Set all to 0"
Gray Shading	0%

2. Press F7 to return to the document screen.
3. Press Alt-F9, B, C. In the Definition: Text Box screen, change the settings to the following:

Anchor Type	Page, Number of pages to skip: 0
Vertical Position	Set Position, 6 3/4"
Horizontal Position	Margin, Left
Size	Set Both, 2" wide × 1.45" high

(The decimal figure was determined by experimentation.)

4. Press E; the text box editor appears. Change the font to 12-point Palatino Bold.
5. Create the downward-pointing triangle graphic by pressing Ctrl-V (Compose). At the `Key =` prompt, type *6,30* (6, comma, 30). Then press Enter.
6. Press the space bar, type *Air Hoists*, and press Enter.
7. Repeat steps 5 and 6 to complete the list.
8. Press F7 twice to return to the document screen.
9. Create a text box for a second product list at the bottom of the right side of the screen by pressing Alt-F9, B, C. In the Definition: Text Box screen, change the settings to the following:

Anchor Type	Page, Number of pages to skip: 0
Vertical Position	Set Position, 6 3/4"
Horizontal Position	Set Position, 6"
Size	Set Both, 2" wide × 1.45" high

10. Press F7 to return to the document screen.

11. To copy the text from the box you created earlier to the box on the right, press Alt-F9, B, E, 1, Enter, E. Press Alt-F4 (Block), Home, Home, the down-arrow key, Ctrl-F4, B, C, F7, F7. Press Alt-F9, B, E, 2, Enter, E, Enter to insert the copy in the text box editor.
12. Press F7 twice to return to the document screen.

Creating the Logotype

To create the logotype, do the following:

1. Change the font to 24-point Palatino Bold and set a tab to position the logotype about 1/4 inch to the right of the image of the gears. Press Shift-F8, L, T; press the right-arrow key to move the cursor two spaces to the right of the `+1` marker on the tab ruler; press L.
2. Press F7 twice to return to the document screen.
3. Press Enter, press Tab three times, and type *INDUSTRIAL*. Press Enter, press Tab three times, and type *TOOL & HOIST*.
4. Before pressing Enter at the end of the line, change the font to 12-point Palatino Bold.
5. Press Enter, press Tab three times, and type the next line (*SALES*...), including the inverted triangles.

   To create the upside-down triangles, press Ctrl-V (Compose); at the `Key =` prompt, type *6,30* (6, comma, 30) and press Enter. Press the space bar once between each triangle and the following word; press the space bar three times between SALES and SERVICE and the following triangles.
6. Before pressing Enter to move to the next line, change the font to 9-point Palatino.
7. Press Enter, press Tab three times, and type the address, pressing the space bar twice between the street, city/state/ZIP, and phone number.
8. Before you press Enter at the end of the address line, change the font to 12-point Palatino; then press Enter three times.

Creating the Body of the Memo

Use the underline key to create the lines that follow the labels TO:, FROM:, DATE:, TIME:, RE:, and COMMENTS:, and align the labels flush right at the start of each line. How can you align the labels flush right at the start of each line? It's simpler than you may think, and you can use the method whenever you want to create lines of equal length with flush-right labels.

To align the labels flush right and to create the lines following the label, do the following:

1. Change the Tab Align character to a blank space (a single press of the space bar). Press Shift-F8, O, D; then press the space bar, Enter, F7. WordPerfect inserts a [Decml/Algn Char::,,] code in the Reveal Codes screen.

2. To create the first horizontal line with its flush-right label, press Tab, Ctrl-F6 (Tab Align). WordPerfect displays the message Align char = in the status line.

3. Type *TO:*. As you type, the characters move to the left.

4. Turn on Reveal Codes (Alt-F3), press the space bar, and press the underline key to create the horizontal line.

   Press the underline key slowly, one tap at time. When WordPerfect reaches the end of the line, the program moves the line down and inserts a [SRt] (soft return) code after the label. You must make WordPerfect move the horizontal line back up to the TO: label.

5. With the cursor still at the end of the horizontal line, press Backspace once; then press the up-arrow key to move the cursor onto the [SRt] code.

6. Press the space bar and then Del to delete the [SRt] code. If WordPerfect moves the line and removes the [SRt] code, you are finished.

   If WordPerfect removes the space you just entered, retains the [SRt] code, and moves the cursor down to the horizontal line, press Home, the right-arrow key, Backspace, the up-arrow key, the space bar, Del. Repeat the process until WordPerfect moves the horizontal line to its proper position, next to the label.

7. To save to a temporary file the line you just created, move the cursor to the start of the horizontal line and press Alt-F4, Home, Home, the right-arrow key, F10. Type the name of a temporary file and press Enter.
8. To create the next line, press Enter twice; then press Tab, Ctrl-F6 (Tab Align). WordPerfect displays the `Align char =` message in the status line.
9. Type *FROM:* and press the space bar.
10. To retrieve the horizontal line, press Shift-F10, type the name of the temporary file containing the copy of the horizontal line, and press Enter. The line appears next to the label.
11. Press Home, Home, and the right-arrow key to move to the end of the line. Press Enter, Enter, and repeat the process to enter the rest of the labels.
12. After you create the last line with a flush-right label (`RE:`), press Enter twice and type the next line label (*COMMENTS:*).
13. Press the space bar; then turn on Reveal Codes (Alt-F3).
14. Press the underline key (slowly!) until WordPerfect moves the line down and inserts a `[SRt]` code after the label. Repeat the process described in steps 4, 5, and 6 to return the horizontal line to the right of the label.
15. Press Enter twice. To create the first blank line below the last label (`COMMENTS:`), turn on Reveal Codes (Alt-F3) and press the underline key until WordPerfect inserts a `[DSRt]` (dormant soft return) code.
16. Press Backspace slowly until the `[DSRt]` code disappears. Repeat the process for the remaining lines on the page, checking your progress with View Document (Shift-F7, V).

Copying the Design

When you are satisfied with the design on the left side of the page, copy the design into a box on the right side of the page by doing the following:

1. Turn on Reveal Codes (Alt-F3) and press Home, Home, Home, and the up-arrow key to move the cursor to the top of

the screen, preceding the hidden codes; then move the cursor so that it follows the `[Text Box:2;;]` code.

2. Press Alt-F9, B, C. In the Definition: Text Box screen, change the settings to the following:

Anchor Type	Page, Number of pages to skip: 0
Vertical Position	Top
Horizontal Position	Set Position, 6"
Size	Auto Both, 4.7" (wide) × 7.45" (high)

The Size figures—4.7" (wide) × 7.45" (high)—appear only after you copy the page design into the box editor.

3. Press F7 to return to the editing screen.
4. With Reveal Codes turned on, move the cursor onto the `[Font:Palatino Bold 24pt]` code. Press Alt-F4; press Home, Home, the down-arrow key, Ctrl-F4, B, C.
5. Press Home, Home, Home, and the up-arrow key and move the cursor onto the `[Text Box:3;;]` code.
6. Press Alt-F9, B, E, 3, E, Enter to insert the copy of the page design into the box.
7. Press F7 twice to return to the document screen. Use View Document (Shift-F7, V) to check your work.

Memo Form No. 2: Service Call Table

A look at the Reveal Codes screen for the memo form in figure 14.2 is indeed revealing: just 14 codes and no text! Except for paper size/type and margin codes, the entire form, including the tables, is contained in graphic boxes. A major advantage of using text boxes instead of columns to place two copies of a design side by side on a page is that WordPerfect doesn't enable you to place tables in columns.

With WordPerfect's table feature, you can create all kinds of business forms, and memo forms are no exception. By adding and deleting cells and lines, you can create virtually any arrangement of lines and boxes for text entry. This sample memo uses a table for a customer service call record.

To begin creating the design, choose a landscape paper size/type and set the margins. Press Shift-F8, P, S; move the cursor to `Standard - wide` and press Enter. Then press M; type *.3*"; press Enter; type *1/2*"; press Enter, Enter, L, M; type *1/2*"; press Enter; type *6*"; and press Enter, F7.

Creating the Graphics

To create a box for the graphic image of a sun on the left side of the page, do the following:

1. Press Alt-F9, B, O. In the Options: Text Box screen, change the settings to the following:

Border Style	Set all to None
Outside Border Space	Set all to 0"
Inside Border Space	Set all to 0"
Gray Shading	0%

2. Press F7 to return to the document screen.
3. Press Alt-F9, B, C. In the Definition: Text Box screen, change the settings to the following:

Filename	SUN.WPG
Anchor Type	Page, Number of pages to skip: 0
Vertical Position	Top
Horizontal Position	Margin, Left
Size	Set Width/Auto Height 7/8" wide × 0.918" (high)

4. Press F7 to return to the document screen.

LightWorks Industrial Lighting Wholesale & Retail

Incandescent · Fluorescent · Quartz · Mercury Vapor
Miniature · Metal Halide · High Pressure Sodium
Sealed Beams · Photo Lamps · Stage & Studio

SERVICE/DELIVERY CALL MEMO DATE ____

Customer	Phone	Job	Time

Call for Next-Day Delivery.
Voice: (800) · 999 · 8888
Fax: (321) · 678 · 5170

1073 E. Market Blvd. N.
Platte City · ND 50303

LightWorks Industrial Lighting Wholesale & Retail

Incandescent · Fluorescent · Quartz · Mercury Vapor
Miniature · Metal Halide · High Pressure Sodium
Sealed Beams · Photo Lamps · Stage & Studio

SERVICE/DELIVERY CALL MEMO DATE ____

Customer	Phone	Job	Time

Call for Next-Day Delivery.
Voice: (800) · 999 · 8888
Fax: (321) · 678 · 5170

1073 E. Market Blvd. N.
Platte City · ND 50303

FIG. 14.2 A memo containing tables.

TIP

You can place images in figure boxes or text boxes. This figure is in a text box because it is convenient to have boxes numbered consecutively in Reveal Codes. (Whether you place an image in a text or figure box, WordPerfect includes the graphic image file name in the hidden code, that is, `[Text Box:1;SUN.WPG;]`.)

Creating the Logotype

To create the box for the company name and subtitle, do the following:

1. Press Alt-F9, B, C. In the Definition: Text Box screen, change the settings to the following:

Anchor Type	Page, Number of pages to skip: 0
Vertical Position	Set Position, .4"
Horizontal Position	Set Position, 1 3/8"
Size	Set Both, 3 9/16" wide × 1" high
Wrap Text Around Box	No

2. Press E. In the box editing screen, create the company name and subtitle. Next, define two newspaper columns, one to hold "LightWorks" and the other for "Industrial Lighting/ Wholesale & Retail."
3. Press Alt-F7, C, D. Change the margins to 0 inch, 1 3/4 inch, 1 13/16 inch, 3 9/16 inch.
4. Press F7, O to turn on columns and return to the text box editor.
5. Change the font to 29-point Avant Garde Gothic Demi.

   Notice that the letters in `LightWorks` are spaced very closely. Because large fonts tend to appear loose, you must tighten the spacing with the Word/Letter Spacing feature. For this memo, make the letters extra tight for a "designed" effect.

6. To tighten the space between letters, press Shift-F8, O, P, W, O, P; type *90*; and press Enter, F7.
7. Type *Light*.
8. Some letters, such as the "W" and "o" in LightWorks require particular attention to their spacing. For this memo, space the letters individually. Press Shift-F8, O, P, W, O, P; type *75*; press Enter, F7 to change the letter spacing.
9. Type *W*.
10. Change the letter spacing by pressing Shift-F8, O, P, W, O, P; type *90*; and press Enter, F7.
11. Type *orks*.
12. Return letter spacing to normal by pressing Shift-F8, O, P, W, O, O, F7.
13. Press Enter (Hard Page) to move the cursor to the top of the second column and change the font to 12-point Avant Garde Gothic Demi.
14. Press Shift-F8, O, A, U; type *3/8"*; and press F7 to use the Advance feature to position the subtitle.
15. Type *Industrial Lighting*, press Enter, and type *Wholesale & Retail*.
16. Press F7 twice to return to the document screen.

Creating the Product List and Company Address

To create a box for the product list, do the following:

1. Press Alt-F9, B, C. In the Definition: Text Box screen, change the settings to the following:

Anchor Type	Page, Number of pages to skip: 0
Vertical Position	Set Position, 9/16"
Horizontal Position	Set Position, 1 3/8"
Size	Auto Both, 5" (wide) × 0.83" (high)
Wrap Text Around Box	No

WordPerfect enters the dimensions of the text box after you create the text.

2. Press E. In the text box editor, enter the text for the product list. Change the font to 8-point Avant Garde Gothic Book, press Enter twice, and type the list as shown in figure 14.2.

   To create the bullets between items, press Ctrl-V (Compose); at the Key = prompt, type *4,3* (4, comma, 3) and press Enter. Press Enter at the end of each line.

3. Press F7 twice to return to the document screen.

To create a box for the company's phone number and address at the bottom of the page, do the following:

1. Press Alt-F9, B, C. In the Definition: Text Box screen, change the settings to the following:

Anchor Type	Page, Number of pages to Skip: 0
Vertical Position	Bottom
Horizontal Position	Margin, Left
Size	Auto Both, 2.25" (wide) × 0.915" (high)

   WordPerfect enters the dimensions for the box after you create the text.

2. Press E. In the box editor, type the text. Change the font to 9-point Avant Garde Gothic Demi and type *Call for Next-Day Delivery*.

3. Press Enter and type the next line, using Compose to create the bullets that separate the parts of the phone number.

4. Press F7 twice to return to the document screen.

Creating the Table

To create the table, do the following:

1. Create a box for the table by pressing Alt-F9, B, C. In the Definition: Text Box screen, change the settings to the following:

Anchor Type	Page, Number of pages to skip: 0
Vertical Position	Set Position, 1 3/8"

Horizontal Position	Margin, Left
Size	Set Width/Auto Height, 4.5" wide × 5.53" (high)

WordPerfect inserts the box dimensions after you create the text.

2. Press E. In the text box editor, create the table by pressing Alt-F7, T, C. At the `Number of Columns:` prompt, type *4* and press Enter. At the `Number of Rows:` prompt, type *19* and press Enter.

   The top row of the table holds the title (SERVICE/DELIVERY CALL MEMO...DATE) in a single borderless cell, which you will create soon.

3. When you create a table, WordPerfect displays the Table Edit menu. Press O, P, F, Enter, to specify a table as wide as the margins.

4. Move the cursor into the top left cell. Press Alt-F4 and press the right-arrow key three times to highlight the top row of cells.

5. Press J, Y to join the cells in the top row.

6. With the cursor in the top row, press L, A, N to erase the lines on the top and sides of the cell.

7. Press F7 to leave the Table Edit menu.

8. Change the font to 12-point Avant Garde Gothic Demi and type *SERVICE/DELIVERY CALL MEMO*.

   Use the underline key to create the date entry line.

9. Press Alt-F6 (Flush Right) and type *DATE*; then press the underline key 12 times to create a horizontal line for the date.

10. Move the cursor into the left cell in the second row. Press Alt-F7 to display the Table Edit menu.

11. Press Alt-F4 and the right-arrow key three times to highlight the row. Press L, B, D to make a double line under the cells.

    Press Alt-F4 and the left-arrow key three times to highlight the row. Press L, J, D to make a double line over the cells.

12. Use Ctrl plus the right-arrow key and Ctrl plus the left-arrow key to adjust the size of the cells.

> **TIP**
>
> If you use Ctrl plus the arrow keys to change cell size, adjust the size of the rightmost cell first. If you enlarge other cells, WordPerfect may "squeeze" the rightmost cell to a minimum size and not enable you to enlarge this cell without first shrinking other cells.

13. Press F7 to leave the Table Edit menu.
14. Move the cursor into the left cell in row two, change the font to 9-point Avant Garde Gothic Demi, press Shift-F6 (Center), and type *Customer*.
15. Repeat the process to type the rest of the labels in row two, as shown in figure 14.2.
16. Press F7 twice to return to the document screen.

Copying the Memo

You now can create boxes for the figure and text on the right side of the page. An easy way to begin is to copy the codes for the figure and text boxes you created and then edit the horizontal position settings in the box definition screens.

To copy boxes for the figure and text, do the following:

1. Turn on Reveal codes (Alt-F3). Move the cursor to the first text box code (`[Text Box:1;SUN.WPG;]`). Press Alt-F4 (Block). Press Home, Home, and the down-arrow key to highlight all the box codes.
2. Press Ctrl-F4, B, C, Enter to insert a copy of the codes at the end of the document.
3. To edit the Horizontal Position settings for the boxes, move the cursor onto the `[Text Box:6;;]` code and press Alt-F9, B, E, Enter. In the Definition: Text Box screen, change the Horizontal Position setting to Set Position, 6 7/8".
4. Press F7 to return to the document screen.
5. Move the cursor onto the next box code (`[Text Box:7; SUN.WPG;]`) and press Alt-F9, B, E, Enter. In the Definition:

Text Box screen, change the Horizontal Position setting to 6 inches.

6. Press F7 to return to the document screen.
7. Move the cursor onto the next box code (`[Text Box:8;;]`) and press Alt-F9, B, E, Enter. In the Definition: Text Box screen, change the Horizontal Position setting to 6".
8. Press F7 to return to the document screen.
9. Move the cursor onto the next box code (`[Text Box:9;;]`) and press Alt-F9, B, E, Enter. In the Definition: Text Box screen, change the Horizontal Position setting to 6 7/8".
10. Press F7 to return to the document screen.
11. Move the cursor onto the next box code (`[Text Box:10;;]`) and press Alt-F9, B, E, Enter. In the Definition: Text Box screen, change the Horizontal Position setting to 6".
12. Press F7 to return to the document screen.
13. Check your work in the View Document Screen (Shift-F7, V).

15

Producing Time Sheets

Like memo forms and fax covers, time sheets can be as simple or as complex as you want to make them. The samples in this chapter provide two simple designs that you can customize for horizontal or vertical company letterheads.

Time Sheet No. 1: Employee Billable Hours

The time sheet pictured in figure 15.1 uses a table placed in a text box to set the form area clearly apart from the letterhead. The effect is professional, although the design is quite simple.

You can adapt the basic layout to place many other forms on vertical or horizontal letterhead. The design also shows you how to place a table in a column, which WordPerfect usually doesn't enable you to do, by first placing the table in a box.

Creating the Table

When you design the table, you start by setting the margins and defining the columns. Follow these steps:

1. Press Shift-F8, P, M; type *1/2"*; press Enter; type *1/2"*; press Enter, Enter, L, M; type *1/2"*; press Enter; type *1/2"*; and then press Enter, F7.

   Next, you define two newspaper-style columns: one for the box and table and one for the letterhead.

Weekly Billable Hours

____

Employee Name

Date	*Client*	*Project*	*Time*
		Billable Hours	

Granite Ridge Company

Architects

♦

418 Wide Road

Sparks, NV 80987-3482

(707) 876-5432

FIG. 15.1 *The first time sheet shows an employee's billable hours.*

2. Press Alt-F7, C, D. In the Text Column Definition screen, change the margins to 1/2", 6", 6 1/4", and 8". Press F7, O to turn on columns and return to the document screen.

   Now you can define the text box that holds the table and provides a frame for the table and heading (*Weekly Billable Hours*).

3. Press Alt-F9, B, O. In the Options: Text Box screen, make the following settings:

Border Style	Set all to Single
Outside Border Space	Set all to 0"
Inside Border Space	Set all to 1/8"
Gray Shading	0%

4. Press F7 to return to the document screen and then press Alt-F9, B, C. In the Definition: Text Box screen, make the following settings:

Anchor Type	Page, Number of pages to skip: 0
Vertical Position	Top
Horizontal Position	Column(s) 1, Full
Size	Set Height/Auto Width, 5.5" (wide) ×10"

5. Press E. In the text box editing screen, type the header text and create the table. Change the font to 12-point Times Roman Bold and type *Weekly Billable Hours*.

6. Press Enter twice and use the underline key to create a horizontal line. The length of the line depends on your printer but try pressing the underline key 40 times. You can adjust the line length later after checking your results in the View Document screen (Shift-F7, V).

7. Press Enter, change the font to 10-point Times Roman Bold, and type *Employee Name*.

8. Press Enter twice. To define the table, press Alt-F7, T, C. At the `Number of Columns` prompt, type *4* and press Enter. At the `Number of Rows` prompt, type *29* and press Enter.

9. WordPerfect displays the Table Edit menu. Press F7 to leave the menu and enter table text entry mode.

   Move the insertion point to the top left cell, change the font to 10-point Times Roman Bold Italic, press Shift-F6 (Center), type *Date*, and then press Tab to move to the next cell. Repeat the process to type the rest of the labels in the first row.

10. With the insertion point in the table, press Alt-F7 to display the Table Edit menu. Press O, P, F, Enter to size the table to the full width of the text box.

11. Move the insertion point into the top left cell (*Date*). Press Alt-F4, Home, Home, and the down-arrow key to highlight all cells in the table. Press L, A, S to format the entire table with single lines.

12. Move the insertion point into the top left cell. Press Alt-F4, Home, and the right-arrow key to highlight the top row. Press L, A, N to turn off the lines in the top row. Use Ctrl and the arrow keys to adjust the width of the columns.

TIP

Adjusting column widths is generally easier if you start with the rightmost column, because if you enlarge other columns to the maximum size that WordPerfect allows, the program may no longer enable you to enlarge the rightmost cells.

13. Move the insertion point into the bottom left cell. If the Table Edit menu isn't displayed, press Alt-F7. Press Alt-F4 and the right-arrow key twice to highlight the first three cells of the bottom row. Press L, I, N to delete the interior lines. Press Alt-F4, Home, and the left-arrow key to highlight the first three cells again. Press L, B, N to turn off the line at the bottom of the table. Press L, L, N to turn off the line on the left side of the bottom row.

14. Move the insertion point into the third cell from the left in the bottom row. Press F7 to turn off the Table Edit menu. Press Alt-F6 (Flush Right) and type *Billable*. Press Enter, Alt-F6 (Flush Right) and type *Hours*.
15. Press F7 twice to return to the document screen.

Creating the Letterhead

Now you can create the letterhead to the right of the table. Follow these steps:

1. Press Ctrl-Enter (Hard Page) to move the insertion point to the top of the second column. Press Enter five times to create white space at the top of the column.
2. Use Advance to position the large black triangle. Press Shift-F8, O, A, R and then type *11/64*". Change the font to 180-point Times Roman and then use Compose to create the graphic image of the triangle. Press Ctrl-V; at the `Key =` prompt, type *6,29* (6, comma, 29, with no space before or after the comma); and then press Enter.

> **TIP**
>
> In the steps that follow, positioning the triangle graphic image precisely over the horizontal line is a matter of experimentation. If you worry that designers have access to secret techniques that make placing design elements especially easy, take comfort. Whether they use PageMaker or WordPerfect, whether they measure with a ruler or by moving on-screen guidelines with a mouse, they must all take time to measure and adjust repeatedly to achieve a precise effect.

3. Before you press Enter after the triangle image, change the font to 10-point Times Roman Italic.
4. Before pressing Enter, define the horizontal line below the triangle image. Press Alt-F9, L, H. In the Graphics: Horizontal Line screen, make the following settings:

Horizontal Position	Center
Vertical Position	Baseline
Length of Line	1 1/2"
Width of Line	1/40"
Gray Shading	100%

5. Press F7 to return to the document screen.

6. Press Enter and use Advance to position the insertion point for the first line of text. Press Shift-F8, O, A, U and then type *5/16*". Then press Enter, F7.

   (***Note:*** Like the placement of the triangle, the Advance Up distance of 5/16" was arrived at by trial and error.)

7. Press Shift-F8, L, J, C, Enter, F7 to center-justify the text that follows. Type *Granite Ridge Company*.

8. Before pressing Enter at the end of the line, change the leading (line spacing) to create the spacing shown in figure 15.1. Press Shift-F8, O, P, L, Enter; type *8p*; and press Enter, F7. (Don't forget the *p*, or WordPerfect deletes inches instead of points, and the lines print on top of each other.)

9. Press Enter, type *Architects*, and press Enter again.

10. To create the small diamond that separates the company name and address, first change the font to 12-point Times Roman and then use Compose to create the image. Press Ctrl-V. At the `Key =` prompt, type *6,96* and then press Enter.

11. Before pressing Enter to end the line, change the font to 10-point Times Roman Italic. Press Enter and type the address as shown in figure 15.1, pressing Enter between lines.

12. After you type the phone number, but before you press Enter to end the line, return the leading (line spacing) to normal. Press Shift-F8, O, P, L, Enter; type *0* (zero); and then press Enter, F7.

13. Press Enter twice. Define the horizontal line at the bottom of the letterhead by pressing Alt-F9, L, H. In the Graphics: Horizontal Line screen, make the following settings:

Horizontal Position	Center
Vertical Position	Baseline
Length of Line	1 1/2"
Width of Line	1/40"
Gray Shading	100%

14. Press F7 to return to the document screen.

Time Sheet No. 2: Project and Personnel Hours

The second time sheet, shown in figure 15.2, combines project billing and internal office timekeeping information. You can customize this example by placing tables with related purposes but very different designs on the same page.

Creating the Letterhead

To begin the design, set the top and bottom margins and then create the letterhead. Follow these steps:

1. Press Shift-F8, P, M; type *3/4*"; press Enter; type *1*"; and then press Enter, F7.
2. For the letterhead, press Shift-F6 (Center) and change the font to 18-point Palatino Bold.

   Create the first graphic image—a Zapf Dingbat. If you don't have Zapf Dingbats in a printer font or soft font, you can choose another symbol.
3. Press Ctrl-V. At the `Key =` prompt, type *12,60* and then press Enter.
4. Press the space bar once and change the font to 30-point Palatino Bold.

✣ WOOD WIZARDS ✣ CUSTOM CABINETRY ✣

11839 MESA VERDE ROAD TEMPE, AZ 87654-9876 (333) 234-5973

PROJECT HOURS

Project	M	T	W	T	F	Sa	Su	Total
							Billable Hours	

PERSONNEL HOURS

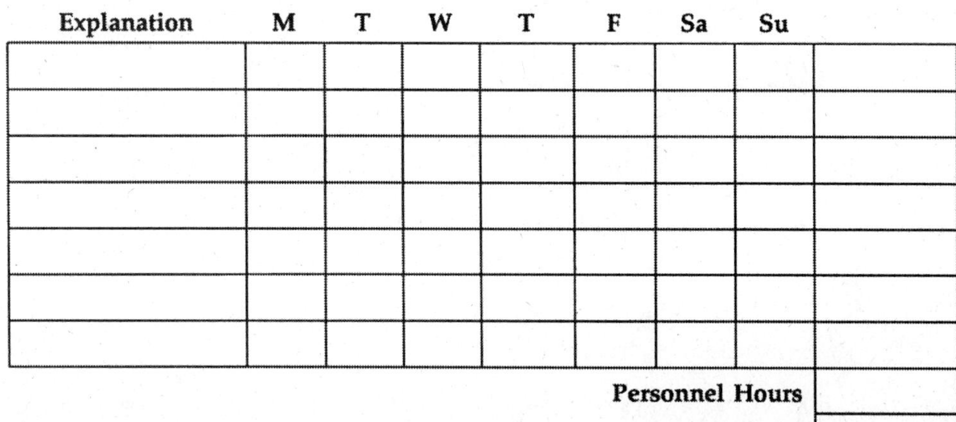

Explanation	M	T	W	T	F	Sa	Su	
							Personnel Hours	
							Total Hours	

FIG. 15.2 A time sheet for project and personnel hours.

> **TIP**
>
> Because large fonts generally look too loosely spaced, use the Word and Letter Spacing feature to tighten logotypes. Certain letter pairs create particularly troublesome letter spacing—the *W* and *o* in *Wood* are prime examples. (Others are *Y* and *T*, followed by any lowercase letter.)

5. Press Shift-F8, O, P, W, O, P; type *80*; press Enter, F7; and then type *W*.
6. Change the font to 18-point Palatino Bold. Adjust the letter spacing for the rest of the word (*ood*). Press Shift-F8, O, P, W, O, P; type *90*; press Enter, F7; and then type *ood*.
7. Press the space bar once, change the font to 30-point Palatino Bold, and type *W*. Change the font to 18-point Palatino Bold and type *izards*. Press the space bar twice and create another graphic symbol as described in step 3.

8. Press the space bar twice, change the font to 30-point Palatino Bold, and type *C*. Change the font to 18-point Palatino Bold and then type *ustom*. Press the space bar, change the font to 30-point Palatino Bold, type *C*, change the font to 18-point, and type *abinetry*.
9. Return letter spacing to normal by pressing Shift-F8, O, P, W, O, O, F7.
10. Press the space bar and create another graphic symbol, as described in step 3.
11. Press Enter, Shift-F6 (Center); change the font to 12-point Palatino; and type the address (*11839 MESA VERDE ROAD...*), pressing the space bar twice between the street, city/state/ZIP, and phone number.

Creating the Tables

Now you can create the tables. Follow these steps:

1. Press Enter four times, change the font to 12-point Palatino Bold, and type *PROJECT HOURS*.

2. Press Enter. Define the table by pressing Alt-F7, T, C. At the `Number of Columns` prompt, type *9* and press Enter. At the `Number of Rows` prompt, type *10* and press Enter.
3. Press F7 to leave the Table Edit menu. Use the arrow keys to move the insertion point to the upper left cell. Press Shift-F6 (Center) and type *Project*. Repeat the process for the remaining cells in row one, pressing Tab to move to the next cell.
4. Press Alt-F7 to display the Table Edit menu. Press Home twice and the up-arrow key to move the insertion point to the upper left cell. Press Alt-F4, Home, Home, and the down-arrow key to highlight the entire table. Press L, A, S to format the table with single lines.
5. If the Table Edit menu isn't displayed, press Alt-F7. Move the insertion point into the top left cell. Press Alt-F4, Home, and the right-arrow key to highlight the top row. Then press L, A, N to remove the lines.
6. Move the insertion point into the bottom left cell. If the Table Edit menu isn't displayed, press Alt-F7. Press Alt-F4 and then press the right-arrow key seven times to highlight the first eight cells of the bottom row. Press L, I, N to delete the interior lines. Press Alt-F4, Home, and the left-arrow key to highlight the first eight cells again. Press L, B, N to turn off the line at the bottom of the table. Press L, L, N to turn off the line at the left side of the bottom row.
7. Move the insertion point into the lower right cell and press L, B, D to create a double line at the bottom of the cell.
8. Move the insertion point in to the fourth cell from the right side of the bottom row of the table. Press Alt-F4 (Block) and the right-arrow key twice to block three cells. Then press J to join three cells for the "Billable Hours" label.
9. Move the insertion point into the second cell from the right in the bottom row. Press F7 to turn off the Table Edit menu. Press Alt-F6 (Flush Right) and type *Billable Hours*.
10. Adjust the width of the columns. Press Alt-F7. Move the insertion point to the right cell in any row and press Ctrl and the left-arrow key and Ctrl and the right-arrow key to adjust the width of the column. If WordPerfect will not enable you to change the width of the column, move to another column

first and decrease its width. Repeat the process for each column, using the arrow keys to move between columns.

TIP

When adjusting column widths, working from right to left is easier, because if you adjust a column to the left to the maximum size WordPerfect allows, the program may not enable you to increase the width of a cell to the right.

To create the second table, you need to copy the first one:

1. Turn on Reveal Codes (Alt-F3) and move the insertion point onto the `[Font:Palatino Bold 12pt]` code preceding the table title. Press Alt-F4 and move the insertion point to the right of the `[Tbl Off]` code at the end of the table. Press Ctrl-F4, B, C, Enter, Enter to retrieve a copy of the table and to insert it one line below the first table.
2. Edit the table title and labels as shown in figure 15.2.

16

Producing Credit Forms

You can adapt many designs in this book for completely different uses. The credit forms described here, for example, provide starting points for customized message forms, invoices, complex memos, and questionnaires.

Both forms are more complex than the forms described so far. If you follow the steps to create these forms, you can learn useful tips for creating your own complex forms.

Credit Form No. 1: A Credit Application

This form uses four separate tables to organize information under different headings. As figure 16.1 shows, the tables are separated by blank lines. Imagine what the form would look like if you joined the tables together.

Joining tables, in fact, is the most efficient way to create complex tables. One WordPerfect 5.1 user even reproduced page one of Internal Revenue Service Form 1040 using multiple, joined tables.

ocean stream aquarium

1000 Freshwater Way

Saline, FL 33333-4444

305 930 3983

Credit Application

BUSINESS INFORMATION

NAME OF BUSINESS	TYPE OF BUSINESS ☐ Corporation ☐ Partnership ☐ Proprietorship
ADDRESS	CONTACT PERSON
CITY/ST/ZIP	TELEPHONE

BANK REFERENCE

NAME OF BANK	CONTACT PERSON
BRANCH	ADDRESS
CHECKING ACCT. NO.	TELEPHONE

TRADE REFERENCES

FIRM NAME	CONTACT NAME	TELEPHONE	YRS. ACCT. OPEN

CONFIRMATION OF ACCURACY

I hereby certify that the information in this credit application is correct. The information included in this application is for use by Ocean Stream Aquarium in determining the amount and conditions of credit to be extended. I understand that Ocean Stream may also use the other sources of credit which it considers necessary in making this determination. Further I hereby authorize the bank and trade references listed in this application to release the information necessary to assist Ocean Stream Aquarium in establishing a line of credit.

Applicant's Signature ______ Applicant's Title ______ Today's Date ______

FIG. 16.1 A credit application form.

Creating the Letterhead

Begin the design by setting the margins and adding the letterhead. Follow these steps:

1. Set the margins by pressing Shift-F8, P, M. Then type *1/2*" and press Enter. Type *1/2*" again and then press Enter, Enter, L, M; type *1/2*"; press Enter; type *1/2*"; and then press Enter, F7.

   The company's letterhead uses two text boxes—one for the shaded "water" and one for the "tank."

2. First, create the shaded box. Press Alt-F9, B, O and in the Options: Text Box screen, make the following settings:

Border Style	Set all to None
Outside Border Space	Set all to 0"
Inside Border Space	Set all to 0"
Gray Shading	20%

TIP

This book has advised you to avoid placing text over screens darker than 10 percent because darker screens reduce readability. A possible exception, as this design shows, is very short text of secondary importance (address and phone number), set in a heavy boldfaced font.

You can selectively break most design rules. Try 10 percent and 6 percent screens and see which one you like better.

3. Press F7 to return to the document screen and then press Alt-F9, B, C. In the Definition: Text Box screen, make the following settings:

Anchor Type	Page, Number of pages to skip: 0
Vertical Position	Set Position, 2"
Horizontal Position	Margin, Left
Size	Set Both, 1 3/4" wide × 8 1/2" high

4. Press F7 to return to the document screen.

5. Now create the tall box with heavy borders in the letterhead. Press Alt-F9, B, O. In the Options: Text Box screen, make the following settings:

Border Style	Set all to Thick
Outside Border Space	Set all to 0"
Inside Border Space	Set all to 0"
Gray Shading	0%

6. Press F7 to return to the document screen and then press Alt-F9, B, C. In the Definition: Text Box screen, make the following settings:

Anchor Type	Page, Number of pages to skip: 0
Vertical Position	Top
Horizontal Position	Margin, Left
Size	Set Both, 1 3/4" wide × 10" high

7. Press E. Change the font to 24-point Avant Garde Gothic Demi.

   Notice in figure 16.1 that the company name's logotype is line spaced very tightly. In the next step, you use the Leading Adjustment feature to create this effect.

8. Press Shift-F8, O, P, L, Enter, Enter and then type *–6p*. Press Enter, F7. (If you forget the *p*, WordPerfect deletes inches instead of points, and the lines print on top of each other.)

9. Press Enter and turn on center justification by pressing Shift-F8, L, J, C, Enter, F7. Type the company name (*ocean stream aquarium*), pressing Enter between words. Before pressing Enter after *aquarium*, return the leading to normal by pressing Shift-F8, O, P, L, Enter; typing *0*; and then pressing Enter, F7.

10. Press Enter four times to insert space between the name and address. Change the font to 9-point Avant Garde Gothic Demi and type the address, pressing Enter three times between lines. Press F7 twice to return to the document screen.

11. To create the figure of waves at the bottom of the letterhead box, press Alt-F9, F, O. In the Options: Figure screen, make the following settings:

Border Style	Set all to None
Outside Border Space	Set all to 0"
Inside Border Space	Set all to 0"
Gray Shading	0%

Creating the Form

Now you can create the form that appears to the right of the letterhead. Follow these steps:

1. Press F7 to return to the document screen. Press Alt-F9, F, C. In the Definition: Figure screen, make the following settings:

Filename	WATER.WPG
Anchor Type	Page, Number of pages to skip: 0
Vertical Position	Bottom
Horizontal Position	Margin, Left
Size	Set Both, 1 3/4" wide × 1 1/4" high

2. Press F7 to return to the document screen.
3. Press Enter three times and Alt-F6 (Flush Right). Change the font to 24-point Avant Garde Gothic Book and type *Credit Application*.
4. Press Enter and define the table. Press Alt-F7, T, C. At the `Number of Columns` prompt, type *2*. At the `Number of Rows` prompt, type *4*.

   WordPerfect places you in the table with the Table Edit menu displayed.
5. Specify single lines for the table. Press Alt-F4, Home, Home, the down-arrow key, L, A, S. Join the cells in the first row (*BUSINESSS INFORMATION*). Move the cursor to the upper left cell and press Alt-F4, Home, and the right-arrow key to highlight the first row. Press J, Y to join the cells.

6. Format the cell with a 10-percent shaded screen. Press O, G; type *10*; and press Enter, Enter, L, S, O. Press F7 to turn off the Table Edit menu.
7. Use the arrow keys to move the insertion point into the top cell. Change the font to 12-point Avant Garde Gothic Demi and type the heading *BUSINESS INFORMATION*.
8. Press the down-arrow key to move the insertion point into the left cell in row two. Change the font to 8-point Avant Garde Gothic Book and type the cell label *NAME OF BUSINESS*.
9. Press Tab to move the insertion point into the right cell in row two. Type the cell label *TYPE OF BUSINESS*. Press Enter twice and the space bar three times. Create the first check box by pressing Ctrl-V. At the `Key =` prompt, type *4,38* (4, comma, 38, with no space before or after the comma) and then press Enter.

TIP

Several check boxes of varied sizes are in the WordPerfect character sets, including the following: 4,38; 4,48; 4,49; 5,24; 6,93.

10. Press the space bar, type *Corporation*, press the space bar nine times, create another check box, press the space bar, and then type *Partnership*. Press Enter. Repeat for the next check box and label (*Proprietorship*).
11. Press Enter once after the word *Proprietorship* to add white space at the bottom of the cell.
12. Type the remaining table labels as shown in figure 16.1. Be sure to press Enter twice after each cell label, to give the user room to write the required information.

Creating the Second Table

The second table is essentially the same as the first. Two alternate methods of creating the table are given: you can copy the first table or create a table from scratch. Do the following:

1. Move the insertion point after the `[Tbl Off]` code, press Enter twice, and define the second table (*BANK REFERENCE*). Press Alt-F7, T, C. At the `Number of Columns` prompt, type *2*. At the `Number of Rows` prompt, type *4*. This table is formatted exactly the same as thc table at the top of the page, so repeat steps 5 through 12 to create the shaded label cell and type the labels but omit step 9 because check boxes are not required for the second table.

   Alternatively, copy the first table by moving the cursor onto the `[Tbl Def...]` code; pressing Alt-F4; moving the cursor onto the `[Tbl Off]` code at the end of the table; and pressing Ctrl-F4, B, C. Press Enter to retrieve the copy of the table and then press Enter twice to insert space between the tables. Edit the cell labels as shown in figure 16.1.

2. For the third table (*TRADE REFERENCES*), move the insertion point below the second table and press Enter twice. Press Alt-F7, T, C. At the `Number of Columns` prompt, type *4* and press Enter. At the `Number of Rows` prompt, type *5* and press Enter.

   Format the table with single lines by pressing L, A, S.

3. Format the first two rows as described in steps 5 through 12, but press Shift-F6 (Center) before typing each label in the second row.

4. To create the fourth table, *CONFIRMATION OF ACCURACY*, move the insertion point below the third table, press Enter twice, and define the table. Press Alt-F7, T, C. At the `Number of Columns` prompt, type *1* and press Enter. At the `Number of Rows` prompt, type *2* and press Enter.

5. Format the top cell as described in steps 5 through 7.

6. Press F7 to turn off the Table Edit menu. Press the down-arrow key to move the insertion point into the bottom cell. Change the font to 10-point Avant Garde Gothic Book and type the text as shown in figure 16.1 (*I hereby certify...*).

7. After you finish typing the text, but before pressing Enter at the end of the last line (*...line of credit*), change the font to 8-point Avant Garde Gothic Book.

8. Press Enter twice. Use the underline key to create the horizontal lines above *Applicant's Signature*, *Applicant's Title*,

and *Today's Date*. Separate the lines by pressing Tab so that you easily can align the labels under the lines. Adjust the line length by checking your work in the View Document screen (press Shift-F7, V).

9. Press Enter at the end of the last horizontal line and type the labels (*Applicant's Signature*, and so on), using Tab to align each label under its line.

Credit Form No. 2: A Credit Memo

This form uses a single table to organize information in cells that span several columns and/or rows (see fig. 16.2).

Notice that each cell is created by joining or dividing cells. WordPerfect 5.1 does not enable you to divide a single cell without simultaneously dividing all the cells in its column. To create complex tables with cells of varying widths in each row, you must create a table with a large number of columns and then selectively join cells; or create two or more tables, each of which may contain just a single row, and place them together so that they appear as a single table. (This process is described in the WordPerfect Workbook.)

Creating the Letterhead

You begin the form by first setting the margins and creating the letterhead. Follow these steps:

1. Press Shift-F8, P, M; type *.3*"; press Enter; type *1/2*"; press Enter, Enter, L, M; type *3/4*"; press Enter; type *3/4*"; and then press Enter, F7.

   The margins now are set. Next you create the letterhead.

2. Change the font to 60-point New Century Schoolbook Bold.

   Notice in the logotype that the first *P* in *Paper* is placed below the baseline. You use the Advance feature to create that effect.

PAPER CHASE

OFFICE SUPPLIES & BUSINESS EQUIPMENT

CREDIT MEMO

CREDIT TO:		CREDIT MEMO NO:
		TODAY'S DATE:
		SALESPERSON:
		DEPARTMENT:

INVOICE NO:	INVOICE DATE:	ORDER NO:

QUANTITY	NUMBER	DESCRIPTION	PRICE	AMOUNT

RECEIVED BY:	REASON CREDIT ISSUED:

Country Club Center 5110 Madison Ave., Suite 400 Angel's Bar, OK 76555-8900 (501) 887-4637

FIG. 16.2 An order/credit form.

3. Press Shift-F8, O, A, D; type *1/4"*; press Enter, F7; and then type *P*. Now advance the insertion point back up to the previous baseline, ready to type the rest of the company name. Press Shift-F8, O, A, U; type *1/4"*; and press Enter, F7.

4. Change the font to 30-point New Century Schoolbook Bold.

   Notice in figure 16.2 that the letters in the company name are widely spaced. Use the Word/Letter Spacing feature in the next step to create that effect.

5. Press Shift-F8, O, P, W, O, P; type *200*; and press Enter, F7. Press the space bar and then type *APER*. (Don't forget to press the space bar first.) Press the space bar twice and then type *CHASE*.

6. Before pressing Enter at the end of the line, change the font to 7-point New Century Schoolbook Bold. Press Enter twice.

7. Press Shift-F8, O, A, U; type *3/16"*; and then press Enter, F7. Use Advance again to move the subtitle 3/4" to the right. Press Shift-F8, O, A, R; type *3/4"*; and press Enter, F7.

8. Press Shift-F8, O, P, W, Enter, P; type *225*; and press Enter, F7. Type *OFFICE SUPPLIES & BUSINESS EQUIPMENT*, pressing the space bar three times between words. Change the letter spacing back to normal. Press Shift-F8, O, P, W, Enter, O, F7.

   Next, you type the company's address at the bottom of the page. Use Advance to position the text and another Advance code to move back up near the top of the page to create the table.

> **TIP**
>
> Using Advance to position the address at the bottom of the page prevents the address from being moved onto the next page if you later add rows to the table.

9. Press Shift-F8, O, A, I; type *10"*; and then press Enter, F7.

10. To create the horizontal line at the bottom of the page, press Alt-F9, L, H. In the Graphics: Horizontal Line screen, make the following settings:

Horizontal Position	Center
Vertical Position	Baseline
Length of Line	5 1/2"
Width of Line	1/40"
Gray Shading	100%

11. Press F7 to return to the document screen.
12. Press Enter twice, change the font to 8-point New Century Schoolbook Bold, press Shift-F6 (Center), and type the address (*Country Club Center...*). Press the space bar twice between street, city/state/ZIP, and phone number.
13. Use Advance to move the insertion point back up near the top of the page. Press Enter, Shift-F8, O, A, I; type *2"*; and then press Enter, F7.

Creating the Form's Table

To finish the document, create the table by following these steps:

1. Type the table title. Change the font to 14-point New Century Schoolbook Bold and type *CREDIT MEMO*.
2. Press Enter and define the table. Press Alt-F7, T, C. At the `Number of Columns` prompt, type *5*. At the `Number of Rows` prompt, type *23*.
3. WordPerfect creates the table and displays the Table Edit menu. Change the table width to extend between the margins by pressing O, P, F, Enter.
4. Format the entire table with single lines. Press L, A, S.
5. Join four cells in the first column to create the box for the *CREDIT TO:* label. Use the arrow keys to move the insertion point into the top left cell. Press Alt-F4 and press the down-arrow key three times and then press J, Y. Press L, S, O to turn shading on and accept the default 10 percent shading.
6. Press Home and the right-arrow key to move the insertion point to the top right cell. Press Alt-F4, the left-arrow key, J, Y to join to two upper right cells.

Repeat the process for the cells in figure 16.2 labeled *TODAY'S DATE:*, *SALESPERSON:*, *DEPARTMENT:*, and *ORDER NO:*.

7. Move the insertion point into the left column and down to the fifth row. Join two cells to create the single cell in figure 16.2 labeled *INVOICE NO:*.

   With the insertion point in the left cell, press Alt-F4, press the right-arrow key to highlight both cells, and press J, Y to join the cells.

8. Now place 10 percent shading in the cells across row six (*QUANTITY*, *NUMBER*, and so forth). Move the insertion point into the left cell in row six, press Alt-F4, Home, and the right-arrow key to highlight the row. Then press L, S, O to apply shading to all the cells in the row.

9. Create the two wide cells in the bottom row (*RECEIVED BY:* and *REASON CREDIT ISSUED:*). Press Home and the down-arrow key to move the insertion point to the bottom row. Press Home and the left-arrow key to move the insertion point to the left cell. Press Alt-F4 and the right-arrow key to highlight the first two cells. Then press J, Y to join the two cells. Press the right-arrow key to move the insertion point into the second cell, press Alt-F4, and then press the right-arrow key twice to highlight the three cells on the right side of the row. Then press J, Y to join the cells.

   Adjust the width of the cells. If you start at the right side of the table, adjusting cells is easier. If you increase the width of cells on the left side of the table to the maximum width that WordPerfect allows, the program may not enable you to increase the width of other cells.

10. Move the insertion point into the top right cell and press Ctrl and the left-arrow key and Ctrl and the right-arrow key to adjust the size of the column.

TIP

WordPerfect may not show the width of columns accurately in the table editing or document editing screen. To view cell widths as they print, use View Document (Shift-F7, V).

11. Repeat step 10 to adjust the widths of the remaining columns. To adjust the columns and cells in the middle of the table (*INVOICE NO:*, *INVOICE DATE:*), move the insertion point into those cells and then press Ctrl and the left-arrow key and Ctrl and the right-arrow key to fine-tune the size.

12. Move the insertion point into the upper left cell, change the font to 7-point New Century Schoolbook Bold, press Enter to insert white space at the top of the cell, and then press Shift-F6 (Center). Then type *CREDIT TO:*, pressing Enter, Shift-F6 between the words.

13. Type the labels for the rest of the table as shown in figure 16.2. Remember to press Enter at least once after each label, to allow room for the information requested.

Producing Organizational Charts

17

The Line Draw feature is not the most efficient way to create an organizational chart with WordPerfect, because the feature has several drawbacks. Line Draw makes entering text difficult, for example, because you easily can displace line segments when entering text. The feature also doesn't work with PostScript printers.

In practice, the Table feature provides a nearly ideal solution, even for complex organizational charts, because you can align chart elements much more easily. Although you cannot use the Table feature to create tables with circles or diagonal lines, for many applications, you can replace circles and diagonals with appropriately formatted table cells or print text in graphic circles from the DrawPerfect Figure Library.

Organizational Chart No. 1: A Project Plan

The chart in figure 17.1 looks as though it was created with Line Draw. In fact, the chart consists entirely of table cells.

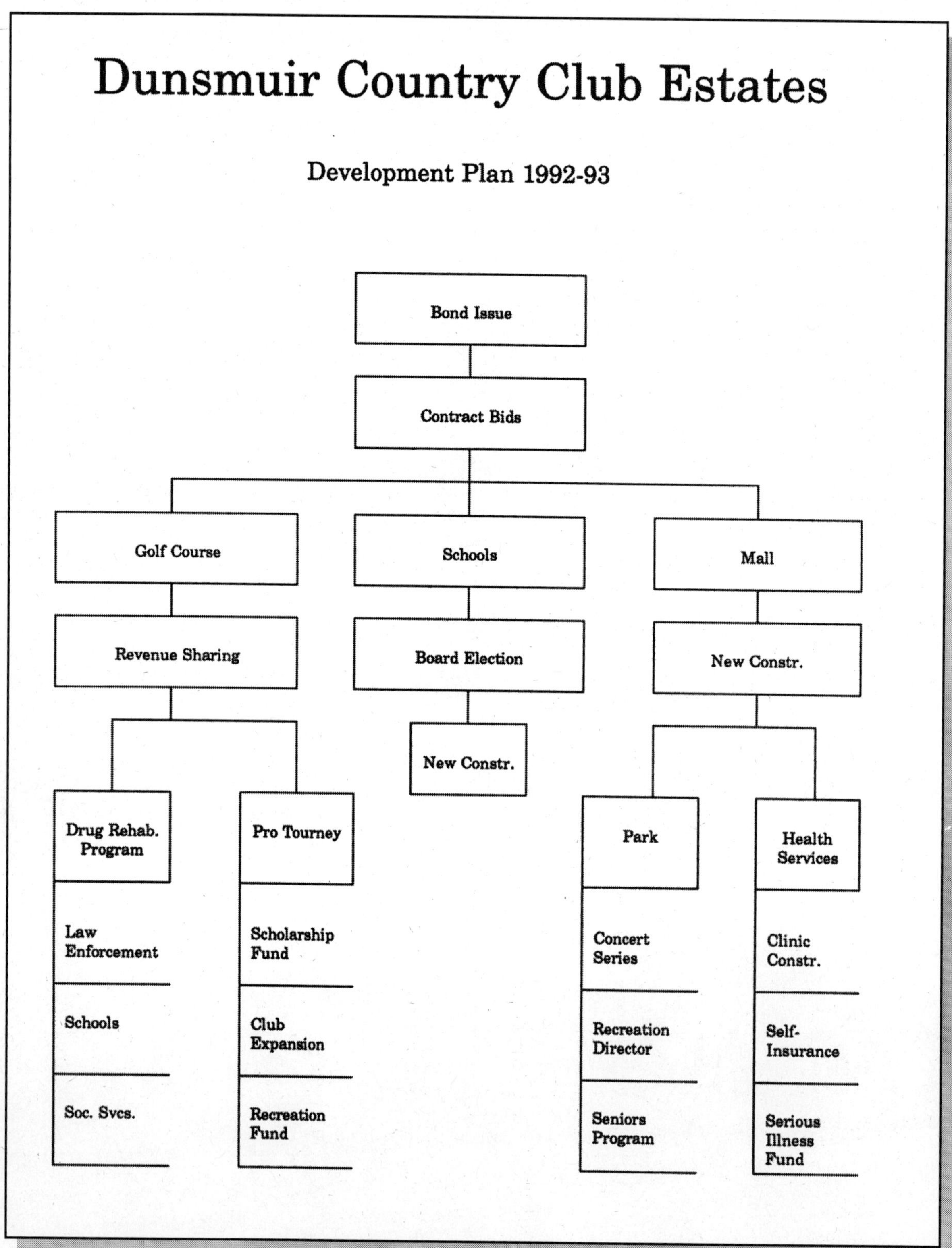

FIG. 17.1 A planning chart consisting of table cells.

TIP

The first step to creating organizational charts (or charts of any kind) with WordPerfect is to create and print a blank table with many rows and columns for pencil-and-paper planning. Write in cell contents, mark connecting lines in colored pen or pencil, and then use Table Edit mode to delete cells and lines as needed.

Creating the Heading

Begin creating the sample chart in figure 17.1 by setting the margins and typing the heading. Follow these steps:

1. Press Shift-F8, P, M. Type *1/2*"; press Enter; type *1/2*"; and then press Enter, F7.

   The margins are now set for 1/2".

2. Change the font to 18-point New Century Schoolbook. Then press Shift-F6 (Center) and type *Dunsmuir Country Club Estates* for the heading.

3. Press Enter twice. Change the font to 14-point New Century Schoolbook, press Shift-F6 (Center), and then type *Development Plan 1992-93* for the subtitle.

Creating the Table

Now you can begin to format the table. Follow these steps:

1. Press Enter four times and define the table. Press Alt-F7, T, C. At the `Number of Columns` prompt, type *15* and press Enter. At the `Number of Rows` prompt, type *30* and press Enter.

2. WordPerfect displays the Table Edit menu. Format the entire table with single lines. Move the insertion point to the upper left cell, press Alt-F4, Home, Home, and the down-arrow key to highlight the table. Then press L, A, S to convert all lines to single lines.

3. Specify table width between left and right page margins. Press O, P, F, Enter. Press F7 to leave the Table Edit menu.

TIP

Most charts must be symmetrical, like the chart in figure 17.1. To create a symmetrical chart that has a centered top cell (*Bond Issue*) consisting of three joined cells, define a table with an odd number of columns. If the top cell consists of four joined cells, create a table with an even number of columns. WordPerfect enables you to create tables with up to 32 columns and 32,765 rows.

4. Print the table (Shift-F7, P). On the printed copy of the table, write the proposed chart text in cells and mark connecting lines heavily or in colored pen or pencil.

Deleting Lines in the Chart

When you begin creating a chart, first type the text in cells and then join cells as needed. Typing the text first provides a helpful template when you begin to remove lines selectively.

Then, to delete lines from the table, follow these steps:

1. Change the font to 9-point New Century Schoolbook and type the text in the table.

   If the Table Edit menu is displayed, press F7 to close it. Move the insertion point into the top row and find the center cell or cells.

2. Join cells as needed for the first labeled cell (*Bond Issue*). To join cells, place the insertion point in the first cell; press Alt-F4; use arrow keys to highlight the cells to be joined; and then press J, Y.

3. With the insertion point in the table, press Alt-F7 to turn on Table Edit mode. Use the Table Edit features to join cells and delete cell borders, following the example in figure 17.1.

The rules for deleting single and multiple cell borders aren't explained in the WordPerfect reference manual. That omission is not surprising, because the explanation is far harder to understand than the process warrants. Which lines WordPerfect deletes depends on whether a single cell or a block of cells is selected;

whether the selected cell or cells are located in top, bottom, left, right, or enclosed rows or columns; or whether the selected area includes corner cells.

You quickly can learn how to delete lines if you practice a little, using the following procedures. Fortunately, restoring lines that you mistakenly delete is easy: highlight the cell(s) again and choose L (Lines), A (All), and a line format (Single, Double, Dashed, Dotted, Thick, or Extra Thick).

The general procedures for deleting cell borders are as follows:

- To delete lines in a single cell, press Alt-F7 to display the Table Edit menu, move the insertion point to the cell whose lines you want to delete, press L (Lines), and then press L (Left), T (Top), or A (All). Press N (None) to delete the selected line(s).
- To delete lines in multiple cells, move the insertion point to the first cell in the group, press Alt-F4 (Block), and use the arrow keys to highlight the cells. Press L (Lines), and then press L (Left), R (Right), T (Top), B (Bottom), I (Inside), O (Outside), or A (All). Press N (None) to delete the specified lines.

Again the results vary depending on where the cell or cells are located. When in doubt, work with one cell at a time. Instead of selecting Lines, All, None for an entire row, for example, delete lines for one cell at a time.

Organizational Chart No. 2: A Timeline Chart

Project planning software is wonderful, but for the occasional timeline chart, WordPerfect's Table feature works fine. This sample chart uses a horizontal (landscape) format to fit nine wide columns comfortably on the page.

The first organizational chart (in fig. 17.1) has a vertical format but easily can have a horizontal layout. With timeline charts, you have no real choice, because time runs horizontally. Shaded cells indicate project phases. Retaining vertical lines helps the reader to see clearly when each phase begins and ends.

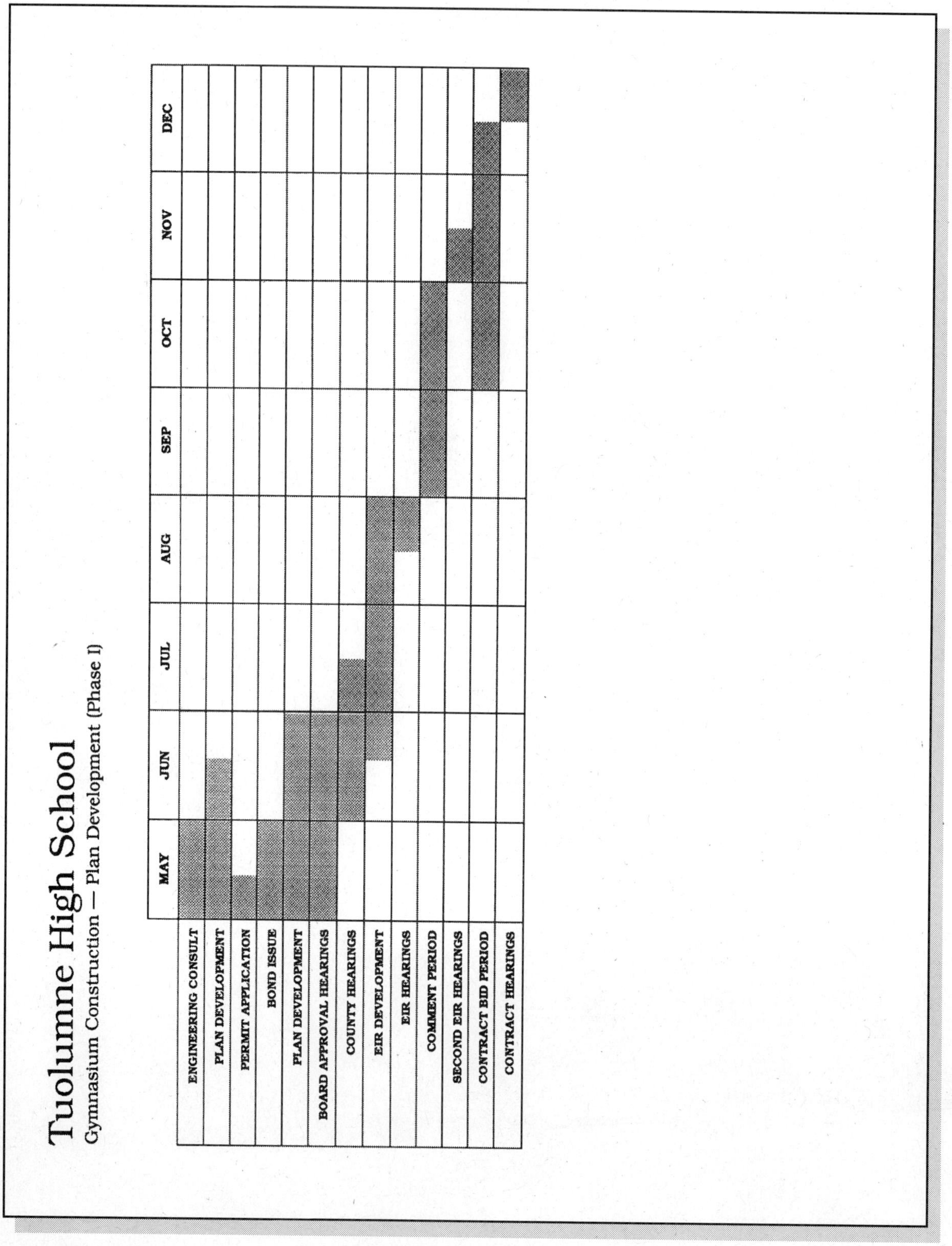

Tuolumne High School

Gymnasium Construction — Plan Development (Phase I)

	MAY	JUN	JUL	AUG	SEP	OCT	NOV	DEC
ENGINEERING CONSULT								
PLAN DEVELOPMENT								
PERMIT APPLICATION								
BOND ISSUE								
PLAN DEVELOPMENT								
BOARD APPROVAL HEARINGS								
COUNTY HEARINGS								
EIR DEVELOPMENT								
EIR HEARINGS								
COMMENT PERIOD								
SECOND EIR HEARINGS								
CONTRACT BID PERIOD								
CONTRACT HEARINGS								

FIG. 17.2 An organizational chart showing the timeline of a project.

If you need more precise placement of shaded cells (a project ends on June 13, for example), you can increase the number of columns (up to 32) and selectively shade cells and delete cell borders. Notice in figure 17.2 that some project phases end in the middle of the month ("PLAN DEVELOPMENT" ends in mid-June, for example). The shaded bar has been extended halfway into the June column by erasing the middle cell borders in two columns under the June heading.

Creating the Chart

To begin creating the design, choose a landscape paper size/type and set the borders. Follow these steps:

1. Press Shift-F8, P, S. Move the insertion point to the Standard Wide landscape definition supplied with WordPerfect and then press Enter. Press P, M; type *1/2"*; press Enter; type *1/2"*; press Enter, Enter, L, M; type *1/2"*; press Enter; type *1/2"*; and then press Enter, F7.

2. Press Enter four times to leave white space at the top of the page. Change the font to 24-point Bookman Light and type the main chart heading, *Tuolumne High School*.

3. Change the font to 12-point Bookman Light. Press Enter. For the subtitle, type *Gymnasium Construction — Plan Development (Phase I)*.

   To create the true typesetter's em dash between "Gymnasium Construction" and "Plan Development (Phase I)," press Ctrl-V. At the `Key =` prompt, type *4,34* (4, comma, 34 with no space before or after the comma). Then press Enter.

4. Press Enter three times and then Alt-F7, T, C. At the `Number of Columns` prompt, type *20* and press Enter. At the `Number of Rows` prompt, type *14* and press Enter.

Changing the Cell Borders

In its final form, the chart clearly doesn't have 20 rows. Creating varied column widths by joining cells is much easier than using Ctrl and the arrow keys in Table Edit mode.

In figure 17.2, the left column (*ENGINEERING CONSULT*, and so on) was created by joining four columns of cells, and the monthly columns (*MAY*, *JUN*, and so forth) were created by erasing the borders between two columns and joining two cells for the headers.

Using Ctrl and the arrow keys in Table Edit mode is a frustrating process because when you change the width of one cell with Ctrl and the arrow keys, WordPerfect changes the width of other cells that you already have sized. The process also is imprecise because WordPerfect doesn't display cell widths accurately in the document or table editing screens, and you must print your work or use View Document to check your progress.

To change the cell borders, follow these steps:

1. Use the arrow keys to move the insertion point into the upper left corner of the table. If the Table Edit menu isn't displayed, press Alt-F7. Press Alt-F4 (Block), Home, Home, and the down-arrow key to highlight the table. Press L, A, S to replace all borders with single lines.

2. Move the insertion point into the upper left cell. If the Table Edit menu isn't displayed, press Alt-F7. Press Alt-F4 and then press the right-arrow key three times to highlight the left four cells. Press L, A, N to erase the inside, top, and left borders of the highlighted cells.

3. Press the down-arrow key, Home, Home, and the left-arrow key to move the insertion point into the left cell of the second row. Press Alt-F4 and press the right-arrow key three times to highlight the first four cells in row two. Press J, Y to join the cells. Repeat to create wide cells for the remaining project category headings.

4. To join two cells for the first column label cell, begin by pressing Home, Home, and the up-arrow key to move the insertion point to the top left cell.

   Press the right-arrow key four times to move the insertion point into the fifth cell from the left. Press Alt-F4 and the right-arrow key to highlight two cells. Press J, Y to join the two cells. Repeat for the rest of the column label cells (*JUN*, *JUL*, and so on).

Next, you delete cell borders to create wide cells under the column headings.

5. Move the insertion point into the cell that holds the *MAY* label. Press the down-arrow key and then the right-arrow key to move the insertion point into the right cell in row two below the label cell. Press Alt-F4 (Block) and then press Home and the down-arrow key to highlight the column. Press L, L, N to delete the left borders of the highlighted cells. Repeat for the rest of the columns under the month labels.

6. If the Table Edit menu is on-screen, press F7 to close it. Move the insertion point into the first label cell (*MAY* in fig. 17.2). Change the font to 9-point Bookman Demi, press Shift-F6 (Center), and type *MAY*. Repeat the process for the rest of the header cells, pressing Tab to move to the next cell.

   Next, you type the project stage labels.

7. Press Home, Home, Home, and the left-arrow key to move to column one. Use the down-arrow key to move the insertion point into the first project stage label cell (*ENGINEERING CONSULT*, and so forth). Change the font to 8-point Bookman Demi, press Alt-F6 (Flush Right), and type the label. Repeat for the rest of the project stage labels.

   Now you shade cells to indicate the duration of each project stage.

8. Press Alt-F7 to display the Table Edit menu. Move the insertion point to the first cell in the *MAY* column, next to *ENGINEERING CONSULT*. Press Alt-F4 and then the right-arrow key once to highlight two cells. Press L, S, O to turn on shading for the cell. Repeat for the rest of the shaded cells.

You don't see the shading in the Table Edit or Document editing screens, but you can preview your progress in the View Document screen (Shift-F7, V).

Longhorn Sports

December 28-31
8-11 am

You're among the top 25% of our customers for 1992! In appreciation of your support, you're invited to a special closed-door year-end sale.

Save up to 50% on our famous maker brands. Top-of-the-line items in all sports drastically reduced.

Shoes
Avia, Nike, Puma, Brooks, Converse, ASICS, Reebok, Vans, New Balance, Adidas, Saucony, LA Gear, Sperry, Rockport

Pro Team Gear
NFL, NBA, NL, AL, NHL

Exercise Equipment
Tunturi, Soloflex, Nautilus, Nordic Track

Sports Outfitting
Running, Cycling, Canoeing, X-C Skiing, Racquet Sports, Swimming, Tennis, Aerobics, Cross-Training

Longhorn Sports
12482 Altissima Blvd.
El Dorado, CO 80004
(555) 789-0123

Part IV

Creating Sales Documents

Includes

18

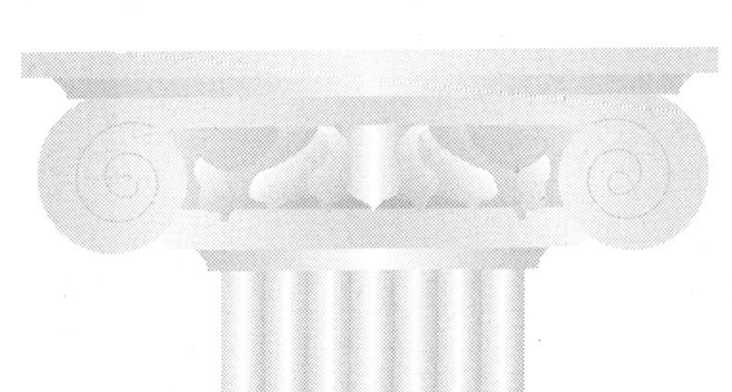

Producing Flyers

Flyers must attract attention and provide enough information to cause people to act. Large headlines and eye-catching art are obligatory. Many flyers, however, also require a great deal of copy. You can resolve the apparent conflict between art and text with a tight, orderly design.

Flyer No. 1: A Financial Seminar for Retirees

The standard 8 1/2-by-11-inch page presents certain design problems for flyers. When space is tight, the temptation is to cram as much information on the page as possible by using a small font and running text across the entire page. Because long lines make text hard to read, chances are people will not read a flyer designed this way.

Figure 18.1 shows a much more readable design, with the text presented in landscape mode. Folded in the middle, this flyer also can make an interesting mailer. The design of this flyer is sophisticated, but simple. Like other examples shown throughout this book, this flyer shows how much design you can get from simple font changes and a few lines.

Bernard Atkinson presents

Markets for Maturity

Planning for Your secure future

Sacramento Golden Bear Inn
October 19, 1992
10 am - 5 pm

Call today to reserve your place!

How flexible will your finances be in the senior years of life?

Hi omnes lingua, institutis, legibus inter se differunt. Gallos ab Aquitanis Garumna flumen, a Belgis Matrona et Sequana dividit. Horum omnium fortissimi sunt Belgae, propterea quod a cultu atque humanitate provinciae longissime absunt, minimeque ad eos mercatores saepe commeant atque ea quae ad effeminandos animos pertinent important, proximique.

Tax-free bonds? IRA rollover? Pension plan? Profit sharing?

Que de causa Helvetii quoque reliquos Gallos virtute praecedunt, quod fere cotidianis proeliis cum Germanis contendunt, cum aut suis finibus eos prohibent, aut ipsi in eorum finibus bellum gerunt. Eorum una pars, quam Gallos obtinere dictum est, initium capit a flumine Rhodano; continetur Garumna flumine, Oceano, finibus Belgarum.

Whom can you trust with your money?

Attingit etiam ab Sequanis et Helvetiis flumen Rhenum; vergit ad septentriones. Belgae ab extremis Galliae finibus oriuntur; pertinent ad Inferiorem partem fluminis Rheni; spectant in septentriones et orientem solem. Aquitania a Garumna flumine ad Pyrenaeos montes et eam partem.

Bernard Atkinson & Associates (916) 999-3210

FIG. 18.1 A more readable flyer.

Setting Up the Flyer

To create the flyer, do the following:

1. Choose a landscape paper size by pressing Shift-F8, P, S; then move the cursor to `Standard - Wide` and press Enter, F7.
2. Set the margins by pressing Shift-F8, L, M; typing *.5"*; pressing Enter; typing *.5"*; pressing Enter, Enter, P, M; typing *7/8"*; pressing Enter; typing *0"*; and pressing Enter, F7.

   Note: If you are using a laser printer, WordPerfect changes the 0" margin setting to 0.3". Typing *0"* is quicker than typing *0.3"*.
3. To create the two thick horizontal lines, press Alt-F9, L, H. In the Graphics: Horizontal Line screen, change the settings to the following:

Horizontal Position	Full
Vertical Position	Set Position, .5"
Width of Line	1/16"
Gray Shading	100%
4. Press F7 to return to the document screen. Press Alt-F9, L, H. In the Graphics: Horizontal Line screen, change the setting to the following:

Horizontal Position	Full
Vertical Position	Set Position, 7.5"
Width of Line	1/16"
Gray Shading	100%

   Press F7 to return to the document screen.

Adding Text in Columns

The next thing you must do is create two horizontal newspaper-style columns. You can set up horizontal newspaper-style columns by doing the following:

1. Press Alt-F7, C, D. In the Text Column Definition screen, change the setting to the following:

   Distance Between Columns 5/8"

2. Press F7 to exit the menu; press O to turn on columns.

To type the text in column one, do the following:

1. Change the font to 18-point Palatino, press Alt-F6 (Flush Right), and type *Bernard Atkinson presents*.
2. Press Enter twice, change the font to 72-point Palatino, press Alt-F6 (Flush Right), and type *Markets*.
3. Press Enter, Alt-F6 (Flush Right) and type *for*.
4. Press Enter, press Alt-F6 (Flush Right), and type *Maturity*.
5. Press Enter, change the font to 36-point Palatino Italic, press Enter, press Alt-F6 (Flush Right), and type *Planning for*.
6. Press Enter, press Alt-F6 (Flush Right), and type *Your secure future*.
7. Press Enter twice, change the font to 14-point Palatino Bold, press Alt-F6 (Flush Right), and type *Sacramento Gold Bear Inn*.
8. Press Enter, Alt-F6 (Flush Right) and type *October 19, 1992*.
9. Press Enter, Alt-F6 (Flush Right) and type *10 am - 5 pm*

To type the text in column two, do the following:

1. Press Ctrl-Enter (Hard Page). Specify a ragged right margin by pressing Shift-F8, L, J, L, F7; change the font to 18-point Palatino Bold Italic; and type the first section heading: *How flexible will your finances be in the senior years of life?*
2. Change the font to 18-point Palatino, press Enter twice, and type the first paragraph of body text.
3. Repeat the process for the remainder of column two. Check your work in Document View (Shift-F7, V).
4. When you reach the end of column two, turn off columns by pressing Alt-F7, C, F.

Adding the Finishing Touches

To finish the flyer, do the following:

1. Press Enter three times to move the cursor down below the bold horizontal line. Create a column definition identical to the one created at the top of column one. Turn columns on.
2. Press Ctrl-F8, A, I and change the font to 14-point Palatino Italic. Type *Call today to reserve your place!*
3. Press Ctrl-Enter (Hard Page) to move to the second column. Change the font to 14-point Palatino and type *Bernard Atkinson & Associates (916) 999-3210*. (Insert two spaces between the name and phone number.)

Flyer No. 2: A Sporting Goods Preferred Customer Sale

Like the first flyer, this flyer uses two columns, but in portrait instead of landscape mode (see fig. 18.2). This flyer also uses a gray screen and imported graphic image as visual elements.

If you follow the steps of this complex design, you can learn several useful tricks—such as the following—that can be applied to other documents:

- Placing lines over boxes
- Placing type across columns
- Placing a graphic image across columns
- Placing text over a graphic image
- Creating a column with a gray shade
- Sizing a graphic image
- Using several lines, boxes, and images on the same page
- Adjusting kerning (letter spacing) and word spacing
- Fine-tuning leading (line spacing)
- Creating invisible (borderless, unshaded) boxes.
- Placing one box over another

Longhorn Sports

December 28-31
8-11 am

You're among the top 25% of our customers for 1992! In appreciation of your support, you're invited to a special closed-door year-end sale.

Save up to 50% on our famous maker brands. Top-of-the-line items in all sports drastically reduced.

Shoes
Avia, Nike, Puma, Brooks, Converse, ASICS, Reebok, Vans, New Balance, Adidas, Saucony, LA Gear, Sperry, Rockport

Pro Team Gear
NFL, NBA, NL, AL, NHL

Exercise Equipment
Tunturi, Soloflex, Nautilus, Nordic Track

Sports Outfitting
Running, Cycling, Canoeing, X-C Skiing, Racquet Sports, Swimming, Tennis, Aerobics, Cross-Training

Longhorn Sports
12482 Altissima Blvd.
El Dorado, CO 80004
(555) 789-0123

FIG. 18.2 A flyer containing a gray screen and imported graphics.

To maintain your sanity while designing complex documents, you should adopt a calm, organized, step-by-step approach. Understanding the logical order that WordPerfect imposes on the design process also helps. For example, when you use the page anchor type for boxes, you must place all box codes at the top of the page. As a result, a neat batch of box codes appears on the first line of the page. Because the codes are in one location, you easily can find a particular code that needs to be checked or changed.

Professional designers, whether they use old-fashioned cut-and-paste methods or the advanced techniques provided by desktop publishing software such as Aldus PageMaker or Ventura Publisher, lay out the foundation first. Although you can begin your flyer by working on any element (text, boxes, lines, or graphic images), designing first the underlying page (or *grid* as designers call it) makes sense. Begin by setting margins that differ from the defaults. If the page includes columns, define the columns next.

After the foundation is laid, you must make another choice: whether to enter text or graphics boxes first. If you enter the text first, you must leave approximately enough space for graphic images. If you create the graphics boxes first, you can enter the text later. Whether you enter the text or graphics boxes first, however, having to use Document View and Reveal Codes to fine-tune the placement of boxes and text is virtually guaranteed.

Laying the Foundation

To create the flyer, you first must set the margins and define the columns by doing the following:

1. To set the margins, press Shift-F8, L, M; type *.5"*; press Enter; type *.5"*; press Enter, Enter, P, M; type *.5"*; press Enter; type *.5"*; and press Enter, F7.

2. To set the columns, press Alt-F7, C, D; then press Enter to accept the default values in the Text Column Definition menu and press O to turn on the defaults.

To create the shaded box in column two, do the following:

1. Press Alt-F9, B, O. In the Options: Text Box menu, change the settings to the following:

Border Style	Set all to None
Outside Border Space	Set all to 0"
Inside Border Space	Set all to .2"
Gray Shading	6%

Research shows that screens darker than 10 percent interfere with the legibility of text.

2. Press F7 to return to the document screen.
3. Press Alt-F9, B, C. In the Definition: Text Box menu, change the settings to the following:

Anchor Type	Page, Number of pages to skip: 0
Vertical Position	Top
Horizontal Position	Columns, 2, Full
Size	Set Both, 3.5" wide × 10" (high)

4. Press F7 to return to the document screen.

If you check your work with View Document (Shift-F7, V), you can see that WordPerfect has created a shaded text box in column two.

Entering Text

This flyer uses two graphic images: a starburst containing the text "Year-End Preferred Customer Sale!" and a box containing the company's logo, a steer's head. As stated earlier, you can place the graphic images or the text first. For this example, you create the text first. Because the store name (Longhorn Sports) is in a text box, the text begins with "Year-End Preferred Customer Sale!"

Column One

To create the text, do the following:

1. Press Enter 12 times, switch to 10-Point Palatino, and press Enter seven more times.

TIP

Switching to a small font such as 10-Point Palatino enables you to fine-tune the vertical spacing of display text by pressing Enter.

2. Switch to 20-point Palatino Bold Italic. Press Enter once more, press the space bar 16 times, and type *Year-End*.
3. Press Enter, press the space bar 11 times, and type *Preferred Customer*.
4. Press Enter, press the space bar 17 times, switch to 56-point Palatino Bold Italic, and type *Sale!*.
5. Press Enter, change the font to 10-point Palatino, and press Enter five times.
6. Press Shift-F8, L, J, R, F7 to turn on right-justification.

TIP

To right-justify or center just a few lines of text, using Alt-F6 and Shift-F6 is quicker. To justify an entire page or column, turning on the justification with the Format Line menu is easier.

7. Set a leading adjustment of –2 points to tighten the line spacing for the date and time text by pressing Shift-F8, O, P, L, Enter; typing *–2p*; and pressing Enter, F7.
8. Change the font to 24-point Palatino Bold Italic and type *December 28-31*.
9. Press Enter and turn leading adjustment off by pressing Shift-F8, O, P, L, Enter, 0, Enter, F7.
10. Type *8-11 am*.
11. Press Enter twice and change the font to 16-point Palatino. Type *You're among the top 25%* and press Enter.
12. Type the rest of this paragraph, formatting it as shown in figure 18.2. Be sure to press Enter at the end of each line.

Remember, you don't need to use Alt-F6 (Flush-Right) because flush-right justification is turned on.

13. After you complete this paragraph, press Enter twice; press Ctrl-F8, A, I to turn on italics; and press F6 to turn on Bold.

> **TIP**
>
> No difference exists between choosing bold italics by changing the base font to 16-point Palatino Bold Italics or turning on italics and bold as described. In either case, WordPerfect switches to the bold italics font for the current typeface.

14. Type *Save up to 50%*; then press the right-arrow key twice to turn off bold and italics.
15. Type the rest of the paragraph, pressing Enter at the end of each line, as shown in figure 18.2.

Column Two

Although a great deal more text needs to be typed, the text in the body of the document is completed. Because you created the right column as a text box, you enter the text for column two in the graphics text box editor.

To enter text in the graphics text box editor, do the following:

1. Press Alt-F9, B, E, 1, Enter, E to get to the graphics box editing screen.
2. Press Enter twice and turn on right justification by pressing Shift-F8, L, J, R, F7. Change the font to 20-point Palatino Bold Italic.
3. Press Enter seven times and type *Shoes*.
4. Press Enter, change the font to 14-point Palatino, and type the rest of the paragraph, as shown in figure 18.2.
5. Press Enter three times, change the font to 20-point Palatino Bold Italic, and type *Pro Team Gear*.
6. At this point, you can use a trick mentioned several times in previous designs in this book. Instead of repeatedly making the same font choices, block the first section with its font

codes and save a copy to a file. To type each new section, retrieve the file and edit the text. Using this technique, type the text for the Pro Team Gear, Exercise Equipment, and Sports Outfitting sections in column two.

7. After you finish the product listings, press Enter six times (to leave room for the steer's head) and change the font to 16-point Palatino.

8. Change the justification to centered by pressing Shift-F8, L, J, C, F7.

9. Type *Longhorn Sports*, press Enter, and type the address and phone number, pressing Enter between lines.

   Press F7 twice to return to the document screen.

Using Graphics

You have typed all the text, except for the store's name, which is in a text box. You now can work on the remaining graphic lines and boxes, which include the following:

- The heavy horizontal lines at the top and bottom of the flyer
- The star burst in column one
- The steer's head in column two
- The store name, which is enclosed in a text box

Adding the Lines

The horizontal lines are easy to create. You can create these lines by doing the following:

1. Move the cursor to top of the document, just after the code for the first text box (the shaded box in column two).

TIP

Remember, when you use a page anchor type for boxes, you must place the box codes on the first line of the page. You also should place any line codes on the first line so that you can turn on Reveal Codes and press Home, Home, and the up-arrow key to move the cursor to the top of the page if you need to find a box or line code.

2. Press Alt-F9, L, H. In the Graphics: Horizontal Line menu, change the settings to the following for the line at the top of the page:

Horizontal Position	Set Position, .5"
Vertical Position	Set Position, 5/8"
Length	7.7"
Width of Line	.05"
Gray Shading	100%

3. Press F7 to return to the document screen; then press Alt-F9, L, H. In the Graphics: Horizontal Line menu, change the settings to the following for the line at the bottom of the page:

Horizontal Position	Set Position, .5"
Vertical Position	Set Position, 10 1/4"
Length	7.7"
Width of Line	.05"
Gray Shading	100%

4. Press F7 to return to the document screen.

TIP

To keep box and line codes orderly, group them in Reveal Codes. Place the codes for this new box just after the codes for the previous box (the shaded box in column two).

Adding the Text Box

To create the box containing the store name in large letters at the top of the page, do the following:

1. Turn on Reveal Codes (Alt-F3) and move the cursor just after the code for Text Box 1.
2. Press Alt-F9, B, O. In the Options: Text Box menu, change the settings to the following:

Border Style	Set all to None
Outside Border Space	Set all to 0"
Inside Border Space	Set all to 0"
Gray Shading	0%

3. Press F7 to return to the document screen.

4. Press Alt-F9, B, C. In the Definition: Text Box screen, change the settings to the following:

Anchor Type	Page, Number of pages to skip: 0
Vertical Position	Set Position, .8"
Horizontal Position	Set Position, .5"
Size	Set Both, 7.5" wide × 3" high
Wrap Text Around Box	No

5. Press E. In the graphic box edit screen, create the text for the store title.

TIP

When you make type very large, the letter spacing may look unnaturally loose. To make large type appear properly kerned (letter spaced), use the letter spacing feature described in step 6.

6. To change the letter spacing to tighten up the text, press Shift-F8, O, P, W, P; type *90%*; press Enter, P; type *90%*; and press Enter, F7.

7. Change the font to 84-point Palatino and type *L*. Change the font to 70-point Palatino and type *onghorn* and press the space bar.

8. Change the font to 84-point Palatino and type *S*. Change the font to 70-point Palatino and type *ports*.

9. Press F7 twice to return to the document screen.

10. Check your work in View Document (Shift-F7, V).

Adding the Starburst

Now you can create the starburst in column one. The starburst graphic is from the figure library that comes with DrawPerfect. You can order several figure libraries for use with WordPerfect. For information, call WordPerfect Corporation.

To create the starburst, do the following:

1. Press Alt-F9, F, O. In the Options: Figure screen, change the settings to the following:

Border Style	Set all to None
Outside Border Space	Set all to 0"
Inside Border Space	Set all to 0"
Gray Shading	0%

2. Press F7 to return to the document screen.

3. Press Alt-F9, F, C. In the Definition: Figure screen, change the settings to the following:

Filename	BURST-6.WPG
Anchor Type	Page, Number of pages to skip: 0
Vertical Position	Set Position, 3.13"
Horizontal Position	Set Position, .3"
Wrap Text Around Box	No

   Before WordPerfect accepts a file name for a figure, the figure must be located in the subdirectory designated in Setup/Location of Files for graphic files (the default is C:\WordPerfect51\GRAPHICS). You can type a file name and path at the `Filename` prompt, but it is much more convenient to save graphic images in the subdirectory designated for graphic images. Because figure libraries take up a great deal of room, you can save disk space by retrieving into the GRAPHICS subdirectory only those images you plan to use. To retrieve graphic images stored on floppy disks, type the drive, subdirectory path, and file name at the `Filename` prompt.

   Note: The graphic images used in this book are from the DrawPerfect Figure Library. The figures supplied with

WordPerfect 5.1 are limited in number and scope. WordPerfect users may purchase several DrawPerfect figure libraries by calling WordPerfect Corporation.

Because the figure is tilted downward at the right side and is not the right shape for the flyer text, you must edit the figure with the graphic image editor. To edit the figure, do the following:

1. Press E to edit the figure. WordPerfect displays the image in the graphics image editing screen.
2. Press S (Scale). At the `Scale X:` prompt, type *120* to make the box 120% longer. Press Enter and at the `Scale Y:` prompt, press Enter to accept the default of 100%.
3. Press R (Rotate). At the `Enter number of degrees:` prompt, type *–20* and press Enter to rotate the figure 20° counterclockwise.

   Press N at the `Mirror image?` prompt.
4. Press F7 twice to return to the document screen.
5. Check your work in View Document (Shift-F7, V).

Adding the Logo Graphic

To insert the figure of the bull's head in column two, do the following:

1. Turn on Reveal Codes (Alt-F3) and move the cursor to the right of the code for the first figure box (the store title).
2. Press Alt-F9, F, C. In the Definition: Figure screen, change the settings to the following:

Filename	BEEF.WPG
Anchor Type	Page, Number of pages to skip: 4
Vertical Position	Set Position, 7.88"
Horizontal Position	Columns, 2, Center
Size	1.25" wide × 1" high
Wrap Text Around Box	No

   Because the bull's head appears unnaturally elongated, use the figure editor to make the head wider.

3. To edit the bull's head, press E. In the graphic image editor, press S (Scale) to change the dimensions of the figure.
4. At the `Scale X:` prompt, type *150* and press Enter. At the `Scale Y:` prompt, press Enter to accept the default of 100%. Press F7 twice to return to the document screen.
5. Check your work with View Document (Shift-F7, V).

19

Producing Brochures

As always, when you design a brochure, you must keep the intended audience in mind. Because brochures are used primarily to advertise goods and services, you must make the brochure appeal to the people you want to attract. Several things impact the design of a brochure: the time investment required, the financial investment required, and the familiarity of the audience with the product or service.

Brochures for services that require a significant investment of time or money usually must include a great deal of information in order to "make the sale." The amount of knowledge your audience has with the service being advertised also can determine the content and design of your brochure. A brochure announcing a medical conference, for example, may need to include very little sell copy because doctors are highly motivated to improve their skills. A brochure touting a major investment opportunity for middle-income families, on the other hand, must contain verbal and visual information.

Brochure No. 1: Service Information

This brochure educates the reader about the dangers of power line spikes, the company's line analysis, and the available protection services. The brochure must educate the reader about power line surges and evoke a response in an informative, but economical, way. The design of this brochure shows how you can pack a great deal of copy onto a single 8 1/2-by-11-inch page without overburdening the reader. The brochure is laid out on two landscape pages and poses some interesting design challenges, such as the header that extends across the entire four-column spread (see figs. 19.1 and 19.2).

Defining the Page

The first step in defining the underlying page design is to choose a landscape form and set margins by doing the following:

1. Press Shift-F8, P, S. In the Format: Paper Size/Type menu, move the cursor to `Standard - Wide`, which is a landscape form provided with WordPerfect. Press Enter and then F7 to return to the document screen.

2. Set the margins by pressing Shift-F8, P, M; typing *1/2*"; pressing Enter; typing *1/2*"; pressing Enter, Enter, L, M; typing *1/2*"; pressing Enter; typing *1/2*"; and pressing Enter, F7.

If a page design includes graphic lines and/or boxes, you should create these next and enter text afterwards. After you create the lines and boxes, you can print a copy of the page. With this printout, you can measure text margins and display type positions accurately in relation to the printed positions of the lines and boxes.

Adding Design Elements

To create the shaded vertical bar and horizontal lines on page 1 of the brochure, do the following:

1. Press Alt-F9, L, V. In the Graphics: Vertical Line screen, change the settings to the following:

Horizontal Position	Set Position, 5 3/4"
Vertical Position	Full Page
Width of Line	3/4"
Gray Shading	20%

2. Press F7 to return to the document screen.

Computer
Power
Conditioning
Service
2890 Pine Tree Avenue
Grass Valley, CA 95945
(916) 265-3700

COMPUTER POWER CONDITIONING SERVICE

Office Power Protection

Are your computers, copiers, faxes at risk?
Research shows 50-70% of computer downtime is caused by substandard office electrical power.

As office machines proliferate in the workplace, utility power is stretched and becomes "dirty" and subject to damaging surges and spikes. In fact, many popular office machines induce sags and spikes in the electrical power supply: copiers, laser printers, air-conditioners, coffee makers, microwave ovens.

Poor power quality causes costly downtime, and can degrade the performance of office machines and computers and shorten their working lifespans.

Power line quality analysis is a complex subject, requiring study of crest factors, clamping voltages, modified sine waves, transients, spikes, and other factors. At Ridge Electric, we're equipped to analyze these factors and recommend the line-conditioning solutions you need.

FIG. 19.1 Page 1 of a service brochure.

Line-conditioning Systems and What They Do

Surge Suppressors provide front-line defense against damaging overvoltage (surges), impulses (spikes), noise, and lightning-induced overloads. High-quality surge suppressors are a must for sensitive electronic equipment such as faxes, copiers, printers, and especially computers. Surge suppressors vary widely in the level of protection they provide. Ridge Electric installs only equipment rated for maximum protection and reliability.

Voltage Regulators keep the power to your business machines and computers at a constant level. When power drops to brownout-levels (90 volts or less), a voltage regulator guarantees that your computer gets the 120 volts it was designed for. (Brownouts can cause severe damage to electronic circuit boards.)

Power Conditioners combine a high-quality surge suppressor with a voltage regulator in a single box. The power conditioner provides top-level power isolation, plus noise filtering and surge suppression. The only protection these units don't offer is uninterruptible power. If your main need is for a clean power supply, this product is your best bet.

Uninterruptible Power Supplies, also called battery backup systems. When the power goes down in your office, a UPS gives you time to save your computer data. A high-end unit will allow you to continue working for several hours or even an entire day while the power is down. Uninterruptible power supplies provide the most complete protection you can have, because they include surge, spike and noise suppression, power isolation, voltage regulation, and emergency power. The UPS eliminates 99% of all power problems experienced by computer users, and is a particularly valuable solution for safeguarding local area network systems. Software supplied with the UPS will actually log off all users, close all files, and do a safe system shut-down. Uninterruptible power supplies are also widely used to keep business telephone systems operating during blackouts.

Individualized Solutions Protect You Best

Because every office environment has it own, unique power supply profile, protecting your business machines is best accomplished by an individualized analysis and line conditioning plan.

That's where Ridge Electric can help. ***We offer a free, half-hour consultation at your site.*** We will analyze your electrical supply and recommend the right surge suppressor, voltage regulator, power conditioner, or UPS to protect your valuable electronic business systems. In addition, we offer a complete turnkey solution that includes monitoring, consultation, installation, and ongoing service.

Call (916) 265-3700 to talk about your power conditioning needs.

A Case Study: Solving Line Power Problems at Hills Flat Lumber

Hills Flat Lumber Co., a major business in the Grass Valley area, struggled with embarrassing computer glitches that randomly shut down their point-of-sale system until Ridge Electric analyzed the power supply and discovered that machinery was being cycled on and off hundreds of times a day, causing power spikes. After installing line-conditioning and UPS equipment, downtime was reduced to zero.

FIG. 19.2 Page 2 of the service brochure.

3. Press Alt-F9, L, H. In the Graphics: Horizontal Line screen, change the settings as indicated; then press F7 to return to the document screen. Repeat this step four times for each of the four lines, entering the settings as shown in the following table:

Horizontal Position	5"	5"	5"	5"
Vertical Position	1/2"	1 1/8"	1 3/4"	2 3/8"
Length	4"	4"	4"	4"
Width	1/16"	.013"	.013"	.013"
Gray Shading	100%	100%	100%	100%

Note: .013" is the default line width and is listed, therefore, in decimal notation—the way WordPerfect displays it in the menu.

Adding Text to Page One

To create the text for page one, do the following:

1. Define newspaper-style columns for this page only (the second page uses different column specifications). Press Alt-F7, C, D. In the Text Column Definition menu, change the settings to the following:

Type	Newspaper
Number of Columns	2
Margins	1/2", 4 1/8", 6 7/8", 10.5"

2. Press F7, O to turn columns on.
3. Move the cursor down to the bottom of page one by pressing Shift-F8, O, A, D and typing *5 1/2"*. Press Enter, F7.

TIP

Using Advance to move the insertion point to the bottom of the page is better than using Enter. Editing in the Reveal Codes screen is easier if most of the hidden codes are together in one compact section at the top of the file. Using Advance prevents the address from being separated from the rest of the codes by several hard returns.

4. Press Tab four times and change the font to 14-point Helvetica Bold. Type *Computer* and press Enter.
5. Type the rest of the company title as shown in figure 19.1. Be sure to press Tab four times before each line and press Enter once after each line. For the street address, city, state, ZIP, and phone number, use 10-point Helvetica.
6. After you type the address, press Ctrl-Enter to move to the next column.
7. Switch to 28-point Helvetica Bold; press Shift-F8, O, A, I; and type *3/4"*. Press Enter and then F7 to position the top of the next line of text (COMPUTER) 3/4" from the top of the page. Type *COMPUTER* and press Enter.
8. Press Shift-F8, O, A, I and type *1 3/8"*. Press Enter and then F7 to position the top of the next line of type 1 3/8" below the top of the page. Type *POWER* and press Enter.
9. Press Shift-F8, O, A, I and type *2"*. Press Enter and then F7 to position the top of the next line of type two inches below the top of the page. Type *CONDITIONING* and press Enter.
10. Press Shift-F8, O, A, I; type *2 5/8"*; and press Enter, F7 to position the top of the next line of type 2 5/8 inches below the top of the page. Type *SERVICE* and press Enter.
11. Switch the font to 20-point Helvetica Bold. Press Shift-F8, O, A, D; type *1/8"*; and press Enter, F7 to move the insertion point down 1/8". Type *Office Power Protection*. Press Enter five times.

    (These Advance figures were determined by trial and error.)
12. Switch the font to 12-point Helvetica Bold and type *Are your computers, copiers, faxes at risk?* Press Enter and switch the font to 10-point Times Roman.

    The columns on the first page are wide, and the font in the second column is too small for the column width. You can make the type readable, however, by adding extra space between lines and paragraphs.
13. Press Shift-F8, O, P, L; type *1p*; press Enter; type *4p*; and press Enter, F7 to add one point of extra leading between lines and four points between paragraphs.

Remember to add the *p*; otherwise, WordPerfect inserts one inch of extra space between lines and four inches of extra space between paragraphs!

14. Type the text on the first page. At the end of the page, press Alt-F7, C, F to turn columns off. If the cursor is at the end of the page, WordPerfect moves the cursor to the next page. If not, press Ctrl-Enter to insert a hard page break and move the cursor to page two.

Adding Text to Page Two

To design page two of the brochure, do the following:

1. Give page two of the brochure a slightly different look by setting new top and bottom margins. Press Shift-F8, P, M; type *5/8"*; press Enter; type *5/8"*; and press Enter, F7.

   Now you can create the shaded box in column four. Actually, the *box* is a thick vertical line. You use a line instead of a box because WordPerfect cannot print horizontal lines over the box.

   Because of a program bug, you must enter the line at the top of the page, ahead of other codes; otherwise, WordPerfect moves the line to the following page.

2. To create the wide vertical line, press Alt-F9, L, V. In the Graphics: Vertical Line screen, change the settings to the following:

Horizontal Position	Set Position, 8 1/4"
Vertical Position	Set Position, 1/2"
Length of Line	7 1/4"
Width of Line	2 1/4"
Gray Shading	5%

   Do not set gray shading to more than 10 percent. Even 10 percent shading makes the text hard to read.

3. Press F7 to return to the document menu.

4. To create the horizontal lines across the top of the page, press Alt-F9, L, H. In the Graphics: Horizontal Line screen,

change the settings to the following (perform this step three times, using the settings for the top, middle, and bottom lines, respectively):

	Top	*Middle*	*Bottom*
Horizontal Position	Full	Full	Full
Vertical Position	1/2"	1 1/8"	1 3/4"
Width of Line	1/16"	.013"	.013"
Gray Shading	100%	100%	100%

(WordPerfect's default Width of Line setting, .013", is listed in decimal notation.)

Next, you must create a text box to hold the sidebar. Because normal column margins don't leave enough space between the sidebar text and gray screen edges and because WordPerfect doesn't enable you to set margins within a column, you must use a text box to enter text instead of typing the sidebar copy as part of the main text.

To create the sidebar, do the following:

1. Press Alt-F9, B, O. In the Options: Text Box screen, set the border style to None for all borders, the inside border space to .2" for all borders, and the gray shading to 0 percent. Press F9.

2. Press Alt-F9, B, C, E. In the text box editor, type the text of the sidebar. Use 14-point Helvetica Bold for the sidebar heading and 10-point Times Roman Bold for the text.

To enter the heading at the top of the page, do the following:

1. Change the font to 28-point Helvetica Bold and position the top of the first line of text 3/4" from the top of the page by pressing Shift-F8, O, A, I; typing *3/4*"; and pressing Enter, F7. Type *Line-conditioning Systems* and press Enter.

2. Position the top of the next line 1 3/8" from the top of the page, type *and What They Do*, and press Enter twice.

To type the text in columns one through three, do the following:

1. Define four columns for the page by pressing Alt-F7, C, D. In the Text Column Definition screen, change the settings to the following:

Type	Newspaper
Number of Columns	4
Margins	1/2", 2 3/4", 3", 5 1/4", 5 3/4", 8", 8 1/2", 10 1/2"

2. Press F7, O to turn columns on and return to the document screen.
3. Change the font to 14-point Helvetica Bold, type *Surge Suppressors*, press Enter, change the font to 10-point Times Roman, and type the text in columns one through three, as shown in figure 19.1.

   Be sure to use 14-point Helvetica Bold for the subheadings.

Brochure No. 2: Business Seminar

The sample brochure shown in figures 19.3 and 19.4 announces a seminar on improving business relationships.

This brochure's design doesn't contain any new challenges in using WordPerfect features; however, the design does use old, familiar features in interesting ways. Two overlapping figure boxes hold the images of a sun and a handshake, for example. The thick horizontal line on the front page runs across space designated for text columns. As as you design documents with WordPerfect, you spend most of your time fine-tuning the spacing of text, lines, and graphics.

Creating Page One

To create the first page of this brochure, do the following:

1. Press Shift-F8, P, S; then move the cursor to the `Standard - Wide` paper definition that comes with WordPerfect and press Enter, F7 to choose a landscape (horizontal) paper size and type.
2. Set the margins by pressing Shift-F8, P, M; typing *1/2"*; pressing Enter; typing *1/2"*; pressing Enter, Enter, L, M; typing *1/2"* ; pressing Enter; typing *1/2"* ; and pressing Enter, F7.

THREE WAYS TO LEARN:
1.
Gallia est omnis divisa in partes tres, quarum unam incolunt Belgae, aliam Aquitani, tertiam qui ipsorum lingua Celtae, nostra Galli appellantur.
2.
Hi omnes lingua, institutis, legibus inter se differunt. Gallos ab Aquitanis Garumna flumen, a Belgis Matrona et Sequana dividit. Horum omnium fortissimi sunt Belgae, propterea quod a cultu atque humanitate.
3.
Que de causa Helvetii quoque reliquos Gallos virtute praecedunt, quod fere cotidianis proeliis cum Germanis contendunt, cum aut suis finibus eos prohibent, aut ipsi in eorum finibus bellum gerunt. Eorum una pars, quam Gallos obtinere dictum est, initium capit.
Paul C. Withers Presents
Building Harmony in Business Relationships
An All-Day Workshop
Tamara Hot Springs Resort
July 20, 1992
9 am - 5 pm

FIG. 19.3 Page 1 of a business seminar brochure.

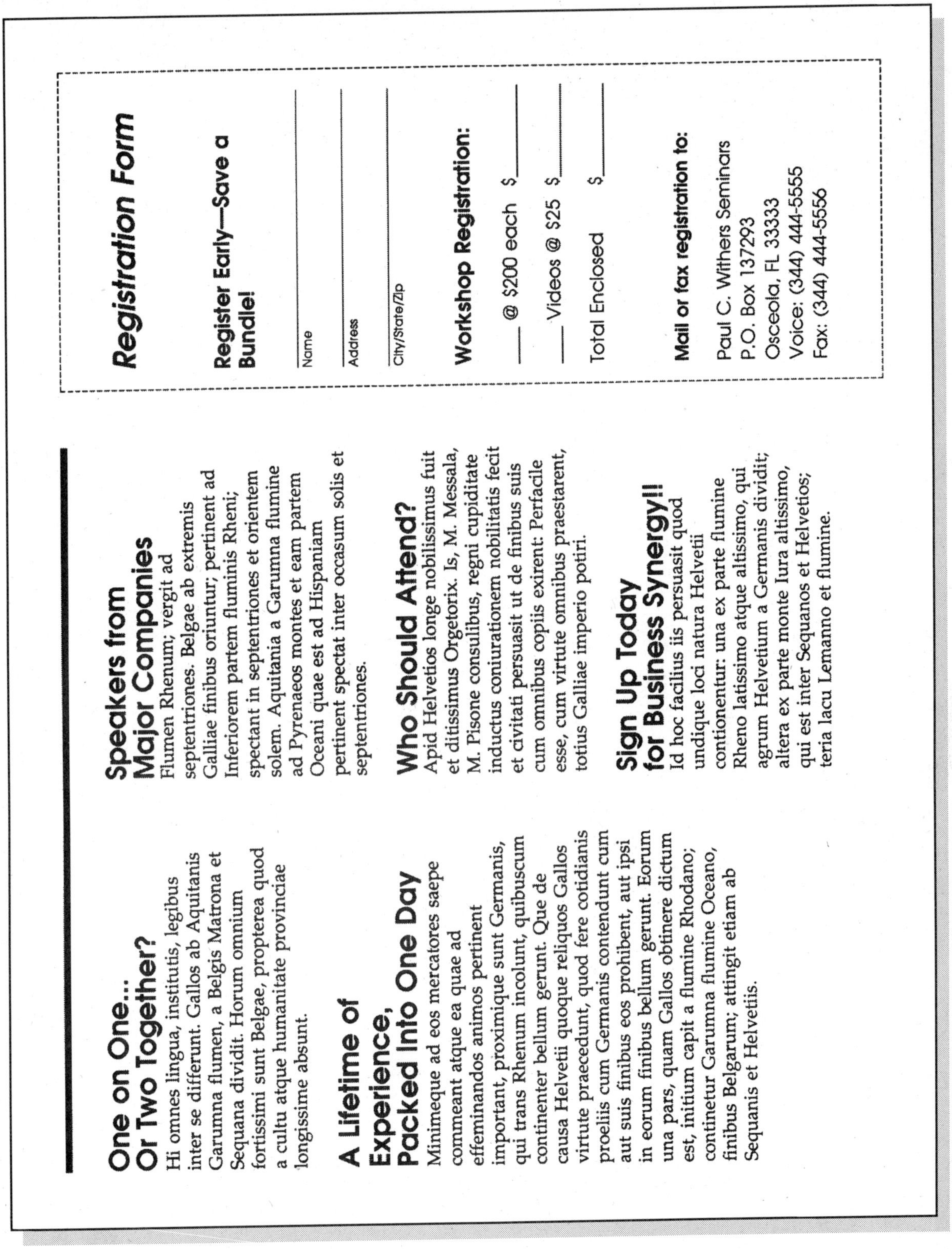

One on One... Or Two Together?

Hi omnes lingua, institutis, legibus inter se differunt. Gallos ab Aquitanis Garumna flumen, a Belgis Matrona et Sequana dividit. Horum omnium fortissimi sunt Belgae, propterea quod a cultu atque humanitate provinciae longissime absunt.

A Lifetime of Experience, Packed Into One Day

Minimeque ad eos mercatores saepe commeant atque ea quae ad effeminandos animos pertinent important, proximique sunt Germanis, qui trans Rhenum incolunt, quibuscum continenter bellum gerunt. Que de causa Helvetii quoque reliquos Gallos virtute praecedunt, quod fere cotidianis proeliis cum Germanis contendunt cum aut suis finibus eos prohibent, aut ipsi in eorum finibus bellum gerunt. Eorum una pars, quam Gallos obtinere dictum est, initium capit a flumine Rhodano; continetur Garumna flumine Oceano, finibus Belgarum; attingit etiam ab Sequanis et Helvetiis.

Speakers from Major Companies

Flumen Rhenum; vergit ad septentriones. Belgae ab extremis Galliae finibus oriuntur; pertinent ad Inferiorem partem fluminis Rheni; spectant in septentriones et orientem solem. Aquitania a Garumna flumine ad Pyrenaeos montes et eam partem Oceani quae est ad Hispaniam pertinent spectat inter occasum solis et septentriones.

Who Should Attend?

Apid Helvetios longe nobilissimus fuit et ditissimus Orgetorix. Is, M. Messala, M. Pisone consulibus, regni cupiditate inductus coniurationem nobilitatis fecit et civitati persuasit ut de finibus suis cum omnibus copiis exirent: Perfacile esse, cum virtute omnibus praestarent, totius Galliae imperio potiri.

Sign Up Today for Business Synergy!!

Id hoc facilius iis persuasit quod undique loci natura Helvetii contionentur: una ex parte flumine Rheno latissimo atque altissimo, qui agrum Helvetium a Germanis dividit; altera ex parte monte Iura altissimo, qui est inter Sequanos et Helvetios; teria lacu Lemanno et flumine.

Registration Form

Register Early—Save a Bundle!

____
Name

____
Address

____
City/State/Zip

Workshop Registration:

____ @ $200 each $________

____ Videos @ $25 $________

Total Enclosed $________

Mail or fax registration to:

Paul C. Withers Seminars
P.O. Box 137293
Osceola, FL 33333
Voice: (344) 444-5555
Fax: (344) 444-5556

FIG. 19.4 Page 2 of a business seminar brochure.

3. Define the thick horizontal line by pressing Alt-F9, L, H. In the Graphics: Horizontal Line screen, change the settings to the following:

Horizontal Position	Full
Vertical Position	Set Position, 2 1/2"
Width of Line	1/8"
Gray Shading	100%

4. Press F7 to return to the document screen.

Now you can place the figures of the sun and the handshake, both of which come from the DrawPerfect Figure Library. To insert the graphics, do the following:

1. Press Alt-F9, F, O. In the Options: Figure screen, change the settings to the following:

Border Style	Set all to None
Inside Border Space	Set all to 0"

2. Press F7 to return to the document screen.
3. Press Alt-F9, F, C. In the Definition: Figure screen, change the settings to the following:

Filename	HANDS-2.WPG
Anchor Type	Page, Number of pages to skip: 0
Vertical Position	Set Position, 2.95"
Horizontal Position	Set Position, 7.56"
Size	Set Both, 2" wide × 2" high
Wrap Text Around Box	No

4. Press F7 to return to the document screen.
5. Press Alt-F9, F, C. In the Graphics: Figure screen, change the settings to the following:

Filename	SUN.WPG
Anchor Type	Page, Number of pages to skip: 0
Vertical Position	Top
Horizontal Position	Set Position, 7"

Size	Set Both, 3" wide × 3" high
Wrap Text Around Box	No

6. Press F7 to return to the document screen.

To define three newspaper-style columns, do the following:

1. Press Alt-F7, C, D. In the Text Column Definition screen, change the settings to the following:

Type	Newspaper
Number of Columns	3
Margins	1/2", 3 1/2", 4", 7", 7 1/2", 10 1/2"

2. Press Enter, O to turn columns on and return to the document screen.

To enter the text, do the following:

1. Press Enter 14 times to move the cursor down to the insertion point for the start of the text. Change the font to 14-point Avant Garde Gothic Demi and type *THREE WAYS TO LEARN:*.

2. Press Enter twice, change the font to 30-point Avant Garde Gothic Demi, type *1.* and press Enter.

3. Change the font to 10-point Palatino and type the first section of body text. Repeat these font specifications for the other numbered paragraphs in the first panel.

4. Press Ctrl-Enter (Hard Page) *twice* to move the cursor to the top of column three.

5. Press Enter 27 times to move the insertion point below the figures in the third column. Change the font to 14-point Avant Garde Gothic Book and type *Paul C. Withers Presents*.

6. Press Enter twice, change the font to 24-point Avant Garde Gothic Demi, and tighten the leading (line spacing) by specifying two points less space between lines. Press Shift-F8, O, P, L, Enter; type *–2p*; and press Enter, F7.

   Remember to include the small *p*; otherwise, WordPerfect inserts two inches less space between lines, turning the text into gibberish.

7. Type *Building* and the remaining lines of the workshop title, as shown in figure 19.3. Be sure to press Enter between lines.

TIP

Many (if not all) headings look better when the letter and line spacing is tightened, especially if you use fonts larger than 18 points. This Avant Garde font is fairly tight and not too big; therefore, you need to adjust only the leading.

8. Before you press Enter at the end of the last line, change the font to 14-point Avant Garde Gothic Book.
9. Press Enter twice and type *An All-Day Workshop*. Press Enter again.
10. Type the rest of the subheading, as shown in figure 19.3. Be sure to press Enter after each line.

TIP

If you switch to a smaller font before pressing Enter, WordPerfect inserts less space after the current line than it would if you left the much larger 24-point font in effect.

Creating Page Two

Now that the first page of the brochure is done, you can create the second page (refer to fig. 19.4). To create page two of the brochure, do the following:

1. From page one, press Ctrl-Enter (Hard Page) to move to the first column on the reverse side of the page.
2. Define the horizontal line at the top of the page by pressing Alt-F9, L, H. In the Graphics: Horizontal Line screen, change the settings to the following:

Horizontal Position	Left
Vertical Position	Set Position, 1/2"
Length of Line	6 1/2"
Width of Line	1/16"

3. Press F7 to return to the document screen.
4. To create the text box in the third column, which holds the sidebar, press Alt-F9, B, O. In the Options: Text Box screen, change the settings to the following:

Border Style	Set all to Dashed
Outside Border	Set all to 0"

   Remember, you must create page-anchored boxes on the first line of the page; otherwise, WordPerfect moves the boxes to the following page.
5. Press F7 to return to the document screen.
6. To create the box for the sidebar, press Alt-F9, B, C.
7. In the Definition: Text Box screen, make the following settings:

Anchor Type	Page, Number of pages to skip: 0
Vertical Position	Set Position, 1/2"
Horizontal Position	Set Position, 7 1/2"
Size	Set Both, 2 7/8" wide × 7 1/2" high

8. Press E, and in the text box editor, create the text for the registration form.

TIP

If you fail to set the outside borders to 0", WordPerfect places the box borders lower than the horizontal line by the amount of the top border width and higher than the bottom of the text area by the amount of the bottom border width.

To create the text for the sidebar, do the following:

1. With the cursor anywhere in the document, press Alt-F9, B, E, 1, Enter, E. In the text box editor, you can type the text for the registration form (described in the next steps).
2. Change the font to 20-point Avant Garde Gothic Demi Oblique, press Enter, and type *Registration Form*.

3. Press Enter three times, change the font to 14-point Avant Garde Gothic Demi, and type *Register Early Save a Bundle!*

> **TIP**
>
> Always use typographic hyphens. To insert the hyphen in `Early—Save`, press Ctrl-V (Compose), type *4,34* (4, comma, 34), and press Enter. If your printer can print graphics, it can print, in the location you entered the code, a true hyphen (also called an *em dash* because it is the same width as the lowercase character *m* in the current typeface).

4. Press Enter twice, change the font to 8-point Avant Garde Gothic Book, press the underline character 45 times to create the first line of the registration form. Press Enter and type *Name*.

> **TIP**
>
> Three ways exist to create lines for response forms. Using the underline character is by far the easiest. Another method uses the table feature, and the remaining method uses Flush Right. Both of these methods involve a great deal of trial and error to position lines correctly. Placing the labels (`Name`, `Address`, and so on) under the lines can save time.

5. Press Enter twice, type another horizontal line, and repeat these steps to create the remainder of the fill-in section of the registration form.
6. After typing *City/State/Zip*, press Enter four times, change the font to 14-point Avant Garde Gothic Demi, type *Workshop Registration:*, and press Enter twice.
7. Change the font to 12-point Avant Garde Gothic Book, press the underline character four times, press the space bar, type *@ $200 each*, press Alt-F6 (Flush Right), type *$*, press the underline character 10 times, and press Enter twice.
8. Type the remaining lines of this section, repeating the format described in step 7.

9. Press Enter four times, change the font to 12-point Avant Garde Gothic Demi, and type *Mail or fax registration to:*.
10. Press Enter twice; change the font to 12-point Avant Garde Gothic Book; press Shift-F8, O, P, L, Enter; type *2p*; and press Enter, F7 to increase the leading by two points to add space between the lines of the address.
11. Type the address, as shown in figure 19.4.
12. Press F7 twice to return to the document screen. Check your work with View Document (Shift-F7, V).

To begin adding the text, complete the following steps:

1. Press Enter twice, change the font to 18-point Avant Garde Gothic Demi, and make a leading adjustment of -2p by pressing Shift-F8, O, P, L, Enter; typing *–2p*; and pressing Enter, F7.
2. Type *One on One...* and press Enter; then type *Or Two Together?*
3. Before you press Enter at the end of the second line of the bold heading, press Shift-F8, O, P, L, Enter, 0, Enter, F7 to change the leading adjustment back to 0.
4. Press Enter, change the font to 12-point Palatino, and type the first section of body text.

   Repeat these heading and text settings for each of the paragraphs on the page. You can work quickly if you block the font codes and text for the first heading, save them to a file, and then retrieve and edit them for each new section.

TIP

After you design a section of a document, you should check View Document before printing a copy of the page. Small, easily corrected mistakes can wreak havoc with formatting, and printing text that contains such errors is a waste of time. If you accidentally insert a hard return before a page-anchored box, for example, WordPerfect prints the box on the following page, making the printed copy useless.

20

Producing Product and Price Lists

Organization is the word that must spring to mind when one thinks of creating price and product lists. Unfortunately, organization also is the quality that often is lacking in these lists. Most people have dealt with poorly planned product and price lists that pack too much information onto a page and use poorly differentiated fonts for headings and lists. Poorly organized price and product lists are hard to read and easy to ignore.

You can create and format a well-organized list by asking the right questions. Does your price list require descriptive text, photographs, or line drawings? Which subject categories need to be set clearly apart? After you plan the basic structure—in your mind first, then in rough sketches—you can choose the most effective design tools for the job.

These tools include type, space, and illustrations. Because space for lists is often at a premium, you may decide to make the type small, but readable. To conserve space, you also can set off categories with shaded bars.

Product and Price List No. 1: A Photographic Hardware Price List

This price list contains a great deal of copy, but no illustrations. By creatively using lines, boxes, and typography, you can put quite a bit of type on the page without overwhelming the reader. Creating this list requires a delicate balancing act.

Adding Design Elements

To create the list shown in figure 20.1, you must do the following:

1. Set 1/2" margins on all sides of the page by pressing Shift-F8, P, M; typing *1/2"*; pressing Enter; typing *1/2"*; pressing Enter, Enter, L, M; typing *1/2"*; pressing Enter; typing *1/2"*; and pressing Enter, F7.

2. To create the heavy line at the top of the page, press Alt-F9, L, H. In the Graphics: Horizontal Line screen, change the settings to the following:

Horizontal Position	Full
Vertical Position	Set Position, 1/2"
Width of Line	1/16"
Gray Shading	100%

3. Press F7 to return to the document screen.

   Obviously, you cannot create lines unless you know where the lines should go. Until you are satisfied with the position of the type, for example, creating the gray line over "New! Advanced Control Unit" doesn't make sense. The line creation keystrokes are given here, however, to remind you to position line and box codes at the top of the page, where you can find them easily.

BLITZLICHT

PRODUCTS FOR THE PHOTO PRO

Products and Prices Spring 1992

Studio Flash Systems

BL 4800 Studio Flash **$1500.00**
Includes 4800 unit, 5" umbrella reflector, protective cover, sync cord, power cable.

BL 3600 Studio Flash **$1250.00**
Includes 3600 unit, 5" umbrella reflector, protective cover, sync cord, power cable.

BL 2400 Studio Flash **$1000.00**
Includes 2400 unit, 5" umbrella reflector, protective cover, sync cord, power cable.

Reflectors and Umbrellas

11" Diameter Reflector **$25.00**
Very effective for situations requiring long-throw, narrow-beam lighting. Bright finish.

20" Diameter Reflector **$35.00**
Good choice for portraits requiring moderate light definition and feathering. (Medium-soft portrait light.) Removable center shield for bouncelight.

42" Silver Bounce Umbrella **$35.00**
Very high output, with smooth, even coverage. Best choice for portraits. Soft bouncelight source for beauty, products. Gives very wide coverage.

New! Advanced Control Unit

BlitzChip Control Box **$150.00**
Controls up to six Blitzlicht strobes from central console. Vary power, modeling, dump.

WARRANTY

Blitzlicht guarantees to repair or replace, free of charge, for a period of two years, any part found to be defective due to faulty materials or workmanship.

TERMS AND CONDITIONS

Blitzlicht products are shipped with an unconditional 30-day money-back guarantee.

On credit card orders, please include expiration date and a phone number where we can reach you during the day. For fastest service, order on our toll-free line using your Mastercard or VISA.

All prices subject to change without notice.

BLITZLICHT
4321 E. Meadowlark
Farmer's Mill, WI 54321
Voice: (508) 987-2345
Fax: (508) 987-2344

Call toll-free:
1-800-987-6543

FIG. 20.1 A well-designed price list.

TIP

A line, not a text box, is used to create the screen over "New! Advanced Control Unit" because lines are much easier to work with than boxes. To edit text that is part of a box, you must use the graphics box text editor, which requires a greater number of keystrokes. Placing a line over the type is much simpler. For this reason, a line—a very fat one—was used to create the shading over the text in column two.

4. To create the line over "New! Advanced Control Unit," press Alt-F9, L, H. In the Graphics: Horizontal Line screen, change the settings to the following:

Horizontal Position	Set Position, 15/16"
Vertical Position	Set Position, 9 1/10"
Length of Line	3 7/8"
Width of Line	4/10"
Gray Shading	6%

   Press F7.

TIP

Gray shading darker than 10 percent decreases readability; shading of 5 to 6 percent is usually dark enough to set apart section titles or sidebars.

5. To create the vertical shaded line over column two, press Alt-F9, L, V. In the Graphics: Vertical Line screen, change the settings to the following:

Horizontal Position	Set Position, 5"
Vertical Position	Set Position, 2 15/16"
Length of Line	7.3"
Width of Line	2 9/16"
Gray Shading	6%

6. To create the box that surrounds the page, press Alt-F9, B, O. In the Options: Text Box screen, change the settings to the following:

Border Style	Set all to Single
Outside Border Space	Set all to 0"

7. Press F7 to return to the document screen.
8. Press Alt-F9, B, C. In the Definition: Text Box screen, change the settings to the following:

Anchor Type	Page, Number of pages to skip: 0
Vertical Position	Set Position, 2 1/4"
Horizontal Position	Margins, Full
Size	Set Both, 7 1/2" wide × 8 1/4" high
Wrap Text Around Box	No

9. Press F7 to return to the document screen.
10. Define the text columns by pressing Alt-F7, C, D. In the Text Column Definition screen, change the settings to the following:

Margins	1", 4 7/8", 5 1/4", 7 1/2"

11. Press F7, O to turn columns on and return to the document screen.
12. Press Enter twice to insert space below the heavy horizontal line.

Adding Text to Column One

Now that the margins, shaded screens, and boxes have been created, you are ready to enter the text. To enter the text, do the following:

1. Change the font to 40-point Avant Garde Gothic Demi.
2. The letters in "BLITZLICHT" are widely spaced, using the Word/Letter Spacing feature. To create this effect, press

Shift-F8, O, P, W, Enter, P; type *120*; and press Enter, F7 to set letter spacing to 120% of optimal.

3. Type *BLITZLICHT* and press Enter.

4. Change the font to 12-point Avant Garde Gothic Demi and type *PRODUCTS FOR THE PHOTO PRO*. (Leave letter spacing at 120 percent.)

5. Press Enter twice and press Shift-F8, O, P, W, Enter, O, F7 to reset letter spacing to normal.

6. Set the font to 18-point Avant Garde Gothic Book and type *Products and Prices Spring 1992*.

7. Press Enter three times, change the font to 18-point Avant Garde Gothic Demi, and type *Studio Flash Systems*. Before you press Enter, change the font to 12-point Avant Garde Gothic Demi.

8. Press Enter twice and type *BL 4800 Studio Flash*. Press Alt-F6 (Flush Right) and type *$1500.00*.

9. Press Enter, change the font to 12-point Avant Garde Gothic Book, and type *Includes 4800 unit, 5" umbrella reflector, protective cover, sync cord, power cable.*

10. Enter the remainder of the first column. Repeat the format described in steps 8 and 9. Be sure to press Enter twice between items.

    (You can save time if you block the first item, including font codes, save it to a file, and retrieve and edit it for each new section.)

    At the end of the next-to-last item, "42" Silver Bounce Umbrella," press Enter twice to place the next heading inside the wide, shaded horizontal line. (Actually, the text was placed first, and then the line was created and positioned correctly over the text by experimenting with the Vertical Position setting.)

    For the last heading in the column, "New!...," change the font to 18-point Avant Garde Gothic Demi. Then change the font to 12-point Avant Garde Gothic Demi, press Enter twice, and format the next heading, "BlitzChip," the same as the other headings in the column.

TIP

When trying to make list items stand out, don't overdo it. The first draft of this list used heavy black lines for the text box and a thicker line at the top of the page. The items in the list had square bullets. The page looked too black; the bold section and item titles alone provided plenty of emphasis. A good guideline for designing tasteful documents is "just enough is enough."

11. When you reach the bottom of column one, press Ctrl-Enter (Hard Page) to move to the next column.

Adding Text to Column Two

To enter the text for the sidebar in the right column, you need to use the Advance to Line function to move the insertion point down to the first line of text ("WARRANTY") and then do the following:

1. Press Shift-F8, O, A, I; type *3.11*"; and press Enter, F7.

   To determine what distance to enter at the `Adv. to line` prompt, move the cursor to the text in column one ("BL 4800 Studio Flash") that is parallel to the first line in column 2 ("WARRANTY") and read the `Ln` message in the status line.

TIP

When you use Advance to Line to even up the tops of columns, remember that Advance to Line specifies the distance to the top of the text. If you specify different font sizes for text at the top of the columns, the first lines align at the top, but not at the baseline. Although you can try to align the baselines by inserting an Advance code, this method may not work because WordPerfect doesn't enable you to enter Advance increments smaller than 1/100". The Advance to Line function works in step 12 because the same 12-point font size was used in the first line of both columns.

2. Change the font to 12-point Avant Garde Gothic Demi and type *WARRANTY*.
3. Press Enter twice, set the font to 10-point Avant Garde Gothic Book, and type the next paragraph (*Blitzlicht guarantees...*).
4. Press Enter three times, change the font to 12-point Avant Garde Gothic Demi, and type *TERMS AND CONDITIONS*.
5. Press enter twice, change the font to 10-point Avant Garde Gothic Book, and type the next three paragraphs (*Blitzlicht products...*). Press Enter twice between paragraphs.
6. Press Enter seven times. Change letter spacing to 120 percent of normal to add space to "BLITZLICHT" at the bottom of column two by pressing Shift-F8, O, P, W, Enter, P; typing *120*; and pressing Enter, F7.
7. Change the font to 14-point Avant Garde Gothic Demi and type *BLITZLICHT*; then set letter spacing to normal by pressing Shift-F8, O, P, W, Enter, O, F7.
8. Press Enter, change the font to 14-point Avant Garde Gothic Book, and type the address and telephone numbers. Be sure to press Enter between lines.
9. Press Enter twice, change the font to 14-point Avant Garde Gothic Demi, and type *Call toll-free:*.
10. Press Enter and type *1-800-987-6543*.

This product list is finished. You can check your work with View Document (Shift-F7, V).

Product and Price List No. 2: A Computer Supply Price Sheet

The list shown in figure 20.2 holds too much information to be effectively organized with the format used in the preceding list (refer to fig. 20.1).

The organization for this list of publishing supplies enables a great deal of information to be included on one sheet of paper. The "relaxed and roomy" design is possible by reducing the text to a small but readable size (9 points); in addition, the WordPerfect table feature, in combination with cell shading, is used to organize the copy. Finally, to fit the maximum amount of text on the page, the left and right margins are set as small as possible. As a result, the page is packed with information, but doesn't look it. In fact, even more copy can be placed in this list.

TIP

When you are pressed for space, reduce the left and right margins before taking space out of the top and bottom margins. Extremely narrow top and bottom margins make documents look crammed onto the page. If you must reduce the top and bottom margins, take more space out of the top margin first.

Setting Up the List

To create this price list, do the following:

1. Press Shift-F8, L, M; type *1/2*"; press Enter; type *1/2*"; press Enter, Enter, P, M; type *0*"; press Enter; type *0*"; and press Enter, F7 to set the margins.

TIP

Left and right margins are set at 0" because it is quicker than typing *0.3*", the minimum value for laser printers. If you are not using a laser printer, set the margins to .3" or 1/3".

2. To create the text box for the list heading, press Alt-F9, B, O. In the Options: Text Box screen, change the settings to the following:

Border Style	None, None, Thick, Thick
Gray Shading	6%

Publisher's PC

Suppliers to the Publishing Industry
8888 Midamerica Dr. ♦ Suite 402 ♦ Indianapolis, IN 46666

GRAPHIC DESIGN SOFTWARE PRICE LIST — JANUARY 1993

MACINTOSH

Graphic Design

PUBLISHER	TITLE	VERSION	PRICE
Adobe	Illustrator	3.0	349.00
	Streamline	2.0	127.00
Aldus	Freehand	3.0	383.00
Aldus	PageMaker	4.0	489.00
	Design Team		849.00

PUBLISHER	TITLE	VERSION	PRICE
Caere	OmniPage		465.00
Xerox	Ventura (PC)	3.0	479.00
	Ventura (MAC)		479.00

Typography

PUBLISHER	TITLE	VERSION	PRICE
Adobe	ATM/Align	4.0	149.00
Broderbund	Typestyler		117.00
5th Generation	Suitcase		100.00

IBM

Graphic Design

PUBLISHER	TITLE	VERSION	PRICE
Adobe	Illustrator	1.1	299.00
	Streamline	1.1	129.00
Corel	CorelDRAW!	2.0	369.00
Micrografx	Designer		443.00
	Charisma		335.00

PUBLISHER	TITLE	VERSION	PRICE
WordPerfect	DrawPerfect	2.0	120.00
ZSoft	PC Paintbrush IV+		113.00
	Publishers PBrush		298.00

Publishing

PUBLISHER	TITLE	VERSION	PRICE
Aldus	PageMaker	4.0	489.00
Caere	OmniPage 386	3.0	465.00
	OmniDraft/Spell		100.00
	OmniProof		119.00

PUBLISHER	TITLE	VERSION	PRICE
Datacopy/Xerox	Grey F/X	1.1	295.00
Digital Comp	db Publisher Pro		495.00
Xerox	Ventura Publisher	3.0	489.00

SHIPPING INFORMATION:

- Orders shipped Airborne Overnight unless UPS Ground delivers next day.
- Same-day shipping on in-stock items.

CALL TOLL-FREE: 1-800-134-5678
INTERNATIONAL: (555) 987-6543

FIG. 20.2 A well-designed price list that contains a wealth of information.

3. Press F7 to return to the document screen. Press Alt-F9, B, C. In the Graphics: Text Box screen, change the settings to the following:

Anchor Type	Page, Number of pages to skip: 0
Vertical Position	Top
Horizontal Position	Margins, Full
Size	7.5" wide × .8" high
Wrap Text Around Box	Yes

4. Press E. In the text box editor, define columns. Press Alt-F7, C, D. In the Text Column Definition screen, set margins of 0", 3", 3 5/8", and 7.17". (WordPerfect enters this last decimal figure when you accept the default for the right margin of column two.) Press F7, O, to turn columns on.

Entering the Text

You need to enter the text from the text box editor. To enter the text, do the following:

1. Set the font to 36-point Times Roman Bold and type *Publisher's PC*. Press Ctrl-Enter (Hard Return) to move to the next column.
2. Set the font to 9-point Helvetica Bold, press Enter, and use Advance to move the insertion point up .031". (This figure was arrived at by experimentation.) Press Shift-F8, O, A, U; type *.31*"; and press Enter, F7.
3. Type *Suppliers to the Publishing Industry*, press Enter, and type the address.
4. To create the diamonds in the address, press Ctrl-V (Compose). At the `Key =` prompt, type *6,96* and press Enter.
5. Press F7 twice to return to the document screen.
6. Press Enter, change the font to 12-point Helvetica Bold, and type *GRAPHIC DESIGN SOFTWARE PRICE LIST—JANUARY 1993*.

7. To create the typesetter's em dash between the words and the date, press Ctrl-V (Compose), type *4,34* and press Enter.
8. Press Enter and define the table. Press Alt-F7, T, C, 1, Enter; type *10*; and press Enter again. This process creates a table with 1 column and 10 rows.

   Change the outside table borders to single lines. Press Alt-F4 and use the arrow keys to highlight the entire table. Press L, A, S, F7 to format the table with single lines and return to the document screen.
9. Move the cursor into the top row of the table, change the font to 12-point Helvetica Bold, and type *MACINTOSH*.
10. To add a gray screen to the cell, with the cursor in the cell that contains `MACINTOSH`, press Alt-F7 to display the Table Edit options. Press O.
11. In the Table Options screen, set Gray Shading to 6 percent. Press F7 to return to the Table Options menu and press L, S, O to turn gray shading on.
12. Press F7 to return to the document screen.
13. Move the cursor down to the next cell, change the font to 9-point Helvetica Bold, press Enter, and type *Graphic Design*.
14. Move the cursor down to the next cell; press Alt-F7 to display the Table Edit options; and press P, C, 2, Enter, F7 to split the cell. Press Enter to add space at the top of the cell.
15. Change the font to 8-point Helvetica Bold and type the column headings (*PUBLISHER*, *VERSION*, *PRICE*), separating them by pressing F4 (Indent). You can adjust the spacing after you type a few lines of product text.

TIP

You must use F4 (Indent) because Tab moves you to the next cell.

To enter the product text, do the following:

1. Press Enter twice, change the font to 9-point Times Roman, and type the first line of product text (*Adobe*, *Illustrator*, *3.0*, *349.00*), pressing F4 (Indent) between entries).

   Type the first four lines of product text. To move the cursor to the cell to the right, press Tab. To return to the cell to the left, press Shift-Tab.

2. Type the rest of the table, repeating the font settings and cell splitting procedure. Press the right-arrow key to get beyond the end of the table (the `[Tbl Off]` code).

3. Boldface text is easier to read if you add extra space between lines. For the shipping information below the chart, add two points of extra leading by pressing Shift-F8, O, P, L, Enter; typing *2p*; and pressing Enter, F7. (Don't forget the *p*; otherwise, WordPerfect adds two inches!)

4. Before you press Enter, change the font to 10-point Helvetica Bold; then press Enter, type *SHIPPING INFORMATION:*, and press Enter again.

5. To create the square bullet that precedes "Orders shipped..." press Ctrl-V (Compose), type *4,2* and press Enter. Format the rest of the text with bullets and capital letters as shown in figure 20.2.

Technical Perspectives Series

Paper No. 32

Should Small Companies Invest in Connectivity?

Ray Blanda
Senior Vice President
Advanced Design Department
Omegacom Corporation

January 15, 1991

Abstract

EQUIPMENT FAILURES VS. WORK group communication convenience: what are the real tradeoffs? Computer hardware from today's blue chip venders (and, surprisingly, from several no-name clonemakers) minimizes the dangers of work group interconnectivity.

The advantages are manifold: rapid communication, instantaneous group-approved document changes, increased sense of participation and cooperation. The technology has proved 100% reliable in environments where important data are backed up on fast tape drives at least four times daily, and where the LAN is designed for fast switch-on of standby servers.

Communicating With the Future

Part V

Creating Long Documents

Includes

21. Producing Reports
22. Producing Booklets
23. Creating Instruction Sheets

21

Producing Reports

Just 10 years ago, most reports were designed with an IBM Selectric typewriter. The font was Courier; the margins were 1 1/2" all around, and headlines were typed in boldface. Charts, diagrams, and photographs were pasted in.

Today, several years after the advent of the laser printer, no one dares submit laser-printed reports formatted in three readable columns to certain government agencies, just because all contract proposals have been typed double-spaced for 75 years. Good reasons may exist for not bucking tradition: your report may land on the desk of some finicky bureaucrat who has just lunched on pickles and pastrami and whose dyspeptic judgments could put you out of work.

On the other hand, you do not need to create unreadable reports when such large issues are not at stake. The sample report in figure 21.1 takes a conservative approach to report design, but the report in figure 21.2 represents a more radical design (but appropriate in its context). In this chapter, you learn to produce each of these reports.

Report No. 1: An Investment Proposal

Laser-printed text cannot be double-spaced like typewritten text, so your reports must find other ways to make reading easier. The sample in figure 21.1 uses a two-column format with wide borders and with section titles in column one.

AgriGanic Growers Association

14259 State Route 93
Alondra, TX 77241
(789) 012-5432

Authors

George Anderby
Terra Linda Farms

Alice DeLongi
Fruit 'N Fertilizer Farm and Feed Supply

John Ritter
Tri-State Organic Produce Growers

Grace Tenor
Texas State Organic Growers Association

Jim Towers
Star Certified Dairy Co-Op

Andrew Wyatt
Eldorado Poultry Ranch

Rio Bravo/South Bend Experimental Farm Land Purchase Proposal

Summary

Of air-born honey, gift of heaven, I now take up the tale. Upon this theme no less look thou, Maecenas, with indulgent eye. A marvellous display of puny powers, high-hearted chiefs, a nation's history, its traits, its bent, its battles and its clans, all, each, shall pass before you, while I sing. Slight though the poet's theme, not slight the praise, so frown not heaven, and Phoebus hear his call.

The Proposal

First find your bees a settled sure abode, where neither winds can enter (winds blow back the foragers with food returning home) nor sheep and butting kids tread down the flowers, nor heifer wandering wide upon the plain dash off the dew, and bruise the springing blades. Let the gay lizard too keep far aloof his scale-clad body from their honied stalls, and the bee-eater, and what birds beside, and Procne smirched with blood upon the breast from her own murderous hands.

Eldorado 1500-Acre Purchase Option

For these roam wide wasting all substance, or the bees themselves strike flying, and in their beaks bear home, to glut those savage nestlings with the dainty prey. But let clear springs and moss-green pools be near, and through the grass a streamlet hurrying run, some palm-tree o'er the porch extend its shade, or huge-grown oleaster, that in Spring, their own sweet Spring-tide, when the new-made chiefs lead forth the young swarms, and, escaped their comb, the colony comes forth to sport and play, the neighbouring bank may lure them from the heat, or bough befriend with hospitable shade.

FIG. 21.1 Three-page, conservatively designed investment proposal. (Part 1 of 3)

Rio Bravo/South Bend
Experimental Farm
Land Purchase Proposal

P. 2

Four Views

1. O'er the mid-waters, whether swift or still, cast willow-branches and big stones enow, bridge after bridge, where they may footing find and spread their wide wings to the summer sun, if haply Eurus, swooping as they pause, have dashed with spray or plunged them in the deep.

2. And let green cassias and far-scented thymes, and savory with its heavy-laden breath bloom round about, and violet-beds hard by sip sweetness from the fertilizing springs. For the hive's self, or stitched of hollow bark, or from tough osier woven, let the doors be strait of entrance; for stiff winter's cold congeals the honey, and heat resolves and thaws, to bees alike disastrous; not for naught so haste they to cement the tiny pores that pierce their walls, and fill the crevices with pollen from the flowers, and glean and keep to this same end the glue, that binds more fast than bird-lime or the pitch from Ida's pines.

3. Oft too in burrowed holes, if fame be true, they make their cosy subterranean home, and deeply lodged in hollow rocks are found, or in the cavern of an age-hewn tree. Thou not the less smear round their crannied cribs with warm smooth mud-coat, and strew leaves above; but near their home let neither yew-tree grow, nor reddening crabs be roasted, and mistrust deep marish-ground and mire with noisome smell, or where the hollow rocks sonorous ring, and the word spoken buffets and rebounds.

4. What more: When now the golden sun has put winter to headlong flight beneath the world, and oped the doors of heaven with summer ray, forthwith they roam the glades and forest o'er, rifle the painted flowers, or sip the streams, light-hovering on the surface. Hence it is with some sweet rapture, that we know not of, their little ones they foster, hence with skill work out new wax or clinging honey mould.

The Payoff Plan

So when the cage-escaped hosts you see float heavenward through the hot clear air, until you marvel at yon dusky cloud that spreads and lengthens on the wind, then mark them well; for the 'tis ever the fresh springs they seek and bowery shelter: hither must you bring the savoury sweets I bid, and sprinkle them, bruised balsam and the wax-flower's

FIG. 21.1 Three-page, conservatively designed investment proposal. (Part 2 of 3)

Rio Bravo/South Bend
Experimental Farm
Land Purchase Proposal

P. 3

lowly weed, and wake and shake the tinkling cymbals heard by the great Mother: on the anointed spots themselves will settle, and in wonted wise seek of themselves the cradle's inmost depth.

Investor Commitments 1992-93

	10/92-12/92	1/93-4/93	5/93-8/93	9/93-12/93
J. Allison	200.00	300.00	400.00	500.00
K. Baxby	4000.00	4000.00	4000.00	4000.00
G. Bortner	2500.00	2500.00	2500.00	2500.00
F. Rondo	200.00	200.00	200.00	400.00
S. Tangrin	500.00	5000.00	5000.00	10000.00
L. Ullyot	3000.00	3000.00	3000.00	3000.00
A. Wetherby	1000.00	2000.00	1000.00	4500.00
Totals by Quarter	15900.00	17000.00	16600.00	22400.00
Grand Total				71900.00

But if in battle they have hied them forth—for oft 'twixt king and king with uproar dire fierce feud arises, and at once from far you may discern what passion sways the mob, and how their hearts are throbbing for the strife; Hark! the hoarse brazen note that warriors know chides on the loiterers, and the ear may catch a sound that mocks the war-trump's broken blasts; then in hot haste they muster, then flash wings, sharpen their pointed beaks and knit their thews, and round the king, even to his royal tent, throng rallying, and with shouts defy the foe.

The Three-Year Plan

Of air-born honey, gift of heaven, I now take up the tale. Upon this theme no less look thou, Maecenas, with indulgent eye. A marvellous display of puny powers, high-hearted chiefs, a nation's history, its traits, its bent, its battles and its clans, all, each, shall pass before you, while I sing. Slight though the poet's theme, not slight the praise, so frown not

FIG. 21.1 Three-page, conservatively designed investment proposal. (Part 3 of 3)

Page One

Begin creating page one of the report by setting the margins and creating a header:

1. To set the left and right margins, press Shift-F8, L, M. Type *7/8*" and press Enter. Type *1.5*" and press Enter, Enter to set the left and right margins.
2. Press P, H, A, P to enter the header editing screen.
3. Change the font to 14-point Times Roman and type the first line of header text *Rio Bravo/South Bend*.
4. Press Alt-F6 (Flush Right), type *P*, press Ctrl-B to enter a page number code (^B), and press Enter.
5. Type the rest of the header, pressing Enter at the end of each line as shown in figure 21.1.
6. Press Enter after the last line to insert extra space between the header and body text.
7. Press F7, U, A, F7 to suppress header printing on page one and return to the editing screen.

Next, you need to define the columns for page one. Complete the following steps:

1. Press Alt-F7, C, D. In the Text Column Definition screen, choose newspaper-style columns.
2. Set the margins to *7/8*", *2 1/2*", *3*", and *7*".
3. Press F7, O to turn columns on and return to the editing screen.

Next, you need to create the horizontal line at the top of the AgriGanic Growers Association address and member list:

1. Press Enter 10 times to move the cursor down the page.
2. Press Alt-F9, L, H and in the Graphics: Horizontal Line screen, make the following settings:

Horizontal Position	Full
Vertical Position	Baseline
Width of Line	1/16"
Gray Shading	100%

3. Press F7 to return to the document screen.

To create the Association name, complete the following steps:

1. Press Enter three times to position the cursor.
2. Press Shift-F8, L, J, C, F7 to turn on center justification and return to the document screen.
3. Change the font to 18-point Times Roman Bold and type *AgriGanic*.
4. Press Enter and type the remainder of the association name.

To create the association address, do the following:

1. Press Enter, change the font to 9-point Times Roman Bold, and press Enter.
2. Type the address as shown in figure 21.1, pressing Enter after each line.
3. At the end of the address, press Enter twice, type *Authors*, and press Enter twice.

To create the list of members, do the following:

1. Type the first member's name, *George Anderby,* and press Enter.
2. Press Ctrl-F8, A, I to turn italics on and type *Terra Linda Farms*.
3. Press the right-arrow key to turn italics off, press Enter twice, and type the next member's name and affiliation.
4. Use the same fonts and format for the remainder of the member list.
5. After the last line in the list "*Eldorado Poultry Ranch*," press Enter twice.

To create another horizontal line, do the following:

1. Press Alt-F9, L, H and in the Graphics: Horizontal Line screen, make the following settings:

Horizontal Position	Full
Vertical Position	Baseline
Width of Line	1/16"
Gray Shading	100%

2. Press F7 to return to the document screen; then press Ctrl-Enter (Hard Page) to move the cursor to the top of column two.

3. Change the font to 24-point Times Roman and press Enter once to insert extra space at the top of the page.

To create the report title, do the following:

1. Press Shift-F8, L, J, L, F7 to turn on left justification and return to the document screen.

2. Type *Rio Bravo/South Bend* and press Enter.

3. Type the remainder of the report title, pressing Enter at the end of each line.

To complete page one, do the following:

1. Press Enter twice, change the font to 16-point Times Roman, and type *Summary*.

2. Press Enter, change the font to 12-point Times Roman, and type the first section of text, *Of air-born honey....* Type the remainder of page one, using the same format.

   The dummy text used in several of the sample documents is from Virgil's seventh Georgic, translated by James Rhoades, in *Great Books of the Western World,* Encyclopedia Britannica, 1952, Vol. 13.

3. When you reach the end of the text on page one, turn columns off by pressing Alt-F7, C ,O. Press Ctrl-Enter (Hard Page) to begin page two.

Page Two

Notice the format changes on page two of figure 21.1. In the remainder of the report, the report headings are placed in the left margin beside the text. To complete the report up to the table at the top of page three, follow these steps:

1. Define parallel columns by pressing Alt-F7, C, D. In the Text Column Definition screen, specify parallel columns.

   Set the margins to *7/8"*, *1 1/2"*, 2", and 7". Press Enter, O to turn columns on and return to the document screen.

2. Change the font to 16-point Times Roman and type the first heading *Four Views*.
3. Create the report text on page two as shown in figure 21.1. Press Ctrl-Enter (Hard Page) to move to column two, change the font to 12-point Times Roman, and type *1*.
4. Then press F4 (Indent) and type the first section of body text, *O'er the mid-waters....*
5. Type the remainder of the report text, up to the table on page three, using the same format for text and headings.

   To begin the next item, "The Payoff Plan," press Ctrl-Enter at the end of step 4.

Page Three

To create the table at the top of page three of figure 21.1, follow these steps:

1. When you are ready to insert the table, press Alt-F7, C, F to turn off columns.
2. To change the left and right margins temporarily to center the table on the page, press Shift-F8, L, M; type *1 1/2*"; press Enter; type *1 1/2*"; and press Enter to set 1 1/2-inch margins.

   Press F7 to return to the document screen.
3. To create the table title, press Enter, change the font to 16-point Times Roman Bold, press Shift-F6 (Center), and type the title *Investor Commitments 1992-93*.
4. To create the column headings, press Enter twice and change the font to 12-point Times Roman Bold. Use the Tab key and the space bar to position the column headings, *10/92-12/92....* You can fine-tune the positioning after typing the numbers in columns.
5. To fill in the table, press Enter twice and change the font to 12-point Times Roman. Begin the first line by typing *J. Allison*.

TIP

Aligning table columns with a proportionally spaced font selected is impossible without using Decimal Tab. You can switch to a nonproportionally spaced font such as Courier, but your tables look much better set in the same face as the body text.

6. To type the figures using the Decimal Tab format, press Tab to move the cursor to the tab stop just before the tab stop where you want to type a number. Press Ctrl-F6 (Tab Align) to advance the cursor to the next tab stop. WordPerfect displays an `Align char. =` prompt in the status line.

   Begin typing the number. As you type, the numbers move to the left. After you type the period—inserting a decimal point—all further numbers you type are moved to the right.

7. After you finish typing the table, insert lines under the columns as shown in figure 21.1, by moving the cursor to the empty line under the last table entry, *A. Wetherby*, and pressing Alt-F9, L, H.

   In the Graphics: Horizontal Line screen, make the following settings:

Horizontal Position	Set Position, 3"
Vertical Position	Baseline
Length of Line	3.73"

   The Length of Line setting, 3.73", was arrived at by experimentation.

8. Press F7 to return to the document screen.

9. Move the cursor to the line below the figures for "Totals by Quarter" and create another line by pressing Alt-F9, L, H.

   In the Graphics: Horizontal Line screen, make the following settings:

Horizontal Position	Set Position, 3"
Vertical Position	Baseline
Length of Line	3.7"

10. Press F7 to return to the document screen.

To create the double line under the Grand Total figure, move the cursor to the line below Grand Total and change the line leading to make the double lines print close together. Then do the following:

1. Press Shift-F8, O, P, L, Enter.
2. Type *–10p* and press Enter, F7. Remember to include the *p*, or WordPerfect decreases line spacing by 10 inches!
3. Create the first line by pressing Alt-F9, L, H. In the Graphics: Horizontal Line screen, make the following settings:

Horizontal Position	Set Position, 6 1/16"
Vertical Position	Baseline
Length of Line	5/8"

4. Turn on Reveal Codes (Alt-F3) and press the Backspace key to delete the code for the horizontal line you just created. Then press F1, 1 to restore the code. Press Enter, F1, 1 to create a copy of the horizontal line.
5. Press Enter twice and return the leading to normal. Then press Shift-F8, O, P, L.
6. Press Enter, type *0*", and press Enter.
7. Press F7 and Enter three times to return to the document screen.

To change the margins back to the previous values, do the following:

1. Press Shift-F8, L, M.
2. Type *7/8*", press Enter, type *1 1/2*", and press Enter.
3. Press F7 to return to the document screen.
4. To turn columns on again, press Alt-F7, C, O. Press Ctrl-Enter to move the cursor into column two.

Report No. 2: A Research Handout

The sample report shown in figure 21.2 informs potential purchasers of local area network equipment about technical issues in setting up a LAN. The company that commissioned the study sells LAN equipment and wants the report to look authoritative, but friendly. The format is, therefore, orderly (competent), but the typeface (Palatino) and decorative use of lines give the report an informal, approachable (friendly) touch.

Page One

Begin creating page one of the report, shown in figure 21.2, by setting the margins:

1. Press Shift-F8, L, M.
2. Type *1 1/2*"; press Enter; type *1 1/2*"; and press Enter, Enter to set the right and left margins.
3. Press P, M; type *1/2*"; press Enter; type *3*"; and press Enter.
4. Press F7 to return to the document screen.

Placing Horizontal Lines at the Top of the Page

To create the two horizontal lines at the top of the page, follow these steps:

1. Press Alt-F9, L, H and in the Graphics: Horizontal Line screen, make the following settings:

Horizontal Position	Set Position, 1 1/2"
Vertical Position	Set Position, 1/2"
Length of Line	2"
Width of Line	1/8"
Gray Shading	100%

Technical Perspectives Series

Paper No. 32

Should Small Companies Invest in Connectivity?

Ray Blanda
Senior Vice President
Advanced Design Department
Omegacom Corporation

January 15, 1991

Abstract

EQUIPMENT FAILURES VS. WORK group communication convenience: what are the real tradeoffs? Computer hardware from today's blue chip venders (and, surprisingly, from several no-name clonemakers) minimizes the dangers of work group interconnectivity.

The advantages are manifold: rapid communication, instantaneous group-approved document changes, increased sense of participation and cooperation. The technology has proved 100% reliable in environments where important data are backed up on fast tape drives at least four times daily, and where the LAN is designed for fast switch-on of standby servers.

FIG. 21.2 Authoritative but friendly report. (Part 1 of 3)

Introduction

HI OMNES LINGUA, institutis, legibus inter se differunt. Gallos ab Aquitanis Garumna flumen, a Belgis Matrona et Sequana dividit. Horum omnium fortissimi sunt Belgae, propterea quod a cultu atque humanitate provinciae longissime absunt, minimeque ad eos mercatores saepe commeant atque ea quae ad effeminandos animos pertinent important, proximique sunt Germanis, qui trans Rhenum incolunt, quibuscum continenter bellum gerunt.

Que de causa Helvetii quoque reliquos Gallos virtute praecedunt, quod fere cotidianis proeliis cum Germanis contendunt, cum aut suis finibus eos prohibent, aut ipsi in eorum finibus bellum gerunt.

The Problem

EORUM UNA PARS, quam Gallos obtinere dictum est, initium capit a flumine Rhodano; continetur Garumna flumine, Oceano, finibus Belgarum; attingit etiam ab Sequanis et Helvetiis flumen Rhenum; vergit ad septentriones. Belgae ab extremis Galliae finibus oriuntur; pertinent ad Inferiorem partem fluminis Rheni; spectant in septentriones et orientem solem. Aquitania a Garumna flumine ad Pyrenaeos montes et eam partem Oceani quae est ad Hispaniam pertinent; spectat inter occasum solis et septentriones.

Apid Helvetios longe nobilissimus fuit et ditissimus Orgetorix. Is, M. Messala, M. Pisone consulibus, regni cupiditate inductus coniurationem nobilitatis fecit et civitati persuasit ut de finibus suis cum omnibus copiis exirent: Perfacile esse, cum virtute omnibus praestarent, totius Galliae imperio potiri. Id hoc facilius iis persuasit quod undique loci natura Helvetii contionentur: una ex parte flumine Rheno latissimo atque altissimo, qui agrum Helvetium a Germanis dividit; altera ex parte monte Iura altissimo, qui est inter Sequanos et Helvetios; teria lacu Lemanno et flumine Rhodano, qui provinciam nostram ab Helvetiis dividit.

The Solutions

HIS REBUS FIEBAT ut et minus late vagarentur et minus facile finitimis bellum inferre possent; qua ex parte homines bellandi cupidi magno dolore afficiebantur. Pro multitudine autem hominum et pro gloria bellie atque fortitudinis angustos se fines habere arbitrabantur, qui in longitudinem milia passuum CCXL, in latitudinem CLLXXX patebant.

His rebus adducti et auctoritate Orgetorigis permoti constitu erunt ea quae ad proficiscendum pertinerent comparare, iumentorum et carrorum quam maximum numerum coemere, sementes quam maximas facere, ut in itinere copia frumenti suppeteret, cum proximis vicitatibus pacem et amicitiam confirmare.

Hardware Gifts, Givens, Gripes

AD EAS RES conficiendas biennieum sibi satis esse duxerunt; in tertium annum profectionem lege confirmant. Ad eas res conficiendas Orgetorix deligitur. Is sibi legationem ad civitates suscipit. In eo itinere persuadet Castico, Catamantaloedis filio, Sequano, cuius pater regnum in Sequania multos annos obtinuerat et a senatu populi Romani amicus appellatus erat, ut regnum in civitate sua occuparet, quod pater ante habuerat; itemque Dumnorigi Haeduo, fratri Diviciaci, qui eo tempore.

FIG. 21.2 Authoritative but friendly report. (Part 2 of 3)

3

Typical Cost Breakdown

EA RES EST HEVETIIS per indicium enuntiata. Moribus suis Orgetorigem ex vinculis cansam dicere coegerun; damnatum poenam sequi oportebat, ut igni cremaretru. Die constituta causae dictionis Orgetorix ad iudicium omnem suam familiam, ad homionum milia decem, undique coegit, et omnes clientes obaeratosque suos, quorum magnum numerum habebat, eodem conduxit; per eos, ne causam diceret, se eripuit. Cum civitas ob eam rem incitata armis ius suum exsequi conaretur, multitudinemque hominum ex agris magistratus cogerent, Orgetorix mortuus est; neque abest suspicio, ut Helvetii arbitrantur, quin ipse sibi mortem consciverit.

Conclusion

POST EIUS MORTEM nihilo minus Helvetii id quod constituerant facere conantur, ut e finibus suis exeant. Ubi iam se ad eam rem paratos esse arbitrati sunt, oppida sua omnia, numero ad duodecim, vicos ad quadringentos, relique privata, aedificia incendunt; frumentum omne, praeterquam quod secum portaturi erant, comburunt, ut, domum reditionis spe sublata, paratiores ad omnia pericula subeunda essent; trium mensium molita cibaria sibi quemque domo efferre iubent. Persuadent Rauracis et Tulingis et Latobrigis, finitimis, uti eodem usi consilio, oppidis suis vicisque exustis, una cum iis proficiscantur; Boiosque, qui trans Rhenum incoluerant et in agrum oricum transierant Noreiamque oppugnabant, receptos ad se socios sibi asciscunt.

FIG. 21.2 Authoritative but friendly report. (Part 3 of 3)

2. Press F7 to return to the document screen.
3. Press Alt-F9, L, H and in the Graphics: Horizontal Line screen, make the following settings:

Horizontal Position	Full
Vertical Position	Set Position, .7"
Width of Line	1/40"
Gray Shading	100%

4. Press F7 to return to the document screen.

Adding the Vertical Lines

To create the vertical lines at the left and right sides of the page, do the following:

1. For the vertical line at the left side of the page, press Alt-F9, L, V and in the Graphics: Vertical Line screen, make the following settings:

Horizontal Position	Set Position, 1 3/8"
Vertical Position	Set Position, 1.93"
Length of Line	6"
Width of Line	.013"
Gray Shading	100%

2. Press F7 to return to the document screen.

TIP

If you were creating this design on your own, you would position the text first, before creating the vertical lines. However, to keep the description of the design process orderly, design steps are described in the order in which codes occur in the Reveal Codes screen. In some cases, this order helps you avoid placing codes in the wrong position. In all cases, this order helps you form the habit of placing box and line codes at the top of the current page when possible, so you can find them later without searching in the Reveal Codes screen.

3. For the shorter vertical line at the right side of the screen, press Alt-F9, L, V and in the Graphics: Vertical Line screen, make the following settings:

Horizontal Position	Set Position, 7 1/8"
Vertical Position	Set Position, 6.04"
Length of Line	1.87"
Width of Line	.013"
Gray Shading	100%

   The decimal figures were arrived at by experimentation.

4. Press F7 to return to the document screen.

Placing Horizontal Lines at the Bottom of the Page

To create the horizontal lines at the bottom of the page, do the following:

1. Press Alt-F9, L, H and in the Graphics: Horizontal Line screen, make the following settings:

Horizontal Position	Set Position, 1 1/2"
Vertical Position	Set Position, 8 3/4"
Length of Line	2"
Width of Line	1/8"
Gray Shading	100%

2. Press F7 to return to the document screen.
3. Press Alt-F9, L, H and in the Graphics: Horizontal Line screen, make the following settings:

Horizontal Position	Full
Vertical Position	Set Position, 8.95"
Width of Line	1/40"
Gray Shading	100%

4. Press F7 to return to the document screen.

Creating the Company Logo

The company logo is placed in a box, rather than typing it as regular text on the page so that body text—the title, abstract, and so forth—can be edited without moving the logotype. When you place a page-anchored box, it stays put.

1. Press Alt-F9, B, O and in the Options: Text box screen, make the following settings:

Border Style	Set all to None
Outside Border Space	Set all to 0"
Inside Border Space	Set all to 0"
Gray Shading	0%

2. Press F7 to return to the document screen. Press Alt-F9, B, C and in the Graphics: Text Box screen, make the following settings:

Anchor Type	Set Position, 3"
Vertical Position	Set Position, 9 1/16"
Horizontal Position	Set Position, 3"
Size	Set Both, 4 1/2" wide × 1 1/2" high

3. Press E.
4. In the text box editor, change the leading and letter spacing to make *Omegacom* and *Corporation* print close together. Press Shift-F8, O, P, L, Enter; type *–0.181*; press Enter, W, O, P; type *90*; and press Enter, F7.
5. Press F7 to return to the editing screen.
6. Change the font to 60-point Palatino and press Tab.
7. Type *Omegacom*. Press Enter, Tab and type *Corporation*.
8. Change the font to 12-point Palatino.
9. Press Enter, Tab, Tab, Tab and type *Communicating With the Future*.
10. Press F7 twice to return to the document screen.

Filling in the Text

The text of figure 21.2 now can be completed. Do the following:

1. Change the font to 10-point Palatino and press Enter three times.
2. Type *Technical Perspectives Series*, press Enter twice, and type *Paper No. 32.*
3. Change the font to 30-point Palatino Italic, press Enter twice, and type *Should Small*. Format the rest of the title as shown in figure 21.2.
4. After typing the word *Connectivity?*, press Enter twice and change the font to 10-point Palatino. Type *Ray Blanda*, press Enter, and format the rest of the author data as shown in figure 21.2.
5. After typing the word *Corporation*, press Enter twice and type *January 15, 1991*.
6. Change the font to 30-point Palatino Italic, press Enter three times, type *Abstract*, and press Enter.
7. Change the font to 12-point Palatino and press Shift-F8, L, J, L, F7 to obtain ragged right margins.
8. Press Tab and type the first paragraph of body text, with *EQUIPMENT FAILURES VS. WORK* in all caps.
9. Type the remainder of the text on page one, as shown in figure 21.2.

Page Two

At the top of page two, shown in figure 21.2, change the top and bottom margins, create a header and a footer, define newspaper-style columns, and place vertical lines on the page. Then you fill in the text.

Begin page two by setting new top and bottom margins:

1. Press Shift-F8, P, M.
2. Type *1/2*" and press Enter.
3. Type *1*" and Enter.
4. Press F7 to return to the document screen.

Adding Vertical Lines

Create the vertical lines by following these steps:

1. For the vertical line on the left side of the page, press Alt-F9, L, V and in the Graphics: Vertical Line screen, make the following settings:

Horizontal Position	Set Position, 1 3/8"
Vertical Position	Set Position, 1 1/4"
Length of Line	8.19"
Width of Line	.013"
Gray Shading	100%

2. Press F7 to return to the document screen.
3. Now create the vertical line at the right side of the page by pressing Alt-F9, L, V and in the Graphics: Vertical Line screen, make the following settings:

Horizontal Position	Set Position, 7 1/8"
Vertical Position	Set Position, 1 1/4"
Length of Line	8.19"
Width of Line	.013"
Gray Shading	100%

4. Press F7 to return to the document screen.

Creating the Header

Create the header containing the horizontal lines and page numbers appearing at the top of the page.

1. For the thick horizontal line, press Shift-F8, P, H, A, P to enter the Header A editing screen.
2. Press Alt-F9, L, H and in the Graphics: Horizontal Line screen, make the following settings:

Horizontal Position	Left
Vertical Position	Set Position, 1/2"
Length of Line	2"
Width of Line	1/8"

3. Press F7 to return to the Header A editing screen.
4. For the thin horizontal line, press Alt-F9, L, H. In the Graphics: Horizontal Line screen, make the following settings:

Horizontal Position	Full
Vertical Position	Set Position, .65"
Width of Line	1/40"

5. Press F7 to return to the Header A editing screen.
6. Press Alt-F6 (Flush Right), change the font to 12-point Palatino Bold, and press Ctrl-B to insert a page number code (^B).
7. Press Enter to add extra space between the header and text.
8. Press F7 to return to the Format:Page screen.

Creating the Footer

Create the footer containing the horizontal lines and running footer text appearing at the bottom of the page:

1. Press F, A, P to enter the footer editing screen.
2. Change the font to 10-point Palatino Bold Italic and type the footer text: *Should Small Companies Invest in Connectivity?*.
3. For the wide horizontal line, press Alt-F9, L, H. In the Graphics: Horizontal Line screen, make the following settings:

Horizontal Position	Right
Vertical Position	Baseline
Length of Line	2"
Width of Line	1/8"
Gray Shading	100%

4. Press F7 to return to the Footer A editing screen.
5. Advance the cursor down 1/16-inch to create space between the first (thick) horizontal line in the footer and the second (thin) line by pressing Shift-F8, O, A, D and typing *1/16*".
6. Press Enter, F7 to return to the editing screen.

7. Press Alt-F9, L, H and in the Graphics: Horizontal Line screen, make the following settings:

Horizontal Position	Full
Vertical Position	Baseline
Width of Line	1/40"

8. Press F7 twice to return to the document screen.

Adding a Nonprinting Comment

You have inserted many hidden formatting codes at the top of page two. To ensure that you don't move them when you edit the report, insert a nonprinting comment at the top of page two. Follow these steps:

1. In Reveal Codes (Alt-F3), move the cursor to the first position on page two and press Ctrl-F5, C, C.
2. In the Document Comment editing screen, type a reminder, such as *<MULTIPLE FORMATTING CODES here.>*.
3. Press F7 to return to the document screen.

Filling in the Text

The text of figure 21.2 now can be completed. Follow these steps:

1. Define newspaper-style columns by pressing Alt-F7, C, D. In the Text Column Definition screen, set the margins to *1 1/2"*, *4"*, *4 1/2"*, *7"*.

   Press F7, O to turn columns on and return to the document screen.
2. Change the font to 24-point Palatino Italic and type the first section heading *Introduction*.
3. Change the font to 10-point Palatino, press Enter, and press Tab.
4. Press Ctrl-F8, A, C to turn on small caps and type the first few words of the paragraph *Hi omnes lingua*.
5. Press the right-arrow key to turn small caps off and type the remainder of the paragraph.

6. Continue typing text and section headings, using the same spacing and fonts.

Page Three

In page three of the report, shown in figure 21.2, the section titled "Conclusion" is separated from the rest of the text by two horizontal lines, and newspaper-style columns are turned off.

1. At the end of the second-to-last section of the report, *"Typical Cost Breakdown,"* press Enter and turn columns off by pressing Alt F7,C, F.
2. For the thick horizontal line, press Alt-F9, L, H and in the Graphics: Horizontal Line screen, make the following settings:

Horizontal Position	Left
Vertical Position	Baseline
Length of Line	2"
Width of Line	1/8"

3. Press F7 to return to the document screen.
4. For the thin horizontal line, press Alt-F9, L, H and in the Graphics: Horizontal Line screen, make the following settings:

Horizontal Position	Full
Vertical Position	Set Position, 3.29"
Width of Line	1/40"

5. Press F7 to return to the document screen.
6. Move the cursor to the top of the page and suspend the printing of a footer for the final page of the report by pressing Shift-F8, P, U, F, Y.
7. Press Ctrl-Home and the up-arrow key to move to the top of the page. Press F7 to return to the document screen.

TIP

You cannot create a nonprinting comment at the top of the page to remind you not to move the footer suspension code when you edit the report or use the design again, because WordPerfect does not enable you to create a comment with columns turned on. However, you can place a comment at the end of the report, where you see the comment when you edit the last page.

8. Press Home, Home, and the down-arrow key to move to the end of the report. With the cursor at the end of the report, press Ctrl-F5, C, C and type the comment text.
9. Press F7 to return to the document screen.
10. Press Enter three times, change the font to 24-point Palatino Italic, and type the last section heading *Conclusion*.
11. Change the font to 10-point Palatino and press Enter.
12. Press Tab, Ctrl-F8, A, C to turn on small caps and type the first three words of the last section.
13. Press the right-arrow key to turn off small caps and type the remainder of the section.

22

Producing Booklets

Booklets are extremely varied, from simple handouts to elaborate four-color catalogs. In all cases, the designers' main concern is to transfer information from the page to the readers. Booklets are longer than flyers and brochures, so design factors affecting readability require special attention. The type must be readable; section headings and artwork give the reader a quick overview of the contents; and the design must be consistent and visually pleasing.

Most booklets are printed in landscape mode on 8 1/2" × 11" paper to create side-by-side 5 1/2" × 8" pages. The small format prevents placing too many visual elements on the page, because elaborate layouts create a busy, agitated look.

Booklet No. 1: Informational Pamphlet

The four-page booklet shown in figure 2.1 informs the reader about professional engineering services. Because the subject is a practical, down-to-earth service, the design needs to communicate information harmoniously and effectively. You need a very different design if, for example, you sell nontoxic perfumes and want to convey a trendy, high-fashion image.

For most business purposes, this generic design can serve as a take-off point from which to customize your booklets. For example, you can replace the photographs with line drawings, use fewer, larger photographs or drawings, eliminate artwork altogether, change the typeface, or use a two-column format.

Helvetii possent: se suis copiis suoque exercitu illis regna conciliaturum confirmat. Hac oratione adducti inter se fidem et ius iurandum dant et, regno occupato, per tres potentissimos ac firmissimos populos totius Galliae sese potiri posse sperant.

CEQA/NEPA Compliance/Regulatory and Permitting Assistance

Et omnes clientes obaeratosque suos, quorum magnum numerum habebat, eodem conduxit; per eos, ne causam diceret, se eripuit. Cum civitas ob eam rem incitata armis ius suum exsequi conaretur, multitudinemkque hominum ex agris magistratus cogerent, Orgetorix mortuus est; neque abest suspicio, ut Helvetii arbitrantur, quin ipse sibi mortem consciverit.

Air Quality Evaluation and Remedial Design

Persuadent Rauracis et Tulingis et Latobrigis, finitimis, uti eodem usi consilio, oppidis suis vicisque exustis, una cum iis proficiscantur; Boiosque, qui trans Rhenum incoluerant et in agrum oricum transierant Noreiamque oppugnabant, receptos ad se socios sibi asciscunt.

Ea res est Hevetiis per indicium enuntiata. Moribus suis Orgetorigem ex vinculis cansam dicere coegerun; damnatum poenam sequi oportebat, ut igni cremaretru. Die constituta causae dictionis.

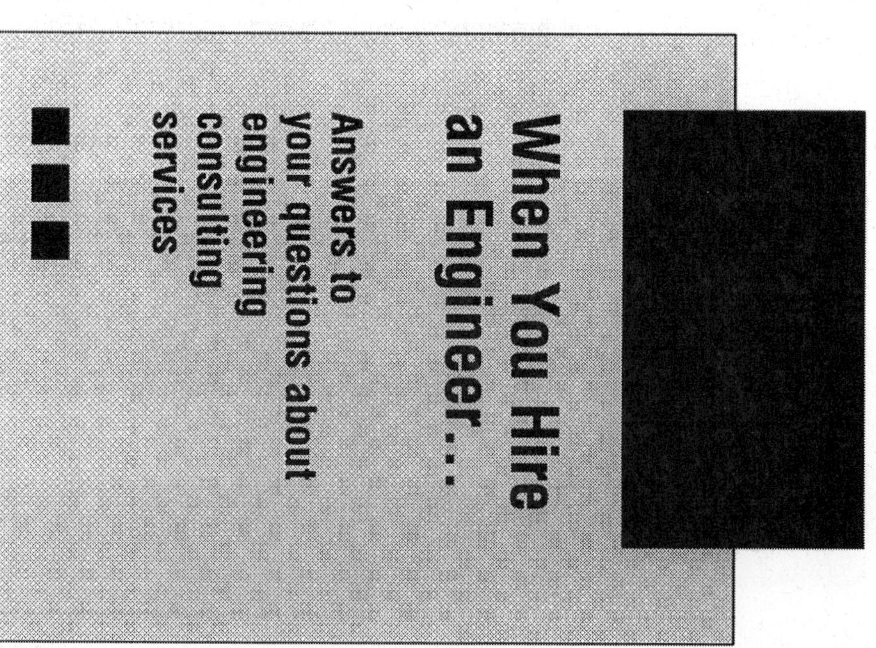

When You Hire an Engineer...
Answers to your questions about engineering consulting services
Consulting Engineers Association of Nebraska
15124 Grand Prairie Road, Suite 502
Omaha, NE 66766
(503) 788-6655

FIG. 22.1 Professional information booklet. (Part 1 of 2)

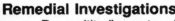

Hi omnes lingua, institutis, legibus inter se differunt. Gallos ab Aquitanis Garumna flumen, a Belgis Matrona et Sequana dividit. Horum omnium fortissimi sunt Belgae, propterea quod a cultu atque humanitate provinciae longissime absunt, minimeque ad eos mercatores saepe commeant atque ea quae ad effeminandos animos pertinent important, proximique sunt Germanis, qui trans Rhenum incolunt, quibuscum continenter bellum gerunt.

Remedial Investigations

Pro multitudine autem hominum et pro gloria bellie atque fortitudinis angustos se fines habere arbitrabantur, qui in longitudinem milia passuum CCXL, in latitudinem CLLXXX patebant.

Apid Helvetios longe nobilissimus fuit et ditissimus Orgetorix. Is, M. Messala, M. Pisone consulibus, regni cupiditate inductus coniurationem nobilitatis fecit et civitati persuasit ut de finibus suis cum omnibus copiis exirent: Perfacile esse, cum virtute omnibus praestarent, totius Galliae imperio potiri. Id hoc facilius iis persuasit quod undique loci natura Helvetii contionentur: una ex parte flumine Rheno latissimo atque altissimo, qui agrum Helvetium a Germanis dividit; altera ex parte monte Iura altissimo, qui est inter Sequanos et Helvetios; teria lacu Lemanno et flumine Rhodano, qui provinciam nostram ab Helvetiis dividit. His rebus fiebat ut et minus late vagarentur et minus facile finitimis bellum inferre possent; qua ex parte homines bellandi cupidi magno dolore afficiebantur.

Solid and Hazardous Waste Management/Feasibility Studies

His rebus adducti et auctoritate Orgetorigis permoti constitu erunt ea quae ad proficiscendum pertinerent comparare, iumentorum et carrorum quam maximum numerum coemere, sementes quam maximas facere, ut in itinere copia frumenti suppeteret, cum proximis vicitatibus pacem et amicitiam confirmare. Ad eas res conficiendas biennieum sibi satis esse duxerunt; in tertium annum profectionem lege confirmant.

Chemical and Process Engineering

Ad eas res conficiendas Orgetorix deligitur. Is sibi legationem ad civitates suscipit. In eo itinere persuadet Castico, Catamantaloedis filio, Sequano, cuius pater regnum in Sequania multos annos obtinuerat et a senatu populi Romani amicus appellatus erat, ut regnum in civitate sua occuparet, quod pater ante habuerat; itemque Dumnorigi Haeduo, fratri Diviciaci, qui eo tempore principatum in civitate obtinebat ac maxime plebi acceptus erat, ut idem conaretur persuadet, eique filiam suam in matrimonium dat.

Environmental and Civil Engineering

Perfacile factu esse illis probat conata perficere, propeterea quod ipse suae civitatis imperium obtenturus esset: Non esse dubium quin totius Galliae plurimum

FIG. 22.1 Professional information booklet. (Part 2 of 2)

The booklet has a photograph on the cover and a small photograph with each section. The commercial printer creates halftone negatives from the photographs and places them in positions indicated by the black boxes shown in figure 22.1. When you have the booklet quick-printed, consider having the halftone PMTs made from your photographs and paste them into the black squares with a glue stick or rubber cement. A *PMT (Photomechanical Transfer)* is a positive image shot through a halftone screen. If you use photographs in your booklets, consult your printer for the appropriate process.

Placing Text—Pages One through Three

Because text flows over onto page three, do the layout of the inside pages first and the cover last.

Choosing Paper Size and Setting Margins

To begin creating the booklet, choose a landscape paper size and type and set the margins:

1. To choose the paper type, press Shift-F8, P, S. In the Paper Size/Type list, highlight the `Standard - Wide` type supplied with WordPerfect and press Enter twice.
2. Press Enter, P, M; type *3/4"*; and press Enter.
3. Type *3/4"* and press Enter to set the top and bottom margins.
4. Press Enter, L, M; type *3/4"*; and press Enter.
5. Type *3/4"* and press Enter to set the left and right margins.
6. Press F7 to return to the document screen.

Placing Bullets at the Top of Page One

Three black text boxes are used to create the three black bullets in the upper left corner of the page. Using Compose (Ctrl-V) is a quicker method to create the bullets, but using text boxes is a more precise method to control box position and size. Follow these steps:

1. Press Alt-F9, B, O. In the Options: Text Box screen, make the following settings:

Border Style	Set all to None
Outside Border Space	Set all to 0"
Inside Border Space	Set all to 0"
Gray Shading	100%

2. Press F7 to return to the document screen.
3. Press Alt-F9, B, C. In the Definition: Text Box screen, make the following settings:

Anchor Type	Page, Number of pages to skip: 0
Vertical Position	Top
Horizontal Position	Set Position, 3/4"
Size	Set Both, 1/4" wide × 1/4" high

4. Press F7 to return to the document screen.
5. Press Alt-F9, B, C. In the Definition: Text Box screen, make the following settings:

Anchor Type	Page, Number of pages to skip: 0
Vertical Position	Top
Horizontal Position	Set Position, 1 1/8"
Size	Set Both, 1/4" wide × 1/4" high

6. Press F7 to return to the document screen. Press Alt-F9, B, C. In the Definition: Text Box screen, make the following settings:

Anchor Type	Page, Number of pages to skip: 0
Vertical Position	Top
Horizontal Position	Set Position, 1 1/2"
Size	Set Both, 1/4" wide × 1/4" high

7. Press F7 to return to the document screen.

Placing the Drop Cap

Now create the large *drop cap* at the start of the text. Follow these steps:

1. Press Alt-F9, B, O. In the Options: Text Box screen, make the following settings:

Border Style	Set all to None
Outside Border Space	Set all to 0"
Inside Border Space	Set all to 0"
Gray Shading	0%

2. Press F7 to return to the document screen.
3. Press Alt-F9, B, C. In the Definition: Text Box screen, make the following settings:

Anchor Type	Page, Number of pages to skip: 0
Vertical Position	Set Position, 1 3/8"
Horizontal Position	Margin, Left
Size	Set Both, 5/8" wide × 3/4" high
Wrap Text Around Box	Yes

4. Press E. In the box editing screen, create the drop cap letter by changing the font to 60-point Helvetica Bold and typing *H*. Press F7 twice to return to the document screen.

Adding the First Section Text

Use Advance to move the insertion point for typing body text next to the drop cap:

1. Press Enter three times.
2. Press Shift-F8, O, A, D; type *.188*"; and press Enter, F7.
3. The figure *.188*" was arrived at by experimentation.

Define newspaper-style columns to place two columns (pages) of text on an 11-by-8 1/2-inch landscape sheet of paper:

1. Press Alt-F7, C, D. In the Text Columns Definition screen, change the margins to *3/4", 5 1/4", 5 3/4", 10 1/4"*.
2. Press F7, O to turn on columns and return to the document screen.
3. Change the font to 12-point Helvetica.
4. Type the first section of body text.

> **TIP**
>
> Although sans serif fonts aren't generally as readable as serif fonts, Helvetica is chosen for this brochure, because Helvetica is very readable and enables use of a relatively small font size and a great deal of type on the page, thanks to its very large x-letter height. Also, Helvetica is suitable for the brochure's subject matter, engineering.

Adding Photograph Boxes and Text

The second section contains the first photograph box. A text box is used to create a black square for the photograph. The paragraph text box anchor type is used so that WordPerfect can adjust the position of the box during editing. Follow these steps:

1. At the end of the first section, press Enter twice.
2. Press Alt-F9, B, O. In the Options: Text Box screen, make the following settings:

Border Style	Set all to None
Outside Border Space	Set all to 0"
Inside Border Space	Set all to 0"
Gray Shading	100%

3. Press F7 to return to the document screen.
4. Press Alt-F9, B, C. In the Definition: Text Box screen, make the following settings:

Anchor Type	Paragraph
Vertical Position	0"
Horizontal Position	Left
Size	Set Both, 1 1/8" wide × 1 1/4" high

5. Press F7 to return to the document screen.
6. Change the font to 14-point Helvetica Bold and type the section title *Remedial Investigations*. Press Enter.
7. Change the font to 12-point Helvetica and type the body text.
8. Type the remainder of pages one through three, using the same fonts and format.
9. Turn off columns by pressing Alt-F7, C, F.

Creating the Front Page

When you reach the end of the copy on page three, create the front page. Begin by setting the margins as follows:

1. Press Shift-F8, L, M; type *3/4";* and press Enter.
2. Type *.3"* and press Enter to set the left and right margins.
3. Press F7 to return to the document screen.

Create the large, shaded box that contains text. Follow these steps:

1. Press Alt-F9, B, O. In the Options: Text Box screen, make the following settings:

Border Style	Set all to Single
Outside Border Space	Set all to 0"
Inside Border Space	Set Left to 1/2", Right to 1/2", Top and Bottom to 0".
Gray Shading	6%

2. Press F7 to return to the document screen.
3. Press Alt-F9, B, C. In the Definition: Text Box screen, make the following settings:

Anchor Type	Page, Number of pages to skip: 0
Vertical Position	Set Position, 2 1/8"
Horizontal Position	Set Position, 6 3/8"
Size	Set Both, 4" wide × 5" high
Wrap Text Around Box	Yes

4. Press E. In the box editing screen, type the title and subtitle. Press Enter six times to move the start of the text down in the box. Change the font to 30-point Helvetica Condensed Bold and type *When You Hire*. Press Enter and type *an Engineer....*
5. Press Enter twice, change the font to 20-point Helvetica Condensed Bold, and type the subtitle *Answers to...*, pressing Enter between lines.
6. After typing *services*, press F7 twice to return to the document screen.

Create the three bullets at the top and bottom of the screen. Follow these steps:

1. Press Alt-F9, B, O. In the Options: Text Box screen, make the following settings:

Border Style	Set all to None
Outside Border Space	Set all to 0"
Inside Border Space	Set all to 0"
Gray Shading	100%

2. Press F7 to return to the document screen.
3. Press Alt-F9, B, C. In the Definition: Text Box screen, make the following settings:

Anchor Type	Page, Number of pages to skip: 0
Vertical Position	Top
Horizontal Position	Set Position, 6 7/8"
Size	Set Both, 1/4" wide × 1/4" high

4. Press F7 to return to the document screen.
5. Press Alt-F9, B, C. In the Definition: Text Box screen, make the following settings:

Anchor Type	Page, Number of pages to skip: 0
Vertical Position	Top
Horizontal Position	Set Position, 7 1/4"
Size	Set Both, 1/4" wide × 1/4" high

6. Press F7 to return to the document screen.
7. Press Alt-F9, B, C. In the Definition: Text Box screen, make the following settings:

Anchor Type	Page, Number of pages to skip: 0
Vertical Position	Top
Horizontal Position	Set Position, 7 5/8"
Size	Set Both, 1/4" wide × 1/4" high

8. Press F7 to return to the document screen.
9. Press Alt-F9, B, C. In the Definition: Text Box screen, make the following settings:

Anchor Type	Page, Number of pages to skip: 0
Vertical Position	Set Position, 6 5/8"
Horizontal Position	Set Position, 6 7/8"
Size	Set Both, 1/4" wide × 1/4" high

10. Press F7 to return to the document screen.
11. Press Alt-F9, B, C. In the Definition: Text Box screen, make the following settings:

Anchor Type	Page, Number of pages to skip: 0

Vertical Position	Set Position, 6 5/8"
Horizontal Position	Set Position, 7 1/4"
Size	Set Both, 1/4" wide × 1/4" high

12. Press F7 to return to the document screen.
13. Press Alt-F9, B, C. In the Definition: Text Box screen, make the following settings:

Anchor Type	Page, Number of pages to skip: 0
Vertical Position	Set Position, 6 5/8"
Horizontal Position	Set Position, 7 5/8"
Size	Set Both, 1/4" wide × 1/4" high

14. Press F7 to return to the document screen.

Create the small black box for the photograph at the top of the page. Follow these steps:

1. Press Alt-F9, B, C. In the Definition: Text Box screen, make the following settings:

Anchor Type	Page, Number of pages to skip: 0
Vertical Position	Set Position, 1 1/4"
Horizontal Position	Set Position, 6 7/8"
Size	Set Both, 2 7/8" wide × 1 5/8" high

2. Press F7 to return to the document screen.

Type the address at the bottom of the page. Follow these steps:

1. Use the Advance feature to move the insertion point to the bottom of the page. Press Enter, Shift-F8, O, A, I. Type *7 1/4"* and press Enter, F7 to return to the document screen.
2. Change the font to 10-Point Helvetica Condensed Bold and press Enter.
3. To advance the insertion point to a position flush-left with the three black bullets at the bottom of the shaded screen,

press Shift-F8, O, A, P; type *6 7/8"*; and press Enter, F7 to return to the document screen.

4. Type the first line of the address *Consulting...* and press Enter.

5. Advance the cursor to position 6 7/8" again, type the next line, and repeat the procedure for the remainder of the address.

Booklet No. 2: Handout for Nature-Awareness Workshops

Both of the designs described in this chapter are suitable for longer booklets. The steps for creating the first sample were adapted from the design process for a short, four-page booklet. The text was laid out on two sides of a single 8 1/2-by-11-inch sheet, so the pages were in position, ready to print in two passes through the printer.

This example describes a process for designing longer booklets. Booklets that span more than one sheet of paper are laid out in signature order. For example, if you want to produce an eight-page booklet with two pages printed on each side of an 8 1/2-by-11-inch sheet in landscape mode, you must print the pages in the following order:

	Side 1		*Side 2*	
	Left	***Right***	***Left***	***Right***
Sheet 1	4	5	6	3
Sheet 2	2	7	8	1

You cannot place text in signature order with WordPerfect without writing an extremely complex macro. For this example, the standard design procedure of printing each page on its own sheet is followed. Then you, or a commercial printer, can tape the pages in signatures, ready for the printer's cameraman.

Figure 22.2 shows five pages of the second sample booklet.

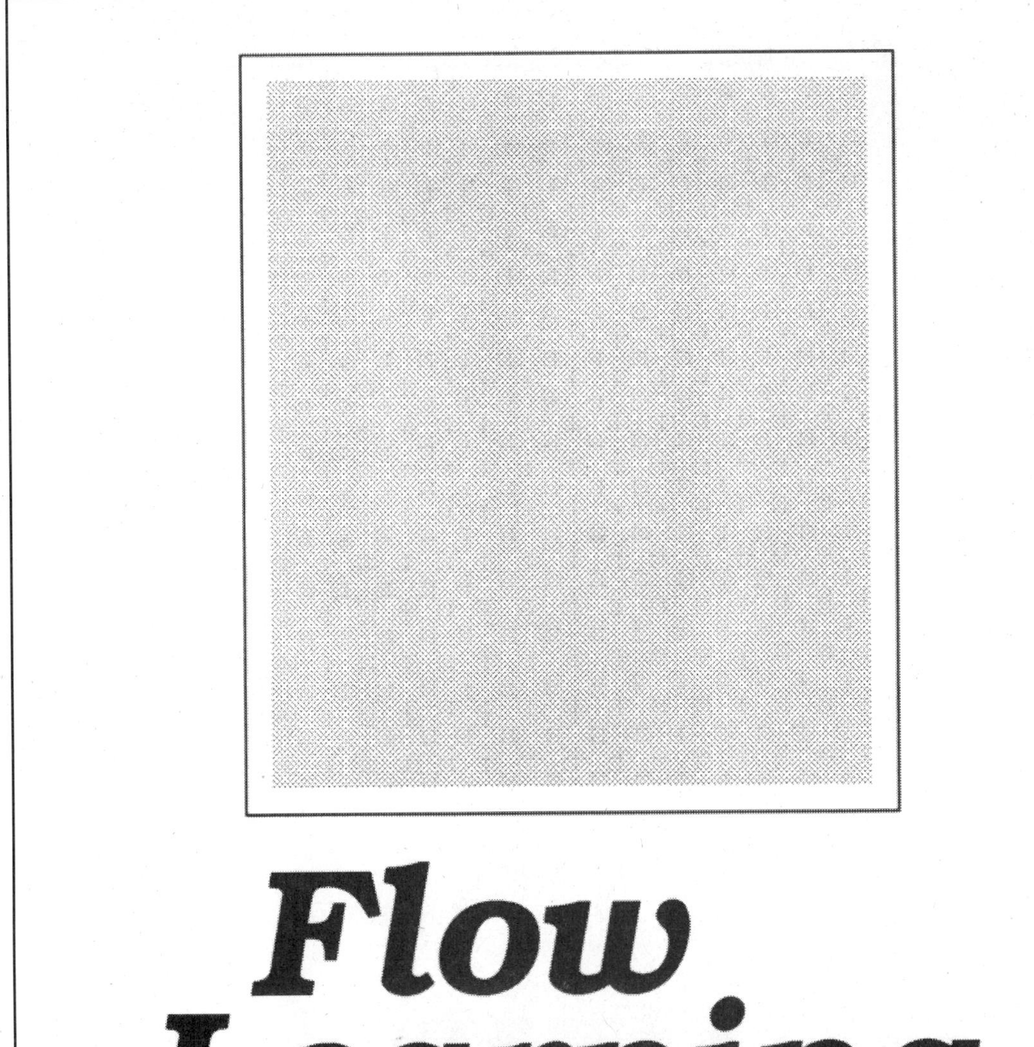

Flow Learning

A Guide to
Nature-Awareness Activities
for Parents, Teachers,
and Recreation Workers

FIG. 22.2 Multiple page booklet. (Part 1 of 5)

How Flow Learning Works

WHEN YOU'RE OUT IN NATURE, do you sometimes have trouble opening up to your surroundings? A direct experience of nature is something few of us ever have, even if we spend lots of time outdoors.

Feeling nature's moods, its power, its subtle, incredible joys, takes calmness, attention, and most of all, an awakened, enthusiastic, open heart. No wonder so few of us have had that experience; the pace of life today, the intertwining involvements with their attendant worries, draw our attention outward, into restlessness and self-preoccupation.

Flow Learning is a wonderful tool that can help us have a richer experience of the world around us, whether we're in a redwood forest, city park, or a garden that's been decorated by a loving hand.

Children love the outdoors. Yet parents and teachers are often frustrated in their attempts to help kids connect with nature in mature and sensitive ways. And that's where Flow Learning comes in. It takes children where they are—full of a sense of fun and with boundless, but often undirected, energy—and leads them step by step through fun-filled activities onto levels of deep, focused awareness.

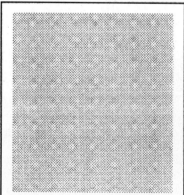

Joseph Cornell, who invented Flow Learning, is fond of quoting the great Japanese conservationist Tanaka Shozo who said: "The question of rivers is not a question of rivers but of the human heart."

FIG. 22.2 Multiple page booklet. (Part 2 of 5)

Paths to Nature Awareness

A Review of the Stages of Flow Learning

Every outdoor game and activity, no matter who invented it or how many centuries ago it was born, has a unique mood. Some games are exciting. Some demand deep, focused attention. Others are calm and reflective. Still others have the power to uplift and inspire.

■ ***OTTER GAMES*** are energetic and full of fun. The otter is the only animal that plays—constantly!—throughout its adult life. Nature's embodiment of rollicking good times, it's a perfect symbol for the first stage of Flow Learning: *Awaken Enthusiasm!*

■ ***CROW GAMES*** are active and observant. Crows are intelligent rascals, always alert to what's happening in their surroundings. The crow embodies the spirit of the second stage of Flow Learning: *Focus Attention.*

■ ***BEAR GAMES*** are reflective and absorbing. In the religion of the Plains Indians, the bear is a symbol of introspection. Bears lead quiet, solitary lives, and they're very curious. Games that capture our attention belong to the third stage of Flow Learning: *Direct Experience.*

■ ***DOLPHIN GAMES*** are inspiring. They lift us into a mood of quiet, joyful appreciation. Dolphins are mystical animals, but they're very social as well. A dolphin that loses contact with its pack will die of loneliness. What better symbol for the fourth stage of Flow Learning: *Share Inspiration.*

FIG. 22.2 Multiple page booklet. (Part 3 of 5)

Games for Flow Learning

The games listed here will give you a start with Flow Learning. You'll find 40 more games in Joseph Cornell's book *Sharing Nature With Children.*

■ ***ANIMALS! ANIMALS! (Otter/Crow)*** Place animal picture cards face down on the ground and ask the players to choose a card. Then tell them they'll have to imitate the animal on their card, and the other players will guess which animal they've chosen. Then have one player at a time act out their animal's typical behavior. The players can hold the animal's typical pose for a few seconds then begin moving like the animal, but without making any sounds. In large groups 5-10 players can perform at the same time.

■ ***THE CAMERA GAME (Bear)*** Have the players pair off in twos. One player plays the photographer and the other plays the camera. The camera keeps his eyes closed until the photographer sees an interesting subject. The photographer then taps the camera on the shoulder, and the camera opens its shutter (eyes) until the photographer taps again to close the shutter (3-5 seconds makes a good exposure). Tell the players to be creative, choosing weird camera angles, panning during exposure, taking closeups. You can play The Camera Game with a group if you lead the players with a rope. (Keep the players far enough apart so they don't trip over each other.)

■ ***NATURE MEDITATIONS (Dolphin/Bear)*** Before playing this game you should write inspiring nature sayings on 3x5 cards, one saying per card. Each card should also give an activity connected with the saying. (Joseph Cornell's book *Listening to Nature*

FIG. 22.2 Multiple page booklet. (Part 4 of 5)

contains 30 quotations with activities.) A beautiful setting helps the players enter into the spirit of the game. Allow 10 minutes for quiet reflection, then call the group together and ask questions about their experiences to encourage sharing between the players.

■ ***BIRDS OF THE AIR (Dolphin)*** Singing and reciting poetry are wonderful ways to share nature with others. Joseph Cornell says that when he's out in the wilderness he spends hours hiking and silently repeating the words of the following poem that he wrote:

The Birds of the Air

The birds of the air are my brothers,
All flowers my sisters, the trees are my friends.
All living creatures, mountains and streams,
I take into my care.
For this green earth is our mother.
Hidden in the sky is the spirit above.
I share one life with all who are here;
To everyone I give my love.
To everyone I give my love.

For more information about Flow Learning, for a list of teaching resources, or for workshop schedules, call Dawn Publications: 1-800-545-7475. The Education for Life Foundation, which sponsors Sharing Nature workshops, has developed a complete system of education that combines character development with comprehensive academic training. Inquiries about the curriculum, traveling workshops, and training programs for teachers are welcome. Call: (916) 292-3775.

FIG. 22.2 Multiple page booklet. (Part 5 of 5)

To begin creating the design, set the margins:

1. Press Shift-F8, L, M; type *5/8*"; and press Enter.
2. Type *5 7/8*" and press Enter, Enter to set the left and right margins.
3. Press, P, M; type *1/2*"; and press Enter
4. Type *1/2*" and press Enter to set the top and bottom margins.
5. Press F7 to return to the document screen.

First Page

Next, you can place the photograph box on the front page. Notice that unlike the photograph boxes in the first example, this one isn't solid black, rather it has an interior 6% screen that is indented on all sides. For this booklet, the designer will order halftone PMTs from the printer. A *PMT* is a positive copy of a photograph sized by the printer's cameraman and shot through a graphic line screen so that you can paste it in place. The printer then can make a negative of the entire page, including the already-screened photographs, without having to shoot the photographs separately.

The inlaid gray screen helps you to position the PMT accurately when you are using a glue stick or rubber cement.

Adding the Photograph Box and Inlaid Screen

To create the photograph box and the inlaid screen, follow these steps:

1. Press Alt-F9, B, O. In the Options: Text Box screen, make the following settings:

Border Style	Set all to None
Outside Border Space	Set all to 0"
Inside Border Space	Set all to 0"
Gray Shading	6%

2. Press F7 to return to the document screen.
3. Press Alt-F9, B, C. In the Definition: Text Box screen, make the following settings:

Anchor Type	Page, Number of pages to skip: 0
Vertical Position	Set Position, 1 3/8"
Horizontal Position	Set Position, 1 1/4"
Size	Set Both, 2 7/8" wide × 3 1/4" high

4. Press F7 to return to the document screen.
5. Press Alt-F9, B, O. In the Options: Text Box screen, make the following settings:

Border Style	Set all to Single
Outside Border Space	Set all to 0"
Inside Border Space	Set all to 0"
Gray Shading	0%

6. Press F7 to return to the document screen.
7. Press Alt-F9, B, C. In the Definition: Text Box screen, make the following settings:

Anchor Type	Page, Number of pages to skip: 0
Vertical Position	Set Position, 1 1/4"
Horizontal Position	Set Position, 1 1/8"
Size	Set Both, 3 1/8" wide × 3 1/2" high

8. Press F7 to return to the document screen.

Next, you need to select a landscape paper size and type. Complete the following steps:

1. Press Shift-F8, P, S.
2. In the Paper Size/Type screen, highlight the `Standard - Wide` definition that comes with WordPerfect and press Enter.
3. Press F7 to return to the document screen.

Creating a Header for Even-Numbered Pages

The header text for the even-numbered pages is different than the header text for the odd-numbered pages. To create a header that prints only on even-numbered pages, follow these steps:

1. Press Shift-F8, P, H, A, V and enter the Header A editing screen.
2. Change the font to 12-point ITC Bookman Demi.
3. Press Ctrl-B to insert a page number code (^B) and press the space bar twice.
4. Type *Flow Learning* and press Alt-F6 (Flush Right).
5. Create the small square bullet. Press Ctrl-V (Compose). At the `Key =` prompt, type *12,110* and press Enter.
6. Use Advance to move the insertion point up 5/8" to make the line in the header print snugly under the text by pressing Shift-F8, O, A, U; typing *5/8"*; and pressing Enter, F7.
7. Create a horizontal line for the header. Press Alt-F9, L, H. In the Graphics: Horizontal Line screen, make the following settings:

Horizontal Position	Full
Vertical Position	Baseline

8. Press F7 three times to return to document screen.

Creating a Header for Odd-Numbered Pages

To create a header that prints only on odd-numbered pages, follow these steps:

1. Press Shift-F8, P, H, B, O and enter the Header B editing screen.
2. Change the font to 12-point ITC Bookman Demi.
3. Create the decorative square bullet. Press Ctrl-V (Compose). At the `Key =` prompt, type *12,110* and press Enter.

The Zapf Dingbat symbols are mapped to WordPerfect character set 12 if you are using a PostScript printer. For a list of the Zapf Dingbat Compose code assignments, see Appendix B. If you are not using a PostScript printer, you can choose a different graphic symbol from one of the other WordPerfect character sets, which are listed in Appendix P of the *WordPerfect Reference* manual.

4. Press Alt-F6 (Flush Right) and type *Flow Learning*.

5. Press the space bar twice, press Ctrl-B to insert a page numbering code (^B), and press Enter.

6. Use advance to move the insertion point for the line to fit snugly under the text by pressing Shift-F8, O, A, U; typing *1/16*"; and pressing Enter, F7.

7. Define the horizontal line. Press Alt-F9, L, H. In the Graphics: Horizontal Line screen, make the following settings:

Horizontal Position	Full
Vertical Position	Baseline

8. Press F7 to return to the Header B editing screen.

9. Press F7, U, A, F7 to suppress header printing for the first page and return to the document screen.

Placing Text

You now are ready to fill in the text. Follow these steps:

1. Press Enter. Change the font to 60-point ITC Bookman Demi Italic and press Enter, Tab.

2. To reduce the line spacing to make the words *Flow* and *Learning* fit tightly together, press Shift-F8, O, P, L, Enter. Type *–15p* and press Enter. Press F7 to return to the document screen.

3. Type *Flow*, press Enter, and type *Learning*.

4. To return the line spacing to normal, press Shift-F8, O, P, L, Enter. Type *0* and press Enter. Press F7 to return to the document screen.

5. Press Enter, Tab and change the font to 14-point ITC Bookman Demi Italic. To create the small black bullet above the subtitle, press Ctrl-V (Compose). At the `Key =` prompt, type *12,110* and press Enter.
6. Type the subtitle text, *A Guide to...*, as shown in figure 22.2, press enter between lines, and press Tab at the start of each line.
7. At the end of the subtitle, press Enter, Tab and create another bullet below the subtitle. Press Ctrl-V (Compose). At the `Key =` prompt, type *12,110* and press Enter.
8. Press Ctrl-Enter (Hard Page) to move to the top of the next page.

Page Two

In addition to text, page two has a photograph box with a shaded inset box for easier photograph placement.

Adding the Photograph Box

To create the box at the bottom of page two, follow these steps:

1. Press Alt-F9, B, O. In the Options: Text Box screen, make the following settings:

Border Style	Set all to Single
Outside Border Space	Set all to 0, except set Right to 1/8"
Inside Border Space	Set all to 0"
Gray Shading	0%

2. Press F7 to return to the document screen.
3. Press Alt-F9, B, C. In the Definition: Text Box screen, make the following settings:

Anchor Type	Page, Number of pages to skip: 0
Vertical Position	Set Position, 6"

Horizontal Position	Set Position, 3/4"
Size	Set Both, 2" wide × 2 1/8" high

4. Press F7 to return to the document screen.

To create the shaded inset box, follow these steps:

1. Press Alt-F9, B, O. In the Options: Text Box screen, make the following settings:

Border Style	Set all to None
Outside Border Space	Set all to 0"
Inside Border Space	Set all to 0"
Gray Shading	6%

2. Press F7 to return to the document screen.
3. Press Alt-F9, B, C. In the Definition: Text Box screen, make the following settings:

Anchor Type	Page, Number of pages to skip: 0
Vertical Position	Set Position, 6 1/8"
Horizontal Position	Set Position, 7/8"
Size	Set Both, 1 3/4" wide × 1 7/8" high

4. Press F7 to return to the document screen.

Placing Text

To complete this page with the text, follow these steps:

1. Change the font to 16-point ITC Bookman Demi Italic and type *How Flow Learning Works*. Change the font to 12-point ITC Bookman Light
2. Use Advance to move the insertion point down 1/16" to adjust the starting position for the line of text. Press Shift-F8, O, A, D; type *1/16*"; and press Enter, F7 to return to the document screen.

3. Press Enter, Tab and type the first few words of body text in caps, *WHEN YOU'RE OUT IN NATURE,* and type the remainder of the page as shown in figure 22.2.
4. At the end of the page, press Ctrl-Enter (Hard Page) to move to the top of the next page.

Page Three

To Create the shaded box with text on page three, follow these steps:

1. Press Alt-F9, B, O. In the Options: Text Box screen, make the following settings:

Border Style	Set all to Single
Outside Border Space	Set all to 0"
Inside Border Space	Set all to 1/8"
Gray Shading	6%

2. Press F7 to return to the document screen.
3. Press Alt-F9, B, C. In the Definition: Text Box screen, make the following settings:

Anchor Type	Page, Number of pages to skip: 0
Vertical Position	Top
Horizontal Position	Set Position, 3/4"
Size	Set Both, 4 1/2" wide × 7" high

4. Press E to enter the text box editor and begin to type the text for the shaded box.
5. Change the font to 16-Point ITC Bookman Demi Italic, press Enter, and type the main heading *Paths to Nature Awareness*.
6. Press Enter, change the font to 12-point ITC Bookman Demi, and type the subtitle, *A Review of the Stages of Flow Learning*.
7. Advance the cursor down to adjust the position of the first line of body text. Press Shift-F8, O, A, D. Type *1/16*" and press Enter. Press F7 to return to the editing screen.

8. Press Enter, Tab; change the font to 10-point ITC Bookman Light; and type the introductory paragraph, *Every outdoor game....*
9. Press Enter twice, press Shift-F4 (Indent), and create a square bullet. Press Ctrl-V (Compose). At the `Key =` prompt, type *12,110*.
10. Press the space bar, change the font to 10-point ITC Bookman Demi Italic, and type the first subheading, *OTTER GAMES*.
11. Press the space bar, change the font to 10-point ITC Bookman Light, and type the body text of the first section.
12. Type the remainder of the page with the same fonts and formatting. When you finish the page, press F7 twice to return to the document screen.
13. Press Ctrl-Enter (Hard Page) to move to the next page.

Page Four

Page four and the first half of page five are all text. Follow these steps:

1. Change the font to 16-point ITC Bookman Demi Italic and type the section heading at the top of page four, *Games for Flow Learning*.
2. Press Enter, Tab; change the font to 12-point Bookman Light; and type the introductory paragraph *The games listed here....*
3. At the end of the paragraph, press Enter, Tab and create a square bullet. Press Ctrl-V, and at the `Key =` prompt, type *12,110*.
4. Press Enter. Press the space bar, change the font to 12-point ITC Bookman Demi Italic, and type the first paragraph heading, *ANIMALS!....*
5. Press the space bar, change the font to 12-point ITC Bookman Light, and type the body text, *Place animal picture....*
6. Type the rest of the section (it extends onto page five) using the same fonts and formatting.

Adding the Photograph Box to Page Five

When you reach the end of the section, format the poem, *The Birds of the Air,* with a photograph box:

1. Press Enter and create the box. Press Alt-F9, B, O. In the Options: Text Box screen, make the following settings:

Border Style	Set all to None
Outside Border Space	Set all to 0 except set Left to 1/8"
Inside Border Space	Set all to 0"
Gray Shading	100%

2. Press F7 to return to the document screen.
3. Press Alt-F9, B, C. In the Definition: Text Box screen, make the following settings:

Anchor Type	Paragraph
Vertical Position	Offset from top of paragraph, 1/4"
Horizontal Position	Right
Size	Set Both, 1 1/2" wide × 1 3/4" high

4. Press F7 to return to the document screen.

Completing the Text

1. Press Enter, change the font to 9-point ITC Bookman Demi Italic, and specify right justification by pressing Shift-F8, L, J, R, F7.
2. Type the poem as shown in figure 22.2 by pressing Enter at the end of each line.
3. At the end of the poem, press Enter three times and change justification to Left by pressing Shift-F8, L, J, L, and F7.
4. Press Tab, change the font to 12-point ITC Bookman Light, and type the final paragraph, *For more information....*

23

Creating Instruction Sheets

Some people are born with a mission to make their mark in the annals of medical research. For others, their mission is to write better instruction sheets. Poorly designed instruction sheets waste time and leave the reader with a bad impression of your company.

Like other documents in this book, clear organization is a prime consideration in the creation of instruction sheets. An excellent organizational aid is WordPerfect's tables feature used in the first example (see fig. 23.1). In the second example, boxes and shading are used to convey a sense of order.

Instruction Sheet No. 1: Company Policy Memorandum

This instruction sheet is posted in the company's shipping department, to remind employees how to handle sensitive customer interactions. Mr. Magdeburg wants the instructions followed, so the design must make things easy for the reader.

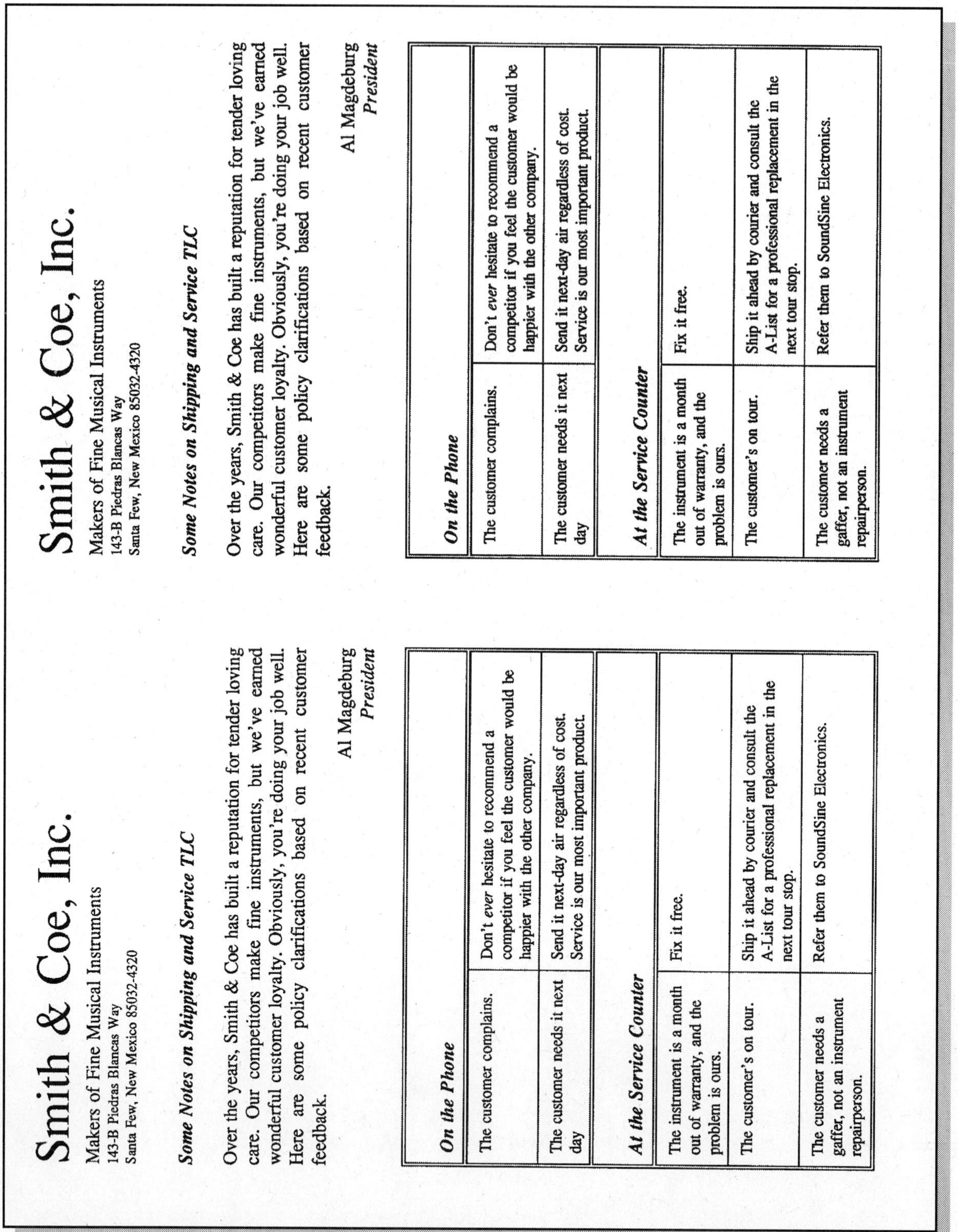

Smith & Coe, Inc.

Makers of Fine Musical Instruments
143-B Piedras Blancas Way
Santa Few, New Mexico 85032-4320

Some Notes on Shipping and Service TLC

Over the years, Smith & Coe has built a reputation for tender loving care. Our competitors make fine instruments, but we've earned wonderful customer loyalty. Obviously, you're doing your job well. Here are some policy clarifications based on recent customer feedback.

Al Magdeburg
President

On the Phone	
The customer complains.	Don't *ever* hesitate to recommend a competitor if you feel the customer would be happier with the other company.
The customer needs it next day	Send it next-day air regardless of cost. Service is our most important product.
At the Service Counter	
The instrument is a month out of warranty, and the problem is ours.	Fix it free.
The customer's on tour.	Ship it ahead by courier and consult the A-List for a professional replacement in the next tour stop.
The customer needs a gaffer, not an instrument repairperson.	Refer them to SoundSine Electronics.

Smith & Coe, Inc.

Makers of Fine Musical Instruments
143-B Piedras Blancas Way
Santa Few, New Mexico 85032-4320

Some Notes on Shipping and Service TLC

Over the years, Smith & Coe has built a reputation for tender loving care. Our competitors make fine instruments, but we've earned wonderful customer loyalty. Obviously, you're doing your job well. Here are some policy clarifications based on recent customer feedback.

Al Magdeburg
President

On the Phone	
The customer complains.	Don't *ever* hesitate to recommend a competitor if you feel the customer would be happier with the other company.
The customer needs it next day	Send it next-day air regardless of cost. Service is our most important product.
At the Service Counter	
The instrument is a month out of warranty, and the problem is ours.	Fix it free.
The customer's on tour.	Ship it ahead by courier and consult the A-List for a professional replacement in the next tour stop.
The customer needs a gaffer, not an instrument repairperson.	Refer them to SoundSine Electronics.

FIG. 23.1 *Instruction sheet outlining company policy.*

With a *two-up* layout like this one, the normal procedure would be to create newspaper-style columns and place a copy of the text in each of the two side-by-side columns on the page. However, WordPerfect does not enable you to place tables in columns. An alternative is to create the text in the left column of the page and then copy this text into a borderless text box on the right side of the page.

The text box code for the box on the right side of the page should appear at the top of the page. After the text is completed, create the text box and put the code at the top of the page.

Setting the Margins

To begin creating the sample, choose a paper type and set the margins. Follow these steps:

1. Press Shift-F8, P, S. In the Paper Size/Type screen, highlight the `Standard - Wide` definition that comes with WordPerfect and press Enter.
2. Press M, type *1/2"*, and press Enter.
3. Type *1/2"* and press Enter to set the top and bottom margins.
4. Press Enter, L, M; type *1/2"*; and press Enter.
5. Type *5 7/8"* and press Enter to set the left and right margins.
6. Press F7 to return to the document screen.

Creating the Letterhead and Body Text

The top half of the column contains a letterhead followed by a brief message from the president. To create the letterhead, follow these steps:

1. Change the font to 30-point Times Roman and type the company name, *Smith & Coe, Inc.*.
2. Press Enter, change the font to 12-point Times Roman, and type the subtitle, *Makers of....*

3. Change the font to 9-point Times Roman, press Enter, and type the address, pressing Enter between lines.

To create the message from the president, do the following:

1. Press Enter three times, change the font to 12-point Times Roman Bold Italic, and type the subject heading, *Some Notes....*
2. Press Enter twice, change the font to 12-point Times Roman. Turn on full justification by pressing Shift-F8, L, J, F.
3. Press F7 to return to the document screen.
4. Type the body text of the memo, *Over the years....*

To add the signature to the message, do the following:

1. After the body text, press Enter, Alt-F6 (Flush Right), and type the writer's name, *Al Magdeburg*.
2. Press Enter, Alt-F6 (Flush Right), Ctrl-F8, A, I to turn on italics. Type the title, *President*.
3. Press the right-arrow key to turn off italics.

Creating the Table

The table in the bottom half of the column provides easy to read directions for responding to customers. To create the table, follow these steps:

1. Press Enter twice and define the table by pressing Alt-F7, T, C.

   At the `Number of Columns` prompt, type *2* and press Enter.

   At the `Number of Rows` prompt, type *7* and press Enter.
2. WordPerfect places you in the table editor. You can use Ctrl plus the arrow keys to adjust the column widths now or after you have entered text in the table.
3. Press O, P, F, G; type *0*; and press Enter, F7.
4. Press F7 to leave the table editing mode.
5. With the cursor in the top left table cell, press Enter to create extra space at the top of the cell. Change the font to 12-point Times Roman Bold Italic and type the first section heading, *On the Phone*.

To join the cells in the top row, do the following:

1. Press Alt-F7 to enter the table editor.
2. Press Alt-F4 and the right-arrow key to highlight the two cells in the top row. Then press J, Y to join the cells (remove the vertical line between them).
3. Press L, A, D, F7 to format the cell with double lines and to leave the table editing mode.

To complete the table, do the following:

1. Move the cursor to the left cell in the second row, by pressing Tab. Change the font to 10-point Times Roman and type the text as shown in figure 23.1, *The customer complains.*
2. Press Tab to move to the right cell in the second row and type the text.
3. Press Tab to move to the left cell in the third row and type the text in both cells in row three as shown in figure 23.1.
4. Format the rest of the table and enter the text as shown in figure 23.1, using the same formatting and fonts.

Adding the Second Column Text Box

Next, create a text box on the right side of the page and copy into it the text and table you created. Follow these steps:

1. Press Home, Home, Home, and the up-arrow key to move the cursor to the top of the document, ahead of any other formatting codes.
2. Press the right-arrow key three times to place the cursor to the right of the margin codes.
3. Press Alt-F9, B, O. In the Options: Text Box screen, make the following settings:

Border Style	Set all to None
Outside Border Space	Set all to 0"
Inside Border Space	Set all to 0"
Gray Shading	0%

4. Press F7 to return to the document screen.
5. Press Alt-F9, B, C. In the Definition: Text Box screen, make the following settings:

Anchor Type	Page, Number of pages to skip: 0
Vertical Position	Top
Horizontal Position	Set Position, 5.94"
Size	Set Both, 4.63" wide × 7 1/2" high

   The decimal figures were arrived at by experimentation.
6. Press F7 to return to the document screen.
7. Press Home, Home, Home, and the up-arrow key to move the cursor to the top of the document.
8. Press Alt-F4 (Block). Press Home, Home, and the down-arrow key to move the cursor to the end of the document.
9. Press Ctrl-F4, B, C to indicate a block move.
10. Press Alt-F9, B, E, 1, Enter, E, Enter to insert the text in the box.
11. Press F7 to return to the document screen.

Check your work by printing a copy.

Instruction Sheet No. 2: Product Assembly Directions

The instruction sheet shown in figure 23.2 uses boxes and shading to create a visual impression of order. The assembly guide is easy to follow, thanks to the use of bullets and boldface to show the steps.

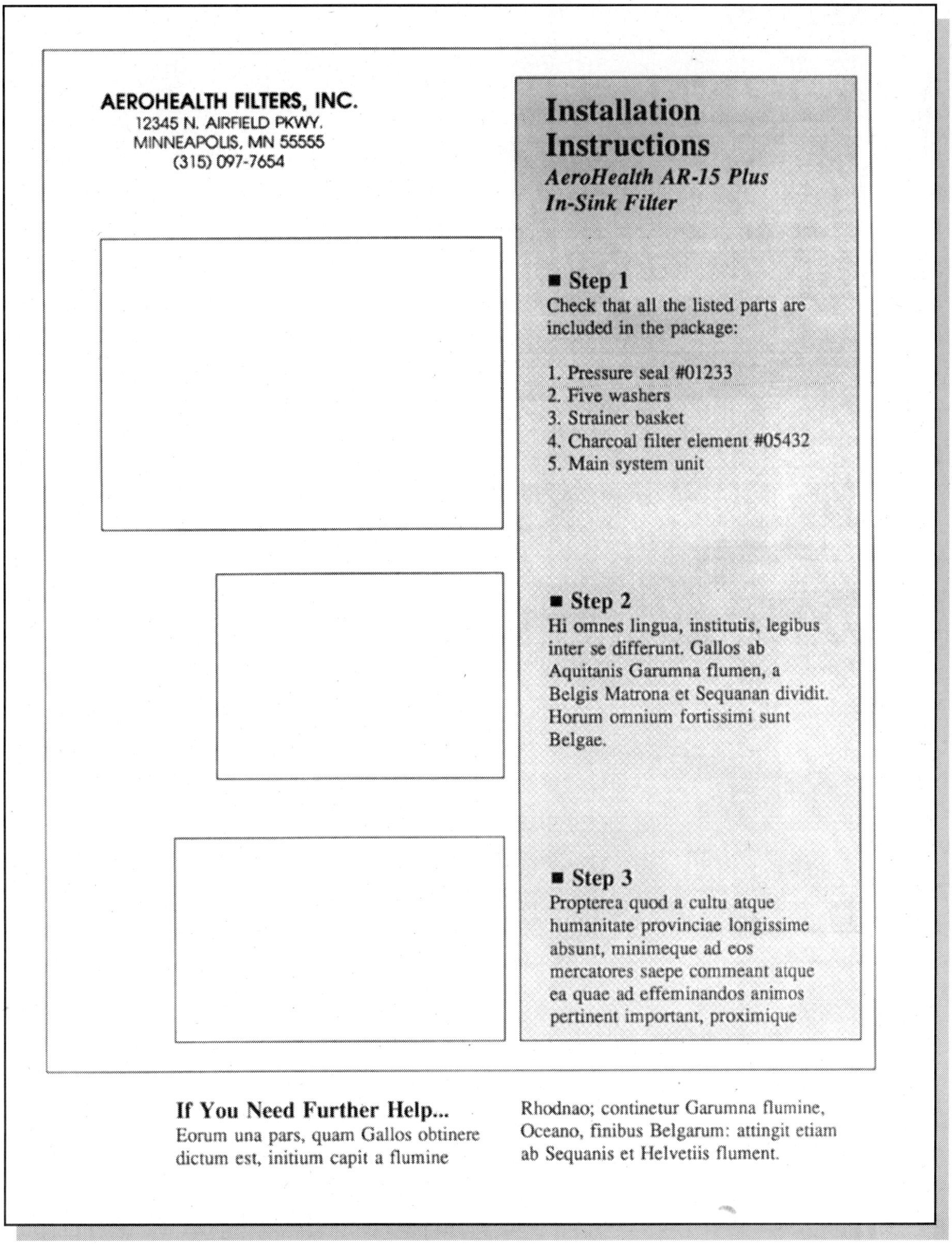

AEROHEALTH FILTERS, INC.
12345 N. AIRFIELD PKWY.
MINNEAPOLIS, MN 55555
(315) 097-7654

Installation Instructions

AeroHealth AR-15 Plus In-Sink Filter

■ Step 1

Check that all the listed parts are included in the package:

1. Pressure seal #01233
2. Five washers
3. Strainer basket
4. Charcoal filter element #05432
5. Main system unit

■ Step 2

Hi omnes lingua, institutis, legibus inter se differunt. Gallos ab Aquitanis Garumna flumen, a Belgis Matrona et Sequanan dividit. Horum omnium fortissimi sunt Belgae.

■ Step 3

Propterea quod a cultu atque humanitate provinciae longissime absunt, minimeque ad eos mercatores saepe commeant atque ea quae ad effeminandos animos pertinent important, proximique

If You Need Further Help...

Eorum una pars, quam Gallos obtinere dictum est, initium capit a flumine Rhodnao; continetur Garumna flumine, Oceano, finibus Belgarum: attingit etiam ab Sequanis et Helvetiis flument.

FIG. 23.2 Organized, easy-to-follow assembly guide.

Setting the Margins

To begin creating the sample, set the margins. Follow these steps:

1. Press Shift-F8, P, M.
2. Type *5/8*", press Enter, type *5/8*", and press Enter, Enter to set the top and bottom margins.
3. Press L, M; type *5/8*"; press Enter; type *5/8*"; and press Enter to set the left and right margins.
4. Press F7 to return to the document screen.

Creating the Company Name and Address

Create a borderless box in the upper left corner of the page for the company name and address. Follow these steps:

1. Press Alt-F9, B, O. In the Options: Text Box screen, make the following settings:

Border Style	Set all to None
Outside Border Space	Set all to 0"
Inside Border Space	Set all to 0"
Gray Shading	0%

2. Press F7 to return to the document screen.
3. Press Alt-F9, B, C. In the Definition: Text Box screen, make the following settings:

Anchor Type	Page, Number of pages to skip: 0
Vertical Position	Set Position, 1"
Horizontal Position	Set Position, .813"
Size	Set Both, 2 7/8" wide × 3/4" high

   The decimal figure for Horizontal Position was arrived at by experimentation.

4. Press E.

   In the text box editor, type the company name and address.

5. Press Shift-F6 (Center) and change the font to 13-point Avant Garde Gothic Demi.
6. Type *AEROHEALTH FILTERS, INC.* Press Enter and change the font to 10-point Avant Garde Gothic Book.
7. Press Shift-F6 (Center) and type *12345 N. AIRFIELD PKWY.*
8. Type the remainder of the address, pressing Shift-F6 (Center) before each line and pressing Enter between lines.
9. Press F7 twice to return to the document screen.

Adding a Shaded Box for Assembly Instructions

WordPerfect can be finicky about the order in which unshaded and shaded boxes are placed. When boxes are placed in the wrong order, the program may move one or more boxes to the next page. Although a firm rule for correct box placement is not available, placing shaded boxes at or near the start of a series of box codes seems to work. Create the long, shaded vertical box for the assembly instructions with the following steps:

1. Press Alt-F9, B, O. In the Options: Text Box screen, make the following settings:

Border Style	Set all to Single
Outside Border Space	Set all to 0"
Inside Border Space	Left 1/4", Right 1/4", Top 0", Bottom 0"
Gray Shading	6%

2. Press F7 to return to the document screen.
3. Press Alt-F9, B, C. In the Definition: Text Box screen, make the following settings:

Anchor Type	Page, Number of pages to skip: 0
Vertical Position	Set Position, 7/8"
Horizontal Position	Set Position, 4 3/4"
Size	Set Both, 3" wide × 8 1/4" high

4. Press E to enter the text box editor and press Enter.
5. Change the font to 20-point Times Roman Bold and type the main heading, *Installation Instructions*.
6. Change the font to 14-point Times Roman Bold Italic, press Enter, and type the next two lines, *AeroHealth AR-15 Plus...*, pressing Enter between lines.
7. Press Enter three times and change the font to 14-point Times Roman Bold.
8. Press Ctrl-V (Compose). At the `Key =` prompt, type *4,2* and press Enter. Press the space bar and type *Step 1*.
9. Press Enter, change the font to 12-point Times Roman and type the first section of text—*Check that all...*—through the fifth section—*Main system unit*.
10. Press Enter six times and type the next section using the same format and fonts.
11. Press F7 twice to return to the document screen.

Fine-tune the vertical spacing of the steps with View Document when you finish entering the text. If a `Too much text` message appears when you press F7 to leave the text box editor, the text you have entered would extend the box past the end of the page, which is not allowed. Tighten the spacing by deleting one or more hard returns, and/or shorten the text by editing.

Creating Three Vertically Stacked Boxes

Create the three boxes to the left of the shaded box, starting with the top one. (You do not have to start with the top one, but it seems logical to do so.) Follow these steps:

1. Press Alt-F9, B, O. In the Options: Text Box screen, make the following settings:

Border Style	Set all to Single
Outside Border Space	Set all to 0"

Inside Border Space	Set all to 0"
Gray Shading	0%

2. Press F7 to return to the document screen.
3. For the top box, press Alt-F9, B, C. In the Definition: Text Box screen, make the following settings:

Anchor Type	Page, Number of pages to skip: 0
Vertical Position	Set Position, 2 1/4"
Horizontal Position	Set Position, 1 1/8"
Size	Set Both, 3 1/2" wide × 2 1/2" high

The decimal figure for Horizontal Position was arrived at by experimentation.

4. Press F7 to return to the document screen.
5. For the center box, press Alt-F9, B, C. In the Definition: Text Box screen, make the following settings:

Anchor Type	Page, Number of pages to skip:0
Vertical Position	Set Position, 5 1/8"
Horizontal Position	Set Position, 2 1/8"
Size	Set Both, 2 1/2" wide × 1 3/4" high

6. Press F7 to return to the document screen.
7. For the bottom box, press Alt-F9, B, C. In the Definition: Text Box screen, make the following settings:

Anchor Type	Page, Number of pages to skip:0
Vertical Position	Set Position, 7 3/8"
Horizontal Position	Set Position, 1 3/4"
Size	Set Both, 2 7/8" wide × 1 3/4" high

8. Press F7 to return to the document screen.

Creating the Page Border

Finally, create the big box that surrounds the other boxes. Follow these steps:

1. Press Alt-F9, B, O.
2. In the Options: Text Box screen, make the following settings:

Border Style	Set all to Single
Outside Border Space	Set all to 0"
Inside Border Space	Set all to 0"
Gray Shading	0%

3. Press Alt-F9, B, C.
4. In the Definition: Text Box screen, make the following settings:

Anchor Type	Page, Number of pages to skip: 0
Vertical Position	Top
Horizontal Position	Margin, Right
Size	Set Both, 7 1/4" wide × 8 3/4" high
Wrap Text Around Box	Yes

5. Press F7 to return to the document screen.

Placing Text at the Bottom of the Page

A note is placed in two newspaper-style columns at the bottom of the page for anyone needing additional help. Follow these steps:

1. Press Enter, Alt-F7, C, D.
2. In the Text Column Definition screen, set the margins to *1 3/4"*, *4 1/2"*, *4 3/4"*, and *7 3/4"*.
3. Press Enter, O, F7 to turn columns on and return to the document screen.

4. Change the font to 14-point Times Roman Bold.
5. Type the first line, *If You Need Further Help....*
6. Change the font to 12-point Times Roman, press Enter, and type the remainder of the text.

west bay

senior runner

January 1993 · Volume 1 · Number 1

Dr. Allen in San Jose

Hi omnes lingua, institutis, legibus inter se differunt. Gallos ab Aquitanis Garumna flumen, a Belgis Matrona et Sequana dividit. Horum omnium fortissimi sunt Belgae, propterea quod a cultu atque humanitate provinciae longissime absunt, minimeque ad eos mercatores saepe commeant atque ea quae ad effeminandos animos pertinent important, proximique sunt Germanis, qui trans Rhenum incolunt, quibuscum continenter bellum gerunt.

New Feature

Que de causa Helvetii quoque reliquos Gallos virtute praecedunt, quod fere cotidianis proeliis cum Germanis contendunt, cum aut suis finibus eos prohibent, aut ipsi in eorum finibus bellum gerunt. Eorum una pars, quam Gallos obtinere dictum est, initium capit a flumine Rhodano; continetur Garumna flumine, Oceano, finibus Belgarum; attingit etiam ab Sequanis et Helvetiis flumen Rhenum; vergit ad septentriones. Belgae ab extremis Galliae finibus oriuntur; pertinent ad Inferiorem partem fluminis Rheni; spectant in septentriones et orientem solem.

Gearing Up

Aquitania a Garumna flumine ad Pyrenaeos montes et eam partem Oceani quae est ad Hispaniam pertinent; spectat inter occasum solis et septentriones.

Apid Helvetios longe nobilissimus fuit et ditissimus Orgetorix. Is, M. Messala, M. Pisone consulibus, regni cupiditate inductus coniurationem nobilitatis fecit et civitati persuasit ut de finibus suis cum omnibus copiis exirent: Perfacile esse, cum virtute omnibus praestarent, totius Galliae imperio potiri. Id hoc facilius iis

Elmo Blatz sets new 10K record in 80-90 veterans' age group.

persuasit quod undique loci natura Helvetii contionentur: una ex parte flumine Rheno latissimo atque altissimo, qui agrum Helvetium a Germanis dividit; altera ex parte monte Iura altissimo, qui est inter Sequanos et Helvetios; teria lacu Lemanno et flumine Rhodano. Que de causa Helvetii quoque reliquos Gallos contendunt, cum aut suis finibus eos. Eorum una pars, quam Gallos.

Women's Racing

Qui provinciam nostram ab Helvetiis dividit. His rebus fiebat ut et minus late vagarentur et minus facile finitimis bellum inferre possent; qua ex parte homines bellandi cupidi magno dolore afficiebantur. Pro multitudine autem hominum et pro gloria bellie atque fortitudinis angustos se fines habere arbitrabantur, qui in longitudinem milia passuum CCXL, in latitudinem CLLXXX patebant.

His rebus adducti et auctoritate Orgetorigis permoti constitu erunt ea quae ad proficiscendum pertinerent comparare, iumentorum et carrorum quam maximum numerum coemere, sementes quam maximas facere, ut in itinere copia frumenti suppeteret, cum proximis vicitatibus pacem et amicitiam confirmare. Ad eas res conficiendas biennieum sibi satis esse duxerunt; in tertium annum profectionem lege confirmant. Ad eas res conficiendas Orgetorix deligitur. Is sibi legationem ad civitates suscipit. In eo itinere persuadet Castico, Catamantaloedis filio, Sequano, cuius pater regnum in Sequania multos annos obtinuerat et a senatu populi Romani amicus appellatus.

Age Group Mileage

	September	October	November	December
40-50	3542	3769	3824	3953
60-70	1905	1954	2012	2124
80-90	743	759	764	865

Congratulations to Scot Phalen, age 65, who ran the Bay City Point-to-Point 10K in 1:04:32.23!

Part VI

Creating Newsletters

Includes

Producing Simple Newsletters

24

Not very long ago, people believed that you couldn't create newsletters with WordPerfect. WordPerfect hadn't yet acquired the features that make publishing attractive newsletters possible, and few who tried to create newsletters with WordPerfect had the required design skills.

As laser printers and desktop publishing software proliferated, people realized that design experience is a critical factor, not merely an expensive frill.

You *can* create attractive newsletters with WordPerfect. The examples in this chapter and the next chapter prove that you can, and the sample in figure 24.1 shows that even simple newsletters can look great, if they are carefully designed.

This newsletter creates a good impression first and foremost because it is orderly. Few other desktop-publishing projects reward attention to detail as richly as newsletters do.

You probably will find it hard to believe the little things that drive professional designers wild: designs that do not *stick* to the grid; headings that do not line up with the tops of photos; drop caps that do not align with the baseline of the following text; and so on.

Attention to detail pays off tremendously. There is a moment when, if you have done everything right, the design snaps into place, and the overall impression becomes subtly professional and reaches a new level of visual appeal.

west bay

senior runner

January 1993 · Volume 1 · Number 1

Dr. Allen in San Jose

Hi omnes lingua, institutis, legibus inter se differunt. Gallos ab Aquitanis Garumna flumen, a Belgis Matrona et Sequana dividit. Horum omnium fortissimi sunt Belgae, propterea quod a cultu atque humanitate provinciae longissime absunt, minimeque ad eos mercatores saepe commeant atque ea quae ad effeminandos animos pertinent important, proximique sunt Germanis, qui trans Rhenum incolunt, quibuscum continenter bellum gerunt.

New Feature

Que de causa Helvetii quoque reliquos Gallos virtute praecedunt, quod fere cotidianis proeliis cum Germanis contendunt, cum aut suis finibus eos prohibent, aut ipsi in eorum finibus bellum gerunt. Eorum una pars, quam Gallos obtinere dictum est, initium capit a flumine Rhodano; continetur Garumna flumine, Oceano, finibus Belgarum; attingit etiam ab Sequanis et Helvetiis flumen Rhenum; vergit ad septentriones. Belgae ab extremis Galliae finibus oriuntur; pertinent ad inferiorem partem fluminis Rheni; spectant in septentriones et orientem solem.

Gearing Up

Aquitania a Garumna flumine ad Pyrenaeos montes et eam partem Oceani quae est ad Hispaniam pertinent; spectat inter occasum solis et septentriones.

Apid Helvetios longe nobilissimus fuit et ditissimus Orgetorix. Is, M. Messala, M. Pisone consulibus, regni cupiditate inductus coniurationem nobilitatis fecit et civitati persuasit ut de finibus suis cum omnibus copiis exirent: Perfacile esse, cum virtute omnibus praestarent, totius Galliae imperio potiri. Id hoc facilius iis

Elmo Blatz sets new 10K record in 80-90 veterans' age group.

persuasit quod undique loci natura Helvetii contionentur: una ex parte flumine Rheno latissimo atque altissimo, qui agrum Helvetium a Germanis dividit; altera ex parte monte Iura altissimo, qui est inter Sequanos et Helvetios; teria lacu Lemanno et flumine Rhodano. Que de causa Helvetii quoque reliquos Gallos contendunt, cum aut suis finibus eos. Eorum una pars, quam Gallos.

Women's Racing

Qui provinciam nostram ab Helvetiis dividit. His rebus fiebat ut et minus late vagarentur et minus facile finitimis bellum inferre possent; qua ex parte homines bellandi cupidi magno dolore afficiebantur. Pro multitudine autem hominum et pro gloria bellie atque fortitudinis angustos se fines habere arbitrabantur, qui in longitudinem milia passuum CCXL, in latitudinem CLLXXX patebant.

His rebus adducti et auctoritate Orgetorigis permoti constitu erunt ea quae ad proficiscendum pertinerent comparare, iumentorum et carrorum quam maximum numerum coemere, sementes quam maximas facere, ut in itinere copia frumenti suppeteret, cum proximis vicitatibus pacem et amicitiam confirmare. Ad eas res conficiendas biennieum sibi satis esse duxerunt; in tertium annum profectionem lege confirmant. Ad eas res conficiendas Orgetorix deligitur. Is sibi legationem ad civitates suscipit. In eo itinere persuadet Castico, Catamantaloedis filio, Sequano, cuius pater regnum in Sequania multos annos obtinuerat et a senatu populi Romani amicus appellatus.

Age Group Mileage

	September	October	November	December
40-50	3542	3769	3824	3953
60-70	1905	1954	2012	2124
80-90	743	759	764	865

Congratulations to Scot Phalen, age 65, who ran the Bay City Point-to-Point 10K in 1:04:32.23!

FIG. 24.1 A simple newsletter that proves you can create attractive newsletters with WordPerfect. (Part 1 of 4)

2 West Bay **senior runner**

Alice Niksen (68) ran Mile-High Marathon in 3:10:15 club age group PR.

Axel's Saturday Morning Club

Erat, ut regnum in civitate sua occuparet, quod pater ante habuerat; itemque Dumnorigi Haeduo, fratri Diviciaci, qui eo tempore principatum in civitate obtinebat ac maxime plebi acceptus erat, ut idem conaretur persuadet, eique filiam suam in matrimonium dat.

Perfacile factu esse illis probat conata perficere, propeterea quod ipse suae civitatis imperium obtenturus esset: Non esse dubium quin totius Galliae plurimum Helvetii possent: se suis copiis suoque exercitu illis regna conciliaturum confirmat. Hac oratione adducti inter se fidem et ius iurandum dant et, regno occupato, per tres potentissimos ac firmissimos populos totius Galliae sese potiri posse sperant.

Hi omnes lingua, institutis, legibus inter se differunt. Gallos ab Aquitanis Garumna flumen, a Belgis Matrona et Sequana dividit. Horum omnium fortissimi sunt Belgae, propterea quod a cultu atque humanitate provinciae longissime absunt, minimeque ad eos mercatores saepe commeant atque ea quae ad effeminandos animos pertinent important, proximique sunt Germanis.

Age Group News

Moribus suis Orgetorigem ex vinculis cansam dicere coegerun; damnatum poenam sequi oportebat, ut igni cremaretru. Die constituta causae dictionis Orgetorix ad iudicium omnem suam familiam, ad homionum milia decem, undique coegit, et omnes clientes obaeratosque suos, quorum magnum numerum habebat, eodem conduxit; per eos, ne causam diceret, se eripuit. Cum civitas ob eam rem incitata armis ius suum exsequi conaretur, multitudinemkque hominum ex agris magistratus cogerent, Orgetorix mortuus est; neque abest suspicio, ut Helvetii arbitrantur, quin ipse sibi mortem consciverit.

Post eius mortem nihilo minus Helvetii id quod constituerant facere conantur, ut e finibus suis exeant. Ubi iam se ad eam rem paratos esse arbitrati sunt, oppida sua omnia, numero ad duodecim, vicos ad quadringentos, relique privata, aedificia praeterquam quod secum portaturi erant, comburunt, ut, domum reditionis spe sublata, paratiores ad omnia pericula subeunda essent; trium mensium molita cibaria sibi quemque domo efferre iubent. Persuadent Rauracis et Tulingis et Latobrigis, finitimis.

Jocks & Docs

Uti eodem usi consilio, oppidis suis vicisque exustis, una cum iis proficiscantur; Boiosque, qui trans Rhenum incoluerant et in agrum oricum transierant Noreiamque oppugnabant, receptos ad se socios sibi asciscunt.

Erant omnino itinera duo quibus itineribus domo exire possent: unum per Sequanos, angustum et difficile, inter montem Iuram et flumen Rhodanum, vix qua singuli carri ducerentur; mons autem altissimus impendebat, ut facile perpauei prhibere possent: alterum per provinciam nostram, multo facilius atque expeditius, propterea.

On Track

Quod inter fines Helvetiorum et Alklobrogum, qui nuper pacati erant, Rhodanus fluit, isque non nullis locis vado transitur. Extremum oppidum Allobrogum est proximumque Helvetiorum finibus Genava.

Ex eo oppido pons ad Helvetios pertinet. Allobrogibus sese vel persuasuros, quod nondum bono animo in populum Romanum viderentur, existimabant, vel vi coacturos ut per suos fines eos ire paterentur. Omnibus rebus ad profectionem comparatis, diem dicunt qua die ad ripam Rhodani omnes conveniant. Is dies erat a.d.v. Kal. April., L. Pisone A. Gabinio consulibus. Eorum una pars, quam Gallos obtinere dictum est, initium

FIG. 24.1 A simple newsletter that proves you can create attractive newsletters with WordPerfect. (Part 2 of 4)

capit a flumine Rhodano; continetur Garumna flumine, Oceano, finibus Belgarum; attingit etiam ab Sequanis et Helvetiis flumen Rhenum; vergit ad septentriones.

Childcare Circle

Aquitania a Garumna flumine ad Pyrenaeos montes et eam partem Oceani quae est ad Hispaniam pertinent; spectat inter occasum solis et septentriones.

Apid Helvetios longe nobilissimus fuit et ditissimus Orgetorix. Is, M. Messala, M. Pisone consulibus, regni

Nutritionist Patricia Labelle will speak at Hurley Center January 20, 8 p.m.

cupiditate. inductus coniurationem nobilitatis fecit et civitati persuasit ut de finibus suis cum omnibus copiis exirent: Perfacile esse, cum virtute omnibus praestarent, totius Galliae imperio potiri. Id hoc facilius iis persuasit quod undique loci natura Helvetii contionentur: una ex parte flumine Rheno latissimo atque altissimo, qui agrum Helvetium a Germanis dividit; altera ex parte monte Iura altissimo, qui est inter Sequanos et Helvetios; teria lacu Lemanno et flumine Rhodano, qui provinciam nostram ab Helvetiis dividit. His rebus flebat ut et minus late vagarentur et minus facile finitimis bellum inferre possent; qua ex parte homines bellandi cupidi magno dolore afficiebantur. Inductus coniurationem nobilitatis fecit et civitati persuasit ut de finibus suis cum omnibus copiis exirent.

Caesar, quod memoria tenebat L. Cassium consulem occisum exercitumque eius ab Helvetiis poulsum et sub iugum missum, concedendum non putabat; neque homines inimico animo, data facultate per provinciam itineris faciendi, temperaturos ab iniuria et maleficio existimabat.

Diets Don't Work

Provinciae toti quam maximum potest militum numerum imperat (erat omnino in Gallia ulteriore legio una), pontem qui erat ad Genavam iubet rescindi. Ubi de eius adventu Helvetii certiores facti sunt, legatos ad eum mittunt, nobilissimos civitatis, cuius legationis Nammeius et Verucloetius principem locum obtinebant, qui dicerent sibi esse in animo sine ullo maleficio iter per provinciam facere, propterea quod aliud iter haberent nullum; rogare ut eius voluntate id sibi facere liceat.

Health Series

Tamen, ut spatium intercedere posset, dum milites quos imperaverat convenirent, legatis respondit diem se ad deliberandum sumpturum; si quid vellent, ad Id. April. reverterentur.

Hi omnes lingua, institutis, legibus inter se differunt. Gallos ab Aquitanis Garumna flumen, a Belgis Matrona et Sequana dividit. Horum omnium fortissimi sunt Belgae, propterea quod a cultu atque humanitate provinciae longissime absunt, minimeque ad eos mercatores saepe commeant atque. Dictum est, initium capit a flumine Rhodano; continetur Garumna flumine, Oceano, finibus Belgarum; attingit etiam.

Family runs at Loren Hills make childcare a non-issue.

coming events

Phone Oren Robertson for details and carpool arrangements for events: 423-9876.

january

- 7 Masters Invitational
- 14 SloPoke Fun Run
- 15 Devil May Care 10K
- 21 Fool's Gold 50K
- 22 Orlaga Youth Benefit 20K
- 28 Winter Carnival 5, 10, 20K

february

- 4 Mothers' Marathon
- 4 WBSR Hillside Carnival
- 5 Tule Trail to W. Beach 30K
- 5 Inkadinka 20K
- 11 Fast & Furious 25K
- 12 E. Wilford 15-miler
- 18 Father & Son 10K
- 18 1992 Blue Ribbon Marathon
- 25 Wild 'N Wooly X-C (20K)

FIG. 24.1 A simple newsletter that proves you can create attractive newsletters with WordPerfect. (Part 3 of 4)

4 West Bay senior runner

Energy & Sports Physiology

Concedendum non putabat; neque homines inimico animo, data facultate per provinciam itineris faciendi, temperaturos ab iniuria et maleficio existimabat. Tamen, ut spatium intercedere posset, dum milites quos imperaverat convenirent, legatis respondit diem se ad deliberandum sumpturum; si quid vellent, ad Id. April. reverterentur.

Aquitania a Garumna flumine ad Pyrenaeos montes et eam partem Oceani quae est ad Hispaniam pertinent; spectat inter occasum solis et septentriones.

Apid Helvetios longe nobilissimus fuit et ditissimus Orgetorix. Is, M. Messala, M. Pisone consulibus, regni cupiditate inductus coniurationem nobilitatis fecit et civitati persuasit ut de finibus suis cum omnibus copiis exirent: Perfacile esse, cum virtute omnibus praestarent, totius Galliae imperio potiri. Id hoc facilius iis persuasit quod undique loci natura Helvetii contionentur: una ex parte flumine Rheno latissimo atque

Ab extremis Galliae finibus oriuntur; pertinent ad Inferiorem partem fluminis

Apid Helvetios longe nobilissimus fuit et ditissimus Orgetorix.

Erant omnino itinera duo quibus itineribus domo exire possent.

agrum Helvetium a Germanis dividit; altera ex parte monte Iura altissimo, qui est inter Sequanos et Helvetios; teria lacu Lemanno et flumine Rhodano, qui provinciam nostram ab Helvetiis

dividit. His rebus fiebat ut et minus late vagarentur et minus facile finitimis bellum inferre possent; qua ex parte homines bellandi cupidi magno dolore afficiebantur. Pro multitudine autem hominum.

west bay
senior runner
589 South North Avenue
San Francisco, CA 94100-9876

U.S. Postage
PAID
Permit No. 000
San Francisco, CA

Address Correction
and Forwarding Requested

FIG. 24.1 A simple newsletter that proves you can create attractive newsletters with WordPerfect. (Part 4 of 4)

This chapter and the next are mostly about attention to detail. Following the step-by-step processes of creating simple and complex newsletters, you will learn skills that will help you improve the appearance of your other designs.

Creating Page One

To begin creating the simple newsletter, you need to set the margins by pressing Shift-F8, P, M; typing *1/2"*; pressing Enter; typing *1/2"*; pressing Enter, Enter, L, M; typing *1/2"*; pressing Enter; typing *1/2"*; and pressing Enter, F7.

Creating the Table

To create a text box for the "Age Group Mileage" table in the lower right corner of page one, complete the following steps:

1. Press Alt-F9, B, O. In the Options: Text Box screen, make the following settings:

Border Style	Set all to Thick
Outside Border Space	Set Top to 3/32" and set the rest to 0"
Inside Border Space	Set all to 1/4"
Gray Shading	0%

2. Press F7 to return to the document screen and then press Alt-F9, B, C. In the Definition: Text Box screen, make the following settings:

Anchor Type	Page, Number of pages to skip: 0
Vertical Position	Bottom
Horizontal Position	Margins, Right
Size	Set Both, 4 15/16" wide × 2 5/8" high

3. Press E, and in the text box editor, type the text for the table. Press Shift-F6 (Center), change the font to 14-point Bookman Demi, and type the box heading (*Age Group Mileage*).

4. Press Enter, change the font to 8-point Bookman Demi, and press Enter again.

To set tab stops for the centered table column headings—September, October, November, and December—complete the following steps:

1. Press Shift-F8, L, T. On the tab ruler, press Ctrl-End to delete all the existing tab stops.
2. Move the tab ruler cursor to the fourth dot to the right of the +1" marker and press C to create a centered tab stop. Press the space bar 13 times and press C to insert another tab stop.
3. Repeat the process twice more to insert a total of four tab stops.
4. Press F7 twice to return to the text box editing screen.
5. Press Tab, type *September*, press Tab, type *October*, press Tab, type *November*, press Tab, and type *December*. Notice that WordPerfect centers the column labels on the centered tab stops that you created.
6. Press Enter twice, change the font to 10-point Bookman Light, and type the first row label (*40-50*).

To set flush-right tabs for the number columns, complete the following steps:

1. Press Shift-F8, L, T. On the tab ruler, press Ctrl-End to delete the existing tab stops.
2. Use the right-arrow key to move the cursor to the ^ mark halfway between the +1" and +2" markers. Press R to insert a flush-right tab stop.
3. Press the right-arrow 11 times and press R to insert another tab stop. Repeat twice more for a total of four flush-right tab stops.
4. Press F7 twice to return to the text box editor.

To enter the text, do the following:

1. Press Tab and type the first number, *3542*. As you type, notice that WordPerfect aligns the numbers flush-right on the tab stop that you created earlier. Type the remaining numbers and row labels in the chart.

2. At the end of the chart, press Enter twice and type the text at the bottom of the box, *Congratulations....*

3. Press F7 twice to return to the editing screen.

Creating the Masthead

To create the newsletter masthead, complete the following steps:

1. Change the font to 18-point Helvetica Narrow Bold Oblique.

   Notice that the letters in "west bay" are widely spaced. Use the Word/Letter Spacing feature to create this effect:

2. Press Shift-F8, O, P, W, P; type *175*; press Enter, P; type *200*; and press Enter, F7. Type *west bay* and change word and letter spacing back to normal. Press Shift-F8, O, P, W, O, O, F7.

3. Before pressing Enter at the end of the line, change the font to 96-point Helvetica Narrow Bold Oblique. Press Enter.

4. Use the Advance feature to move the newsletter title ("senior runner") 1/4" up so that it prints snugly under the *kicker* ("west bay"). Press Shift-F8, O, A, U; type *1/4*"; press Enter, F7. Type the title, *senior runner*.

5. To advance the insertion point down 1/16" to print the thin horizontal line close under the title, press Shift-F8, O, A, D; type *1/16*"; and press Enter, F7.

To create the thin horizontal line underneath the newsletter title, complete the following steps:

1. Press Alt-F9, L, H. In the Graphics: Horizontal Line screen, make the following settings:

Horizontal Position	Full
Vertical Position	Baseline
Width of Line	0.013"
Gray Shading	100%

2. Press F7 to return to the document screen.

Next, you need to create the heavy dashed line. WordPerfect does not have a heavy graphics horizontal line, and specifying a very large font doesn't change the size of the thin dashed horizontal line that WordPerfect does have. Therefore, you need to create the line by specifying a large font and using the hyphen key:

1. Change the font to 12-point Helvetica Narrow Bold Oblique, press Enter, and use the Advance command to fine-tune the spacing of the thick, dashed horizontal line under the thin line. Press Shift-F8, O, A, U; type *9/16*"; and press Enter, F7.

2. To change the font to 56-point Helvetica Narrow Bold, press the - key to create the thick, dashed horizontal line across the screen. (Try pressing the dash key 36 times.) If you are working in Reveal Codes, watch the document window. When WordPerfect creates a dash on the next line, press Backspace to erase it.

You use another Advance code to position the dateline, "January 1993...," snugly under the thick, dashed line. Complete the following steps:

1. Press Shift-F8, O, A, U; type *3/4*"; and press Enter, F7.

2. Press Alt-F6 (Flush Right), change the font to 10-point Helvetica Narrow Bold, and type the dateline as shown in figure 24.1.

   To create the bullets between items in the date line, use Compose. Press Ctrl-V and at the `Key =` prompt, type *4,3*. Press Enter.

3. Press Enter four times to insert white space below the newsletter heading.

Defining the Columns

You need to define three newspaper-style columns for the first page of this simple newsletter. WordPerfect places newspaper-style columns much farther apart than the 3/16" that the designer of this newsletter specified, so you need to change that setting when you define columns. Complete the following steps:

1. Press Alt-F7, C, D. In the Text Column Definition screen, specify three newspaper-style columns.

2. Change the `Distance Between Columns` setting to 3/16". WordPerfect adjusts the settings in the Margins section of the menu.

3. Press F7, O to turn columns on and return to the document screen.
4. WordPerfect's default tab settings are too wide for three newspaper-style columns. Change the settings by pressing Shift-F8, L, T. On the tab ruler, press the right-arrow key three times and press L. Press F7 twice to return to the document screen.

Creating the Text Box in Column Two

To define the black text box in column two, complete the following steps:

1. Press Alt-F9, B, O. In the Options: Text Box screen, make the following settings:

Border Style	Set all to None
Outside Border Space	Set all to 0", except Bottom = 3/32"
Inside Border Space	Set all to 0"
Gray Shading	100%

2. Press F7 to return to the document screen. Press Alt-F9, B, C. In the Definition: Text Box screen, make the following settings:

Anchor Type	Page, Number of pages to skip: 0
Vertical Position	Set Position, 2 3/4"
Horizontal Position	Column(s) 2, Full
Size	Set Both, 2 3/8" wide × 2 1/2" high

3. Press C to enter the Box Caption editing screen. Press the Backspace key to delete the automatically generated caption number.

WordPerfect places captions much too close to text boxes. If you use halftone PMTs for your photos, this practice does not cause a problem, but if you have a printer strip in negatives, you will need at least 1/8" between the photo box and the caption. You need to adjust the spacing of the caption with an Advance code in the Box Caption editing screen:

1. Press Shift-F8, O, A, D; type *1/8"*; and press Enter, F7.
2. Change the font to 9-point Bookman Light Italic and type the caption, *Elmo Blatz....*
3. Press F7 twice to return to the document screen.

Entering the Text

This newsletter is informal, so justify the text ragged right by completing the following steps:

1. Press Shift-F8, L, J, L, F7.
2. Change the font to 18-point Helvetica Narrow Bold and type the first article heading, *Dr. Allen....* Before pressing Enter to end the line, change the font to 9-point Bookman Light.
3. Press Enter and type the first article. At the end of the first article, press Enter twice, change the font to 18-point Helvetica Narrow Bold, and type the next article heading, *New Feature*.
4. Before pressing Enter to end the line, change the font to 9-point Bookman Light, press Enter, and type the text of the article. Use this process for all the articles in the newsletter.

Notice how many Advance codes you have used already, and you are only halfway down the first column of page one. If you create newsletters on a regular basis, it may at first drive you crazy to have to adjust spacing so meticulously. If you talk to professional designers who use PageMaker or Ventura Publisher, however, you discover that they must spend a great deal of time adjusting spacing with the utmost care. The results more than justify the work, however, because the human eye quickly picks up the tiniest misalignments.

The next example of nitpicking comes at the end of the first column. When you reach the bottom of the page, press Ctrl-Enter (Hard Page) to move to column two. Inserting a hard page break, rather than letting WordPerfect wrap text to the next column is often better, especially if you will be inserting an Advance code at the top of the new column. If you let WordPerfect wrap the text, the program may move the Advance code if you later edit the copy.

The short text in column two presents a problem. Ideally, every line of text should align with the text in the columns to the left and right. With WordPerfect's Advance tool, you can at least see that the bottoms of columns align. After laying out all the text and boxes on this page, enter various Advance amounts at the top of column two until the bottoms of columns two and three align. Your newsletter front page probably looks different from this one, with articles of different lengths and photos and boxes differently arranged. For the newsletter in figure 24.1, a 1/8" Advance Down command works nicely. To achieve this affect, do the following:

1. Press Shift-F8, O, A, D; type *1/8*"; and press Enter, F7.
2. Type the remaining text in columns two and three, pressing Ctrl-Enter (Hard Page) at the end of each column. Then press Ctrl-Enter (Hard Page) to move the cursor to the top of page two.

Adding a Dividing Line

To create the horizontal line under the photo in the middle of the page, complete the following steps:

1. Turn on Reveal Codes (Alt-F3) and press Home, Home, Home, and the up-arrow key to move the cursor to the top of the file, ahead of all codes. Move the cursor on top of the `[Font:Helvetica Narrow Bold Oblique 18pt]` code.
2. Press Alt-F9, L, H. In the Graphics: Horizontal Line screen, make the following settings:

Horizontal Position	Set Position, 3 1/16"
Vertical Position	Set Position, 5 13/16"
Length of Line	2 11/32"
Width of Line	0.013"
Gray Shading	100%

3. Press F7 to return to the document screen.

Creating Page Headers

Before moving on to page two, create two headers: for odd-numbered and even-numbered pages. First create the header for even-numbered pages by completing the following steps:

1. Turn on Reveal Codes (Alt-F3) and press Home, Home, Home, and the up-arrow key to move the cursor to the top of the document, ahead of all hidden codes.
2. Then use the right-arrow key to move the cursor past the box and line codes, which should be placed in the first line of a document, ahead of header/footer codes. Press Shift-F8, P, H, A, V.
3. In the Header A editing screen, type the text for the header by changing the font to 10-point Helvetica Narrow Bold Oblique, pressing Ctrl-B to insert a page numbering code, ^B; press Tab; and typing *West Bay*. (Type *West Bay* with uppercase initial letters, because lowercase doesn't look good in the headers.)

   Press the space bar twice, change the font to 14-point Helvetica Narrow Bold Oblique, and type *senior runner*.
4. To use Advance to move the insertion point down, press Shift-F8, O, A, D and type *1/32*". Press Enter, F7.
5. To create the horizontal line, press Alt-F9, L, H. In the Graphics: Horizontal Line screen, make the following settings:

Horizontal Position	Full
Vertical Position	Baseline
Width of Line	0.013"
Gray Shading	100%
6. Press F7 to return to the Header A editing screen.
7. Press Enter and use an Advance code to move the cursor up 1/4" to position the heavy dashed line. Press Shift-F8, O, A, U; type *1/4*"; and press Enter, F7.
8. Change the font to 40-point Helvetica Bold and press the dash key to create the heavy dashed line. As you press the dash key, watch the document window, not Reveal Codes.

When WordPerfect moves the cursor to the next line, use Backspace to delete dashes until the cursor moves back up to the dashed line.

9. Press Enter twice to create extra white space below the dashed line in the header. Press F7 twice to return to the document screen.

To create a second header to be printed on odd-numbered pages, do the following:

1. Press Shift-F8, P, H, B, O. You type the text of the header in the Header B editing screen.

2. Change the font to 10-point Helvetica Narrow Bold Oblique. Press Alt-F6 (Flush Right) and type *West Bay*.

3. Press the space bar twice, change the font to 14-point Helvetica Narrow Bold Oblique, and type *senior runner*.

4. Press the space bar eight times and change the font to 10-point Helvetica Narrow Bold Oblique. Press Ctrl-B to have WordPerfect inset a page number.

5. To use an Advance code to move the insertion point down for the thin horizontal line, press Shift-F8, O, A, D; type *5/16*"; and press Enter, F7.

6. Press Alt-F9, L, H. In the Graphics: Horizontal Line screen, make the following settings:

Horizontal Position	Full
Vertical Position	Baseline
Width of Line	0.013"
Gray Shading	100%

7. Press F7 to return to the Header B editing screen.

8. Press Enter and use Advance again to position the heavy dashed line. Press Shift-F8, O, A, U; type *1/4*"; and press Enter, F7.

9. Change the font to 40-point Helvetica Bold and create the heavy dashed line as described earlier. Press Enter twice and press F7, U, A, Enter, F7 to suppress header printing for page one and return to the document screen.

Creating Page Two

If you didn't do so already, press Ctrl-Enter (Hard Page) at the end of page one to move the cursor to the top of page two.

The first thing you need to do for the second page is to create the photo box and text for the first article, "Axel's Saturday Morning Club."

> **TIP**
>
> A bug in WordPerfect 5.1 prevents you from placing a text box over the area where a header prints. However, you can work around this bug by creating the text box code on page one, before the header codes, and specifying an appropriate value for Number of pages to skip in the text box menu.

To create the photo box and place the text for the first article, complete the following steps:

1. Press Home, Home, Home, and the up-arrow key to move the cursor to the top of the document, ahead of all hidden codes.
2. In Reveal Codes, move the cursor to the right of the two margin codes and then create a black box for the photo at the top of page two. Press Alt-F9, B, O.
3. In the Options: Text Box screen, make the following settings:

Border Style	Set all to None
Outside Border Space	Set all to 0", except set Bottom to 1/8"
Inside Border Space	Set all to 0"
Gray Shading	100%

4. Press F7 to return to the document screen. Press Alt-F9, B, C. In the Definition: Text Box screen, make the following settings:

Anchor Type	Page, Number of pages to skip: 1
Vertical Position	Set Position, 1 3/4"

Horizontal Position	Set Position, 1/2"
Size	Set Both, 4 7/8" wide × 3 1/8" high

5. Press C. Press the Backspace key to delete the automatically generated caption number. In the Box Caption editing screen, type the caption by advancing the cursor down 1/8" to create extra space between the box and the caption; pressing Shift-F8, O, A, D; and typing *1/8"*. Press Enter, F7.
6. Change the font to 9-point Bookman Light Italic and type the text, *Alice Niksen....* Press F7 twice to return to the document screen.

Next, you need to create a box for the article text. You can create this box on page two, because it does not overprint the header space, but if you need to edit the text box and/or photo boxes, you will find it more convenient to have the codes placed together. Therefore, create the text box on page one by completing the following steps:

1. Move the cursor to the right of the `[Text Box:1;;[AdvDn:0.125"] ... ]` code for the photo box.
2. Press Alt-F9, B, O. In the Options: Text Box screen, make the following settings:

Border Style	Set all to None, except set Bottom to Single
Outside Border Space	Set all to 0", except set Bottom to 1/4"
Inside Border Space	Set all to 0", except set Bottom to 1/8"
Gray Shading	0%

3. Press F7 to return to the document screen. Press Alt-F9, B, C. In the Definition: Text Box screen, make the following settings:

Anchor Type	Page, Number of pages to skip: 1
Vertical Position	Set Position, 5 3/8"
Horizontal Position	Set Position, 1/2"
Size	Set Both, 4 7/8" wide × 2 3/4" high

4. Press E. In the text box editing screen, you will type the text for the article, using the same spacing and font codes as for the articles you created on page one. You need to set a tab stop for the paragraph first line indents, because the tab stop you set for normal text columns doesn't apply to a text box. If you have set WordPerfect's default to full justification, you need to enter a left justification code (Shift-F8, L, J, L, Enter, F7).

   When you finish typing the text, press F7 twice to return to the document screen.

5. Move the cursor back to page two and create the text as shown in figure 24.1.

Except for the photo and text box that you just created, page two is fairly straightforward. However, the first two columns consisting of the "Age Group News" article are a little tricky, because the heading rides above the two columns, requiring that you align the text in the columns carefully. Complete the following steps:

1. When you reach the bottom of column one, press Ctrl-Enter (Hard Page) to move the cursor to the top of column two.

   If you check your work in View Document (Shift-F7, V), you should see that the next line of body text aligns with the top of the article heading. You want to align column two with the top of column one. Use an Advance Down code to align the columns: Press Shift-F8, O, A, D; type *9/32*"; and press Enter, F7.

TIP

Aligning elements nearly always requires repeated trials until you get the spacing just right. Print a copy of the page, use a ruler to estimate the Advance amount, and then fine-tune your work in View Document, using the 200% view.

2. Type the text for column two, pressing Ctrl-Enter at the bottom to move the cursor to the top of column three.

3. After typing the text in column three, use an Advance code to align the bottom of the column with the bottoms of columns one and two.

4. Move the cursor back to the top of column three and press Shift-F8, O, A, D; type *5/16*"; and press Enter, F7.

Creating Page Three

At the end of column three of page two, press Ctrl-Enter (Hard Return) to move to the top of page three.

Type the text for the end of the article that carries over from page two and the beginning of the first article on page three, "Childcare Circle."

At the beginning of the second paragraph, you need to create a photo box and a caption, "Nutritionist Patricia...." Complete the following steps:

1. Press Alt-F9, B, O. In the Options: Text Box screen, make the following settings:

Border Style	Set all to None
Outside Border Space	Left 0", Right 0", Top 1/8", Bottom 1/8"
Inside Border Space	Set all to 0"
Gray Shading	100%

2. Press F7 to return to the document screen.
3. Press Alt-F9, B, C. In the Definition: Text Box screen, make the following settings:

Anchor Type	Paragraph
Vertical Position	1 1/2"
Horizontal Position	Full
Size	Set Height/Auto Width, 2.37" (wide) × 2 3/8" high

   The Vertical Position specification (1/2") places the box 1/2" down from the top of the paragraph. When you enter a paragraph-anchored box code, WordPerfect moves the code to the left of the first line in the paragraph.

4. Press C. Press the Backspace key to delete the automatically generated box number.
5. In the Box Caption screen, use Advance to move the cursor down 1/8" to create space between the box and caption. Press Shift-F8, O, A, D; type *1/8"*; and press Enter, F7.

6. Change the font to 9-point Bookman Light Italic, and type the caption, *Nutritionist....* Press F7 twice to return to the document screen.

Columns one and two are straightforward. Type the rest of the text in columns one and two, allowing WordPerfect to wrap the text to column two. At the end of column two, press Ctrl-Enter (Hard Page) to move to the top of column three.

At the top of column three on page two, create two boxes for the photo and the schedule, "coming events," by completing the following steps:

1. Press Alt-F9, B, O. In the Options: Text Box screen, make the following settings:

Border Style	Set all to None
Outside Border Space	Set all to 0", except set Bottom to 1/8"
Inside Border Space	Set all to 0"
Position of Caption	Above box, Outside borders
Gray Shading	100%

2. Press F7 to return to the document screen.
3. Press Alt-F9, B, C. In the Definition: Text Box screen, make the following settings:

Anchor Type	Paragraph
Vertical Position	0"
Horizontal Position	Full
Size	Set Height/Auto Width, 2 3/8" (wide) × 1 3/4" high

4. Press C and in the Box Caption editing screen, type the caption. Press the Backspace key to delete the automatically generated box number.
5. Change the font to 9-point Bookman Light Italic and type the text, *Family runs....* Press F7 twice to return to the document screen.

To create a box for the schedule, do the following:

1. Press Alt-F9, B, O. In the Options: Text Box screen, make the following settings:

Border Style	Set all to Dashed
Outside Border Space	Left 0", Right 0", Top 1/8", Bottom 1/8"
Inside Border Space	Set all to 3/16"
Gray Shading	0%

2. Press F7 to return to the document screen.
3. Press Alt-F9, B, C. In the Definition: Text Box screen, make the following settings:

Anchor Type	Paragraph
Vertical Position	0"
Horizontal Position	Full
Size	Auto Both, 2 3/8" (wide) × 4.95" (high)

   WordPerfect adjusts the exact box dimensions (Size), as you enter the text.
4. Press E. In the box editing screen, you type the text.
5. Change the font to 24-point Helvetica Narrow Bold and type *coming events*. Before pressing Enter at the end of the line, change the font to 9-point Helvetica Narrow Bold. Press Enter and type the introduction, *Phone Oren Robertson....*
6. Press Enter twice, change the font to 18-point Helvetica Narrow Bold, and type the first heading, *january*. Before pressing Enter at the end of the line, change the font to 10-point Helvetica Narrow Bold. Press Enter.
7. To set a tab stop for the listings, press Shift-F8, L, T. In the tab ruler, press the right-arrow key five times and press L. Press F7 twice to return to the box editing screen.
8. Type the listings, pressing Indent between dates and race names and using the font settings given in step 6. Press Enter twice between monthly listings. Press F7 twice to return to the document screen.
9. Press Shift-F8, O, P, L, Enter; type *2p*; and press Enter, F7. Press Ctrl-Enter (Hard Page) to move to the top of page four.

Creating Page Four

Page four features a photo layout. When you use several photos together, be sure to space the photo boxes consistently. In this example, notice that the horizontal spaces between photos are the same width and that all four photos are aligned on the vertical white space in the center.

When you create photo layouts, you also should make one photo larger than the others to guide the reader's eye into the layout.

Creating the Photo Layout

First create the black photo box for the upper left photo by completing the following steps:

1. Press Alt-F9, B, O. In the Options: Text Box screen, make the following settings:

Border Style	Set all to None
Outside Border Space	Set all to 0"
Inside Border Space	Set all to 0"
Gray Shading	100%

2. Press F7 to return to the document screen.
3. Press Alt-F9, B, C. In the Definition: Text Box screen, make the following settings:

Anchor Type	Page, Number of pages to skip: 0
Vertical Position	Set Position, 2 7/16"
Horizontal Position	Set Position, 4 1/4"
Size	Set Both, 1 1/8" wide × 15/16" high

4. Press F7 to return to the editing screen.

Notice that this box (the small box at the upper left) has a caption. Because WordPerfect's automatic caption feature enables you to position captions only above or below a photo box, create a text box for this caption later.

To create the upper right box in the photo layout, complete the following steps:

1. Press Alt-F9, B, C. In the Definition: Text Box screen, make the following settings:

Anchor Type	Page, Number of pages to skip: 0
Vertical Position	Set Position, 2 7/16"
Horizontal Position	Set Position, 5 5/8"
Size	Set Both, 2 5/16" wide × 1 7/8" high

2. Press F7 to return to the editing screen.

To create the lower right photo box, do the following:

1. Press Alt-F9, B, C. In the Definition: Text Box screen, make the following settings:

Anchor Type	Page, Number of pages to skip: 0
Vertical Position	Set Position, 4 1/2"
Horizontal Position	Set position, 5 5/8"
Size	Set Both, 2 5/16" wide × 1" high

2. Press C. Press the Backspace key to delete the automatically generated box number.

3. In the Box Caption screen, use Advance to create space between the caption and photo box. Press Shift-F8, O, A, D; type *1/8*"; and press Enter, F7.

4. Change the font to 9-point Bookman Light Italic and type the caption, *Erant omnino*.... Press F7 twice to return to the document screen.

To create the lower left photo box, do the following:

1. Press Alt-F9, B, C. In the Definition: Text Box screen, make the following settings:

Anchor Type	Page, Number of pages to skip: 0
Vertical Position	Set Position, 3 9/16"
Horizontal Position	Set Position, 3 1/16"
Size	Set Both, 2 5/16" wide × 1 15/16" high

2. Press C. Press the Backspace key to delete the automatically generated box number.
3. In the Box Caption screen, use Advance to add 1/8" space between the box and caption. Press Shift-F8, O, A, D; type *1/8*"; and press Enter, F7.
4. Change the font to 9-point Bookman Light Italic and type the caption, *Apid Helvetios*.... Press F7 twice to return to the document screen.

To create a box for the caption to the left of the upper left photo, do the following:

1. Press Alt-F9, B, O. In the Options: Text Box screen, make the following settings:

Border Style	Set all to None
Outside Border Space	Set all to 0", except set Right to 1/ 8"
Inside Border Space	Set all to 0"
Gray Shading	0%

2. Press F7 to return to the document screen.
3. Press Alt-F9, B, C. In the Definition: Text Box screen, make the following settings:

Anchor Type	Page, Number of pages to skip: 0
Vertical Position	Set Position, 2 7/16"
Horizontal Position	Set Position, 3"
Size	Set Both, 1 1/16" wide × 15/16" high

4. Press E. You will type the caption within the text box editing screen. Press Shift-F8, L, J, R, Enter, F7 to turn on right justification.
5. Change the font to 9-point Bookman Light Italic and type the caption, *Ab extremis*.... Press F7 twice to return to the editing screen.

Adding the Postal Information

The only remaining box on page four is for the "U.S. Postage PAID" postal indicia in the lower right part of the screen. Create this box by doing the following:

1. Press Alt-F9, B, O. In the Options: Text Box screen, make the following settings:

Border Style	Set all to None
Outside Border Space	Set all to 0"
Inside Border Space	Set all to 0"
Gray Shading	0%

2. Press F7 to return to the document screen.
3. Press Alt-F9, B, C. In the Definition: Text Box screen, make the following settings:

Anchor Type	Page, Number of pages to skip: 0
Vertical Position	Set Position, 8 1/8"
Horizontal Position	Set Position, 7 1/8"
Size	Set Both, 1" wide × 1 1/4" high

4. Press E. Change the font to 9-point Helvetica Narrow and type the text as shown in figure 24.1, pressing Enter at the end of each line. Press F7 twice to return to the document screen.

Adding a Dividing Line

To create the thin horizontal line that separates the photo layout from the newsletter text, complete the following steps:

1. Press Alt-F9, L, H. In the Graphics: Horizontal Line screen, make the following settings:

Horizontal Position	Set Position, 3 1/16"
Vertical Position	Set Position, 6"
Length of Line	4 7/8"

Width of Line	0.013"
Gray Shading	100%

2. Press F7 to return to the document screen.

Placing the Last Article

To place the article on page four, "Energy & Sports Physiology," complete the following steps:

1. Change the font to 18-point Bookman Demi, type the heading, change the font to 9-point Bookman Light, press Enter, and type the body text of the article. At the bottom of column one, press Ctrl-Enter (Hard Page) to move to the top of column two.

   At the top of column two, you need to enter an Advance code to position the column beneath the horizontal line, under the photo layout. To calculate the distance to advance, print out the page and find a line in column one with which you want to align the top of column two. Move the cursor to that line in the document screen and check the `Ln` indicator in the status line. In figure 24.1, the top of column two is aligned with line 6.17".

2. Press Shift-F8, O, A, I; type *6.17*"; and press Enter, F7.
3. Type the rest of column two. Use View Document and a Hard Page code (Ctrl-Enter) to break the column after the line at the bottom of column two that lines up with the end of column one.
4. Type column three. Edit the text so that all three columns align. At the end of column three, turn columns off. Press Alt-F7, C, F.

Creating the Mailing Section

To create the mailing section at the bottom of page four, do the following:

1. At the end of column three, press Enter four times to add space between the text and the mailer.

2. To create the thin horizontal line across the page above the heavy dashed line, press Alt-F9, L, H. In the Graphics: Horizontal Line screen, make the following settings:

Horizontal Position	Full
Vertical Position	Baseline
Width of Line	0.013"
Gray Shading	100%

3. Press F7 to return to the document screen.

To create the heavy dashed line, do the following:

1. Press Enter and use Advance to move the heavy dashed line close to the thin line. Press Shift-F8, O, A, U; type *3/16"*; and press Enter, F7.
2. Change the font to 40-point Helvetica Bold and use the - key to create the heavy dashed line. Press this key until WordPerfect wraps a dash to the next line. Then use Backspace to delete dashes until WordPerfect returns the cursor up to the dashed line.
3. Change the font to 12-point Helvetica Bold Oblique, type *west bay*, and change the font to 32-point Helvetica Narrow Bold Oblique. Press Enter.
4. Use Advance to move the insertion point up, close to "west bay." Press Shift-F8, O, A, U and type *1/16"*. Press Enter, F7 and type *senior runner*.
5. Change the font to 10-point Bookman Light, press Enter, and use Advance to move the insertion point for the address up, close to "senior runner." Press Shift-F8, O, A, U and type *1/16"*. Press Enter, F7.
6. Type the address, *589 South North Avenue...*, pressing Enter between lines. Press Enter seven times, change the font to 9-point Helvetica Narrow Bold, and type *Address Correction*. Press Enter and type *and Forwarding Requested*.

Producing Complex Newsletters

25

A complex newsletter is an ambitious design project, requiring plenty of patience and commitment to detail. You may not believe that you can create a newsletter like the one in figure 25.1, but figure 25.1 was created with WordPerfect and is ready for you to customize for your own purposes.

This newsletter packs many more design elements onto each page than does the simple newsletter in Chapter 24. The simple newsletter uses an arrangement of lines and type, but every element of the complex newsletter's main heading requires extremely careful design and placement, from the "designed" typography of the title to the precise alignment of the dateline, founding member list, and subtitle.

Notice in the design how everything is laid out with strict attention to the underlying page *grid*:

- The drop cap on page one (the big "H") is carefully aligned at its base with the baseline of a text line to its right and with the baseline of the words "On Rise" to its left.
- The columns at the bottom of the page are aligned at their bottoms. Throughout the newsletter, photo captions are placed exactly the same distance from photo boxes.
- Text that runs around photo boxes is carefully edited so that no paragraph begins in the runaround, creating a jagged effect. (A *runaround* is type that "runs around" the edge of a photo or other design element.)

- On page one, the newsletter title is carefully left-aligned with the text.
- The "FOUNDING MEMBERS" box at the top of the page is right-aligned with the column gutter that runs from top to bottom of the page.
- The distance between text, boxes, and captions and the thin-lined box that surrounds the page is kept equal throughout the newsletter, except at the tops of pages.
- Drop caps are placed as close as possible to the text to their right.
- The newsletter uses full text justification to create a formal, orderly look. Full justification is appropriate for a business newsletter. (Left justification was used for the informal newsletter in Chapter 24.)

Creating this newsletter in WordPerfect took two working days, following the designer's detailed plan. If the newsletter was produced on a regular, monthly schedule, the amount of time needed would soon decrease.

Creating Page One

The first page of the complex newsletter contains the most difficult design challenges. The page consists of a harmonious arrangement of elements that in themselves are quite simple: boxes, lines, and type. However, the designer specified extremely precise placement of lines, boxes, and type. If you adapt the design for your own newsletter, it is important to maintain the same rigorous control of spacing, because the human eye picks up ragged edges and tiny misalignments with hawk-like acuity.

To begin creating the design, set the margins. Press Shift-F8, P, M; type *1/2*"; press Enter; type *1/2*"; press Enter, Enter, L, M; type *1/2*"; press Enter; type *1/2*"; and press Enter, F7.

November 1992 Vol 3 No. 11

FOUNDING MEMBERS

Salkin Construction

Brown Restorers

Vintage Homes, Inc.

THE TRADITIONAL BUILDER

❖ *Newsletter of Peninsula Restorers and Period Builders Association* ❖

Plexes On Rise

Tight money has new buyers moving in together

HI OMNES LINGUA, institutis, legibus inter se differunt. Gallos ab Aquitanis Garumna flumen, a Belgis Matrona et Sequana dividit. Horum omnium fortissimi sunt Belgae, propterea quod a cultu atque humanitate provinciae longissime absunt, minimeque ad eos mercatores saepe commeant atque ea quae ad effeminandos animos pertinent important, proximique sunt Germanis, qui trans Rhenum incolunt, quibuscum continenter bellum gerunt. Que de causa Helvetii quoque reliquos Gallos virtute praecedunt, quod fere cotidianis proeliis cum Germanis contendunt, cum aut suis finibus eos prohibent, aut ipsi in eorum finibus bellum gerunt. Eorum una pars, quam Gallos obtinere dictum est, initium capit a flumine Rhodano; continetur Garumna flumine, Oceano, finibus Belgarum; attingit etiam ab Sequanis et Helvetiis flumen Rhenum; vergit ad septentriones. Belgae ab extremis Galliae finibus oriuntur; pertinent ad Inferiorem partem fluminis Rheni; spectant in septentriones et orientem solem. Aquitania a Garumna flumine ad Pyrenaeos montes et eam partem Oceani quae est ad Hispaniam pertinent; spectat inter occasum solis et septentriones. Apid Helvetios longe nobilissimus fuit et ditissimus Orgetorix. Is, M. Messala, M. Pisone consulibus, regni cupiditate inductus coniurationem nobilitatis fecit et civitati persuasit ut de finibus suis cum omnibus copiis exirent: Perfacile esse, cum virtute. Que de causa Helvetii quoque reliquos Gallos virtute praecedunt. Eorum una pars, quam Gallos obtinere dictum est, initium capit a flumine Rhodano. ❖

Victorian Sunshine Builders specializes in add-on solaria for traditional homes.

Victorian Sunshine

Add-on solaria now a popular trend for older homes

ID HOC FACILIUS iis persuasit quod undique loci natura Helvetii contionentur: una ex parte flumine Rheno latissimo atque altissimo, qui agrum Helvetium a Germanis dividit; altera ex parte monte Iura altissimo, qui est inter Sequanos et Helvetios; teria lacu Lemanno et flumine. Gallos ab Aquitanis Garumna flumen, a Belgis Matrona et Sequana dividit. Horum omnium fortissimi sunt Belgae, propterea quod a cultu atque humanitate provinciae longissime absunt, minimeque ad eos mercatores saepe commeant atque ea quae ad effeminandos animos pertinent important, proximique sunt Germanis, qui trans Rhenum incolunt, quibuscum continenter bellum. Eorum una pars, quam Gallos obtinere dictum est, initium capit a flumine Rhodano; continetur Garumna. ❖

FIG. 25.1 *A complex newsletter created with WordPerfect 5.1. (Part 1 of 4)*

2

Dest and Hess Restore the Asparte Mansion

Contract won on strength of portfolio, say cousins

Built in 1874-76, the Asparte Mansion is a Marsden Vale landmark.

AD EAS RES conficiendas biennieum sibi satis esse duxerunt; in tertium annum profectionem lege confirmant. Ad eas res conficiendas Orgetorix deligitur. Is sibi legationem ad civitates suscipit. In eo itinere persuadet Castico, Catamantaloedis filio, Sequano, cuius pater regnum in Sequania multos annos obtinuerat et a senatu populi Romani amicus appellatus erat, ut regnum in civitate sua occuparet, quod pater ante habuerat; itemque Dumnorigi Haeduo, fratri Diviciaci, qui eo tempore principatum in civitate obtinebat ac maxime plebi acceptus erat, ut idem conaretur persuadet, eique filiam suam in matrimonium dat.

Perfacile factu esse illis probat conata perficere, propeterea quod ipse suae civitatis imperium obtenturus esset: Non esse dubium quin totius Galliae plurimum Helvetii possent: se suis copiis suoque exercitu illis regna conciliaturum confirmat. Hac oratione adducti inter se fidem et ius iurandum dant et, regno occupato, per tres potentissimos ac firmissimos populos totius Galliae sese potiri posse sperant.

Ea res est Hevetiis per indicium enuntiata. Moribus suis Orgetorigem ex vinculis cansam dicere coegerun; damnatum poenam sequi oportebat, ut igni cremaretru. Die constituta causae dictionis Orgetorix ad iudicium omnem suam familiam, ad homionum milia decem. Belgae ab extremis Galliae finibus oriuntur; pertinent ad Inferiorem partem fluminis Rheni; spectant in septentriones et orientem solem. Aquitania a Garumna flumine ad Pyrenaeos montes et eam partem Oceani quae est ad Hispaniam pertinent; spectat inter occasum solis et septentriones. Apid Helvetios longe nobilissimus fuit. ❖

Commercial Contractors Discover 1910

Teak and brass take time but pay well

Newel posts of polished black oak make the Smithson home, built in 1913, an enduring sight.

CUM CIVITAS ob eam rem incitata armis ius suum exsequi conaretur, multitudinemkque hominum ex agris magistratus cogerent, Orgetorix mortuus est; neque abest suspicio, ut Helvetii arbitrantur, quin ipse sibi mortem consciverit. Post eius mortem nihilo minus Helvetii id quod constituerant facere conantur, ut e finibus suis exeant. Ubi iam se ad eam rem paratos esse arbitrati sunt, oppida sua omnia, numero ad duodecim, vicos ad quadringentos, relique privata, aedificia incendunt; frumentum omne, praeterquam quod secum portaturi erant, comburunt, ut, domum reditionis spe sublata, paratiores ad omnia pericula subeunda essent; trium mensium molita cibaria sibi quemque domo efferre iubent. Persuadent Rauracis et Tulingis et Latobrigis, finitimis, uti eodem usi consilio, oppidis suis vicisque exustis, una cum iis proficiscantur; Boiosque, qui trans Rhenum incoluerant et in agrum oricum transierant Noreiamque oppugnabant, receptos ad se socios sibi asciscunt. Erant omnino itinera duo quibus itineribus domo exire possent: unum per Sequanos, angustum et difficile. Id hoc facilius iis persuasit quod undique loci natura Helvetii contionentur: una ex parte flumine Rheno latissimo atque altissimo, qui agrum Helvetium a Germanis dividit; altera ex parte monte Iura altissimo, qui est inter Sequanos et Helvetios; teria lacu Lemanno et flumine Rhodano, qui provinciam nostram ab Helvetiis dividit. ❖

FIG. 25.1 A complex newsletter created with WordPerfect 5.1. (Part 2 of 4)

3

Specialty Styles Turn the Corner

New Mexico? Old South? Maine? Texas? Sense of place keeps builders busy

EXTREMUM OPPIDUM Allobrogum est proximumque Helvetiorum finibus Genava. Ex eo oppido pons ad Helvetios pertinet. Allobrogibus sese vel persuasuros, quod nondum bono animo in populum Romanum viderentur, existimabant, vel vi coacturos ut per suos fines eos ire paterentur. Omnibus rebus ad profectionem comparatis, diem dicunt qua die ad ripam Rhodani omnes conveniant. Is dies erat a.d.v. Kal. April., L. Pisone A. Gabinio consulibus.

Caesari cum id nuntiatum esset, eos per provinciam nostram iter facere conari, maturat ab urbe profisci, et quam maximis potest itineribus in Galliam ulteriorem contendit et ad Genavam pervenit. Provinciae toti quam maximum potest militum numerum imperat (erat omnino in Gallia ulteriore legio una), pontem qui erat ad Genavam iubet rescindi. Ubi de eius adventu Helvetii certiores facti sunt, legatos ad eum mittunt, nobilissimos civitatis, cuius legationis Nammeius et Verucloetius principem locum obtinebant, qui dicerent sibi esse in animo sine ullo maleficio iter per provinciam facere, propterea quod aliud iter haberent nullum; rogare ut eius voluntate id sibi facere liceat.

His rebus adducti et auctoritate Orgetorigis permoti constitu erunt ea quae ad proficiscendum pertinerent comparare, iumentorum et carrorum quam maximum numerum coemere, sementes quam maximas facere, ut in itinere copia frumenti suppeteret, cum proximis vicitatibus pacem et amicitiam confirmare. Ad eas res conficiendas biennieum sibi satis esse duxerunt. ❖

New Mexico adobe in Central City? Yes, in Crosstree Park Estates, near Rock River.

CAESAR, QUOD memoria tenebat L. Cassium consulem occisum exercitumque eius ab Helvetiis poulsum et sub iugum missum, concedendum non putabat; neque homines inimico animo, data facultate per provinciam itineris faciendi, temperaturos ab iniuria et maleficio existimabat. Tamen, ut spatium intercedere posset, dum milites quos imperaverat convenirent, legatis respondit diem se ad deliberandum sumpturum; si quid vellent, ad Id. April. reverterentur.

Perfacile factu esse illis probat conata perficere, propeterea quod ipse suae civitatis imperium obtenturus esset: Non esse dubium quin totius Galliae plurimum Helvetii possent: se suis copiis suoque exercitu illis regna conciliaturum confirmat. Hac oratione adducti inter se fidem et ius iurandum dant et, regno occupato, per tres potentissimos ac firmissimos populos totius Galliae sese potiri posse sperant. Ea Hevetiis per indicium enuntiata. Moribus suis Orgetorigem. Is sibi legationem ad civitates suscipit. In eo itinere persuadet Castico, Catamantaloedis filio, Sequano, cuius pater regnum in Sequania multos annos obtinuerat et a senatu populi Romani amicus appellatus erat, ut regnum in civitate sua occuparet. ❖

Freeport Crafts Sponsors Classes

Three master cabinetmakers offer full schedule

Shop owners give weekend time for master classes.

FIG. 25.1 A complex newsletter created with WordPerfect 5.1. (Part 3 of 4)

Financial Woes Affect Middle-Income Builders Most

Lake Forest area builders not as hard-hit, says realtor Gloria Calabrese

Post eius mortem nihilo minus Helvetii id quod constituerant facere conantur, ut e finibus suis exeant. Ubi iam se ad eam rem paratos esse arbitrati sunt, oppida sua omnia, numero ad duodecim, vicos ad quadringentos, relique privata, aedificia incendunt; frumentum omne, praeterquam quod secum portaturi erant, comburunt, reditionis spe sublata ad ut, domum reditionis spe sublata, paratiores ad omnia pericula subeunda essent; trium mensium molita cibaria sibi quemque domo efferre iubent. Persuadent Rauracis et Tulingis et Latobrigis, finitimis, uti eodem usi consilio, oppidis suis vicisque exustis, una cum iis proficiscantur; Boiosque, qui trans Rhenum incoluerant et in agrum oricum transierant Noreiamque oppugnabant, receptos ad se socios sibi asciscunt. Die constituta causae dictionis Orgetorix ad iudicium omnem suam familiam, ad homionum milia decem, undique coegit, et omnes clientes obaeratosque suos. ❖

Affluent areas have high maintenance activity, as well as new building.

THE TRADITIONAL BUILDER

◆ Newsletter of Peninsula Restorers and Period Builders Association ◆

90012 Alder Way East Grange, MA 02112-9346

Non-profit organization
US Postage
PAID
Permit No. 000
Ash Valley, MA

ADDRESS CORRECTION
AND FORWARDING
REQUESTED

FIG. 25.1 A complex newsletter created with WordPerfect 5.1. (Part 4 of 4)

Creating the Text Boxes

Next, you need to create the six text boxes on page one. When you have many graphic boxes on a page, make a list of them on a sheet of paper with a note about each box's contents. This list will save you time when you need to edit a box. For example, the following list describes the six boxes on page one:

1. November 1992...
2. Traditional Builder...
3. Newsletter of Peninsula...
4. Founding Members...
5. Long photo box, mid-page
6. Photo box, lower left

(The thin-lined box around the page is contained in a header that you create later.)

TIP

Placing the date in a box keeps it from being moved accidentally during later editing sessions, enables you to center the text easily above the box below "FOUNDING MEMBERS," and enables you to place the date text at the top of the file where you can edit it along with other boxes on the page.

To create a box for the issue date at the top of the page, complete the following steps:

1. Press Alt-F9, B, O. In the Options: Text Box screen, make the following settings:

Border Style	Set all to None
Outside Border Space	Set all to 0"
Inside Border Space	Set all to 0"
Gray Shading	0%

2. Press F7 to return to the document screen.
3. Press Alt-F9, B, C. In the Definition: Text Box screen, make the following settings:

Anchor Type	Page, Number of pages to skip: 0
Vertical Position	Set Position, 1/2"
Horizontal Position	Set Position, 3/4"
Size	Set Both, 2 1/8" wide × 3/16" high
Wrap Text Around Box	No

4. Press E. To type the dateline in the text box editing screen, change the font to 8-point New Century Schoolbook, press Shift-F6 (Center), and type the dateline, *November....*

5. Press F7 twice to return to the document screen.

To create a box for the newsletter title, *THE TRADITIONAL BUILDER*, complete the following steps:

1. Press Alt-F9, B, C. In the Definition: Text Box screen, make the following settings:

Anchor Type	Page, Number of pages to skip: 0
Vertical Position	Set Position, 1"
Horizontal Position	Set Position, 3"
Size	Set Both, 4 7/8" wide × 1 1/2" high

2. Press E. To type the title text in the text box editor, use an Advance code to position the text precisely. Press Shift-F8, O, A, D; type *1/8*"; and press Enter, F7.

3. Press Shift-F6 (Center) and change the font to 10-point New Century Schoolbook.

4. Use the Word/Letter Spacing feature to space "THE TRADITIONAL" with widely spaced letters. Press Shift-F8, O, P, W, P; type *250*; press Enter, P; type *225*; press Enter, F7; and type *THE TRADITIONAL*.

5. To adjust the letter spacing for the word "BUILDER," press Shift-F8, O, P, W, O, P; type *90*; and press Enter, F7.

6. Press Enter and use Advance to adjust the insertion point for the word "BUILDER." Press Shift-F8, O, A, U; type *1 1/4*"; and press Enter, F7.

7. Press Shift-F6 (Center), change the font to 96-point New Century Schoolbook, and type *B*. Change the font to 72-point New Century Schoolbook and type *UILDE*. Change the font to 96-point New Century Schoolbook and type *R*.
8. Press Enter to create white space below the heading and then press F7 twice to return to the document screen.

To create a box for the subheading, "Newsletter of...," use box borders to create the thin horizontal lines above and below the subheading:

1. Press Alt-F9, B, O. In the Options: Text Box screen, make the following settings:

Border Style	Left: None, Right: None, Top: Single, Bottom: Single
Outside Border Space	Set all to 0"
Inside Border Space	Set all to 0" except set Top to 1/16"
Gray Shading	0%

2. Press F7 to return to the document screen.
3. Press Alt-F9, B, C. In the Definition: Text Box screen, make the following settings:

Anchor Type	Page, Number of pages to skip: 0
Vertical Position	Set Position, 2 1/8"
Horizontal Position	Set Position, 3"
Size	Set both, 4 7/8" wide × 1/4" high

4. Press E. To type the subheading text in the box editor, press Shift-F6 (Center).
5. Use Compose to create the graphic symbol. Press Ctrl-V. At the `Key =` prompt, type *12,118* and then press Enter.

   The graphic symbol is a Zapf Dingbat, which WordPerfect assigns to character set 12 if you are using a PostScript printer. If you don't have Zapf Dingbats in your printer or a soft font, select another symbol from the WordPerfect extended character set. For example, you can use 5,1 (a black diamond) or 4,46 (a large black box). Appendix B of this book lists the Zapf Dingbats and their Compose assignment codes.

6. Press the space bar after the graphic symbol, change the font to 10-point New Century Schoolbook Italic, and type the subheading, *Newsletter....*
7. Press the space bar, create another graphic symbol, and press F7 twice to return to the document screen.

To create a box for the list of founding members, complete the following steps:

1. Press Alt-F9, B, O. In the Options: Text Box screen, make the following settings:

Border Style	Set all to None, except set Bottom to Thick
Outside Border Space	Set all to 0"
Inside Border Space	Set all to 0"
Gray Shading	10%

2. Press F7 to return to the document screen.
3. Press Alt-F9, B, C. In the Definition: Text Box screen, make the following settings:

Anchor Type	Page, Number of pages to skip: 0
Vertical Position	Set Position, .7"
Horizontal Position	Set Position, 3/4"
Size	Set Both, 2 1/8" wide × 1 11/16" high
Wrap Text Around Box	No

4. Press E. To type the text in the text box editor, press Enter and turn on center justification. Press Shift-F8, L, J, C, F7.
5. Change the font to 8-point New Century Schoolbook Bold and type *FOUNDING MEMBERS*. Press Enter three times and type the list of founding members, pressing Enter twice between names.
6. Press F7 twice to return to the document screen.

For a longer list of founding members, you can adjust the box size. Notice in figure 25.1 that the bottom of the box aligns precisely with the lower thin horizontal line under the subheading. Before changing the box size and changing this alignment, try adjusting the line spacing of the founding members' list with a Leading Adjustment command or type the members' names single-spaced.

To create a black box for the photo in the middle of the page, do the following:

1. Press Alt-F9, B, O. In the Options: Text Box screen, make the following settings:

Border Style	Set all to None
Outside Border Space	Left: 0", Right: 1/8", Top: 0", Bottom: 1/8"
Inside Border Space	Set all to 0"
Gray Shading	100%

   Outside Border Space of 1/8" is needed at the right and bottom of the box to separate the box from surrounding text.

2. Press F7 to return to the document screen.
3. Press Alt-F9, B, C. In the Definition: Text Box screen, make the following settings:

Anchor Type	Page, Number of pages to skip: 0
Vertical Position	Set Position, 4 5/8"
Horizontal Position	Set Position, 1 3/8"
Size	Set Both, 2 5/8" wide × 1 3/4" high

4. Press F7 to return to the document screen.

To create a black box for the photo near the bottom of the page, do the following:

1. Press Alt-F9, B, C. In the Definition: Text Box screen, make the following settings:

Anchor Type	Page, Number of pages to skip: 0
Vertical Position	Set Position, 7 1/4"
Horizontal Position	Set Position, 3/4"
Size	Set Both, 2 1/8" wide × 2" high

2. Press C. Press the backspace key to delete the automatically generated box number.

3. To type the caption in the Box Caption screen, use an Advance code to insert 1/8" space between the box and caption. Press Shift-F8, O, A, D; type *1/8*"; and press Enter, F7.
4. To turn on right justification, press Shift-F8, L, J, R, Enter, F7.
5. Change the font to 10-point New Century Schoolbook Italic and type the caption, *Victorian Sunshine Builders specializes....* Press F7 twice to return to the document screen.

Creating the Headers

Next, you need to create two headers: one to be printed on odd-numbered pages and one to be printed on even-numbered pages.

To create the header to print on odd-number pages, do the following:

1. Press Shift-F8, P, H, A, O. In the Header A editing screen, you create the box that surrounds each page. Press Alt-F9, B, O.
2. In the Options: Text Box screen, make the following settings:

Border Style	Set all to Single
Outside Border Space	Set all to 0"
Inside Border Space	Set all to 0"
Gray Shading	0%

3. Press F7 to return to the Header A editing screen.
4. Press Alt-F9, B, C. In the Definition: Text Box screen, make the following settings:

Anchor Type	Page, Number of pages to skip: 0
Vertical Position	Set Position, 11/16"
Horizontal Position	Margin, Left
Size	Set Both, 7 1/2" wide × 9 3/4" high
Wrap Text Around Box	No

5. Press F7 to return to the Header A editing screen.
6. To create the thick horizontal line that prints above the top line of the box in the header, press Alt-F9, L, H. In the Graphics: Horizontal Line screen, make the following settings:

Horizontal Position	Full
Vertical Position	Set Position, 5/8"
Width of Line	0.013"
Gray Shading	100%

7. Press F7 to return to the Header A editing screen.
8. Change the font to 10-point New Century Schoolbook Bold, which sets the font for page numbers.
9. Press Alt-F6 (Flush Right). Press F7 to return to the Format: Page menu. Press N, P, 4 to tell WordPerfect to print page numbers at the top right and left corners on odd-numbered and even-numbered pages respectively.
10. Press Enter to return to the Format: Page menu. Press U, P, Y, Enter to suppress page numbering for page one and return to the Format: Page menu.

To create a second header to print on even-numbered pages, complete the following steps:

1. Press H, B, V. In the Header B editing screen, create a text box and horizontal line as described in steps 1-7 in the preceding list.
2. Change the font to 10-point New Century Schoolbook Bold.
3. Press F7 twice to return to the document screen.

Placing the First Article

The first article has many elements. Not only do you need to create body text, but you also need to place the main headline and the subhead.

To begin creating the first article, “Plexes On Rise...,” you need to set up the format. Complete the following steps:

1. Press Enter 11 times. To define columns for the article, press Alt-F7, C, D. In the Text Column Definition menu, change the column type to Parallel.
2. Change the margins to 3/4", 2 7/8", 3 1/8", and 7 3/4".
3. Press F7, O to turn columns on and return to the document screen.

To place the main headline and the subhead, complete the following steps:

1. Change the font to 24-point New Century Schoolbook Bold. Turn on right justification. Press Shift-F8, L, J, R, Enter, F7.
2. Use Advance to move the insertion point down 11/64" to align the bottom of the first two lines of the heading with the large drop cap to the right. (The amount of the advance, 11/64", was determined by experimentation.) Press Shift-F8, O, A, D; type *11/64"*; and press Enter, F7.
3. Type *Plexes*. Press Enter and type *On Rise*.
4. Change the font to 14-point New Century Schoolbook Bold, press Enter, and type *Tight money has*. Press Enter and type *new buyers moving in together*, allowing WordPerfect to wordwrap the line automatically. Press Ctrl-Enter to move to the top of the next column.

Next, you need to create the large drop cap, H. The drop cap is contained in a text box:

1. Press Alt-F9, B, O. In the Options: Text Box screen, make the following settings:

Border Style	Set all to None
Outside Border Space	Set all to 0"
Inside Border Space	Set all to 0"
Gray Shading	0%

2. Press F7 to return to the document screen.
3. Press Alt-F9, B, C. In the Definition: Text Box screen, make the following settings:

Anchor Type	Paragraph
Vertical Position	1/8"
Horizontal Position	Left
Size	Set Both, 3/4" wide × 21/32" high

4. Press E. To type the drop cap in the text box editing screen, change the font to 60-point New Century Schoolbook and type *H*. Press F7 twice to return to the document screen.

Next, you need to turn on full justification and type the text of the first article. Do the following:

1. Press Shift-F8, L, J, F, F7.
2. Change the font to 10-point New Century Schoolbook. Press Enter twice to move the text down in relation to the drop cap as shown in figure 25.1.
3. Type the first three words of the text in caps, *I OMNES LINGUA*.
4. At the end of the article, press the space bar and use Compose to insert the same graphic symbol you used for the newsletter subtitle, *Newsletter of Peninsula Restorers....* Press Ctrl-V. At the `Key =` prompt, type *12,118*. Press Enter.

Placing the Second Article

The second article also has a main headline and a subhead. This article, however, is divided into two columns. Before you can create the second article, "Victorian Sunshine...," you need to press Enter twice at the end of the first article.

To create the upper, thick horizontal line between the articles, do the following:

1. Press Alt-F9, L, H. In the Graphics: Horizontal Line screen, make the following settings:

Horizontal Position	Full
Vertical Position	Baseline
Width of Line	1/40"
Gray Shading	100%

2. Press F7 to return to the document screen.

Next, you use Advance to position the second, thinner line. Complete the following steps:

1. Press Shift-F8, O, A, D; type *1/32*"; and press Enter, F7.
2. Press Alt-F9, L, H. In the Graphics: Horizontal Line screen, make the following settings:

Horizontal Position	Full
Vertical Position	Baseline
Width of Line	0.013"
Gray Shading	100%

3. Press F7 to return to the document screen.

To place the heading of the second article, "Victorian Sunshine...", complete the following steps:

1. Press Enter three times. Change the font to 16-point New Century Schoolbook Bold and type *Victorian Sunshine*.
2. Before pressing Enter to end the line, change the font to 12-point New Century Schoolbook Bold. Press Enter and type the subtitle, *Add-on solaria now a popular trend for older homes*.
3. Turn columns off to end the two-parallel column specification. Press Alt-F7, C, F.
4. Press Enter. To define two newspaper-style columns, press Alt-F7, C, D. In the Text Column Definition menu, specify two newspaper-style columns and change the margins to 3 1/8", 5 3/16", 5 9/16", and 7 3/4".
5. Press F7, O to turn columns on and return to the document screen.

To define the vertical line between the columns in the second article, do the following:

1. Press Alt-F9, L, V. In the Graphics: Vertical Line screen, make the following settings:

Horizontal Position	Between Columns, Column 1
Vertical Position	Set Position, 8.55"
Length of Line	1 5/8"
Width of Line	.013"
Gray Shading	100%

2. Press F7 to return to the document screen.

WordPerfect's default initial paragraph indent setting is much too wide for typeset text. This article doesn't contain a paragraph indent, but go ahead and create a better-looking tab setting now so that it can be used later. To change the tab setting, do the following:

1. Press Shift-F8, L, T.
2. In the tab ruler, type an *L* on the fifth dot to the right of the 0" marker.
3. Press F7 to return to the document screen.

WordPerfect uses relative tabs by default. You get the same first-line paragraph indent whether you are typing in column one, two, or three.

To enter the text of this article, do the following:

1. Change the font to 9-point New Century Schoolbook. Type the text of the article, with the first three words in all caps.

   This article doesn't need a large drop cap to draw the eye to the start of the text. The large photo and the headline serve that purpose. Two large drop caps would be design overkill on this already *busy* page.

2. When you get to the bottom of the first column, press Ctrl-Enter (Hard Page) to move to the top of column two.
3. Type the text for column two and end the text with the same Zapf Dingbat or other graphic symbol you used for the first article on the page. Edit the text, if necessary, to make the columns align at the bottom.

   From this point on, the keystrokes for creating the article-ending graphic symbol will not be given. To review the process, see the preceding section on creating text boxes.

4. At the end of page one, press Alt-F7, C, F to turn columns off. Then press Ctrl-Enter (Hard Page) to move to the top of page two.

Note: The font assignments for article headings, subheadings, text, or photo captions also are not repeated in this chapter. They are as follows:

Article headings	16-point New Century Schoolbook Bold
Subheadings	12-point New Century Schoolbook Bold
Article text	9-point New Century Schoolbook
Captions	10-point New Century Schoolbook Italic

Creating the Middle Spread

Page two contains two photos, and page three contains three photos. Notice in figure 25.1 that the two-page spread, pages two and three, was designed as a single entity, with column arrangements, headlines, and photo boxes harmoniously placed on the spread. The design was painstakingly planned:

- The three drop caps form an eye-pleasing triangle. (Notice that the first article on page three does not have a drop cap, because it is not needed to draw the reader's eye to the beginning of the article, and another drop cap would make the design a bit too busy.)
- Small photos are placed in the outside columns on each page, creating a consistent, mirrored design element.
- The article at the bottom of page two runs across two columns, creating eye-relief from an otherwise all-vertical three-column spread. The large photo on page three also breaks up the three-column format and, not coincidentally, mirrors the wide-column article on page two.

Creating Page Two

At the top of page two, create the box for the photo next to the second article on the page. (The photo box for the upper article is contained in a paragraph-anchored text box that you create after the title of the first article.)

To create the photo box for the second article, do the following:

1. Press Alt-F9, B, O. In the Options: Text Box screen, make the following settings:

Border Style	Set all to None
Outside Border Space	Set all to 0"
Inside Border Space	Set all to 0"
Position of Caption	Below box, Outside borders
Gray Shading	100%

2. Press F7 to return to the document screen.
3. Press Alt-F9, B, C. In the Definition: Text Box screen, make the following settings:

Anchor Type	Page, Number of pages to skip: 0
Vertical Position	Set Position, 7 1/8"
Horizontal Position	Set Position, 3/4"
Size	Set Both, 1 7/8" wide × 1 7/8" high

4. Press C. Press the backspace key to delete the automatically generated box number.
5. To type the caption in the Box Caption editing screen, use Advance to space the caption 1/8" from the box. Press Shift-F8, O, A, D; type *1/8*"; and press Enter, F7.
6. Change the font to 10-point New Century Schoolbook Italic.
7. Turn on right justification. Press Shift-F8, L, J, R, F7.
8. Type the caption text allowing WordPerfect to wordwrap the lines. Press F7 twice to return to the document screen.
9. Press Enter twice to create white space at the top of the page.

To define newspaper-style columns for the first article and its heading, complete the following steps:

1. Press Alt-F7, C, D. In the Text Column Definition screen, specify three newspaper-style columns and accept Word-Perfect's margin settings but set the rightmost margin to 7 3/4".
2. Press F7, O to turn columns on and return to the document screen.

To define the vertical lines between columns for the first article on page two, do the following:

1. Press Alt-F9, L, V. In the Graphics: Vertical Line screen, make the following settings:

Horizontal Position	Between Columns, Column 1
Vertical Position	Set Position, 1.77"
Length of Line	3.91"
Width of Line	.013"
Gray Shading	100%

2. Press F7 to return to the document screen.
3. Press Alt-F9, L, V. In the Graphics: Vertical Line screen, make the following settings:

Horizontal Position	Between Columns, Column 2
Vertical Position	Set Position, 1.77"
Length of Line	3.91"
Width of Line	.013"
Gray Shading	100%

4. Press F7 to return to the document screen.

Next, you need to enter the headline for the first article on page two. Complete the following steps:

1. Press Enter and change the font to 16-point New Century Schoolbook Bold.
2. Turn on right justification. Press Shift-F8, L, J, R, F7.
3. Use Advance to move the title up so that the bottom of the fourth line, "Mansion," aligns with the drop cap to the right. Press Shift-F8, O, A, U; type *1/16*"; and press Enter, F7.
4. Type the article title, pressing Enter between lines as shown in figure 25.1. At the end of the article title, before pressing Enter to move to the next line, change the font to 12-point New Century Schoolbook Bold.
5. Press Enter and type the subtitle, pressing Enter at the end of each line.

After the subtitle, create a black box for a photo by doing the following:

1. Press Enter twice and define the box by pressing Alt-F9, B, O. In the Options: Text Box screen, make the following settings:

Border Style	Set all to None
Outside Border Space	Set all to 0"
Inside Border Space	Set all to 0"
Position of Caption	Below box, Outside borders
Gray Shading	100%

2. Press F7 to return to the document screen.
3. Press Alt-F9, B, C. In the Definition: Text Box screen, make the following settings:

Anchor Type	Paragraph
Vertical Position	0"
Horizontal Position	Right
Size	Set Both, 1 1/8" wide × 1 1/4" high

4. Press F7 to return to the document screen and press Enter eight times to move the insertion point beneath the photo box.
5. Use Advance to move the insertion point down 1/16". Press Shift-F8, O, A, D; type *1/16*"; press Enter, F7. Change the font to 10-point New Century Schoolbook Italic and type the caption, pressing Enter after each line as shown in figure 25.1.
6. Press Ctrl-Enter (Hard Page) to move to the top of column two.

Creating a drop cap is a delicate balancing act: aligning the bottom of the drop cap with the baseline of a line of text, making sure that just three text lines print to the right of the drop cap, aligning the tops of the text lines with the vertical lines, and making sure that the bottoms of the vertical lines line up with the bottoms of the columns of text.

To create the drop cap, do the following:

1. Press Enter to move the drop cap down so that roughly 1/3 of the letter A sticks up above the vertical lines. Use Advance to position the drop cap precisely. Press Shift-F8, O, A, D and type *3/32*". Press Enter, F7.
2. To create a text box for the drop cap, press Alt-F9, B, O. In the Options: Text Box screen, make the following settings:

Border Style	Set all to None
Outside Border Space	Set all to 0"
Inside Border Space	Set all to 0"
Gray Shading	0%

3. Press F7 to return to the document screen.
4. Press Alt-F9, B, C. In the Definition: Text Box screen, make the following settings:

Anchor Type	Paragraph
Vertical Position	1/8"
Horizontal Position	Left
Size	Set both, .625" wide × .65" high

5. Press E. To type the drop cap in the text box editing screen, you need to use another Advance code to position the drop cap. Press Shift-F8, O, A, U; type *1/4*"; and press Enter, F7.
6. Change the font to 60-point New Century Schoolbook and type *A*. Press F7 twice to return to the document screen.
7. Change the font to 9-point New Century Schoolbook.
8. Press Enter twice and use Advance to position the first line of text so that the third line's baseline aligns with the bottom of the drop cap. Press Shift-F8, O, A, D; type *3/32*"; and press Enter, F7. Type the first three words in caps.

After aligning the text in column one correctly with the drop cap, continue to type the text in column one. Then do the following:

1. At the bottom of column one, press Ctrl-Enter (Hard Page) to move to the top of column two.

2. At the top of column two, use Advance to align the baseline of the first line of column two with the first line of column one. Press Shift-F8, O, A, D; type *39/64*"; and press Enter, F7.
3. Type the text in column two. Create a graphic symbol at the end of the column.
4. After the graphic symbol, turn off columns. Press Alt-F7, C, F. Then press Enter to insert a blank space above the horizontal line.

At the end of the first article on page two, you need to press Enter and definc the two horizontal lines that separate the articles:

1. Press Alt-F9, L, H. In the Graphics: Horizontal Line screen, make the following settings:

Horizontal Position	Center
Vertical Position	Baseline
Length of Line	7"
Width of Line	1/40"
Gray Shading	100%

2. Press F7 to return to the document screen.
3. Press Enter and use Advance to position the thin line. Press Shift-F8, O, A, D; type *1/32*"; press Enter, F7; and press Alt-F9, L, H. In the Graphics: Horizontal Line screen, make the following settings:

Horizontal Position	Center
Vertical Position	Baseline
Length of Line	7"
Width of Line	0.013"
Gray Shading	100%

4. Press F7 to return to the document screen.

The first thing you need to do to finish the second article on page two is to define parallel columns. Complete the following steps:

1. Press Alt-F7, C, D. In the Text Column Definition screen, specify two parallel columns and accept WordPerfect's default margins.

2. Press F7, O to turn columns on and return to the document screen.
3. Press Ctrl-Enter (Hard Page) to move to the top of column two. Press Enter twice to insert white space at the top of the column.
4. Type the heading and subheading ("Commercial Contractors..."), using the fonts specified earlier. Press Shift-F6 at the start of each line to right-justify the heading and subheading.
5. Press Enter twice and use Advance to position the drop cap. Press Shift-F8, O, A, U; type *1/8"*; and press Enter, F7.
6. To create the vertical line to the left of the column, press Alt-F9, L, V. In the Graphics: Vertical Line screen, make the following settings:

Horizontal Position	Between Columns, Column 1
Vertical Position	Set Position, 7 5/16"
Length of Line	2 27/32"
Width of Line	.013"
Gray Shading	100%

7. Press F7 to return to the document screen.
8. To create a box for the drop cap, press Alt-F9, B, O. In the Options: Text Box screen, make the following settings:

Border Style	Set all to None
Outside Border Space	Set all to 0"
Inside Border Space	Set all to 0"
Gray Shading	0%

9. Press F7 to return to the document screen.
10. Press Alt-F9, B, C. In the Definition: Text Box screen, make the following settings:

Anchor Type	Paragraph
Vertical Position	1/8"
Horizontal Position	Left
Size	Set Both, 5/8" wide × 21/32" high

11. Press E. To type the text in the editing text box, use Advance to position the drop cap. Press Shift-F8, O, A, U; type *1/4*"; and press Enter, F7.
12. Change the font to 60-point New Century Schoolbook and type *C*. Press F7 to return to the document screen.
13. Change the font to 9-point New Century Schoolbook, press Enter twice, and use Advance to position the first line of body text in relation to the drop cap so that the bottom of the drop cap aligns with the third line of text. Press Shift-F8, O, A, D; type *1/16*"; and press Enter, F7.
14. Type the text, capitalizing the first two words, UM CIVITAS. Type the rest of the second article, ending with a graphic symbol. At the end of the page, turn columns off. Press Alt-F7, C, O.
15. Press Ctrl-Enter (Hard Page) to move to the top of page three.

Creating Page Three

Page three of the newsletter, the second page of the middle spread, is designed to complement the elements on page two. Page three contains five text boxes. The first is for the large picture in the upper right corner of the page, and the second is for the caption of that photo.

The designer of the newsletter placed the photo caption in its own box, instead of using the box caption feature, because this placement creates a more stable anchor for the box and caption. When using the caption feature, the designer discovered that when text ran over from the bottom of column two, WordPerfect wrapped it to the top of column three, above the photo caption, and pushed the caption and photo down. Even though column two is edited so that the text ends at the bottom, anchoring the large box and caption solidly is better so that you can freely edit text and captions in columns two and three as needed, without having to worry about changes when moving the photo and caption.

To create the large box for the picture in the upper right corner of page three, do the following:

1. Press Alt-F9, B, O. In the Options: Text Box screen, make the following settings:

Border Style	Set all to None
Outside Border Space	Set all to 0"
Inside Border Space	Set all to 0"
Gray Shading	100%

2. Press F7 to return to the document screen.
3. Press Alt-F9, B, C. In the Definition: Text Box screen, make the following settings:

Anchor Type	Page, Number of pages to skip: 0
Vertical Position	Set Position, 1 1/2"
Horizontal Position	Set Position, 3 5/32"
Size	Set Both, 4 1/2" wide × 2 3/8" high

4. Press F7 to return to the document screen.

To create a box for the caption, do the following:

1. Press Alt-F9, B, O. In the Options: Text Box screen, make the following settings:

Border Style	Set all to None
Outside Border Space	Set all to 0"
Inside Border Space	Set all to 0"
Gray Shading	0%

2. Press F7 to return to the document screen.
3. Press Alt-F9, B, C. In the Definition: Text Box screen, make the following settings:

Anchor Type	Page, Number of pages to skip: 0
Vertical Position	Set Position, 15/16"
Horizontal Position	Set Position, 5"
Size	Set Both, 2 5/8" wide × 1/2" high

4. Enter the caption text. Set right justification by pressing Shift-F8, L, J, R, F7. Change to 10-point New Century Schoolbook Italic. Type the text, pressing Enter between lines and F7 twice after the last line. Press F7 to return to the document screen.

To define three newspaper-style columns for the page, do the following:

1. Press Alt-F7, C, D and in the Text Column Definition screen, specify three newspaper-style columns and change the left and right margin settings to 3/4" and 7 3/4", respectively.
2. Press F7, O to turn columns on and return to the document screen.

To create the vertical line between columns one and two, do the following:

1. Press Alt-F9, L, V. In the Graphics: Vertical Line screen, make the following settings:

Horizontal Position	Between Columns, Column 1
Vertical Position	Set Position, 1 1/2"
Length of Line	8 21/32"
Width of Line	.013"
Gray Shading	100%

2. Press F7 to return to the document screen.

To create the vertical line between columns two and three, do the following:

1. Press Alt-F9, L, V. In the Graphics: Vertical Line screen, make the following settings:

Horizontal Position	Between Columns, Column 2
Vertical Position	Set Position, 4 23/32"
Length of Line	5 7/16"
Width of Line	.013"
Gray Shading	100%

2. Press F7 to return to the document screen.

To place the heading, subheading, and body text for the first article on page three, do the following:

1. Press Enter, Shift-F8, L, J, L, F7; change the font to 16-point New Century Schoolbook Bold; and type the article heading, pressing Enter at the end of each line. Then type the subheading and text using the fonts, justification, and spacing described earlier.
2. At the end of column one, press Ctrl-Enter (Hard Page) to move to the top of column two. Press Enter seven times to insert white space at the top of the page.

To create the double horizontal line under the large photo box, do the following:

1. Press Alt-F9, L, H. In the Graphics: Horizontal Line screen, make the following settings:

Horizontal Position	Set Position, 3 1/8"
Vertical Position	Set Position, 4 11/64"
Length of Line	4 9/16"
Width of Line	1/40"
Gray Shading	100%

2. Press F7 to return to the document screen.
3. Press Alt-F9, L, H. In the Graphics: Horizontal Line screen, make the following settings:

Horizontal Position	Set Position, 3 1/8"
Vertical Position	Set Position, 4 7/32"
Length of Line	4 9/16"
Width of Line	0.013"
Gray Shading	100%

4. Press F7 to return to the document screen.

To create a text box for the drop cap, C, at the top of column two, do the following:

1. Press Alt-F9, B, O. In the Options: Text Box screen, make the following settings:

Border Style	Set all to None
Outside Border Space	Set all to 0"
Inside Border Space	Set all to 0"
Gray Shading	0%

2. Press F7 to return to the document screen.
3. Press Alt-F9, B, C. In the Definition: Text Box screen, make the following settings:

Anchor Type	Paragraph
Vertical Position	1/8"
Horizontal Position	Left
Size	Set Both, .625" wide × 21/32" high

4. Press E. You create the drop cap in the text box editing screen. To use Advance to position the drop cap, press Shift-F8, O, A, U and type *1/8"*. Press Enter, F7.
5. Change the font to 60-point New Century Schoolbook and type *C*. Press Exit twice to return to the document screen.

You need to use Advance to position the first line of text so that the baseline of the third line aligns with the bottom of the drop cap. To place the text for the second article on page three, do the following:

1. Press Shift-F8, O, A, D; type *5/64"*; and press Enter, F7.
2. Type the text of the article in column two, using the font and spacing described earlier in the chapter. At the bottom of column two, press Ctrl-Enter (Hard Page) to move to the top of column three.

To finish page three, do the following:

1. Press Enter five times to position the top line of the column. Use Advance to position the first line of text precisely. Press Shift-F8, O, A, D; type *1/16"*; and press Enter, F7.
2. Press Shift-F8, L, J, L, F7 and type the article title and subtitle, using the fonts and spacing described earlier. At the end of the subtitle, press Enter twice.

3. To create the horizontal photo box below the article title, press Alt-F9, B, O. In the Options: Text Box screen, make the following settings:

Border Style	Set all to None
Outside Border Space	Set all to 0"
Inside Border Space	Set all to 0"
Position of Caption	Below Box, Outside Borders
Gray Shading	100%

   This box doesn't have a caption, but the photo beneath the box does. Set a caption position here so that you do not have to use the Options: Text Box menu twice.

4. Press F7 to return to the document screen.

5. Press Alt-F9, B, C. In the Definition: Text Box screen, make the following settings:

Anchor Type	Paragraph
Vertical Position	0"
Horizontal Position	Full
Size	Set Height, Auto Width, 1.92" (wide) × 1 1/4" high

6. Press F7 to return to the document screen.

7. Press Enter and create the text box for the second photo. Press Alt-F9, B, C. In the Definition: Text Box screen, make the following settings:

Anchor Type	Paragraph
Vertical Position	0"
Horizontal Position	Left
Size	Set Both, 1 1/8" wide × 1 1/2" high

8. Press C. Press the backspace key to delete the automatically generated box number. Type the caption within the Box Caption screen.

9. Use Advance to position the caption 1/8" beneath the box. Press Shift-F8, O, A, D; type *1/8"*; and press Enter, F7.

10. Change the font to 10-point New Century Schoolbook Italic and type the caption, allowing WordPerfect to wordwrap the lines. Press F7 twice to return to the document screen.
11. Turn columns off. Press Alt-F7, C, F.

Check the status line. You have been working close to the bottom of column three. If turning columns off moves you to page four, don't enter a Hard Page code, or WordPerfect inserts a blank page and numbers the new page.

Creating Page Four

The mailer in the bottom half of page four presents special challenges. You need to create a small copy of the newsletter heading and create a box for the postal indicia ("Non-profit organization/ US Postage PAID...").

Creating the Text Boxes

Page four has seven text boxes. They are listed here so that you can see in one place how boxes are used to place various elements on the page:

- Text Box 17 — Black photo box with caption
- Text Box 18 — Large 10% screen box, bottom of page
- Text Box 19 — "The Traditional Builder"
- Text Box 20 — "Newsletter of..."
- Text Box 21 — "90012 Alder Way..."
- Text Box 22 — "Non-profit organization..."
- Text Box 23 — Drop cap ("P")

To create the box for the photo and caption in the upper right corner of the page, do the following:

1. Press Alt-F9, B, O. In the Options: Text Box screen, make the following settings:

Border Style	Set all to None
Outside Border Space	Set all to 0"
Inside Border Space	Set all to 0"
Position of Caption	Below Box, Outside Borders
Gray Shading	100%

2. Press F7 to return to the document screen.
3. Press Alt-F9, B, C. In the Definition: Text Box screen, make the following settings:

Anchor Type	Page, Number of pages to skip: 0
Vertical Position	Set Position, 1 1/4"
Horizontal Position	Set Position, 5 13/16"
Size	Set Both, 1 7/8" wide × 2 3/8" high

4. Press C. Press the backspace key to delete the automatically generated box number. Type the caption in the Box Caption screen.
5. Use Advance to space the caption 1/8" below the box. Press Shift-F8, O, A, D; type *1/8"*; and press Enter, F7. Change the justification to produce a ragged right margin (Shift-F8, L, J, L, F7).
6. Change the font to 10-point New Century Schoolbook Italic and type the caption, pressing Enter at the end of each line as shown in figure 25.1. Press F7 twice to return to the document screen.

To create the large shaded box in the lower half of the screen for the mailer, complete the following steps:

1. Press Alt-F9, B, O. In the Options: Text Box screen, make the following settings:

Border Style	Set all to None
Outside Border Space	Set all to 0"
Inside Border Space	Set all to 0"
Gray Shading	10%

2. Press F7 to return to the document screen.

3. Press Alt-F9, B, C. In the Definition: Text Box screen, make the following settings:

Anchor Type	Page, Number of pages to skip: 0
Vertical Position	Set Position, 5 13/16"
Horizontal Position	Set Position, 3/4"
Size	Set Both, 7" wide × 4 3/8" high

4. Press E. To change the margins from the text box editing screen, press Shift-F8, L, M; type *3/8*"; press Enter; type *5 1/4*"; and press Enter, F7.

5. Change the font to 10-point Helvetica Narrow Bold. Turn on center justification. Press Shift-F8, L, J, C, F7.

6. Press Enter 20 times and type *ADDRESS CORRECTION AND FORWARDING REQUESTED*, pressing Enter between the lines as shown in figure 25.1. Press F7 twice to return to the document screen.

To create the text box for the newsletter name in the return address, complete the following steps:

1. Press Alt-F9, B, O. In the Options: Text Box screen, make the following settings:

Border Style	Set all to None
Outside Border Space	Set all to 0"
Inside Border Space	Set all to 0"
Gray Shading	0%

2. Press F7 to return to the document screen.

3. Press Alt-F9, B, C. In the Definition: Text Box screen, make the following settings:

Anchor Type	Page, Number of pages to skip: 0
Vertical Position	Set Position, 6 1/4"
Horizontal Position	Set Position, 3/4"
Size	Set Both, 4" wide × 1 1/2" high

4. Press E. To type the text for the newsletter name in the text box editing screen, press Shift-F6 (Center) and change the font to 8-point New Century Schoolbook.
5. Change the letter spacing to add space between the letters in "THE TRADITIONAL." Press Shift-F8, O, P, W, P; type *200*; press Enter, P; type *200*; and press Enter, F7. Type *THE TRADITIONAL*.
6. To change the letter spacing to tighten the letters in "BUILDER," press Shift-F8, O, P, W, O, P; type *90*; and press Enter, F7. Press Enter and use Advance to move "BUILDER" close under "THE TRADITIONAL." Press Shift-F8, O, A, U; type *1 1/4*"; and press Enter, F7.
7. Press Shift-F6 (Center), change the font to 60-point New Century Schoolbook, and type *B*. Change the font to 48-point New Century Schoolbook and type *UILDE*.
8. Change the font to 60-point New Century Schoolbook and type *R*. Press Enter to add space after the title. Press F7 twice to return to the document screen.

To create a box for the subtitle of the newsletter, "Newsletter of Peninsula...," you need to specify top and bottom single lines for the long, thin box. Complete the following steps:

1. Press Alt-F9, B, O. In the Options: Text Box screen, make the following settings:

Border Style	Left: None, Right: None, Top: Single, Bottom: Single
Outside Border Space	Set all to 0"
Inside Border Space	Set all to 0", except set Bottom and Top to 1/16"
Gray Shading	0%

2. Press F7 to return to the document screen
3. Press Alt-F9, B, C. In the Definition: Text Box screen, make the following settings:

Anchor Type	Page, Number of pages to skip: 0
Vertical Position	Set Position, 7"

Horizontal Position	Set Position, 1 5/16"
Size	Set Both, 3" wide × 3/16" high

4. Press E. To type the text for the subtitle in the text box editor, change the font to 6-point New Century Schoolbook and press Shift-F6 (Center).
5. Use Compose to create a Zapf Dingbat graphic symbol. Press Ctrl-V. At the `Key =` prompt, type *12,118* and then press Enter.
6. Press the space bar and type the subtitle. Press the space bar and create another graphic symbol. Press F7 twice to return to the document screen.

To create a text box for the organization's return address, complete the following steps:

1. Press Alt-F9, B, O. In the Options: Text Box screen, make the following settings:

Border Style	Set all to None
Outside Border Space	Set all to 0"
Inside Border Space	Set all to 0", except set Top to 1/16"
Gray Shading	0%

2. Press F7 to return to the document screen.
3. Press Alt-F9, B, C. In the Definition: Text Box screen, make the following settings:

Anchor Type	Page, Number of pages to skip: 0
Vertical Position	Set Position, 7 3/16"
Horizontal Position	Set Position, 1 5/16"
Size	Set Both, 3" wide × 3/16" high

4. Press E. To type the address in the text box editor, change the font to 8-point New Century Schoolbook, press Shift-F6 (Center), and type the address, pressing Enter three times between the street address and the town.
5. Press F7 twice to return to the document screen.

To create a box for the non-profit organization mailing indicia, complete the following steps:

1. Press Alt-F9, B, O. In the Options: Text Box screen, make the following settings:

Border Style	Set all to Single
Outside Border Space	Set all to 0"
Inside Border Space	Set all to 1/16"
Gray Shading	0%

2. Press F7 to return to the document screen.
3. Press Alt-F9, B, C. In the Definition: Text Box screen, make the following settings:

Anchor Type	Page, Number of pages to skip: 0
Vertical Position	Set Position, 6 1/8"
Horizontal Position	Set Position, 6 1/4"
Size	Set Both, 1 1/4" wide × 1" high

4. Press E. To type the text in the text box editor, change the font to 8-point Heretical Narrow Bold. Press Enter to add space at the top of the box.
5. Turn on center justification. Press Shift-F8, L, J, C, Enter, F7. Type the text, pressing Enter between the lines as shown in figure 25.1.
6. Press F7 twice to return to the document screen.

Suppressing the Page Number

Notice in figure 25.1 that page four does not have a page number. To suppress page numbering for page four, press Shift-F8, P, U, P, Y, F7.

Placing the Headline and Subhead

Only one article appears on page four. To type the text of the article, you first need to place the article's title and subtitle. Complete the following steps:

1. After the [Suppress:PgNum] code, press Enter twice to add white space at the top of the page.
2. Change the left and right margins to 3/4" to position the title. Press Shift-F8, L, M; type *3/4"*; press Enter; type *3/4"*; and press Enter, F7.
3. Use Advance to align the top of the title with the top of the photo box to the right. Press Shift-F8, O, A, D; type *1/16"*; and press Enter, F7.
4. Change the font to 16-point New Century Schoolbook Bold and type the article title and subtitle, using the fonts and spacing described earlier in this chapter. Press Enter to end the lines as shown in figure 25.1.
5. Use Advance Up to nullify the effect of the Advance Down code you entered earlier. Press Shift-F8, O, A, U; type *1/16"*; and press Enter, F7.
6. After the title and subtitle, press Enter twice to add space above the article text.

Defining the Columns

To define two newspaper-style columns for the article, do the following:

1. Press Alt-F7, C, D. In the Text Column Definition screen, specify two newspaper-style columns and accept WordPerfect's default margin settings.
2. Press F7, O to turn columns on and return to the document screen.

Creating the Vertical Lines

To create two vertical lines after columns one and two, do the following:

1. Press Alt-F9, L, V. In the Graphics: Vertical Line screen, make the following settings:

Horizontal Position	Between Columns, Column 1
Vertical Position	Set Position, 2 23/32"

Length of Line	2 7/32"
Width of Line	.013"
Gray Shading	100%

2. Press F7 to return to the document screen.
3. Press Alt-F9, L, V. In the Graphics: Vertical Line screen, make the following settings:

Horizontal Position	Between Columns, Column 2
Vertical Position	Set Position, 1 1/4"
Length of Line	3 11/16"
Width of Line	.013"
Gray Shading	100%

4. Press F7 to return to the document screen.

Adding the Drop Cap

To create a box for the drop cap, complete the following steps:

1. Press Alt-F9, B, O. In the Options: Text Box screen, make the following settings:

Border Style	Set all to None
Outside Border Space	Set all to 0"
Inside Border Space	Set all to 0"
Gray Shading	0%

2. Press F7 to return to the document screen.
3. Press Alt-F9, B, C. In the Definition: Text Box screen, make the following settings:

Anchor Type	Paragraph
Vertical Position	5/32"
Horizontal Position	Left
Size	Set Both, 9/16" wide × 21/32" high

4. Press E. You create the drop cap in the text box editor.

5. Use Advance to position the drop cap precisely. Press Shift-F8, O, A, U; type *1/8*"; and press Enter, F7.
6. Change the font to 60-point New Century Schoolbook and type *P*. Press F7 twice to return to the document screen.
7. Press Enter, change the font to 9-point New Century Schoolbook, press Enter, and use Advance to position the first line of body text so that the baseline of the third line lines up with the bottom of the drop cap. Press Shift-F8, O, A, D; type *1/16*"; and press Enter, F7.

Placing the Body Text

To place the body text in column one, complete the following steps:

1. At the bottom of column one, press Ctrl-Enter to move to the top of column two. Press Enter twice and use Advance to align the first line of column two with the first line of column one.
2. Press Shift-F8, O, A, D; type *7/64*"; and press Enter, F7. Type the rest of column two, adding a graphic symbol at the end as described earlier.
3. At the end of column two, press Enter twice and turn columns off. Press Alt-F7, C, F.

Adding the Horizontal Lines

To create the double horizontal line above the mailing area, do the following:

1. Press Alt-F9, L, H. In the Graphics: Horizontal Line screen, make the following settings:

Horizontal Position	Set Position, 3/4"
Vertical Position	Set Position, 5 3/4"
Length of Line	7"
Width of Line	1/40"
Gray Shading	100%

Press F7 to return to the document screen.

2. Press Alt-F9, L, H. In the Graphics: Horizontal Line screen, make the following settings:

Horizontal Position	Set Position, 3/4"
Vertical Position	Set Position, 5 13/16"
Length of Line	7"
Width of Line	0.013"
Gray Shading	100%

3. Press F7 to return to the document screen.

If the process of creating complex newsletters seems overly complex, take heart. There are many steps that you need to do only for the first issue: setting up the newsletter logotype, headers, mailer, and font sizes, for example. With each month, creating a newsletter becomes easier.

Glossary of Desktop Publishing Terms

alignment Definition of text edge: flush right, flush left, justified, or centered.

anchoring Placement of boxes at a specific location: on the page or in a paragraph.

ascender The portion of the lowercase letters b, d, f, h, k, l, and t that rises above the height of the letter x. The height of the ascender varies in different typefaces. See *descender*.

ASCII (American Standard Code for Information Interchange) A standard computer character set devised in 1968 to enable efficient data communication and achieve compatibility among different computer devices.

The standard ASCII code consists of 96 displayed upper- and lowercase letters, plus 32 nondisplayed control characters. Because ASCII code includes no graphics characters, most modern computers use an extended character set containing needed characters.

ASCII file A file that contains only characters drawn from the ASCII character set.

attribute A character emphasis, such as boldface or italic, and other characteristics of character formatting, such as typeface and type size. See *formatting sequence*.

automatic font downloading The transmission of disk-based, downloadable printer fonts to the printer, done by an application program as the fonts are needed to complete a printing job.

banner A newsletter title.

baseline The lowest point characters reach (excluding descenders). For example, the baseline of a line of text is the lowermost point of letters like a and x, excluding the lowest points of p and q. See *descender*.

bit-mapped font A screen or printer font in which each character is composed of a pattern of dots. Bit-mapped fonts represent characters with a matrix of dots. To display or print bit-mapped fonts, the computer or printer must keep a full representation of each character in memory. Outline fonts are considered technically superior. See *outline font*.

bit-mapped graphic A graphic image formed by a pattern of pixels (screen dots) and limited in resolution to the maximum screen resolution of the device being used. Bit-mapped graphics are produced by paint programs and some scanners.

bleed A photograph, shaded box, bar, or other element that extends to the edge of the page. Laser-printed pages have a 0.3" margin and may not have bleeds.

blurb A subtitle printed above or below a headline, usually set in a smaller type size than the headline.

body type The font (normally 8- to 12-point) used to set paragraphs of text (distinguished from the typefaces used to set headings, subheadings, captions, and other typographical elements).

boldface A character emphasis visibly darker and heavier in weight than normal type.

brush style A typeface design that simulates script drawn with a brush or broad-pointed pen.

byline An author's name, often including the author's title.

caption Descriptive phrase identifying a photograph, image, chart, or graph.

cartridge A removable module that expands a printer's memory or font capabilities.

cartridge font A printer font supplied in the form of a read-only memory (ROM) cartridge that plugs into a receptacle on Hewlett-Packard LaserJet printers and clones. Unlike down-loadable fonts, the ROM-based cartridge font is immediately available to the printer and does not consume space in the printer's random-access memory (RAM).

CGM (Computer Graphics Metafile) An international graphics file format that stores object-oriented graphics in device-independent form so that you can exchange CGM files among users of different systems (and different programs).

character Any letter, number, punctuation mark, or symbol that can be produced on-screen by pressing a key.

character set The fixed set of keyboard codes that a particular computer system uses. See *ASCII (American Standard Code for Information Interchange)*.

characters per inch (cpi) The number of characters that fit within a linear inch in a given font. Standard units drawn from typewriting are pica (10 cpi) and elite (12 cpi).

clip art A collection of graphics images, stored on disk and available for use in a spreadsheet, page layout, or presentation graphics program.

clustering A method of grouping small visual elements together on the page to create a single, larger illustration; for example, a series of small head-and-shoulder portrait photographs.

color separation Separate color negatives (magenta, cyan, black, and yellow) created by a printer to produce four-color printed images.

compose sequence A series of keystrokes that enables a user to enter a character not found on the computer's keyboard.

composite newsletter A newsletter created with desktop publishing and traditional graphic design techniques; for example, when the newsletter is produced by desktop publishing methods except for photographic halftones, which are pasted into black squares.

condensed type Type narrowed in width so that more characters will fit into a linear inch. In dot-matrix printers, condensed type usually is set to print 17 characters per inch (cpi). See *characters per inch (cpi)*.

constraining A method used by many desktop publishing and draw programs to maintain the original proportions of an image while reducing or enlarging its size.

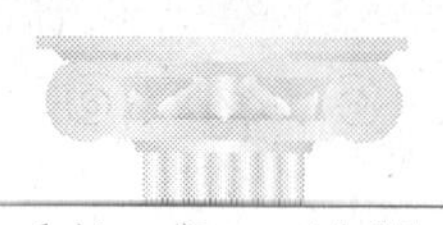

continuous-tone photograph A photographic print, which must be photographed through a halftone screen by the printer before it can be printed

contrast The range of light and dark tones in a text page, graphic image, line drawing, or photograph.

copyfitting The common practice of designing the space for an article and then cutting or expanding the text to fit the allotted space.

Courier A monospace typeface, commonly included as a built-in font in laser printers, that simulates the output of office typewriters.

crop marks Marks on a page or photograph that tell the printer how to trim the page or position the photograph. Some desktop publishing programs can print crop marks on the page automatically.

cropping Sizing a box to eliminate a portion of a photograph, image, chart, and so on.

default font The font that the printer uses unless you instruct otherwise.

descender The portion of a lowercase letter that hangs below the baseline. Five letters of the alphabet have descenders: g, j, p, q, and y. See *ascender*.

desktop publishing (DTP) The use of a personal computer as an inexpensive production system for generating typeset-quality text and graphics. Desktop publishers often merge text and graphics on the same page and print pages on a high-resolution laser printer or typesetting machine.

dingbats Ornamental characters such as bullets, stars, and arrows used to decorate a page.

discretionary hyphen A hyphen that you insert manually and that the program uses to break a word at the end of a line; useful for telling the software where to hyphenate unusual words.

display type A typeface, usually 14 points or larger and differing in style from the body type, that is used for headings and subheadings. See *body type*.

dot leader Pronounced "leeder;" a line of dots (periods) that leads the eye horizontally from one text element to another—for example, from a chapter title to a page number.

dot-matrix printer An impact printer that forms text and graphics images by pressing the ends of pins against a ribbon. Dot-matrix printers are fast, but the output they produce is generally poor quality because the character is not fully formed. Some dot-matrix printers use 24 pins instead of 9, and the quality of their output is better.

dot pitch The size of the smallest dot that a monitor can display on-screen. Dot pitch determines a monitor's maximum resolution.

downloadable font A printer font that must be transferred from the computer's (or the printer's) hard disk drive to the printer's random-access memory before the font can be used.

drop cap A large initial capital letter used to guide the reader's eye to the beginning of body text.

drop shadow A shadow placed behind an image, slightly offset horizontally and vertically, that creates the illusion that the topmost image has been lifted off the surface of the page.

elite A typeface that prints twelve characters per inch. See *pitch*.

em dash A long typographer's dash (—) used to separate phrases. The name indicates that the length of an em dash is the same as the width of the capital M in the current typeface.

em space A horizontal space equal to the width of a capital M in the current typeface.

en dash A typographer's hyphen, equal in width to a capital N in the current typeface.

en space Half an em space.

extended character set A character set that includes extra characters, such as foreign language accent marks, in addition to the standard 256-character IBM character set.

feathering Making very small changes in line spacing to line up the bottoms of adjacent columns of text.

flush left The alignment of text along the left margin, leaving a ragged right margin. Flush left alignment is easier to read than right-justified text.

flush right The alignment of text along the right margin, leaving a ragged left margin. Flush right alignment is seldom used, except for decorative effects or epigrams.

folio Printed next to a document title, the folio indicates issue date, volume, and issue number.

font One complete collection of letters, punctuation marks, numbers, and special characters with a consistent and identifiable typeface, weight (Roman or bold), posture (upright or italic), and font size—for example, Helvetica italic 12. The term, however, often is used to refer to typefaces or font families.

Two kinds of fonts exist: bit-mapped fonts and outline fonts. Each comes in two versions, screen fonts and printer fonts. See *bit-mapped font*, *font family*, *outline font*, *screen font*, *typeface*, *type size*, and *weight*.

font cartridge Some printers accept plug-in font cartridges to add font variations to the printer's repertoire.

font family A set of fonts in several sizes and weights that share the same typeface:

Helvetica Roman 10

Helvetica bold 10

Helvetica italic 10

Helvetica Roman 12

Helvetica bold 12

Helvetica italic 12

Helvetica bold italic 12

font metric The width and height information for each character in a font. The font metric is stored in a width table.

footer A short version of a document's title or other text positioned at the bottom of every page of the document. See *header*.

formatting The process of changing the appearance of a page, by setting margins, choosing fonts, changing line spacing, alignment, column width, headers and footers, and other printed elements.

frame A box. Some desktop publishing and word processing programs use frames to hold various page elements, including body text, graphic images, charts, headers and footers, and so on.

frame-grabber A combination of hardware and software that captures images from a video camera, still video camera, or videocassette.

full justification The alignment of multiple lines of text along the left and the right margins. See *justification*.

graphics mode In IBM and IBM-compatible computers, a mode of graphics display adapters in which the computer can display bit-mapped graphics.

graphics monitor A computer monitor that can display both text and graphic images.

gray scale A series of shades from white to black.

grayscale monitor A monitor that can reproduce many shades of gray, typically 256 or more. Ordinary monitors can display only from 4 to 16 shades of gray.

greeking Many word processing and desktop publishing programs display unreadably small text as solid lines or abstract symbols, called greeked text.

grid The underlying design that establishes a consistent pattern for the position and style of columns, headings, fonts, line spacing, photos, and other document elements.

gutter An additional margin added for two-sided printing to allow room for the binding. An extra margin is added to the left side of odd-numbered (recto) pages and to the right side of even-numbered (verso) pages.

halftone A photo that has been copied through a printer's screen to create an image composed of dots or lines.

hanging indent Paragraph formatting in which the first line extends into the left margin.

hard hyphen A hyphen that prevents software from breaking a word; useful for preventing hyphenation of such words as "anti-inflammatory."

hard space A space used to prevent two words from being separated by wordwrap at the end of a line; for example "Et Al."

header Repeated text, such as a page number and a short version of a document's title, that appears at the top of each page in a document. See *footer*.

Helvetica A sans serif typeface frequently used for display type applications and occasionally for body type. One of the most widely used fonts in the world, Helvetica is included as a built-in font with many laser printers. See *font family* for an example of Helvetica.

high-resolution output Typesetting; generally refers to printing quality of 1200 dots per inch or better.

hyphenation A program feature that automatically hyphenates words based on program rules (algorithmic hyphenation) or a list of hyphenated words (dictionary hyphenation).

image scanner Hardware that converts photos, drawings, or line images into computer-readable graphic files.

indentation The alignment of a paragraph to the right or left of the margins set for the entire document.

initial cap A large letter that indicates the beginning of body text. An initial cap can be dropped (inset) into the text, raised above the first line of text, or printed to the left of the body text.

jumpline Text placed at the bottom of a column of text to guide the reader to the page where the article continues—for example, "Continued on page 5" and "Continued from page 1."

justification The alignment of multiple lines of text along the left margin, the right margin, or both margins. The term justification often is used to refer to full justification, or the alignment of text along both margins.

kerning The reduction of space between certain pairs of characters in display type so that the characters print in an aesthetically pleasing manner.

landscape orientation The rotation of a page design to print text and/or graphics horizontally across the longer axis of the page. See *portrait orientation*.

laser printer A high-resolution printer that uses a version of the electrostatic reproduction technology of copying machines to fuse text and graphic images to the page. See *resolution*.

layout In desktop publishing, the process of arranging text and graphics on a page.

leading The space between lines of type, measured from baseline to baseline. Synonymous with *line spacing*.

left justification The alignment of text along only the left margin. Synonymous with *ragged-right alignment*.

letter-quality printer An impact printer that simulates the fully formed text characters produced by a high-quality office typewriter.

ligature Combinations of letters printed in formal typography as a single letter: for example, ﬀ and ﬂ.

line spacing See *leading.*

linking The capability of some desktop publishing programs to treat text continued from one text frame to another as a single entity so that when text is added or deleted in one frame, the remaining text is automatically reflowed between the frames.

Linotronic Brand name of the best-known PostScript-compatible typesetting machines. The Linotronic typesetters print at 1270 or 2540 dots per inch resolution.

live area The area of a page on which the printing hardware can print. Laser printers require a 0.3" margin around the live area on the page. Printing presses may require a nonprinting "gripper" area used to pull the sheet of paper through the press.

logo A business name, often designed for an artistic effect.

master pages A feature of many desktop publishing programs, master pages provide a foundation for each page of a document and may contain standard rule lines, column guides, borders, headers, and footers.

masthead An area that lists the staff, subscription information, ownership, and address of a newsletter or other publication, generally printed near the front of the issue.

mezzotint A photograph printed through a line or dot screen that adds an interesting texture or pattern to the image.

moire pattern A distracting pattern that may result when the printer makes a halftone screen of an already halftoned photograph.

monospace A typeface such as Courier in which the width of all characters is the same, producing output that looks like typed characters. See *proportional spacing*.

nameplate The title of a newspaper, newsletter, magazine, or other serial publication.

near-letter quality (NLQ) A dot-matrix printing mode that prints typewriter-quality characters. As a result, printers using this mode print slower than other dot-matrix printers.

newspaper-style columns Columns in which text "snakes" from the bottom of one column to the top of the next.

non-breaking space A space that prevents the software from breaking two letters, words, or phrases at the end of a line.

oblique The italic form of a sans serif typeface. See *sans serif*.

OCR (Optical Character Recognition) A hardware and software system that can scan printed text into the computer for editing.

orientation See *landscape orientation* and *portrait orientation*.

orphan A formatting flaw in which the first line of a paragraph appears alone at the bottom of a page. Most word processing and page-layout programs suppress widows and orphans; the better programs enable you to switch widow/orphan control on and off and to choose the number of lines for which the suppression feature is effective. See *widow*.

outline font A printer or screen font in which a mathematical formula generates each character, producing a graceful and undistorted outline of the character, which the printer then fills in at its maximum resolution.

Because mathematical formulas produce the characters, you need only one font in the printer's memory to use any type size from 2 to 127 points.

overstrike The printing of a character not found in a printer's character set by printing one character, moving the print head back one space, and printing a second character on top of the first.

page layout program An application program that assembles text and graphics from a variety of files with which you can determine the precise placement, sizing, scaling, and cropping of material in accordance with the page design represented on-screen.

page orientation See *landscape orientation* and *portrait orientation*.

palette An on-screen display containing the set of colors or patterns that can be used.

pica A unit of measure equal to approximately 1/6 inch, or 12 points. In typewriting and letter-quality printing, a 12-point monospace font that prints at a pitch of 10 characters per inch (cpi).

pitch A horizontal measurement of the number of characters per linear inch in a monospace font, such as those used with typewriters, dot-matrix printers, and daisywheel printers. By convention, pica pitch equals 10 characters per inch, and elite pitch equals 12 characters per inch. See *monospace*, *pica*, and *point*.

pixel The smallest element (a picture element) that a device can display on-screen and out of which the displayed image is constructed. See *bit-mapped graphic*.

placeholder A tool provided with many desktop publishing programs to ensure consistent spacing of headlines, subheads, body text, photos, captions, and other document elements.

PMS (Pantone Matching System) The universal standard for creating colors by mixing red, blue, and green.

point The fundamental unit of measure in typography. 72 points equals an inch.

portrait orientation The default printing orientation for a page of text, with the longest measurement oriented vertically. See *landscape orientation*.

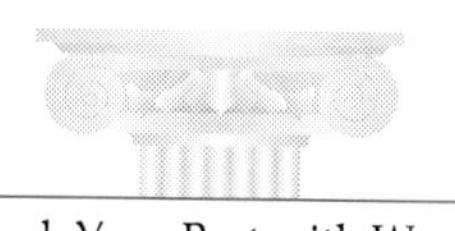

posterization High-contrast effect created by removing the gray mid-tones from a scanned image.

PostScript A sophisticated page description language for medium- to high-resolution printing devices.

PostScript laser printer A laser printer that includes the processing circuitry needed to decode and interpret printing instructions phrased in PostScript.

pre-printing Printing color elements on a page before printing page elements in black in a second pass; an inexpensive way to print nameplates, logos, and other document elements in color.

presentation graphics Text charts, bar graphs, pie graphs, and other charts and graphs, which you enhance so that they are visually appealing and easily understood by your audience. See *presentation graphics program*.

presentation graphics program An application program designed to create and enhance charts and graphs so that they are visually appealing and easily understood by an audience.

printer font A font available for printing, unlike screen fonts available for displaying text on-screen.

process color A standard color that does not require custom ink mixing.

proof Preliminary draft, used to proofread and check layouts.

proportion scale A graphic design tool used to size photos.

proportional spacing The allocation of character widths proportional to the character shape so that a narrow character, such as i, receives less space than a wide character such as m. See *kerning* and *monospace*.

pull quote A quotation printed in large letters to spark interest in an adjoining article

ragged-left alignment The alignment of each line of text so that the right margin is even, but the left remains ragged. Synonymous with *flush right*.

raised cap A large initial capital letter that extends above the first line of text. Raised and drop caps are used to guide the reader's eye to the beginning of body text.

registration mark A printer's guide mark that ensures that color separations used in four-color printing will print in perfect alignment.

resident font A font built into printer hardware—for example, most PostScript printers have 35 resident fonts

resolution A measurement—usually expressed in linear dots per inch (dpi), horizontally and vertically—of the sharpness of an image generated by an output device such as a monitor or printer.

In monitors, resolution is expressed as the number of pixels displayed on-screen. For example, a CGA monitor displays fewer pixels than a VGA monitor, and, therefore, a CGA image appears more jagged than a VGA image. Dot-matrix printers produce output with a lower resolution than laser printers.

reverse type Type or graphic images printed in white on a dark background.

right justification The alignment of text along the right margin and the left margin, producing a superficial resemblance to professionally printed text. The results may be poor, however, if the printer is incapable of proportional spacing; in such cases, right justification can be achieved only by inserting unsightly gaps of two or more spaces between words. For readability, most graphics artists advise computer users to leave the right margin ragged.

rotated type In a graphics or desktop publishing program, text that has been rotated from its normal, horizontal position on the page. The best graphics programs, such as CorelDraw, enable the user to edit the type even after it has been rotated.

rule line Horizontal or vertical lines used to separate text and images. For example, horizontal rule lines often are used to separate a newsletter nameplate from the body text area.

sans serif A typeface that lacks serifs, the fine cross strokes across the ends of the main strokes of a character.

Sans serif typefaces, such as Helvetica, are preferred for display type but are harder to read than serif typefaces, such as Times Roman, when used for body type. See *body type*, *display type*, *serif*, and *typeface*.

scalable font See *outline font*.

scalloped columns An informal design grid in which columns are allowed to end before they reach the bottom of the page.

screen A shade of gray added to a box. Screens darker than 10% interfere with readability of black text; and screens lighter than about 60% may interfere with the readability of reversed (white) text.

screen font A bit-mapped font designed to mimic the appearance of printer fonts when displayed on medium-resolution monitors.

serif The fine cross strokes across the ends of the main strokes of a character.

Serif fonts are easier to read for body type, but most designers prefer to use sans serif typefaces for display type. (The body text in this book is serif text.) See *sans serif*.

script A typeface that resembles handwriting.

separations A negative used in four-color printing. Each layer contains one of the colors used to produce the four-color image.

service bureau A business that provides phototypesetting of desktop published files.

shadow box A box with a shadow that creates the illusion that the box is floating above the page.

sidebar A short section of text accompanying a main article, usually set in a separate box.

slide show A predetermined list of on-screen presentation charts and graphs displayed one after the other.

Some programs can produce interesting effects, such as fading out one screen before displaying another and enabling you to choose your path through the charts available for display. See *presentation graphics*.

soft font See *downloadable font*.

spot color Color applied selectively to rules, boxes, headline text, and so on.

spread Two facing pages.

standing head A headline that introduces a regular feature, such as a department, in a newspaper, newsletter, or magazine.

stroke The thickness of the letters of a font. Typeface stroke variations may include bold, narrow, and heavy.

subscript A number or letter printed slightly below the typing line. See *superscript*.

superscript A number or letter printed slightly above the typing line. See *subscript*.

text file A file consisting of nothing but the standard ASCII characters (with no control characters or higher order characters).

template A file containing the basic formatting commands for a certain type of document. For example, a newsletter template may contain the nameplate, column formatting codes, headers and footers, and so on.

thumbnail A small, hand-drawn or computer-generated sketch of one or more document pages. Some programs can print up to 16 thumbnails on an 8 1/2-by-11-inch page.

TIFF (Tagged Image File Format) The file format used to store scanned images.

tombstone headlines Two headlines that accidentally align horizontally in adjacent columns, creating unwelcome ambiguity for the reader.

trim size The final size of a document page after the pages have been physically trimmed to equal size by the printer.

typeface The distinctive design of a set of type, distinguished from its weight and size.

Typefaces are grouped into two categories, serif and sans serif. Serif typefaces frequently are chosen for body type because they are more legible. Sans serif typefaces are preferred for display type. See *sans serif* and *serif*.

type size The size of a font, measured in points (approximately 1/72 inch) from the top of the tallest ascender to the bottom of the lowest descender. See *pitch*.

type style The weight (such as Roman or bold) or posture (such as italic) of a font—distinguished from a font's typeface design and type size. See *attribute*.

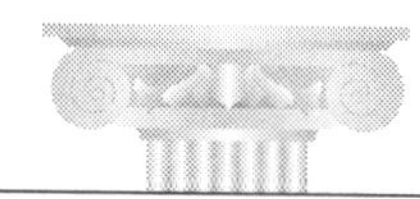

vertical justification Aligning the bottoms of adjacent columns by selectively adding or subtracting small amounts of leading to text or by adding extra space between paragraphs, between text and headings, between photos and text, and so on.

weight The overall lightness or darkness of a typeface design or the gradations of lightness to darkness within a font family.

A type style can be light or dark, and within a type style, you can see several gradations of weight (extra light, light, semilight, regular, medium, semibold, bold, extrabold, and ultrabold). See *typeface*.

widow A formatting flaw in which the last line of a paragraph appears alone at the top of a new column or page.

Most word processing and page layout programs suppress widows and orphans; better programs enable you to switch widow/orphan control on and off and to choose the number of lines. See *orphan*.

word wrap A feature of word processing programs (and other programs that include text-editing features) that wraps words down to the beginning of the next line if they go beyond the right margin.

WYSIWYG (What-You-See-Is-What-You-Get) A design philosophy in which formatting commands directly affect the text displayed on-screen so that the screen shows the appearance of the printed text.

B

Compose Codes for Zapf Dingbats

If you own a PostScript printer, you can create characters from the Zapf Dingbat character set with the WordPerfect Compose feature.

To use compose, press Ctrl-V, type the Compose code for the Dingbat character you want to create, and press Enter. For example, to create a typesetter's em dash (—), press Ctrl-V and at the `Key =` prompt, type *4,34* (4, comma, 34, with no space before or after the comma) and then press Enter.

Depending on your display card, characters you create with compose may be displayed as a solid square on the document screen and as a hollow square on the View Document screen.

When you select a PostScript printer definition, WordPerfect assigns the Dingbats to character set 12. The individual key assignments are not documented in the WordPerfect manual.

If you use a non-PostScript printer or a soft font package that supports Zapf Dingbats, the manual tells you how to access the characters.

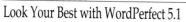

Table B.1
Compose Codes for Zapf Dingbats

Code	*Dingbat*	*Code*	*Dingbat*	*Code*	*Dingbat*
12,33	✁	12,81	✱	12,163	❣
12,34	✂	12,82	✲	12,164	❤
12,35	✃	12,83	✳	12,165	❥
12,36	✄	12,84	✴	12,166	❦
12,37	☎	12,85	✵	12,167	❧
12,38	✆	12,86	✶	12,168	♣
12,39	✇	12,87	✷	12,169	♦
12,40	✈	12,88	✸	12,170	♥
12,41	✉	12,89	✹	12,171	♠
12,42	☛	12,90	✺	12,172	①
12,43	☞	12,91	✻	12,173	②
12,44	✌	12,92	✼	12,174	③
12,45	✍	12,93	✽	12,175	④
12,46	✎	12,94	✾	12,176	⑤
12,47	✏	12,95	✿	12,177	⑥
12,48	✐	12,96	❀	12,178	⑦
12,49	✑	12,97	❁	12,179	⑧
12,50	✒	12,98	❂	12,180	⑨
12,51	✓	12,99	❃	12,181	⑩
12,52	✔	12,100	❄	12,182	❶
12,53	✕	12,101	❅	12,183	❷
12,54	✖	12,102	❆	12,184	❸
12,55	✗	12,103	❇	12,185	❹
12,56	✘	12,104	❈	12,186	❺
12,57	✙	12,105	❉	12,187	❻
12,58	✚	12,106	❊	12,188	❼
12,59	✛	12,107	❋	12,189	❽
12,60	✜	12,108	●	12,190	❾
12,61	✝	12,109	❍	12,191	❿
12,62	✞	12,110	■	12,192	➀
12,63	✟	12,111	❏	12,193	➁
12,64	✠	12,112	❐	12,194	➂
12,65	✡	12,113	❑	12,195	➃
12,66	✢	12,114	❒	12,196	➄
12,67	✣	12,115	▲	12,197	➅
12,68	✤	12,116	▼	12,198	➆
12,69	✥	12,117	◆	12,199	➇
12,70	✦	12,118	❖	12,200	➈
12,71	✧	12,119	◗	12,201	➉
12,72	★	12,120	❘	12,202	➊
12,73	✩	12,121	❙	12,203	➋
12,74	✪	12,122	❚	12,204	➌
12,75	✫	12,123	❛	12,205	➍
12,76	✬	12,124	❜	12,206	➎
12,77	✭	12,125	❝	12,207	➏
12,78	✮	12,126	❞	12,208	➐
12,79	✯	12,161	❡	12,209	➑
12,80	✰	12,162	❢	12,210	➒

Compose Codes for Zapf Dingbats

Code	Dingbat	Code	Dingbat	Code	Dingbat
12,211	➓	12,225	➡	12,239	➯
12,212	➔	12,226	➢	12,241	➱
12,213	→	12,227	➣	12,242	➲
12,214	↔	12,228	➤	12,243	➳
12,215	↕	12,229	➥	12,244	➴
12,216	➘	12,230	➦	12,245	➵
12,217	➙	12,231	➧	12,246	➶
12,218	➚	12,232	➨	12,247	➷
12,219	➛	12,233	➩	12,248	➸
12,220	➜	12,234	➪	12,249	➹
12,221	➝	12,235	➫	12,250	➺
12,222	➞	12,236	➬	12,251	➻
12,223	➟	12,237	➭	12,252	➼
12,224	➠	12,238	➮	12,253	➽
				12,254	➾

C

Decimal Equivalents

When you enter measurements in inches, WordPerfect translates them into decimal equivalents. This procedure may cause problems when you want to compare the lengths of two lines, for example, but you don't have a ruler that measures in hundredths of an inch.

The following table may prove useful in such cases.

Table C.1
Decimal Equivalents

Fraction	*Decimal*	*Fraction*	*Decimal*
1/64	.01	3/16	.18
1/32	.03	13/64	.20
3/64	.04	7/32	.21
1/16	.06	15/64	.23
5/64	.07	17/64	.26
3/32	.09	9/32	.28
7/64	.10	19/64	.29
1/8	.12	5/16	.32
9/64	.14	21/64	.32
5/32	.15	11/32	.34
11/64	.17	23/64	.35

Table C.1
Decimal Equivalents

Fraction	*Decimal*	*Fraction*	*Decimal*
3/8	.37	11/16	.68
25/64	.39	45/64	.70
13/32	.40	23/32	.71
27/64	.42	47/64	.73
7/16	.43	49/64	.76
29/64	.45	25/32	.78
15/32	.46	51/64	.79
31/64	.48	13/16	.81
33/64	.51	53/64	.82
17/32	.53	27/32	.84
35/64	.54	55/64	.85
9/16	.56	7/8	.87
37/64	.57	57/64	.89
19/32	.59	29/32	.90
39/64	.60	59/64	.92
5/8	.62	15/16	.93
41/64	.64	61/64	.95
21/32	.65	31/32	.96
43/64	.67	63/64	.98

Index

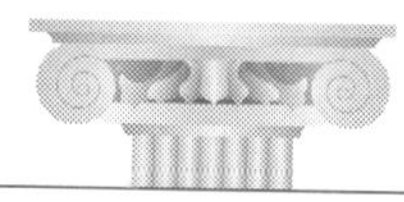

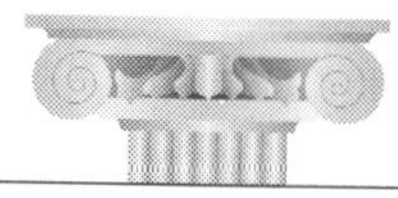

F

G

H

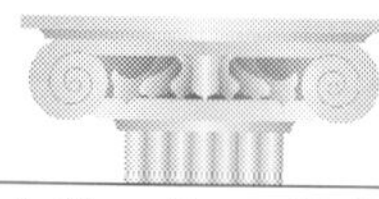

Q–R

S

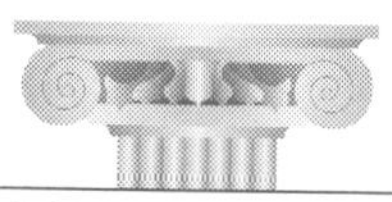

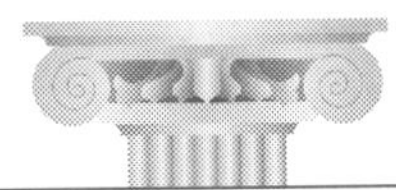

U–V

W

X–Z

Using WordPerfect Is Easy When You're Using Que

Using WordPerfect 5.1, Special Edition

Que Development Group

The classic, #1 best-selling word processing book—only from Que! Includes tear-out command map, icons, margin notes, and cautions.

WordPerfect 5.1

$27.95 USA

0-88022-554-8, 900 pp., 7 3/8 x 9 1/4

WordPerfect 5.1 QuickStart

Que Development Group

A graphics-based, fast-paced introduction to 5.1 essentials! Numerous illustrations demonstrate document production, table design, equation editing, and more.

WordPerfect 5.1

$19.95 USA

0-88022-558-0, 500 pp., 7 3/8 x 9 1/4,

WordPerfect 5.1 Quick Reference

Que Development Group

Instant reference for the operations of WordPerfect 5.1. Alphabetical listings make information easy to find!

WordPerfect 5.1

$8.95 USA

0-88022-576-9, 160 pp., 4 3/4 x 8

Check Out These Other Great Titles!

Using WordPerfect 5

Charles O. Stewart III, et. al.

WordPerfect 5

$27.95 USA

0-88022-351-0, 867 pp., 7 3/8 x 9 1/4

WordPerfect PC Tutor

Que Development Group

Versions 5 & 5.1

$39.95 USA

0-88022-619-6, 350 pp., 7 3/8 x 9 1/4

WordPerfect Power Pack

Ralph Blodgett

WordPerfect 5.1

$39.95 USA

0-88022-520-3, 593 pp., 7 3/8 x 9 1/4

WordPerfect Tips, Tricks, and Traps

Charles O. Stewart III., Daniel J. Rosenbaum, & Joel Shore

WordPerfect 5.1

$24.95 USA

0-88022-557-2, 743 pp., 7 3/8 x 9 1/4

WordPerfect 5.1 QueCards

Que Development Group

Version 5.1

$19.95 USA

0-88022-617-X, 60 cards, 6 1/2 x 9

To Order, Call:
(800) 428-5331
OR
(317) 573-2500

Find It Fast With Que's Quick References!

Que's Quick References are the compact, easy-to-use guides to essential application information. Written for all users, Quick References include vital command information under easy-to-find alphabetical listings. Quick References are a must for anyone who needs command information fast!

1-2-3 for DOS Release 2.3 Quick Reference
Release 2.3
$9.95 USA
0-88022-725-7, 160 pp., 4 3/4 x 8

1-2-3 Release 3.1 Quick Reference
Releases 3 & 3.1
$8.95 USA
0-88022-656-0, 160 pp., 4 3/4 x 8

Allways Quick Reference
Version 1.0
$8.95 USA
0-88022-605-6, 160 pp., 4 3/4 x 8

AutoCAD Quick Reference, 2nd Edition
Releases 10 & 11
$8.95 USA
0-88022-622-6, 160 pp., 4 3/4 x 8

Batch File and Macros Quick Reference
Through DOS 5
$9.95 USA
0-88022-699-4, 160 pp., 4 3/4 x 8

CorelDRAW! Quick Reference
Through Version 2
$8.95 USA
0-88022-597-1, 160 pp., 4 3/4 x 8

dBASE IV Quick Reference
Version 1
$8.95 USA
0-88022-371-5, 160 pp., 4 3/4 x 8

Excel for Windows Quick Reference
Excel 3 for Windows
$9.95 USA
0-88022-722-2, 160 pp., 4 3/4 x 8

Fastback Quick Reference
Version 2.1
$8.95 USA
0-88022-650-1, 160 pp., 4 3/4 x 8

Hard Disk Quick Reference
Through DOS 4.01
$8.95 USA
0-88022-443-6, 160 pp., 4 3/4 x 8

Harvard Graphics Quick Reference
Version 2.3
$8.95 USA
0-88022-538-6, 160 pp., 4 3/4 x 8

Laplink Quick Reference
Laplink III
$9.95 USA
0-88022-702-8, 160 pp., 4 3/4 x 8

Microsoft Word Quick Reference
Through Version 5.5
$9.95 USA
0-88022-720-6, 160 pp., 4 3/4 x 8

Microsoft Works Quick Reference
Through IBM Version 2.0
$9.95 USA
0-88022-694-3, 160 pp., 4 3/4 x 8

MS-DOS 5 Quick Reference
Version 5
$9.95 USA
0-88022-646-3, 160 pp., 4 3/4 x 8

MS-DOS Quick Reference
Through Version 3.3
$8.95 USA
0-88022-369-3, 160 pp., 4 3/4 x 8

Norton Utilities Quick Reference
Norton Utilities 5 & Norton Commander 3
$8.95 USA
0-88022-508-4, 160 pp., 4 3/4 x 8

PC Tools 7 Quick Reference
Through Version 7
$9.95 USA
0-88022-829-6, 160 pp., 4 3/4 x 8

Q&A 4 Quick Reference
Versions 2, 3, & 4
$9.95 USA
0-88022-828-8, 160 pp., 4 3/4 x 8

Quattro Pro Quick Reference
Through Version 3
$8.95 USA
0-88022-692-7, 160 pp., 4 3/4 x 8

Quicken Quick Reference
IBM Through Version 4
$8.95 USA
0-88022-598-X, 160 pp., 4 3/4 x 8

UNIX Programmer's Quick Reference
AT&T System V, Release 3
$8.95 USA
0-88022-535-1, 160 pp., 4 3/4 x 8

UNIX Shell Commands Quick Reference
AT&T System V, Releases 3 & 4
$8.95 USA
0-88022-572-6, 160 pp., 4 3/4 x 8

Windows 3 Quick Reference
Version 3
$8.95 USA
0-88022-631-5, 160 pp., 4 3/4 x 8

WordPerfect 5.1 Quick Reference
WordPerfect 5.1
$8.95 USA
0-88022-576-9, 160 pp., 4 3/4 x 8

WordPerfect Quick Reference
WordPerfect 5
$8.95 USA
0-88022-370-7, 160 pp., 4 3/4 x 8

To Order, Call:
(800) 428-5331 OR (317) 573-2500

Teach Yourself With QuickStarts From Que!

The ideal tutorials for beginners, Que's QuickStart books use graphic illustrations and step-by-step instructions to get you up and running fast. Packed with examples, QuickStarts are the perfect beginner's guides to your favorite software applications.

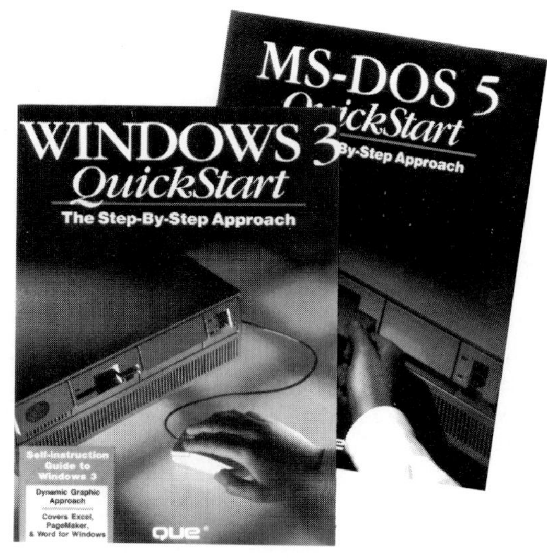

1-2-3 for DOS Release 2.3 QuickStart
Release 2.3
$19.95 USA
0-88022-716-8, 500 pp., 7 3/8 x 9 1/4

1-2-3 for Windows QuickStart
1-2-3 for Windows
$19.95 USA
0-88022-723-0, 500 pp., 7 3/8 x 9 1/4

1-2-3 Release 3.1 + QuickStart, 2nd Edition
Releases 3 & 3.1
$19.95 USA
0-88022-613-7, 569 pp., 7 3/8 x 9 1/4

dBASE IV 1.1 QuickStart,
Through Version 1.1
$19.95 USA
0-88022-614-5, 400 pp., 7 3/8 x 9 1/4

Excel 3 for Windows QuickStart
Version 3 fo rWindows
$19.95 USA
0-88022-762-1, 500 pp., 7 3/8 x 9 1/4

MS-DOS QuickStart, 2nd Edition
Version 3.X & 4.X
$19.95 USA
0-88022-611-0, 420 pp., 7 3/8 x 9 1/4

Q&A 4 QuickStart
Versions 3 & 4
$19.95 USA
0-88022-653-6, 400 pp., 7 3/8 x 9 1/4

Quattro Pro 3 QuickStart
Through Version 3.0
$19.95 USA
0-88022-693-5, 450 pp., 7 3/8 x 9 1/4

WordPerfect 5.1 QuickStart
WordPerfect 5.1
$19.95 USA
0-88022-558-0, 427 pp., 7 3/8 x 9 1/4

Windows 3 QuickStart
Ron Person & Karen Rose

This graphics-based text teaches Windows beginners how to use the feature-packed Windows environment. Emphasizes such software applications as Excel, Word, and PageMaker and shows how to master Windows' mouse, menus, and screen elements.

Version 3
$19.95 USA
0-88022-610-2, 440 pp., 7 3/8 x 9 1/4

MS-DOS 5 QuickStart
Que Development Group

This is the easy-to-use graphic approach to learning MS-DOS 5. The combination of step-by-step instruction, examples, and graphics make this book ideal for all DOS beginners.

DOS 5
$19.95 USA
0-88022-681-1, 420 pp., 7 3/8 x 9 1/4

To Order, Call: (800) 428-5331 OR (317) 573-2500

Learning is Easy with Easy Books from Que!

Easy WordPerfect

Shelley O'Hara

The ideal coverage of WordPerfect for beginners! 4-color illustrations and text as well as before-and-after screen shots illustrate each task. The book also includes a command summary and a glossary.

Version 5.1

$19.95 USA

0-88022-797-4, 200 pp., 8 x 10

Que's Easy Series offers a revolutionary concept in computer training. The friendly, 4-color interior, easy format, and simple explaniations guarantee success for even the most intimidated computer user!

Easy Lotus 1-2-3

Shelley O'Hara

Releases 2.01 & 2.2

$19.95 USA

0-88022-799-0, 200 pp., 8 x 10

Easy Quattro Pro

Shelley O'Hara

Versions 3.X, 4.X, & 5

$19.95 USA

0-88022-798-2, 200 pp., 8 x 10

Easy Windows

Shelley O'Hara

Versions 3 & 4

$19.95 USA

0-88022-800-8, 200 pp., 8 x 10

To Order, Call: (800) 428-5331 OR (317) 573-2500

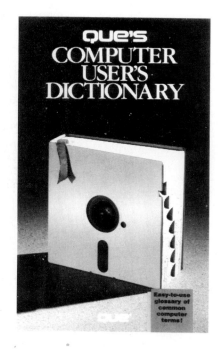